new patterns
new patterns
new patterns
for worship
for worship
for worship

Church House Publishing

Published by   Church House Publishing
                 Church House
                 Great Smith Street
                 London SW1P 3AZ

Copyright ©   *The Archbishops' Council 2002*
                 Second edition 2008
                 Fourth impression 2019

                 978 0 7151 2326 3 (paperback edition)

Printed and bound in the United Kingdom
by Bell and Bain Ltd, Glasgow

Typeset in Gill Sans by Omnific
Designed by Derek Birdsall RDI and John Morgan

Contents

317 Sample Services

Authorization

New Patterns for Worship comprises

＊ alternative services and other material authorized for use until further resolution of the General Synod;

＊ services which comply with the provisions of A Service of the Word and other authorized services;

＊ material commended by the House of Bishops;

＊ material, the use of which falls within the discretion allowed to the minister under the provisions of Canon B 5 and by the rubrics and notes in authorized forms of service.

For details, see page 480.

Canon B 3 provides that decisions as to which of the authorized services are to be used (other than occasional offices) shall be taken jointly by the incumbent and the parochial church council.

Note

Throughout this volume references simply to *Common Worship* refer to the main *Common Worship* volume, *Common Worship: Services and Prayers for the Church of England*. The other *Common Worship* volumes are referred to by their full titles, for example *Common Worship: Pastoral Services*.

Preface

Patterns for Worship was first published in a Synod edition in 1989, but was not published in a commercial edition until 1995. The Synod draft contained what some people considered fairly revolutionary proposals about alternative structures for the Eucharist and Eucharistic Prayers, and the House of Bishops said it was 'mindful of those who want a period of stability in the liturgical life of the Church, and who might be anxious lest the Commission's proposals extend the bounds of choice and variety of liturgical provision more widely than has been customary in the Church of England'. The 1995 edition established the principle followed in *Common Worship* of publishing both commended and authorized material in one volume. It included the newly authorized Service of the Word, Confessions and Absolutions and Affirmations of Faith, but no Eucharistic Prayers were included. This present volume contains the same range of material, and includes the outline for the Eucharist, authorized as A Service of the Word with a Celebration of Holy Communion, together with provision for using a number of thanksgivings as extended prefaces with some of the new Eucharistic Prayers.

What is the difference between *New Patterns for Worship* and *Common Worship*? There are two important features about *New Patterns* which distinguish it from the *Common Worship* volumes. These have led to the publication of a new edition of this book, brought up to date so that it is entirely compatible with *Common Worship*.

First, it is organized in a completely different way from *Common Worship*. It is a directory of resources, organized in such a way that those looking for material for different sections of the service can find and compare possible texts and ideas, all cross-referenced for 'secular' themes as well as for major doctrinal themes and seasons. This is not a new idea. The introduction to *Lent, Holy Week, Easter* in 1984 said, 'We are providing a directory from which choices may be made. We think of this book as a manual to be used with selectivity, sensitivity and imagination.' In 1985 the report by the General Synod Standing Committee, *The Worship of the Church*, called for 'a directory with a wealth of resource material including supplementary material for each of the many points in the service where there is room for the individual's own words. The directory would need to set boundaries to the proposed freedom, and points which might be theologically divisive would have to be watched.' The introduction to *Common Worship* says that the provision for the combination of old and new 'provides for the diverse worshipping needs of our communities, within an ordered structure which affirms our essential unity and common life'. This continued provision for diversity within an authorized structure continues in *Common Worship*, both in the outline structures provided for A Service of the Word and other services, and also in the notes and rubrics which frequently use the phrase 'these or other suitable words'.

Second, *New Patterns for Worship* is designed to educate and train those who plan and lead worship. There are training elements built into each of the resource sections, together with discussion material for PCCs and worship planning groups. Some of the items in the Resource Sections have been deliberately chosen to illustrate different ways of doing things. So there are different ways of handling the Prayers of Intercession, and a number of examples of the same psalm or canticle treated in different ways both for singing and for speaking. At the end of the book there are Sample Services, covering quite a wide range of thematic and seasonal occasions. Sometimes they will be exactly what the user is looking for, and can be copied for local use. Sometimes they are simply outlines illustrating different shapes and creative ideas. The principles behind the basic outline of A Service of the Word imply the need for those who conduct and lead the services to be aware of the theological models that shape our worship, both in the patterns of the services and in the structures of the component parts. These patterns draw worshippers from where they are by means of encounter with the story of what God has done for his people to where we might hope they would be. But the main reason they are there is to illustrate the theory and methods explained in the earlier part of the book, and to stimulate those who plan services locally to produce better worship. Again, one of these services is deliberately dealt with in a number of different ways, so that the effect of different approaches may be seen.

The Liturgical Commission's aim in producing *Patterns for Worship* in 1989 was to meet some of the current needs of the Church's worship, reflected most acutely in Urban Priority Areas and in services (often called 'family services') at which all age groups, including children, are present. We used the already established principle of flexibility to provide forms of worship which could still be recognizable as belonging within the Anglican tradition, while encompassing the enormous variety that exists within the Church at present. Time has moved on. Much of the flexibility and variety is enshrined in *Common Worship*, and this book provides some complementary resources to encourage that. And we now speak of 'all-age worship' rather than 'family services', reflecting the social changes which still continue. But many of the needs are still the same: the need to explore different ways of recognizing and celebrating the presence of God in worship, the need to maintain the unity of the Church while doing so, the need to train more people to share in the planning and preparation of worship, and the need to enjoy God in worship in such a way that others are attracted and join in.

✠ David Sarum
Chairman of the Liturgical Commission

November 2002

Introduction

How to use this book

Worship is not worship until you do it.

Worship books consisting simply of texts to say or sing are like recipes which list ingredients without the instructions for putting them together.

But how do you offer advice and suggest questions to ask about the presentation of the liturgy without putting it all in rubrics, or mandatory stage directions, in the services, or producing a separate manual? Probably the most digestible and least legalistic way of doing it would be to tell stories. So here you have

* the authorized text of A Service of the Word, with notes and instructions about how to put it together;

* a set of Resource Sections providing material, section by section, for each part of a service; and

* the stories of four entirely imaginary churches, at the beginning of each Resource Section. As you read them, you will gather a little of the flavour and style of each church, both rural and urban, with different spaces and resources. You may find you identify more with one than with another, but be prepared to learn from the others. Sometimes the lessons may be how *not* to do it.

What do you want to do?

* To look for items to put into a service, browse through the Resource Sections, using the indexes. You will find an index of the themes followed in each section on pages 59 and 501.

* To find a service for a special occasion, look at the section entitled Sample Services for ideas and suggestions, an outline order of service, or a complete worked-out example.

* To find some help in preparing either of these, read the introductory pages to each Resource Section and each Sample Service.

* To learn more about putting services together, or find ways of helping a PCC or worship planning group to learn more about the decisions they need to take, read the stories of the four churches. The introductory notes and outline discussion starters included in the Planning Worship section of this book are designed to make it a useful educational tool.

How to use the stories

Two or three people could be asked to read a particular section beforehand, in preparation for the discussion; the stories – and possibly the questions below – could be reproduced on a handout given to everyone. A larger meeting would be better divided into groups, possibly with both the questions and the collecting of responses set out on an overhead projector. Ask some questions:

* Can you imagine being present in the situations described?

* What is good or bad about them?

* Do you feel nearer to the experience of one of the four churches?

* Which one?

* Make a list of suggestions which come to you as a result of reading this section.

* Are any of these suggestions possible for us

  a) some time in the future?

  b) right now?

* Do we need variety in how we handle this part of the service week by week, or do we need the security of being consistent?

* Do we need to consult with others before taking action – other church leaders, the PCC, musicians, choir, servers etc.?

Patterns of church life:
Introducing the four imaginary churches

St Ann's is a large suburban church, with a mixed congregation of different ages and backgrounds. There is considerable lay involvement in the leadership of the church, and this is evident in the worship too. The PCC recently spent a day away reviewing the church's worship, and one of the results of this was the setting up of a worship planning group. See the first section of page 25, and Planning and Preparation in General, beginning on page 24.

Sunday worship is the focus of the whole life of this very active church, and a lot of energy is put into preparing for Sunday both by those involved in teaching the different adult and children's groups and by the music and drama groups. Sunday morning worship follows *Common Worship* Order One Holy Communion, but on occasion makes use of the provisions of A Service of the Word with a Celebration of Holy Communion to enable it to feel more like a less formal all-age service. The sermon is done in a variety of ways, for example using videos or dividing the adult members of the congregation into groups. There is a break at the Peace when the children come back from their groups and some non-communicants and enquirers leave without embarrassment.

♣

St Bartholomew's is a lovely medieval country church, small both in size and in congregation. Sharing a vicar with other churches in the group means that the Sunday pattern varies from week to week, and the main service is not always communion. The church is not as insular as it used to be; one or two people sometimes go to services at other churches in the group, and some incomers in the village bring experience of other churches. The main vision of the staff (vicar, deacon and an excellent Reader) is of worship that is accessible to everyone in the village, children included, and that accurately reflects and sums up the life of the community. Some of the congregation would prefer the worship to be a little less related to the community and more of a beautiful oasis, away from the week's troubles – a kind of entering into eternity from which they can emerge refreshed to face the week.

St Christopher's is a large nineteenth-century neo-gothic building in the downtown part of the city. The parish priest lives in the vicarage adjoining the church. The high brick wall which surrounds the church and vicarage also includes the disused school, now used adventurously for a wide range of community activities. The parish priest is the only professional living in the area. The small congregation spend a lot of time together; all of them live locally. Some of them help to run things in the community centre and every morning there are four or five praying, with more for late evening worship, and thirty for communion with hymns and sermon on Tuesday evening. Sunday worship is a culmination and gathering together of the activities, concerns and worship of the week. The social needs of the community are offered to God as easily as they are discussed practically in the pub after church – a kind of extended Peace attended by most of the congregation.

St Dodo's is a church where worship is simply not one of the most important things the church does. It comes low on most people's agenda, though there are occasional heated discussions at the PCC. The demands of different factions and rival views in the church mean that the worship is very bitty, and there is a different kind of service each Sunday in the month, with very few people going every week. The vicar finds little time for preparation and feels it is impossible to involve others in preparing or helping to lead because of the need to keep the balance between the different factions.

Note: There really was a St Dodo. He was the abbot of a monastery in Belgium who died in AD 750. We've chosen him partly because there are no churches dedicated to him in Britain, partly because of the other overtones of his name. But if you find yourself identifying with some of the stories of St Dodo's (and many of them are true) don't despair: you're not extinct yet, and the fact that you are using this book shows that you are well on the way to recovering from deadness.

planning planning planning worship worship worship

Planning Worship

Contents

A Service of the Word:
Authorized Text and Notes

Worship may often make use of the authorized provision for A Service of the Word, which is given here for ease of reference.

A Service of the Word

¶ *Introduction*

A Service of the Word is unusual for an authorized Church of England service. It consists almost entirely of notes and directions and allows for considerable local variation and choice within a common structure. It is important that those who prepare for and take part in A Service of the Word should have a clear understanding of the nature of worship and of how the component parts of this service work together. Leading people in worship is leading people into mystery, into the unknown and yet the familiar. This spiritual activity is much more than getting the words or the sections in the right order. The primary object in the careful planning and leading of the service is the spiritual direction which enables the whole congregation to come into the presence of God to give him glory. Choices must be made responsibly by leaders of this service or by groups planning worship with them, whether the service is an occasional one, or a regular one which may use a service card. The notes and the text of A Service of the Word should be read together as they interpret one another.

The Liturgy of the Word

At the heart of the service is the Liturgy of the Word. This must not be so lightly treated as to appear insignificant compared with other parts of the service. The readings from Holy Scripture are central to this part and, together with the season, may determine the theme of the rest of the worship. At certain times of the year, as Note 5 says, the readings come from an authorized lectionary, so that the whole Church is together proclaiming the major events in the Christian story. Telling that story and expounding it in the 'sermon' can be done in many different and adventurous ways. Some are suggested in Notes 5 and 7, but there are many others. The word 'sermon' is used in the service, and explained in the note, precisely because it would be too limiting to use words like 'address', 'talk', 'instruction', or 'meditation'.

The items in the Liturgy of the Word may come in any order and more than once. So the sermon may be in parts and there may be more than one psalm or song, and of course hymns may be inserted as well. But on most occasions it will be appropriate for this part of the service to have a Creed or Affirmation of Faith as its climax.

Preparation

With the Liturgy of the Word becoming clear it will be easier to see how the Preparation for it, and the response to it in the Prayers, fit in. People need to know when the service has started (Note 1). What happens at the beginning can create the atmosphere for worship and set the tone and mood for what follows. The gathering of the congregation and the call to worship are to be marked by a liturgical greeting between minister and people. Leaders should have worked out exactly where this comes among the singing, Scripture sentence, introduction (perhaps to the theme) and opening prayer. All these should draw the members of the congregation together and focus their attention on almighty God.

This part of the service will usually include the Prayers of Penitence, though these may come later if, for instance, the theme of the Liturgy of the Word appropriately leads to penitence. Authorized Prayers of Penitence include all those confessions and absolutions in *The Book of Common Prayer* and in services in *Common Worship*, together with several other seasonal and thematic forms, mostly for occasional use, which are set out on pages 122–137 of *Common Worship*. The climax of this part of the service is either the Collect or, if that is included in the Prayers, one of the items of praise, a hymn or the Gloria. The Collect does not have to be that of the day; it may be a thematic one based on the readings (in which case it should come immediately before the readings), or be used to sum up the Prayers.

Prayers

Part of the response to the Word is the Creed, but the response should be developed in the Prayers which follow. There are many different options for this part of the service. These range from a series of Collect-type prayers to congregational involvement in prayer groups, visual and processional prayers, with responsive forms and a number of people sharing the leading of intercessions in between. But, whatever the form, it is essential that the Prayers also include thanksgiving. A section of thanksgiving, which may include the spoken word, music and hymns, may be the proper climax to this part of the service.

Conclusion

Many different words have been used for the Conclusion, each of which has something to contribute to our understanding of how the service ends: dismissal, farewell, goodbye, departure, valediction, commission, blessing, ending, going out. What is essential, as with the way the service starts, is that it should have a clear liturgical ending: options are listed in Note 9.

Once the service is planned, leaders will want to check through to ensure that there is the right balance between the elements of word, prayer and praise, and between congregational activity and congregational passivity. Does the music come in the right places? Is there sufficient silence (Note 4)? This is something leaders can be afraid of, or fail to introduce properly. And is there a clear overall direction to the service: is it achieving the purpose of bringing the congregation together to give glory to God?

¶ A Service of the Word

Preparation

The minister welcomes the people with the **Greeting**.

Authorized Prayers of Penitence may be used here or in the **Prayers**.

The Venite, Kyries, Gloria, a hymn, song, or a set of responses may be used.

The **Collect** is said either here or in the **Prayers**.

The Liturgy of the Word

This includes
¶ **readings (or a reading) from Holy Scripture**
¶ a **psalm**, or, if occasion demands, a scriptural song
¶ a **sermon**
¶ an **authorized Creed**, or, if occasion demands, an **authorized Affirmation of Faith**.

Prayers

These include
¶ **intercessions and thanksgivings**
¶ **the Lord's Prayer**

Conclusion

The service concludes with a **blessing, dismissal** or other **liturgical ending**.

¶ A Service of the Word
with a Celebration of Holy Communion

This rite requires careful preparation by the president and other participants, and is not normally to be used as the regular Sunday or weekday service.

Sections marked with an asterisk* must follow an authorized text.

Preparation

The people and the priest:

¶   greet each other in the Lord's name
¶   confess their sins and are assured of God's forgiveness*
¶   keep silence and pray a Collect*

The Liturgy of the Word

The people and the priest:

¶   proclaim and respond to the word of God

Prayers

The people and the priest:

¶   pray for the Church and the world

The Liturgy of the Sacrament

The people and the priest:

¶   exchange the Peace
¶   prepare the table
¶   pray the Eucharistic Prayer*
¶   break the bread
¶   receive Holy Communion

The Dismissal

The people and the priest:

¶   depart with God's blessing.

¶ Notes

In this form of service, the material is described as 'authorized' or 'suitable', which expressions shall have the following meanings:

¶ 'authorized' means approved by the General Synod in accordance with the provisions of Canon B 2.

¶ 'suitable' means a form used at the discretion of the minister conducting the form of service on any occasion, but such that the material so used shall be neither contrary to, nor indicative of any departure from, the doctrine of the Church of England in any essential matter.

This service is authorized as an alternative to Morning Prayer and Evening Prayer. It provides a structure for Sunday services, for daily prayer and for services of an occasional nature.

1 Greeting
The service should have a clear beginning. The liturgical greeting may follow some introductory singing, or a hymn or a sentence of Scripture, and may be followed by a brief introduction or an opening prayer.

2 Prayers of Penitence
Only authorized Prayers of Penitence should be used. They may be omitted except at the Principal Service on Sundays and Principal Holy Days. Authorized forms of Confession and Absolution may be found in *The Book of Common Prayer*, in the services in *Common Worship* and on pages 122–137 of *Common Worship*. See also pages 81–97 in this book. The minister may introduce the Confession with suitable words.

3 Hymns, Canticles, Acclamations and the Peace
Points are indicated for some of these, but if occasion requires they may occur elsewhere.

4 Silence
Periods of silence may be kept at different points of the service. It may be particularly appropriate at the beginning of the service, after the readings and the sermon, and during the prayers.

5 Readings
There should preferably be at least two readings from the Bible, but it is recognized that if occasion demands there may be only one reading. It may be dramatized, sung or read responsively. The readings are taken from an authorized lectionary during the period from the Third Sunday of Advent to the Baptism of Christ, and from Palm Sunday to Trinity Sunday. When A Service of the Word is combined with Holy Communion on Sundays and Principal Holy Days, the readings of the day are normally used.

6   Psalms
     The service should normally include a psalm or psalms. These might
     be said or sung in the traditional way, but it is also possible to use a
     metrical version, a responsive form or a paraphrase such as can be
     found in many current hymn books. The psalm may occasionally be
     replaced by a song or canticle the words of which are taken directly
     from Scripture: a 'scriptural song'.

7   Sermon
     The term 'sermon' includes less formal exposition, the use of drama,
     interviews, discussion, audio-visuals and the insertion of hymns or
     other sections of the service between parts of the sermon. The
     sermon may come after one of the readings, or before or after the
     prayers, and may be omitted except on Sundays and Principal
     Holy Days.

8   Sermon and Creed
     The sermon, and a Creed or authorized Affirmation of Faith may be
     omitted except at the principal service on Sundays and Principal
     Holy Days.

9   Ending
     The service should have a clear ending. This takes one or more of
     the following forms: the Peace, the Grace or a suitable ascription
     or blessing. If a responsive conclusion is used, it comes last.

10   A Service of the Word with a Celebration of Holy Communion
     An order for this is provided (see page 25 of *Common Worship*). The
     notes to the Order for the Celebration of Holy Communion (pages
     158–159 and 330–335 of *Common Worship*) apply equally to this service.
     In particular the Note on Ministries (pages 158–159 of *Common
     Worship*) specifies that the president must be an episcopally ordained
     priest, but indicates that where necessary a deacon or lay person may
     preside over the Preparation and the Liturgy of the Word, including the
     Prayers. The order provided is not prescriptive.

Planning and Preparing a Service of the Word

How to put a service together

1   Structure

The first thing to do is to read the authorized introduction to A Service of the Word on pages 9–10. From this you will see that there are three main sections, like three tubs into which you are going to put the different items in the service; Preparation, The Liturgy of the Word, Prayers. Into these tubs you put the ingredients, the different items in the service. Add to these a beginning and an ending and you have the main outline.

There are four different kinds of ingredients and it is important that there is a balance in the way these are used:

Word │ Prayer │ Praise │ Action

It is a bit like preparing a meal with three courses, plus an appetizer at the beginning and coffee at the end. Each course has a number of different ingredients, which can be used more than once in different combinations in different courses. It is worth noting that for the principal service on a Sunday certain ingredients, which are otherwise optional, are required: an authorized confession and absolution, an authorized creed or affirmation of faith, and a sermon.

The basic structure for A Service of the Word is set out on page 11 and for A Service of the Word with Holy Communion on page 12. For more background on the structure see page 27. It is important to have a clear structure such as that in A Service of the Word, even though the detail may vary from week to week. The emphasis on different parts of the structure may be varied according to the theme.

2   Theme and direction

The Introduction to A Service of the Word says:

> Leading people in worship is leading people into mystery, into the unknown and yet the familiar. This spiritual activity is much more than getting the words or the sections in the right order. The primary object in the careful planning and leading of the service is the spiritual direction which enables the whole congregation to come into the presence of God to give him glory.

Care should be taken to ensure that there is some overall direction, some sense of cohesion, of going somewhere, some development in the congregation's relationship to God, reflected in the service structure. Sometimes this is provided by a clear theme. The theme may be determined by the occasion or season, such as Mothering Sunday or Christmas, or by some local event, such as a patronal festival or jazz festival. The theme will also be regularly determined by the Bible readings. Sometimes no clear overall theme will emerge, and the Bible reading, prayers and praise will be left, like coloured glass in a kaleidoscope, to cast light on one another and to provide, in the interplay of patterns, different pictures for different people in the congregation. The important thing is to recognize which of these routes is being followed. Ask the question, either on your own or in a planning group, 'What do we expect to happen to people in this service? What will be the outcomes in terms of Christian growth, education, deepening appreciation of God, experience of him in worship and praise, and in obedience to his word?' And that outcome, and the development through the service, will be partly determined by giving some attention to the emotional flow of the service. Does it start quietly and build up, start on a 'high' and become reflective, or have a climax in the middle?

3 The Word

The Introduction says this is 'the heart of the service', and this is the best place to begin to look at the ingredients which will sometimes determine the theme for the service.

✳ What are the Bible readings? The authorized Lectionary will be the natural starting point, and must be followed in the periods around Christmas and Easter. This helps to keep the whole church together on the same track as we tell the stories of Jesus' birth, death and resurrection, and the coming of the Holy Spirit. At other times other routes may be followed, such as those in Resource Section C (pages 98–123) or a specially designed local teaching scheme.

✳ If occasion demands, there need only be one reading, except that if the service is Holy Communion, there should be two readings, one of which should be from the Gospels.

✳ How are other readings going to be presented? See page 101 for examples.

✳ What psalms, Scripture, songs or canticles are to be used? Begin to think about music resources and preparation. See pages 125–128 (Psalms) and 35–38 (Music).

✳ Begin to plan the sermon. If the preacher is not part of the planning group, it is important to know the main drift of the sermon so that other items in the service support rather than conflict with this part of the Word. Does it need one 'slot' or more? Note 7 to A Service of the Word (page 14) gives a new interpretation to the word 'sermon' which 'includes less formal exposition, the use of drama, interviews, discussion, audio-visuals and the insertion of hymns or other sections of the service between parts of the sermon'.

4 Prayer

Look at the Prayer section of the service, and also the Preparation section, as both penitence and the collect may be included in the prayers. Note 4 (page 13) reminds us about the need for silence. What form should the prayers take?

* An outline form filled in by the minister
* An outline form with extempore prayer or biddings from the congregation, or from a group
* A litany or responsive intercession
* A series of set prayers

It is best not to mix the forms too much, though a set prayer may be a good way to end or sum up one of the other forms. The Lord's Prayer and a collect should be used at every Sunday service.

5 Praise

Praise may be said or sung. Select hymns, songs or items from the Praise section of *New Patterns* or elsewhere. See pages 220–222 for further ideas. A set of versicles and responses (see pages 225–233 for examples) may be used in the Preparation or elsewhere.

6 Action

This is not the same kind of thing as the other three ingredients; rather, it describes the way in which something is done. For example, dramatic action might interpret the Word, or a procession or dance might help to express praise. So something might be done with music, or followed by silence, or accompanied by visuals, gestures or symbols. There might be a movement by the congregation, such as standing or joining hands, movement with an object, e.g. a candle or Bible, a change in lighting or visual presentation. See pages 279–281 for further examination of this.

The action may be the climax towards which the service moves, or an action that begins the worship and sets the theme for it.

7 Beginning and ending

These are dealt with in the paragraphs headed 'Preparation' and 'Conclusion' in the authorized Introduction to A Service of the Word (pages 10–11), together with Notes 1, 2 and 9 (pages 13–14).

* Decide how the service is to begin and end: each should be clear.

* Decide what is to go into 'The Preparation', and what other material you want to add. Prayers of Penitence, with an authorized form of confession and absolution (see Resource Section B, pages 72–97 and *Common Worship*, pages 122–137), may come here or in 'Prayers'. The collect may also come later in that section.

* Decide whether and where to add a creed or affirmation of faith (see Resource Section E, pages 157–169), notices, collection, invitations or biddings, explanation, silence. See pages 29–32 for some ideas about inserting things like this into services.

* Decide how these ingredients relate to the aim and structure of the rest of the service. For example, prayers of penitence might be part of the preparation at the beginning, to clear away any barrier to hearing God, or they could be the climax towards which the service moves (as in an Ash Wednesday service). The full structure might then look like one of the following samples.

Example 1: A block structure

Items you must include for a Principal Service on Sunday (though individual items and order will vary)		Additional items you may want to add
Preparation		
Greeting	1	Scripture sentence
	2	Hymn
	3	Opening prayer
	4	Invitation
* Confession	5	
* Forgiveness	6	
Word		
	7	Introduction
Old Testament	8	
Psalm or paraphrase	9	
New Testament	10	
	11	Song or hymn
Talk	12	
* Creed	13	
	14	Hymn
Prayer		
* Collect	15	
Form of intercession	16	
Praise		
	17	Versicles and responses
	18	Hymn
Action		
	19	All stand while the candle is carried out
Blessing or ending	20	

* Authorized texts must be used

Example 2: A conversation structure

Word | Prayer | Praise | Action may come many times within the same service. Imagine a conversation between God and the congregation. The **Word** items present what God is saying, and the other three items may be used as the response or reply to God. The service may be built from a series of **Presentation** and **Response** units, like building blocks. This example is from Morning Prayer in *The Book of Common Prayer*:

Presentation	Response
God Speaks	We Speak
Word	
Scripture Sentence	
	Praise
	Hymn of adoration
Word	
Invitation	
	Prayer
	Confession
Prayer	
Declaration of forgiveness	
	Praise
	Open our lips…
	Glory be…
	Canticle
Word	
Psalm	
Old Testament	
	Praise
	Canticle
Word	
New Testament	
	Praise
	Canticle
	Creed
	Lord's Prayer
	Collect
Word	
Sermon	
	Hymn

Themes

A theme may determine the pattern of the worship. The traditional Morning and Evening Prayer pattern allows the word and praise to throw light on each other. A thematic approach very often means that the worship leader decides the way the word is to be heard, and the response that needs to be made. Care must be taken to make sure that the whole service does not become a sermon. This tends to happen when explanations and exhortations introduce every item.

Some examples of a thematic approach

* Maundy Thursday foot-washing

* Baptism service: see pages 363–371

Guidelines

When you have completed the service outline, consider this checklist.
Parts of this are amplified in the descriptive commentary sections that follow.

* Is there a balance between word, prayer, praise and action? For instance the Word section may be top heavy with long readings and long introductions, or too many short readings.

* Is the worship directed to God, addressing him rather than the people?

* Is the structure and direction of the service clear enough for people to know where it is going? Does the service have an overall coherence, or is it just one item after another?

* When is the climax to the service? If there is more than one, is that deliberate? Is the emotional or spiritual climax the same as the climactic moment in terms of music or words or congregational action? There is no 'right' answer, but it helps if service planners are aware of these ways in which the service develops.

* What space is there for reflection or silence in the service?

* How much of the service might be classed as 'entertainment'? Is this justified? Is there a balance between receiving (listening, watching, contemplating) and responding? Check on posture: is there too much sitting down or standing up at one time? Or, conversely, are people bobbing up and down too much? Is there enough action?

* Is the music used in such a way as to further and develop the main thrust of the service? Is there too much musical praise, with too many choir items, or too long a section of choruses from the music group, or hymns too close to one another?

* Does the form of service enable the gifts of a variety of people in the church to be used in both planning and taking part?

* Compare this service with other services in the month. An occasional completely new form of worship may stimulate people to discover new dimensions to their ordinary worship, but a new pattern each week may be confusing and unsettling, particularly to children. If people are familiar with both structure and content of the service, they feel more secure and can take part more easily. For an all-age service, for instance, it may be better to have a standard structure, with 'windows' or 'slots' which can be changed from week to week.

* Especially if you are planning 'family worship', check that the contents do not exclude some in the congregation, e.g. children, single people, the bereaved, members of broken families. It is hurtful and not constructive to require a mixed congregation simply to join in prayers thanking God for our homes and families and all the happiness that parents and children share.

Planning and Preparing Holy Communion

There are basically two parts to the Holy Communion service: the Word and the Sacrament.

The Word part consists of
* the first part of the Holy Communion
  (The Gathering and The Liturgy of the Word)
or
* A Service of the Word (Preparation, The Liturgy of the Word, Prayers).
  This can take the form of Morning or Evening Prayer, or a Family Service.

The Sacrament part consists of
* The Peace
* Preparation of the Table
* The Eucharistic Prayer
* Breaking of the Bread
* Giving of Communion
* The Dismissal

These features are not all of equal weight.

How it works

First decide the structure.

This is well set out on page 12 above, although Note 10 to A Service of the Word (page 14) says that the order provided is not prescriptive. A decision will need to be taken about where to place those ingredients that are normal but may vary in position; for example, where penitence is to come, and where the Peace is shared.

Second, add to this structure:

* Other elements that are compulsory, but may vary in form. All of the authorized forms of confession and absolution from *Common Worship* may be found in Section B. When A Service of the Word with a Celebration of Holy Communion is being used, the readings must be governed by an authorized lectionary, but the Creed could be the Apostles' Creed or an authorized Affirmation of Faith. All those currently authorized may be found in Section E.

* Those ingredients in the service which are not compulsory; e.g. the collect for purity, the Gloria in excelsis, the prayer of humble access, the choice of post communion or another suitable prayer.

* Those parts of the service where 'ad lib' or unofficial material may be used, or where there is provision made in the Resource Sections, e.g. the Greeting, the Prayers of Intercession, the introduction to the Peace, Prayers at the Preparation of the Table, the Post Communion or other suitable or seasonal prayers, the seasonal or other suitable form of blessing.

The Peace

Most modern rites place the Peace between the Prayers and the Preparation of the Table. Note the scope for placing it elsewhere, for example at the beginning or the end of the service, as well as the option to introduce it with other words, which may be composed for the occasion or the locality. See page 271 below.

Preparation of the Table

Customs vary on the solemnity with which this is done. In some places, variable prayers may be used. These should be *preparatory*, as the title for this part implies, and not dramatically overshadow the Eucharistic Prayer.

The Eucharistic Prayer

One of the authorized forms must always be used. A Eucharistic Prayer, whether it takes the form of extended monologue with acclamations, or a dialogue between president and congregation, normally includes the following:

* thanksgiving for creation, redemption and the work of the Spirit
* the memorial prayer for the Church to receive and grow in the life of Christ
* doxology, offering praise to God the Holy Trinity.

These are the 'deep structures' of the prayer. They need to be 'signposted' clearly as the prayer progresses, not least by the tone of voice(s) used as the prayer is proclaimed.

The pattern of the prayer is normally

* an opening dialogue
* an introduction to praise
* an extended act of thanksgiving
* the narrative of the institution of the Lord's Supper
* the memorial prayer
* the prayer for the work of the Spirit
* the concluding doxology.

While this basic pattern is true for all the Eucharistic Prayers in *Common Worship* Order One, an examination of the position of the Sanctus reveals two slightly different structures.

* The traditional Western structure, to which people grew accustomed in the prayers in *The Alternative Service Book 1980*, places the Sanctus at the climax of the preface or extended thanksgiving. It is followed by petition, which also encompasses the narrative of institution. This is the pattern of Prayers A, B, C and E.
* The Trinitarian or Eastern structure followed in Prayers F and G places the Sanctus within the thanksgiving, where it marks the change of focus from Father to Son. In this pattern the narrative of institution marks the shift from praise to petition and the focus on the Holy Spirit comes after it. This Trinitarian pattern is slightly less clear in Prayer D. Prayer H is also

Trinitarian in pattern, but the initial thanksgiving is concluded with the narrative of institution and the Sanctus is the final climax of praise at the end of the prayer.

Within this framework there is scope for variations:

* The Preface: Short Prefaces may be inserted in Eucharistic Prayers A, B and C in Order One, and Extended Prefaces may be used with Eucharistic Prayers A, B and E. See Note 18 on page 333 in *Common Worship*, and also Praise in Resource Section G in this book. Others may be specially composed, provided that they balance the style and overall length of the rest of the prayer.
* Acclamations: four three-line acclamations, each with a specific introductory line, are provided for Eucharistic Prayers A, B, C, E and G, and one of them must be chosen. Optional acclamations are suggested for use in Prayers A and E, and as Note 18 says, other acclamations may be used.
* Chorus or metrical versions of the Sanctus and Doxology may be used, instead of those printed.

In Order One the Eucharistic Prayer leads into the Lord's Prayer, but A Service of the Word with a Celebration of Holy Communion does not specify where the Lord's Prayer should be used, opening up the possibility of using it, for example, in the Prayers of Intercession or in its Order Two position.

Breaking of the Bread

This symbolic action prepares for the sharing of the bread and wine. On Sundays and Principal Holy Days one of the forms of words provided in Order One or Order Two must be used. On other days it may be done in silence or during the Agnus Dei. See Note 20 on page 334 of *Common Worship*.

Invitation to Communion

Forms for this may be found on page 180 of *Common Worship*, but there are no explicit instructions either in the Notes or the Order on page 12 in this book.

Giving of Communion

Local customs vary. However the consecrated bread and wine are shared, it should be done decently and in order.

After Communion

Consecrated bread and wine not required for communion are reverently consumed at the end of the distribution or after the service. This is not a liturgical act and need not be done at the holy table or by the president.

For prayer after communion there is a choice between presidential texts (the authorized Post Communion of the day or another suitable prayer) and congregational texts. Other alternative prayers and dismissals are provided in Resource Section J.

Planning and Preparation in General

Stories from the four churches

St Ann's sent three lay leaders on a diocesan course on preparing worship. As a result they came back wanting to set up a planning group for worship. They brought back with them draft terms of reference for such a group, which were discussed and amended by the PCC (see section opposite). The PCC recognized that this was a move away from the previous pattern, where a different house group had planned and led the worship each week. This had resulted in some inconsistency in the worship, though one good thing about it was that a very wide range of people had been involved, so the new planning group had a long list of people in the church who had worship gifts.

At **St Bartholomew's** the vicar recognizes the difficulty of planning worship for several different country churches. At St Bartholomew's itself the monthly all-age service is planned and led by a group of young parents, two of whom teach in the small Sunday school, so that there is some link between the two. They plan the themes with the vicar six months at a time. This involves deciding on how to handle the theme in terms of teaching, readings, music, prayers and activities. In one village two people have been on a diocesan course on leading worship and can plan a communion service and lead the first part of it until the vicar arrives. In another village the PCC is small enough to discuss worship easily and the vicar has been training some of them to lead the intercessions.

Planning at **St Christopher's** is in the hands of the staff. The vicar uses a blank form (specimen opposite) which gradually gets filled in, from his initial ideas a couple of months ahead, through discussion with the staff and regular meetings with Sunday school leaders, organist and head server. Copies of the form, duly typed, give all concerned a complete menu for each service.

The vicar of **St Dodo's** returned from a (compulsory) diocesan clergy conference, at which worship had been on the agenda, keen to put into practice some of the things he had learnt others were doing. The next Sunday's worship had a different structure, with a new confession, creed and Eucharistic Prayer (and no time for the congregation to be taught about them or even to read quietly through them before having to join in). There were also new songs – which the choir hadn't seen before – in the order of service badly duplicated on dark pink paper. The clearest liturgical refrain in the service was 'You'll find it on your pink slip', which amused everyone but the colour-blind. An angry PCC the next week invoked the provisions of the Worship and Doctrine Measure and insisted on a return to the traditional services. Everyone was hurt and the worship was fossilized.

Worship Planning Group: terms of reference

1   To review and evaluate all aspects of worship at St Ann's, including
    * structures and patterns of worship on Sunday;
    * the relationship between worship and the rest of the life of the church;
    * the teaching and preaching programme and the use of music and drama;
    * the place of children and other groups.

2   To be responsible for the planning and preparation of Sunday worship, including working through other groups such as house groups, choir, music groups, drama group.

3   To ensure that the varied gifts of the congregation are being used in worship.

4   To plan developments in worship and to prepare for regular PCC discussion of worship.

St Christopher's service form: 10.30 a.m. Parish Eucharist

Season/mood:
President:
Assistants:
Standard service:
Setting:

Introit / introductory music / sentence:

Hymn:

Old Testament:
Psalm:
New Testament:
Canticle/song:
Gospel:
Sermon:
Any special requirements e.g. tapes, visuals:
Intercessions: (who? add items...)

Hymn:

Variable items for Liturgy of the Sacrament:
(words/music for peace, preface, before and during distribution)

Hymn:

Post-communion prayer:
Notices (list...)
Blessing/dismissal

Discussion starter/Away Day agenda: our worship

1 Share in twos or threes: what is really good about our worship?

2 Talk or Bible study or discussion:
   * What is worship? Look at the section below, which could be reproduced as a handout.
   * Would we say more, or less, than this? What is our experience?
   * What should our Sunday worship include? What are the basic ingredients for our worship?

3 From this, in twos and threes, list two or three principles which should govern our worship. Share these with the whole group, and see how much agreement there is. Sometimes we disagree on practical decisions about worship because we don't agree on the principles.

4 Next, consider in small groups practical questions such as:
   * How does the worship meet the needs of the elderly, children of different ages, the disabled, those who find reading difficult, those who need to be stretched intellectually?
   * Should there be more freedom (or less?) in our worship?
   * How should we expect to know the presence of God?
   * How could the intercessions be improved?
     Then decide which two items should come top of the group's agenda.

5 With everyone together, list the suggested agenda items, see how much overlap there is, and start with the one with most 'votes'. There will not be time to discuss everything. Some items will need further research: two people could be briefed to bring items back to the PCC.

6 For each item, consider four questions.
   * What resources do we need?
   * What barriers or problems are there in the way of taking action on this?
   * What is the timetable for action?
   * Who is responsible for action?

Discussion handout:
What is worship?

A worship planning group, a PCC or church leaders' group would do well to have some discussion in general terms about worship. Are we agreed about what is worship and what is not, what the ingredients are, what kind of movement, physical, emotional and spiritual, we should expect in worship?

Try completing the sentence, 'Worship is…' Yes, it is giving God his worth, or what he deserves, or glory. 'The true end of man is to glorify God and enjoy him for ever', as Christians said in the seventeenth century. But explore the mechanics of that a bit more: do any of the following paragraphs get near our experience?

Worship is a door open in heaven. We lift up our hearts, listen in to what God is saying, join the angels and archangels and all the saints in heaven in praising God's eternal holiness. We are there and he is here.

Worship is a door open to the inner depths of life. Suddenly, as we worship, there is wholeness, *shalom*, peace, as all the fragmented bits of our being are put into God's perspective. Things make sense, and there is something to hold on to which has hitherto seemed just beyond the grasp of our mind.

Worship is a door open to the rhythms of life. Through festivals, simple rituals, a weekly rhythm, worship marking morning and evening, the whole of life, time and space is claimed for God and given back to him. In the worship he gives it to us again, to use for him, and we know he is concerned with our hopes and fears, politics and problems, families and finance.

Worship is a door to our hearts open in obedience to God. He commands us to worship in spirit and in truth. We respond to the overwhelming majesty of his beauty revealed in creation, to his overwhelming love and grace revealed in his word and in his Son. And as we worship, we are changed…

Now, this is in no sense an agreed definition of worship. Rather, it is intended to stimulate local parish groups and worship leaders to arrive at some agreement on what they expect, or are longing for, in their worship.

Would we say more than this, or less? What is our own experience?

What should our Sunday worship include? What are the basic ingredients for our worship?

Discussion handout:
Service structures – some historical background

A glance at history shows us the pedigree of the different strands of non-eucharistic worship which we find today in the all-age or 'family' service, Morning and Evening Prayer, and the first half of Holy Communion. In the early centuries of the Church's life there are three strands of non-eucharistic worship:

✳ The Word Service (first part of Holy Communion)
✳ Daily Prayer (Morning and Evening Prayer)
✳ Services of Teaching or Instruction.

The evidence here is from the writings of Justin Martyr (who wrote in the middle of the second century) and the *Apostolic Tradition* (written in the early third century, and traditionally ascribed to Hippolytus), but it is also to be found in other places.

Justin's description of The Word Service consists of readings from the prophets or memoirs of the Apostles, read for as long as time allowed. This is followed by a discourse, and common prayer. This core of material is still recognizable in all major traditions, even though other elements were added in the intervening centuries. Usually there is an approach, with prayer and praise, and possibly penitence; then the readings, the last of which is a Gospel reading, followed in turn by a sermon, the creed and intercessions. What sort of 'shape' does this give us? It would be possible to see the climax of such a service either in the reading of the Gospel (even though this is a later addition), or in the intercessions, as the response of faith – the living sacrifice of the Church responding to the Word proclaimed and preached.

The content of daily prayer in the *Apostolic Tradition* is less precise. It is prayer in the heart, with a few people, or many. The emphasis is on the *times* of daily prayer. The later evidence of East and West suggests that the main times were morning and evening, and the service consisted of praise, using fixed psalms, hymns and songs, together with intercession. Later developments included:

* many introductory prayers;
* the continuous recitation of the Psalter;
* readings from Scripture of ever increasing length, along with other Christian writings.

The original core of daily prayer, praise to God at certain times of the day, eventually became obscured, and its structure distorted, by lengthy psalm-singing and readings.

The 'Teaching' type of service centring on instruction in the Word of God is referred to in the *Apostolic Tradition* and may be a direct offspring of the corresponding synagogue service, a Bible study with no particular liturgical shape.

As history proceeds, these three types of service, which major respectively on reading the Word, on prayer and praise, and on teaching, do not remain distinct. At the Reformation, Cranmer reduced the seven medieval 'hours' into Morning and Evening Prayer, combining prayer and praise with an emphasis on reading and teaching the Word.

Before we draw some conclusions from this, a further glance at history suggests that Christians in the early Church were not divided up according to *age*, but rather according to *stage*, so that catechumens (those preparing for baptism, however old they were) were excluded from the Eucharist. Their formal departure at the end of the Word Service would have been a dramatic feature of the liturgy in a large building, probably involving some upheaval in the congregation as a whole. Perhaps we might make similar structural provision today. As they did in the early Church, we are again providing not only for individuals but for whole families to move from a non-Christian to a Christian lifestyle. Should we still be organizing our church life and worship on the assumption that people grow from being less Christian to more Christian in parallel with their age (and so older people but not children are admitted to communion …)?

Additions and insertions

Stories from the four churches

At **St Ann's** there is usually some kind of 'spot' which is particularly suitable for the children before they go out. Sometimes it is a fairly riotous action chorus which (depending on the mood of the service) usually fits best among the introductory choruses. Today there is a brief quiz (with scoring on the projection equipment) on the Old Testament story which is read in church and forms the basis of the teaching when they leave. This naturally comes straight after it is read. Sometimes there is an interview with a member of the congregation, or a visitor or past member of the church (always done with a microphone). Some interviews are lively enough to be done when the children are present, or of particular interest to them, and may come before or after one of the readings; others fit much better as part of the sermon or, more usually, just before the intercessions so that prayer follows naturally from them. Today there is a missionary couple who are returning overseas after home leave, and the farewell prayer and commissioning takes place after communion, immediately before the blessing. Apart from the notices (before the intercessions today) the only other 'insertion' is the laying on of hands for healing, which happens in a non-intrusive way as people come forward to receive communion.

Today is Rogation Sunday at **St Bartholomew's** and the archdeacon is there for Evensong in the afternoon. The congregation have saved up for a new electric organ to replace the old harmonium, and it is dedicated after the second lesson, before the small choir sing an anthem. After the sermon, everyone goes out in a haphazard kind of procession to the lych gate, where a pair of new gates, given in memory of a young farmer killed last year, are blessed. There is prayer for the family, and conversation with them as the procession moves off to the highest point at the top of the churchyard for the Rogationtide blessing of fields, crops, sheep and sea. The blessing of the people, present at the service and in the surrounding village, ends the service. Sometimes an insertion on this scale becomes the focus and climax towards which the worship moves.

The vicar at **St Christopher's** has studied Note 7 of *Common Worship* Holy Communion (*Common Worship* page 331), so silences are inserted at the appropriate points, and the service moves along with a clear and dignified rhythm of music, words and space for reflection. Today, ministers of the Eucharist are being commissioned to take communion to the sick, and this is most appropriately done immediately before the Peace, with some words of explanation, questions to them and a prayer of commissioning. This is the point in the service where the annual commissioning of the PCC and church leaders takes place in April, using some of the Words for Dedication from Resource Section I of *New Patterns*, but other points are used when appropriate. A couple of weeks ago a new head chorister was installed after one of the readings before the choir led the singing of the psalms.

At **St Dodo's** the vicar knows he has a number of different things to get into the service, but has failed to sort out on paper where they should come. It is a Parade Service, and there is a baptism. He announces the first hymn and goes to the sanctuary to collect the assorted Scout and Guide flags which don't begin their slow procession from the back of the church until during the last verse. He gets impatient and flustered, and doesn't get back to his reading desk until after the Reader, trying to be helpful, has said 'Let us pray.' Oh dear! He had meant to welcome the baptismal party and give a few notices. Never mind: there is plenty of time to do this after the second reading because the churchwardens (despite his frantic signalling during the psalm) have failed to come forward with the stand, portable glass sugar-bowl font and water for the baptism. So, having begun the baptism part of the service, he realizes people can't insert the child's name into the prayer (their usual custom) as he has neither welcomed the baptismal party nor presented the child. He invites the parents and godparents to the front and introduces them while the wardens get things ready. To fill in time, he asks them a couple of impromptu questions (he has heard that other churches sometimes do this), but they don't seem very prepared for it, and get embarrassed. To give himself time to think, he puts an extra hymn after the baptism, but forgets that the third hymn is always the one when the collection is taken and so is faced unexpectedly with an approaching column of plate-bearers. In the confusion, he forgets that he had promised one of the Guide leaders that they could present a gift to one of their leaders who is moving away. He remembers just as the flag party are half way down the aisle to collect their flags in the last hymn and – rightly – judges it to be too late.

Interviews

Interviews have some advantages over inviting someone to talk for five minutes:
* the interviewer is in control of the time taken;
* the interviewer can direct the conversation to those things the congregation will be most interested in, and interrupt and curtail boring bits;
* the variety in voices makes them easier to listen to.

How to prepare
* Don't meet to 'talk it over' hours or days beforehand. It will taste like left-overs and be like trying to recapture a spontaneous joke when the circumstances are different. Meeting the victim three or four minutes before is plenty.

- Do some reading and thinking around the background to the interview. Decide on an 'angle'. Be selective in what you want to ask. The informed interviewer can select what is most interesting or relevant to the congregation.
- Have a simple outline you can hold in your mind, perhaps three or four basic questions that can be elaborated. Make sure there is a progression so that they lead on from one to the next.

How to do it
- Use a microphone if one is available.
- Be mobile: face the victim and also turn to the congregation.
- Above all, be interested. If the interviewer is not interested in the answers to the questions, no one else will be. If the interviewer yawns, so will everyone else.

Notices

When in the service?
Sometimes it is tempting to see the notices as nothing more than an annoyance and an intrusion into worship. Perhaps the first thing to do is to recognize their value as part of the shared life of the worshipping community. Only then can questions about the best place for them be addressed, in the context of the structure and flow of the whole service.

Common Worship Holy Communion Note 9 suggests three possible places:

At the beginning:
- Notices can be used to give the congregation some sense of unity, of being part of the same family, as family news and forthcoming events are shared. They can also help to set the atmosphere for worship.
- Some people might miss them by arriving late, saying, 'It's only the notices'; on the other hand the notices may be so attractive and important that people get there in time for them.
- People who go out to the children's groups or the creche can leave for their activities having heard the notices.
- If not well done, they can get the service off to a bad start.
- If at the beginning, they could be done before the president enters (in which case they should be done by someone else) or after the opening greeting (possibly by the president). This might be seen as marking them out as part of the worship, and spiritually important.

Before the intercessions:
- They can be used to prepare and give information for the intercessions, so that people can pray for items of news or events to come.
- It may help to provide a break in the middle of the service.
- Notices here can disrupt the flow of the worship.

At the end:
- Everyone has arrived by then.
- The notices are seen as part of the Christian community going out to serve God in the world: things to fix our eyes on, to pray for, and times to meet again during the week.

* It is too late to pray for these things in this service.
* It may seem disruptive to those who want to go on quietly praying: notices are a community-centred activity, not easily mixed with private prayer. Which is most important at this point in this particular service?

How to do them

* A printed weekly bulletin or notice sheet; if there are spoken notices as well, these should be used to highlight important items, not to add another long collection of details.
* Vary the person who gives the notices: why should it be the function of the person leading the worship?
* Try two people sharing the task as 'presenters', with media-style headlines.
* Use visuals, such as a projector or some drama.
* Be enthusiastic; look at the congregation; remember there is a spiritual purpose to the notices.
* Evaluate and review both the place in the service and the method. Do they outweigh the sermon in length and importance? Do they contribute spiritually to the growth of the church at worship?

Questions to ask when putting something different into the service

* Is this something covered by the Notes in *Common Worship*, or by the examples here?
* Is it such a large item that it will change the feel of the whole service? If so, would it be better to construct a special service?
* What is the effect of this item likely to be on the parts of the service around it? Where will it fit most naturally so that it contributes to and does not halt the flow of the worship? For example, if it is giving information, would this lead into prayer? If it is a special musical contribution, can it replace or be part of a Godward part of the worship? If a procession, can it happen at the beginning or end, or when there is movement anyway in the service?
* Is it going to help or hinder the congregation's sense of God's presence and his purpose for them? If it is likely to hinder, is it really necessary?

Structures and 'specials'

Stories from the four churches

It's the fifth Sunday in the month, and each church is having a special 'family' service, exploring how to use A Service of the Word to help them produce something a bit different from the regular worship.

There are a large number of children and young families present in **St Ann's** for another in their series of thematic services. They have been trying to involve people of all ages in the action of the worship. As the service begins, everyone learns an acclamation:

> **God has set his rainbow in the clouds:**
> **he will remember his covenant for ever.**

Using the suggestion in Resource Section G, this is used as a 'shout' at intervals during the service, a reminder of the theme as the service moves from one section to the next. The drama group have some small pieces of drama, one for each section, based on the Bible story, but the main thrust of the action is to involve the whole congregation. The first section, considering God's problem of confronting sin in the world, leads into the responsive confession for creation (B42). The children in the drama saw and hammer to music, building the ark, and round up the animals into the ark, as the story is read. There is no sermon – the whole service is full of the Word, but there is time for two well-prepared testimonies to God's rescue operation before the service ends with a responsive thanksgiving for creation (G66) and the sharing of the Peace.

At **St Bartholomew's** the planning group have been looking at Example 2 – the conversation structure – in the section above on planning and preparing a Service of the Word (page 19). They have been struck by the idea that Morning Prayer is like a conversation, with God speaking and then the congregation replying, and have decided to use this to help people understand and benefit more from the regular services. Their service outline uses 'Hello', 'Sorry', 'Thank you', 'Please' as the headings for the main sections, held up on large visual aid cards as the service proceeds.

There are two children being baptized at **St Christopher's**, so that provides the overall theme for the worship. The clergy have looked at the *Common Worship* Baptism service, and decided to have a service which is not eucharistic, and which involves people as much as possible. They take as their basis the Holy Communion with Baptism Sample Service in *New Patterns,* ending with the Peace. One of the readings is dramatized, and a procession of children brings in the water, ceremonially poured from a large jug.

The vicar at **St Dodo's** called a meeting of his worship planning group, which has representatives from every organization in the church, many of them enthusiastic to take over the running of worship from the vicar. In generous mood, he said yes to all their ideas for the fifth Sunday all-age service, but didn't think it possible to get them to agree on a common theme and also forgot to make a note of what each was offering. He thinks it's just a matter of adding a few things in to Morning Prayer, but as the service unfolds we are treated to a disorganized concert-like jostling for position between the Guides parading to the front with their flags, the women's meeting (they used to be 'Young Wives') anthem for St Cecilia's Day, a rogue drummer from the youth group who tries to get in on every hymn, three dramatized versions of the Good Samaritan, one in full costume with trip-over lighting effects…
All agree it is a very special service.

Music in Worship

Stories from the four churches

St Ann's has a music planning group which consists of the organist and representative members of the choir, the music group, the worship group, and the clergy. They meet regularly to look at themes for services, special occasions etc., to plan the music three months in advance.

Representatives of this group go to youth events and to diocesan music events so that they keep abreast of new music resources. A training day was recently held in the parish when a tutor from the RSCM came to introduce them to some new music for the *Common Worship* services, and new ways of singing psalms, as they felt that their eucharistic worship was in danger of being stuck in a rut musically. The organist and a member of the congregation who is a music teacher are working together to write some music for the Eucharist which will suit their congregation and musical resources.

The choir and music group have practised a new song, and some of the congregation have learnt it in their home groups. Today the music group is teaching the new song before the service starts, so that it is familiar before it is sung in the service later.

St Bartholomew's organist is very willing and enthusiastic, but only has limited time, as she also plays for the Methodist church down the road. She chooses the music for two Sundays a month, using the RSCM's guide, *Sunday by Sunday*.

The music group (two or three adults and a group of enthusiastic children) have been playing simple music together for a while. Because of their limited resources, they have been accompanying songs in the usual 'hymn slots' in the services, but have also been experimenting with using music in other ways. They have used Taizé chants as responses to the prayers. These chants work well as the music can be adapted to the number and skill of the instrumentalists available. Today they are playing a piece after the readings, when the congregation can have space to reflect on what they have heard. The music is simple enough for the children to join in, yet the skills of the adult musicians are also used in playing and singing the harmonies.

When the music group learn new songs, they are very keen to share them with the congregation. They have made a few mistakes along the way by using too much new material without giving people a chance to learn it, but, by and large, the congregation are pleased at the enthusiasm and commitment of the music group, and are happy to learn new music alongside using the traditional hymns which they know.

St Christopher's have an organ, but no one who can play it. Their large robed choir is now reduced in numbers and its members are all growing old; several can no longer get to church regularly.

There are no other musicians in the congregation, so the church decided to send one of their younger members, who can sing, to have guitar lessons. He is getting more proficient at basic chords and will soon be able to lead and accompany some simple songs for the congregation to sing.

Meanwhile, as they felt that using music adds something special to a service, the congregation have been trying unaccompanied singing. Today the songs are 'The Lord's my shepherd' and 'Amazing grace', which people feel they know well enough to sing confidently. They find singing hymns with a number of long verses difficult to sustain, so they are using music which is simple and short. The response to the prayers today is a sung one from Iona, 'Through our lives and by our prayers, your kingdom come'.

For the Eucharist, they have been contemplating using a simple cantor-led setting for the acclamations, which can be sung unaccompanied.

The organist at **St Dodo's** chooses all the music – without consultation with anyone. He tries to fit in with the theme or season, using the index in *Hymns Ancient and Modern*. He also directs the choir, who are a group of enthusiastic singers, many of whom don't read music. They lead the congregational singing and persevere with Anglican chant, but don't manage many anthems. Sometimes they're tempted to try pieces they hear on CDs made by their cathedral choir – like Schubert's Mass in G. When they tried part of it, it proved far too difficult for them and they faltered and then completely stopped halfway through.

The youth group would like to sing more up-to-date music, so for today's all-age service, the organist has agreed to play 'Sing Hosanna' and 'Shine, Jesus, Shine'. The vicar announces the number of the song, and reads out the first line, but his words are drowned out as the organist, keen to get the modern songs over, starts to play. There is a retired schoolteacher who has offered to involve some of the children who play recorders, and she has taught them to play a song from the Iona community, 'Will you come and follow me'. They haven't had much time to practise, and haven't checked how many verses there are. When they stop playing, the vicar says, 'There's another verse yet,' and there is a long pause while they all get ready to play again.

Teaching the congregation new music

* Be positive: 'We are going to learn a song which fits with today's theme …', not 'I know you don't like learning new music but…'
* Know the music well enough to sing it in the bath yourself.
* Pitch the music at a sensible level to suit everyone – if possible, get somebody to give you a note first.
* If at all possible, use your voice to teach the melody – or at least, an instrument which plays the melody line, not full harmony.
* It may help to sing the whole of a verse to the congregation, so that they get the gist.
* Then learn the music line by line, unaccompanied. You sing a line, and let them sing it straight back to you. Warn them of any tricky bits, or point out where the tune repeats. If they make a mistake, put it right straight away. But always be encouraging.
* Using your hand to show where the notes go up and down can be a helpful guide – both when singing each line to demonstrate, and when encouraging the congregation to sing it back.
* Think about when you're going to teach the new song. Don't do it immediately before it's sung in the service – it breaks the flow of the worship. You could teach it before the service. Ideally, it could be taught the week beforehand, and then rehearsed briefly before the service in the week it is to be sung. If your church has a choir or music group, they can sing the song one week (if it is appropriate to the service), to help people to become more familiar with it.

> Believe in the voice God has given you. It is the voice of an apprentice angel. Believe in the voices God has given other people.
>
> John Bell, Iona Community, in *Heaven Shall not Wait*

Why use music in worship?

* To make the text special, 'different' from everyday speech.
* It is corporate, something we can all join in with, and encourages participation.
* It is memorable, and helps us to remember the words.
* It expresses feelings and emotions in a deeper way than words alone.

How to use music in worship

* To 'break up' a section of a service or a whole service.
  It may be useful as a response after a period of listening, or to allow a change of posture after a period of sitting or kneeling.
* To complement action.
  It is often used to 'cover up' an action, e.g. taking the collection, but is better used in its own right or complementing an action, e.g. singing a meditative prayer while giving people space to light candles or use some other symbolic action.

✳ To heighten our awareness.
Music makes us more aware of shape. Its use can make sound and silence more meaningful, and can give shape to the time we spend in prayer and praise.

Where to use music in worship

✳ Gathering. This is not just music for the entry of the ministers, but music which will help the people of God to gather for worship. Thought needs to be given to the exact position for the music in the opening section of the service.
✳ Praise. The obvious places are the Gloria, Gospel Acclamation and Eucharistic Prayer in a communion service, but praise as a response to God may come at various points and be expressed in different styles of music.
✳ Response, e.g. after the readings and the sermon. How do we use psalms as a response to the readings, and is there a balance of word and song in that part of the liturgy? Music does not always have to have words in order for us to use it to respond to God – just as words do not always need to have a musical setting.
✳ Proclamation of the Gospel. Do sung Gospel Acclamations heighten the expectation of listening to God's word? If they do, should we use music in a similar way around other readings from Scripture, or the sermon?
✳ Affirming our belief. One of the authorized Affirmations of Faith is a hymn. Are there other ways in which we could affirm in song the underlying principles of our belief?
✳ Prayer. Often sung responses are used. What other music would enable us to deepen our collective prayer?
✳ Offering. We offer ourselves and our gifts to God. How do we express the joy of our offering in song?
✳ Contemplation. There should be space for both silence and reflection in our worship. What kinds of music can contribute to that contemplation? Or is this a time for the music of silence?
✳ Sending. We are sent out to the mission of the Church in the world. What kind of music enables and strengthens us for this task?

Questions to ask when choosing music

✳ How does this fit into the overall theme of the service, or the readings?
✳ How does it fit into the shape of the service, e.g. is it suitable for the gathering, or the offertory, or a prayerful response?
✳ How does the music fit with the overall style of the service, e.g. is it a celebratory Eucharist or a meditative Evening Prayer?
✳ Is the music well known to the congregation, or does it need to be introduced to them first?
✳ What resources do we have? What is achievable by our musicians and congregation?

Children in Worship

Stories from the four churches

St Ann's has plenty of rooms and people, and so is able to provide a teaching programme for the children whenever they are not present in church for the whole of the service. At a recent meeting of the PCC, it was felt that although the children benefited from their own groups for teaching, they missed out on experiencing the worship of the whole church. It was decided, therefore, to have more services which were suitable for the whole church community to worship together. The worship planning group were sent off to come up with some ideas for involving the children in the whole of the liturgy. They suggested these areas for consideration:

* Involving the children in preparation for worship – choosing hymns, preparing the holy table, giving out hymn books, joining in a procession, using opening responses which the children can join in (with simple or repetitive responses such as A28).
* Having a worship theme table (see page 41) reflecting the theme of the service at different points in the church building in different seasons.
* Using more visuals in all parts of the service, for example images on OHP or video projection, in the Penitence or Prayer sections or as an accompaniment to one of the readings (see page 41).
* Making sure that some of the Liturgy of the Word actively involves children, either in the presentation of the readings, or in taking part in or responding to the sermon; the Gospel might be preceded or followed by a free adaptation, transposing it to a modern setting, perhaps in dialogue form.
* Making more use of movement, letting the children move around the spaces in the church at appropriate moments, perhaps gathering under the big cross in the north aisle for the Prayers of Penitence, or around the font for the Affirmation of Faith.

They also suggested that some of the worship leaders and planners might visit the church junior school, and find out how interactive the lessons were, to gain more understanding of what the children were used to.

St Bartholomew's has Sunday school two weeks in the month and an all-age worship service once a month. On the fourth Sunday worksheets and pens are provided for the children to complete during the sermon. The worship leaders are working hard to find ways of integrating the children's contributions into a service which has to cater for everyone in the village. Some of the parents involved in planning and leading also teach in the Sunday school, so sometimes the children prepare something one week in Sunday school for use in worship the following Sunday. This week they have produced a collage of loaves and fishes for a temporary altar frontal. The intercessions often involve the children, as well as the rest of the congregation, in writing their own prayers or suggesting topics for prayer. Sometimes symbols are used to help people focus their prayers. A group of mums and older children are willing to cut out paper shapes for prayers to be written on, or to give a lead in preparing items for prayer beforehand, e.g. bringing newspaper cuttings to church as a starting point for the prayers.

There is a music group which sometimes leads the worship. It usually consists of a couple of adults and several children of differing musical abilities playing assorted instruments. Sometimes this makes for interesting sounds, but the congregation are glad to have the children's offerings. The children in turn are very enthusiastic and have a wide range of favourite music encompassing all styles.

St Christopher's has few children, as there are not many living in the parish. Activity sheets based on the lectionary readings are provided for the children who come on Sunday mornings. They refer to what the children will be doing later in the service. People bring their concerns to the church for prayer, and the children are encouraged to join in as well. Some of the older children occasionally read the lessons, or take part with adults in a dramatic reading for several voices. Sometimes a small group of adults and some children meet together a few weeks before a service to prepare banners, or a throw-over frontal for the altar, to reflect the theme of a special service.

The alternative provisions from *Common Worship* are often used, such as a responsive form of confession. The question and answer form of the Creed is used at both all-age services and communion services, so that the children and families who start to come to communion after having come to all-age worship are familiar with at least some of the liturgy. In the communion services where children are present, the shorter Eucharistic Prayers are usually used, and sometimes the children are invited to come and stand around the altar, or help to serve. They regularly use the responsive Prayer at the Preparation of the Table (*Common Worship*, page 292, Prayer 8), as they bring the bread and wine:

> With this bread that we bring
> **we shall remember Jesus.**

They have occasionally experimented with longer insertions at this point (see page 42) and taken advantage of the provision for varying the words of the Preface in some of the Eucharistic Prayers (see Note on Thanksgivings in Resource Section G, page 222).

Today is the monthly all-age service at **St Dodo's**, to which children and families have been invited, and there is a baptism. The young people are taking part in a drama (the Good Samaritan – again!) but once this is over they get restless, as the remainder of the service is not especially geared to them. The baptism sounds like a long monologue, and the music consists of Victorian hymns that are all unfamiliar. The children in the Sunday school have been asked to lead the prayers, so the Sunday school teachers have written them on pieces of paper, and the children have some difficulty reading them. It is also difficult to hear what they are saying as the microphone is not adjusted to their height. There are some Bible story books (given to the church ten years ago) and colouring things at the back of the church, but most of the children are now too old for them, and feel that they have rather outgrown such entertainment.

Ideas for visual accompaniment to readings

* Mime.
* Tableau.
* Drama.
* Dance.
* Puppets (shadow puppets are more easily seen by large numbers).
* Projected slides or OHP transparencies of the story drawn by the children.
* A procession of items referred to in the reading, brought up and arranged in a suitable space near the reader. (This has the advantage that it introduces movement without requiring a great deal of rehearsal. It provides concrete visual images and the people carrying the things up have to listen to the reading so as not to miss their turn.)

Worship theme table

Such a table, with items reflecting the theme or biblical material to be heard in the service, provides a concrete object of interest on arrival and throughout the service, both for children and adults. For example, on the first Sunday in Lent the table is below the pulpit. There is a large cloth covered with sand, in which are strewn a few large pebbles and the odd withering plant. Or on the fourth Sunday after Easter in Year A, there is a green felt cloth, a few toy lambs, a shepherd's crook or a large walking stick, a leather water bottle or perhaps a sheepskin. A group of people is always responsible for the preparation of the theme table and many people in the congregation are now used to contributing suitable items. Sometimes one of the flower arrangers provides an appropriate arrangement to complement the images and sometimes items are used during the address and then replaced.

Preambles before the Eucharistic Prayer

This might be a set of biddings or reasons for giving thanks, spoken by children or others, before the opening dialogue. Jewish-style questions and answers such as the following might be compiled, perhaps to echo the theme of the service. A child might ask the questions, which the president or deacon might answer, and not all questions need be attempted every time.

Q Why do we give thanks and praise to God?

A Because he has created all that is, and he has given us life. He is Lord of all, and yet loves each of us.

Q Why do we remember Jesus?

A Because he was sent from God and he gave up his life for us on the cross. God raised him from the dead so that we might see that death is not the end, but the beginning of a new life, the life Jesus showed us how to live.

Q Why do we use bread?

A Because Jesus took bread at the Last Supper. It is a sign of Jesus feeding us as we share with others around his table.

Q Why do we use wine?

A Because this wine is a sign of Jesus' saving love, poured out for us when he died on the cross.

(or)

Q Who are we remembering and who is here with us?

A Jesus Christ the Lord who lives today.

Q Why do we take this bread?

A To show that his body was given up to death for us.

Q Why do we take this wine?

A To show that Jesus shed his blood for our sins.

Q Why is there one loaf and one cup?

A Because we are one family; we belong to each other like the parts of a body.

Q Why do we come to his table?

A He invites us because he accepts us. We are his people and we share in his heavenly life.

Q For how long will Christians celebrate like this?

A Until Jesus comes to take us to be with God in heaven.

Whatever happens, the actions, style and approach of the president, while being accessible to children, should make clear that the Eucharistic Prayer which follows is addressed to God, in whose presence it is right to be filled with awe. The sense of mystery should not lose out to a chatty educational or instructional approach.

Discussion starter: All-Age Worship

If you have an all-age service in your church, compare it with what is described here.

If you are considering starting an all-age service, these questions and lists might help you compile a statement which begins 'Our all-age worship will be like this....' Try some brainstorming, when people list answers to questions such as:

* What is our aim in starting an all-age service?
* What are the arguments against it?
* What are the arguments in favour?

What is our aim in starting an all-age service?

* Who is the service for? Who might come to all-age worship?
    * Nuclear families with parents and young children.
    * Children from the Sunday School or regular children's activities.
    * Single parent families.
    * Single people.
    * Older people.
    * Those whose children have grown up and moved away.
    * Teenagers.
    * Visitors to the church or area.
    * Younger married couples.
* Is the service basically the Eucharist (Holy Communion) with a new title to emphasize that it is for the whole church community, or that provision is made for children as well as adults?
* Either for this or for a non-eucharistic service, are 'All-Age Worship', 'All-Age Service' or 'All-Age Communion' better titles than the often-used 'Family Service', to stress that people of all ages can worship together? Would it be better to invent a new, local name for the service?
* Is it just a way of giving children's workers a monthly break?

What are the arguments against all-age worship?

* Worship may seem 'childish'; the focus is on children to such an extent that adults are forced to deny their adulthood by joining in.
* If proper care is not taken it can focus so strongly on the nuclear family that it makes those in other styles of household – the single, bereaved, divorced and elderly – feel less part of the church family.
* Both structure and content can be so free and variable that people may see no links with traditional Anglican worship.
* It can fail to act as a 'bridge' to more main-line eucharistic or Morning Prayer worship: some worshippers never move on from the monthly 'all-age service'.

* Worship can become banal, superficial, focused on learning rather than worship, dominated by a strong teaching aim or a 'compere', and provide little God-centred worship.
* It can easily become all-age learning rather than all-age worship, because it is much easier to find resources for the former than the latter.
* Worship depends on the whim of the worship leader because so much is new; and because some people think it is not a 'statutory' service, there is sometimes little or no consultation with the PCC.

What are the arguments in favour of all-age worship?

* All-age worship can provide a place where those unfamiliar with formal worship can begin to feel at home. One reason for this is that it can be a bridge, in reflecting local culture more easily than the rest of the Church's worship. Another reason is that people sometimes welcome the excuse to accompany their children, and then find that they understand teaching which is simple and visual, and sometimes at a more 'introductory' level.
* It is a place where genuine intergenerational activity can take place, with adults and children learning from each other and worshipping together.
* It can help regular church attenders to discover new dimensions in worship.
* It provides an opportunity for people to grow and use their gifts by sharing in planning, leading and contributing to worship.
* It provides a way of introducing new elements into worship (in a congregation likely to be less critical of them?) – drama, dance, audio-visuals, new hymns or methods of teaching.

Space and Colour

Stories from the four churches

St Ann's is a modern building with worshippers seated on movable chairs in a semi-circle around the shallow open dais. The amplification system is excellent and none of the furniture in the building is fixed. A creative group in the church makes banners and throw-away paper visuals which focus on the season or the teaching theme – and the children's groups often contribute their own decorations. Using free-standing screens for some of these means that they need not always be in the same place and can be moved according to the needs of the worship. It also avoids sticky messes on the walls, though occasionally the wall is used, as when they went for a year or so with the words 'Christ has died, Christ is risen, Christ will come again' in well-designed paper letters on the wall behind the holy table.

St Bartholomew's found some years ago that they could increase the sense of space in their tiny church by removing the back row of the choir, moving the front stalls back, and putting carpet right across the chancel and sanctuary. At the same time, they moved the altar forward far enough for the president to get behind it.

More recently, they have looked at the need for somewhere for a very small group to worship on Sunday evenings or for less formal midweek occasions. The result of this has been the transformation of a small side chapel. The floor has been levelled (a sanctuary step had been put in at some stage), an efficient independent heating system installed and the old wooden chairs replaced by stacking cushioned stools, whose upholstery matches the carpet and the new pastel wash on the walls. And the small Jacobean table, restored and no longer boxed in with hangings, is a fitting focus for the seven or eight who gather round. Other 'focus' items include an icon of the Trinity and a single candle. Worshipping in this situation, with a more personal relationship between the members of the congregation and the president, inevitably has an effect on what happens in the larger group on Sundays. It has also been suitable for trying some of the less formal structures in *New Patterns for Worship*.

St Christopher's have only been back in church for a month. They worshipped in the school hall while the church was being re-ordered and decorated, and found this a surprisingly valuable experience. They took a deliberate decision not to cart bits of furniture out of the church into the hall to make the place 'more like church' – they had seen the odd effect of this in another local church which used a community centre, with plastic chairs (each with its embroidered hassock) and metal tables (one of them with a Victorian frontal not quite fitting it), a heavy gothic lectern and sanctuary chairs to match.

Instead, they decided to use the school furniture as it was, with a white cloth on the table and all the links with church centred on the people and the colourful vestments of the ministers. Without hassocks, they stood for the whole of the Eucharistic Prayer – and quite a bit more in the worship – and decided to carry on doing this when they returned to church. Doing without the organ was a good experience, too, and opened up the possibility of using other instruments regularly. A flute, guitar and piano now practise each week for some of the items in each service, and taped music provides the background to receiving communion more often than the organ.

In the re-ordered St Christopher's, the choir stalls have been moved to the west end of the church, behind the congregation. The chancel, cleared of furniture, is made more spacious with a platform built forward of the chancel arch and a carpet unifying the floor area. Gone are the heavy oak clergy desks and ornate bishop's chair; they are replaced by simple seats for the president and his assistants, arranged to face the people. The lectern too is of a simple design. The altar has been brought forward, under the arch, with plenty of space for movement round it. There is also space at the side of the church for a modern one-piece font which is big enough for an adult to stand in and have water poured over her or him and incorporates a bowl at waist height for pouring.

St Dodo's is a bit like an old-fashioned museum, with generations of furnishings and clutter which no one is allowed to touch. The sanctuary houses banners from long-departed church organizations, a large three-dimensional marble monument on one wall, a threadbare strip of carpet with brass fasteners, and a holy table which is not a table but a boxed-in wooden framework to hold ancient frontals (and behind which the flower vases, spare candles and watering can are kept). The modern light oak reading desks (given in memory of a benefactor twenty years ago and therefore immovable – one reason why the table cannot be moved forward) contrast with the dark pine empty choir stalls. And there are some items taken from the now-demolished church in the next parish when it was amalgamated with St Dodo's – an enormous carved oak lectern, which is out of all proportion to the rest of the furnishings, and a large marble font. This was so heavy that a special concrete base had to be built for it at the back of the church (where it is never used). They even found space to cram in a few more pews at the same time, and all without thinking of seeking advice or getting a faculty.

St Ann's checklist

At their monthly worship planning meeting, the St Ann's leaders check through a number of items to do with space, colour and the use of the building:

* Should the seating be in the normal arrangement or do we need to change it – make the aisles wider for a procession or dancing, for instance?
* Are we making the best use of the different spaces?
* Could we, for example, do a dramatic reading from different parts of the building?
* Can we visualize the different colours in use on any one day, in the dress of the ministers, banners and other hangings or visuals? Are there times when we might need to use the coloured stage lights?
* Plot the movement of people in each service, decide if there are clear 'ceremonial routes' for the ministers, e.g. moving to the font for a baptism with a family coming forward. Who is responsible for taking care of mechanical hiccups like moving an overhead projector or microphone stand out of the way?
* What does the church smell and look like? Do we need polish, air freshener or incense?

How St Christopher's moved

1 Some months of teaching about worship led most people to conclude that the present layout could be improved.
2 Vicar and churchwardens met the archdeacon, who outlined possibilities and offered a list of other churches which had made similar changes.
3 The PCC set up a small group to visit other churches, get ideas, take measurements and report back.
4 In a full-scale on-site consultation, the PCC committee, architect, archdeacon and some members of the Diocesan Advisory Committee and the Diocesan Liturgical Committee looked at how the proposed changes might help or hinder the worship – bearing in mind the need for flexibility, since ways of worshipping might change.
5 The PCC rightly thought that it was important for people to have some idea of what it would be like before taking the final decision. They considered asking the architect to produce some artist's impressions of what the church would look like, viewed from different points, which could be mounted on large display boards. But they decided instead on an experimental moving of the furniture (by the congregation and therefore at no cost).
6 After a couple of months the PCC consulted every member of the congregation – which made raising the money easier, as everyone felt they had a stake in the decision.
7 The PCC decided unanimously to apply for a faculty, and discussed carefully how the cost could be cut by doing some of the work themselves.

Small groups

Small groups at worship include not only small Sunday congregations, but those who gather midweek, ministers and others praying daily, and one minister at prayer on his or her own.

St Bartholomew's discussed the importance of:

* The scale of the worship area. A small group may be overwhelmed and made to feel insignificant by a large and lofty building.
* Warmth and comfort. It is easier to worship when people are comfortable.
* Colour. Gentle colours are better in a small space; more strident colours suit distant and dramatic viewing.
* Flexible seating. This can be arranged so that people can look at each other or have as the focus altar table, icon, candle, banner, lectern or Bible.
* Space, so that movement is possible, not only to come and go with ease, but to move during the worship.
* The possibility of using the area for counselling, the ministry of reconciliation, ministry to couples, spiritual direction.

Common Prayer and the Law

Stories from the four churches

St Ann's PCC has recently had to discuss 'Who has the authority to change the worship in our parish church?' This is because a number of people in the church would like to see a return to the Prayer Book for some services. At the beginning of *Common Worship*, on the authorization page (page vii), is a summary of Canon B 3:

> Canon B 3 provides that decisions as to which of the authorized services are to be used (other than occasional offices) shall be taken jointly by the incumbent and the parochial church council. In the case of occasional offices (other than Confirmation and Ordination), the decision is to be made by the minister conducting the service, subject to the right of any of the persons concerned to object beforehand to the form of service proposed.

The spirit of this Canon, and of the Worship and Doctrine Measure on which it is based, is that there should be agreement at local level. This is why there is no provision for appeal under Canon B 3, apart from cases where there is dispute over the form to be used for occasional offices. In cases of disagreement, *The Book of Common Prayer* or a form of service in use for two of the past four years is to be used. So it is important for the PCC to have regular discussions about the church's worship, and come to agreement on questions such as:

* Is the overall pattern of services right? How often is A Service of the Word or A Service of the Word with a Celebration of Holy Communion used?
* Does the PCC want to make specific recommendations on the contents of the service?
* When will the PCC next review the pattern of worship?

St Bartholomew's group of churches has recently been looking at what authority is needed for lay people to conduct services. Canon B 11 (see page 51) speaks of two categories of lay person, as well as Readers: those authorized by the bishop of the diocese (in their diocese this is done after attendance at a group of diocesan courses on worship sponsored jointly by the adult training department and the Diocesan Liturgical Committee), and other suitable lay persons, invited by the incumbent. Because of the existence of the course, the diocesan bishop has given directions that where lay people are to lead worship regularly, they should be those authorized by him. So St Bartholomew's now has four lay people on the course. They are glad that, once authorized, these people will be able to lead not only A Service of the Word, which is the structure for their all-age service, but also the entire

Gathering and Liturgy of the Word sections of Holy Communion on those occasions when the vicar arrives half way through the service (see *Common Worship*, page 159).

In the church school attached to **St Christopher's** there is a real need for a Eucharistic Prayer which the children can understand. The vicar has a copy of some prayers from a non-Anglican church, and has written to the bishop to ask, 'Please will you authorize this Eucharistic Prayer for use with children in our church school?' The bishop replies warmly, enthusiastic about the work in the school, but suggesting that Eucharistic Prayers D, H or E with a special extended preface (see page 42) are used. He encloses a letter from his legal adviser, who says:

> It does not matter legally whether the service is in school or in church. Canon B 1 limits Church of England ministers to using only the services it covers, unless he is claiming that the provisions of Canon B 5 apply, namely that it is a service for which no provision is made in the *Book of Common Prayer* or under Canons B 2 or B 4. Our common understanding is that Canon B 5 cannot be stretched to cover services of Holy Communion even if they are for specific occasions, age groups, or places not specifically provided for in the BCP or Canons B 2 and B 4. So a service of Holy Communion for St Swithun's Day should be regarded primarily as a service of Holy Communion (and therefore coming under Canons B 1 and B 2), and not as a special liturgy for St Swithun (for which the BCP etc. makes no provision, thus leaving the minister to his own discretion under Canon B 5).

The vicar of **St Dodo's** complains at the chapter meeting that the rural dean has used some illegal liturgy in the service which began the meeting. 'Where did that confession and absolution come from?' he asks, and is shown the pages of authorized forms of Confession and Absolution in *Common Worship* (pages 122–137).

Canon B 11.1

Morning and Evening Prayer shall be said or sung in every parish church at least on all Sundays and other principal Feast Days, and also on Ash Wednesday and Good Friday. Each service shall be said or sung distinctly, reverently, and in an audible voice. Readers, such other lay persons as may be authorized by the bishop of the diocese, or some other suitable lay person, may, at the invitation of the minister of the parish or, where the cure is vacant or the minister is incapacitated, at the invitation of the churchwardens say or sing Morning or Evening Prayer (save for the Absolution).

Common prayer in the Church of England

It may help to identify three aspects of the Anglican understanding of common prayer.

1   The valuing of patterns of worship which are recognized as the common possession of the people of God. This does not mean that nothing can change nor that every popular practice must prevail. It does not rule out any local variation. It does mean that worship must not simply be governed by the whim of the minister or the congregation. Corporate patterns of worship must exist and be developed which are recognized by worshippers as their corporate worship. It is therefore appropriate that these are approved and regulated by the Church.

2   The patterns and forms of worship must not be determined purely at the level of the local congregation but must bear witness to participation in the wider common life of the Church. For this reason it is right that common forms such as creeds, collects, confessions, and eucharistic prayers should be followed, as well as common approaches to the shape and content of Christian worship.

3   Patterns of common prayer play an important part in maintaining the unity of the Church in its confession of the Christian faith. For this reason,
     * those authorized to lead worship promise to 'use only the forms of service which are authorized or allowed by Canon' (Declaration of Assent, *Common Worship*, page xi);
     * while ministers have considerable liturgical freedom under Canon B 5, they are charged to ensure such services are 'neither contrary to, nor indicative of any departure from, the doctrine of the Church of England in any essential matter'; the section on page 52 sets out the things which need to be taken into account in assessing whether particular words and actions conform to the doctrine of the Church of England;
     * in recent years the General Synod has taken great care that all liturgical forms that it has authorized can be used with a good conscience by the different traditions in the Church of England.

The doctrine of the Church of England

1   Canon A 5, Of the doctrine of the Church of England, states:

> The doctrine of the Church of England is grounded in the Holy Scriptures, and in such teachings of the ancient Fathers and Councils of the Church as are agreeable to the said Scriptures. In particular such doctrine is to be found in the Thirty-nine Articles of Religion, *The Book of Common Prayer*, and the Ordinal.

This canon is based on the Worship and Doctrine Measure 1974, section 5(1). It is under this Measure that alternative forms of service to those in *The Book of Common Prayer* and the Declaration of Assent for church office holders have been authorized.

2   The Worship and Doctrine Measure 1974 requires that 'every form of service … approved by the General Synod … shall be such as in the opinion of the General Synod is neither contrary to, nor indicative of any departure from, the doctrine of the Church of England in any essential matter' (section 4(1)). Section 4(2) states: 'The final approval by the General Synod of any such Canon or regulation or form of service or amendment thereof shall conclusively determine that the Synod is of such opinion as aforesaid with respect to the matter so approved.'

3   In considering whether any rite is contrary to, or indicative of any departure from, the doctrine of the Church of England in any essential matter, reference should be made to:

i   the Holy Scriptures;

ii   such teachings of the Fathers and the Councils of the Church as are agreeable to the said Scriptures;

iii   the Thirty-nine Articles of Religion, *The Book of Common Prayer* and the Ordinal;

iv   such forms of service, canons and regulations as have received the final approval of General Synod.

Attention will need to be paid to (iv) in weighing matters that have recently been in dispute in the Church of England. Where, in controversial matters, General Synod has taken care not to depart from the teachings or usage found in (iii), this should be respected.

Discussion starter: Common prayer

1   Share together what different people mean by 'common prayer'.
   * Being able to walk into any church in the land and find exactly the same words to follow.
   * Recognizing some common features, some shared experiences, language and patterns or traditions as one does when visiting other members of the same family.
   Even Archbishop Thomas Cranmer recognized the need for cultural diversity in worship from country to country, saying in his Preface to the 1549 *Book of Common Prayer*: 'it often chanceth diversely in diverse countries'. Accepting a variety of forms, dictated by local culture, is part of our Anglican heritage.

2   Make a list of the characteristics of Anglican worship that we might expect to find everywhere. Share these with your neighbour, and compare them with this list drawn up by the Liturgical Commission in 1989.

   Some of the marks which should be safeguarded for those who wish to stand in any recognizable continuity with historic Anglican tradition are:
   * a recognizable structure for worship;
   * an emphasis on reading the word and on using psalms;
   * liturgical words repeated by the congregation, some of which, like the creed, would be known by heart;
   * using a collect, the Lord's Prayer, and some responsive forms in prayer;
   * a recognition of the centrality of the Eucharist;
   * a concern for form, dignity, and economy of words.

   How far are these in evidence in your church's worship?

3   Do you think it is possible to identify a 'core' of Anglican worship? If so, what would it consist of? Try to identify things under two headings:
   * **Structures** At the beginning of almost every new service in *Common Worship* there is a page showing the service structure. The debates on the structures of A Service of the Word and the Holy Communion service have helped us to see those things on which there is agreement across the Church: 'An Anglican service looks something like this.'
   * **Texts** 'An Anglican service contains prayers like this, the ones we know by heart.' These are some of the things that hold us together, but what are they? Share your list with others and see if they are different.

resource sections

resource sections

resource sections

Resource Sections

Contents

Resource Section Themes

In each Resource Section, the resources are grouped according to theme, in the following order.

Theme	Subjects covered
General	General (morning and evening)
Father, Son and Spirit	Trinity, approach to worship
God in creation	Harvest, creation
Christ's coming	Advent
Incarnation	Christmas, Epiphany, light
Cross	Holy Week, Lent
Resurrection	Easter
Ascension	Ascension, kingship
Holy Spirit	Pentecost
Word	Word
Church and mission	Mission, ministry, unity
Christian beginnings	Baptism and Confirmation
Lament	Lent, frustration/pain/anger
Relationships and healing	Reconciliation, family, love
Living in the world	Society, city
Holy Communion	Holy Communion
Heaven	Saints, death, glory
Time	Time

gathering and greeting

A Gathering and Greeting

Stories from the four churches

While the large and lively mixed-age congregation arrive for worship, the **St Ann's** music group plays a selection of thematic hymns and choruses in order to focus people's attention on worship and set the initial mood of the service.

The congregation join in the singing; the song numbers have been printed on the service sheet. The music stops three or four minutes before the ministers enter and take their places. The congregation become quiet, attentive and prayerful – a sense of expectancy is in the air. The minister rises to call the people to worship with the greeting:

> God is spirit.
> **Let us worship him in spirit and truth.**

Then, after the opening hymn of praise, the congregation sit for an imaginative presentation of the notices, done by two people in a 'sharing the news' style. This is regarded as part of the worship, both giving a sense of belonging and bringing all the church's activities into the presence of God. The notices end with a reminder of today's learning themes (for adults, children and young people), some silence and the opening collect.

Other options which **St Ann's** has used for Gathering and Greeting include:
* the giving of the Peace;
* a solo song or hymn;
* some verses from a psalm, sung as an introit by the choir at the back of the church;
* a spoken verse of a song or hymn.

At **St Bartholomew's** the organist quietly plays a simple voluntary based on a seasonal hymn melody on the small village organ while the congregation arrive for worship. The minister has hurried from another village and makes his way to the vestry in order to robe and have a few moments of prayer before the service begins. The churchwarden has taken care to ensure that everything is prepared for worship before the minister arrives and she announces the opening hymn. As the congregation sing, the minister makes his way to his place from the back of the church. At the end of the hymn, he greets the congregation with a seasonal greeting and invites them to join with him in some moments of silence before saying a prayer of preparation for worship.

At **St Christopher's** good quality taped music is relayed gently through the amplification system as the multi-cultural, mixed-age congregation take their seats. The choir is already seated five minutes before the service is advertised to begin. When the taped music ceases, the churchwarden gives out some notices, announces the opening song of praise and invites people to keep a time of silence before the organ plays the first line. As the lights are turned full on, a well-ordered procession of crucifer, acolytes and two ministers enters the church, the deacon holding aloft the Book of the Gospels. As soon as the song is finished, the president welcomes the people with a responsive greeting, announces the theme of the service and invites the people to make their confession.

It is Pentecost at **St Dodo's** and the clergy and choir are hurrying to prepare for worship as the congregation arrive. The organist starts to play a difficult voluntary with some unexpected stops and starts five minutes before the service is advertised to begin. Four minutes after the service should have begun the minister appears at the front of the church, nods at the organist to stop playing, welcomes everyone and realizes that the amplification system is not working. High-pitched feedback jolts everyone awake as the amplification comes to life. No one can hear the announcement of the number of the opening processional hymn. Choir and clergy process slowly in a ragged crocodile to their seats. The minister turns and greets the people again – this time with a liturgical greeting. He then tells everyone to be seated and announces the notices for the week at some length, before inviting the congregation to join him in a prayer of preparation for worship.

Greetings and their meanings

The opening greeting establishes a relationship between the minister and the rest of the congregation. In choosing what to include, the minister will consider the options (including a formal welcome, perhaps followed by more informal comments, a prayer, an acclamation of praise, or a call to worship) and try to use a greeting that is right for the context, and to remember that greetings convey unspoken messages:

* 'Hello!' ('Good morning', 'Welcome, everyone', etc.) is a reflection of shared human ordinariness that links worship with the rest of life.
* 'The Lord be with you – and also with you' speaks of mutual prayer for one another and an expectation of God's presence.
* A sentence of Scripture as the first utterance puts the emphasis firmly on God, but doesn't establish a relationship between worshippers.
* 'I couldn't hear you singing' establishes a (probably unhealthy) relationship of power.

Commentary

> The service should have a clear beginning. The liturgical greeting may follow some introductory singing, or a hymn or a sentence of Scripture, and may be followed by a brief introduction or an opening prayer.
>
> *Note 1, A Service of the Word*

Each church has its own way of making clear that the service is about to start, whether by the entrance of a procession, the start of the first hymn, or the turning on of the overhead projector. Whatever you do, make it clear. There is nothing wrong with some silence before a service, or some music or worship songs to help people prepare themselves, but everyone needs to know when we have stopped being a collection of individuals and are being summoned as a *body* of people to worship God together.

One of the functions of the opening stages of the service is to allow people consciously to bring to God all that is going on in the rest of their lives as they come to worship. The spoken texts can help that; so can silence. The sharing of the Peace might also be an appropriate part of the Gathering and Greeting. Care should also be taken to ensure that the form of greeting or opening prayer flows naturally into what is to follow. A greeting that works well if followed by a hymn of praise might not fit if penitence is to follow.

Notes to the resources

1 More examples of responses that may be suitable for use at the beginning of the service can be found in Resource Section G, 'Praise' (pages 223–233).

2 The resources provided below should be adapted as necessary if the Peace is to be included.

3 'Alleluia' may be added to many of the greetings, for example at Easter and Pentecost.

Greetings, calls to worship and other introductions

General **A**/	The grace of our Lord Jesus Christ, the love of God, and the fellowship of the Holy Spirit be with you **and also with you.**
General **A**2	Welcome in the name of Christ. God's grace, mercy and peace be with you **and also with you.**
General **A**3	The grace and mercy of our Lord Jesus Christ be with you **and also with you.**
General **A**4	Grace, mercy and peace from God our Father and the Lord Jesus Christ be with you **and also with you.** <div align="right">*cf 1 Timothy 1.2*</div>
General **A**5	The Lord of glory be with you. **The Lord bless you.** *(This greeting may be used before or after other introductions.* *'The Lord of glory' may be replaced by other similar phrases, for* *example 'The risen Lord', 'The Lord of mercy', 'The Lord of all* *creation'.)*
General **A**6	Through Christ let us offer our sacrifice of praise to God. **Let our lips proclaim his praise.** <div align="right">*cf Hebrews 13.15*</div>
General **A**7	O Lord, open our lips **and our mouth shall proclaim your praise.** O God, make speed to save us. **O Lord, make haste to help us.** Glory to the Father and to the Son and to the Holy Spirit; **as it was in the beginning is now** **and shall be for ever. Amen.** Praise the Lord. **The Lord's name be praised.** *cf Psalm 51.15; 70.1*

General A8	Praise our God, all you his servants: **those who fear him, both small and great.** *cf Revelation 19.5*

General A9	Praise the name of the Lord; **ascribe greatness to our God.** Lord, open our lips **and we shall praise your name.** *cf Deuteronomy 32.3; Psalm 51.15*

General A10	The Lord our God, the Almighty, reigns. **Let us rejoice and shout for joy, giving God the glory.** Glory to the Father and to the Son and to the Holy Spirit; **as it was in the beginning is now and shall be for ever. Amen.** *cf Revelation 19.6,7*

General A11	The Lord be with you **and also with you.** Let us worship God.

General A12	We come from scattered lives to meet with God. Let us recognize his presence with us. *Silence is kept.* As God's people we have gathered: **let us worship him together.**

General (morning) Incarnation A13	God in Christ has revealed his glory. **Come let us worship.** From the rising of the sun to its setting **the Lord's name is greatly to be praised.** Give him praise, you servants of the Lord. **O praise the name of the Lord!**

General (morning) Resurrection A14	The light and peace of Jesus Christ be with you **and also with you.** The glory of the Lord has risen upon us. **Let us rejoice and sing God's praise for ever.**

General (morning)
Resurrection
A15

This is the day that the Lord has made.
Let us rejoice and be glad in it.

Psalm 118.24

General (evening)
A16

O Lord, we call to you: come to us quickly.
Hear us when we cry to you.

Let our prayers rise up before you like incense.
Let our lifted hands be like an evening sacrifice.

Glory to the Father and to the Son
and to the Holy Spirit;
**as it was in the beginning is now
and shall be for ever. Amen.**

cf Psalm 141.1,2

General (evening)
A17

May the light and peace of Jesus Christ our Lord
be with you.
The Lord bless you.

General (evening)
Resurrection
A18

Jesus Christ is the light of the world:
a light no darkness can quench.

Stay with us, Lord, for it is evening:
and the day is almost over.

Even the darkness is not dark for you:
and the night shines like the day.

Let your light scatter the darkness:
and fill your church with your glory.

cf John 1.5; 8.12; Psalm 139.12; Luke 24.29

General
Father, Son and Spirit
A19

We meet in the name of God:
Father, Son and Holy Spirit.

General
Father, Son and Spirit
A20

We meet in the name of God:
**God the Father,
God the Son,
God the Spirit:
God is one.**

General *Resurrection* *Holy Spirit* **A**21	O Lord, open our lips **and our mouth shall proclaim your praise.** Give us the joy of your saving help **and sustain us with your life-giving Spirit.**

General *Holy Spirit* **A**22	God is spirit. **Let us worship him in spirit and truth.** The Lord is with us. **Let us praise his name together.** *cf John 4.24*

General *Father, Son and Spirit* **A**23	Let us worship God: Father, Son and Holy Spirit. **Amen.** The Lord be with you **and also with you.**

General *Heaven* **A**24	We stand before the throne of God with countless crowds from every nation and race, tribe and language. **Blessing and glory and wisdom,** **thanksgiving and honour, power and might** **be to our God for ever and ever.** **Amen.** *cf Revelation 7.9,12*

General *Living in the world* **A**25	Let everything be said and done in the name of the Lord Jesus, **giving thanks to God through Jesus Christ.** Sing psalms, hymns and sacred songs: **let us sing to God with thankful hearts.** Open our lips, Lord: **and we shall praise your name.** *cf Colossians 3.16,17*

General *Time* **A**26	God is good **all the time.** All the time **God is good.**

Christ's coming *Resurrection* **A**27	Praise God! For the Lord our God the almighty reigns! **Let us rejoice and be glad and give him the glory.** Happy are those who have been invited to the wedding-feast of the Lamb. **Amen. Praise the Lord!** *cf Revelation 19.6,9*

Incarnation
A28

Today we remember Jesus and the story of his birth;
Jesus is our King.
A candle may be lit.
Jesus Christ is the light of the world;
Jesus is our Way.
With Jesus even dark places are light;
Jesus is the Truth.
In Jesus we shall live for ever;
Jesus is our Life.

Incarnation
A29

We meet to celebrate the coming of Christ into the world.
The Word was made flesh, and dwelt among us
and we beheld his glory.

Incarnation
A30

I bring you good news of great joy:
a Saviour has been born to you. Alleluia.
Unto us a child is born,
unto us a Son is given. Alleluia.

[Hear the words of St Luke:
When the angels had gone from them into heaven,
the shepherds said to one another,
'Let us go to Bethlehem and see this thing that has happened
which the Lord has made known to us.'
So they hastened, and found Mary and Joseph,
and the baby lying in a manger.]

He is Christ the Lord. Alleluia.
We worship and adore him. Alleluia.

Resurrection
A31

Alleluia. Christ is risen.
He is risen indeed. Alleluia.

Praise the God and Father of our Lord Jesus Christ:
he has given us new life and hope
by raising Jesus from the dead.

[God has claimed us as his own:
He has made us light to the world.]

Alleluia. Christ is risen.
He is risen indeed. Alleluia.

Ascension
A32

Christ is risen.
He is risen indeed. Alleluia.

Christ has ascended on high.
He reigns for ever. Alleluia.

Lift up your hearts.
We lift them to the Lord. Alleluia.

Heaven
A33

Jesus Christ has made us a kingdom of priests
to serve his God and Father.
To God be glory and kingship for ever and ever.

Grace, mercy and peace be with you
and also with you.

Lament
Relationships
*   and healing*
A34

We meet in the presence of God
who knows our needs,
hears our cries,
feels our pain,
and heals our wounds.

Opening prayers

General
A35
Lord, direct our thoughts, and teach us to pray.
Lift up our hearts to worship you in spirit and in truth,
through Jesus Christ our Lord.
Amen.

General
A36
Faithful one, whose word is life:
come with saving power
to free our praise,
inspire our prayer
and shape our lives
for the kingdom of your Son,
Jesus Christ our Lord.
Amen.

General
A37
Loving God, we have come to worship you.
**Help us to pray to you in faith,
to sing your praise with gratitude,
and to listen to your word with eagerness;
through Christ our Lord.**
Amen.

General
Resurrection
Ascension
A38
Almighty God,
your Son has opened for us
a new and living way into your presence.
Give us new hearts and constant wills
to worship you in spirit and in truth;
through Jesus Christ our Lord.
Amen.

General
Word
A39
Lord, speak to us
that we may hear your word.
Move among us
that we may behold your glory.
Receive our prayers
that we may learn to trust you.
Amen.

General
Living in the world
Time
A40
God of our days and years,
we set this time apart for you.
Form us in the likeness of Christ
so that our lives may glorify you.
Amen.

Father, Son and Spirit
A4I

Holy God,
holy and strong,
holy and immortal:
have mercy on us.
Holy God,
holy and strong,
holy and immortal:
have mercy on us.
Silence
Eternal God, source of all blessing,
help us to worship you
with all our heart and mind and strength;
for you alone are God,
Father, Son and Holy Spirit,
for ever and ever.
Amen.

Holy Spirit
A42

Let us pray.
Come, Holy Spirit,
fill the hearts of your faithful people,
and kindle in us the fire of your love;
through Jesus Christ our Lord.
Amen.

Holy Spirit
Relationships and healing
A43

Be with us, Spirit of God;
nothing can separate us from your love.
Breathe on us, breath of God;
fill us with your saving power.
Speak in us, wisdom of God;
bring strength, healing and peace.
Silence is kept
The Lord is here.
His Spirit is with us.

Holy Spirit
A44

Faithful God,
who fulfilled the promises of Easter
by sending us your Holy Spirit,
and made known to every race and nation the way of
    eternal life;
open our lips by your Spirit,
that every tongue may tell of your glory,
through Jesus Christ our Lord.
Amen.

penitence

B Penitence

Stories from the four churches

At **St Ann's** the Reader invites the congregation to kneel or sit in order
to make their confession. The Reader waits for the people to settle down
before inviting them to call to mind their sins against God and against their
neighbour. After a time of silence for reflection, a sentence of Scripture is
read aloud, the people are invited to confess their sins and one of the
twenty-two authorized forms of Confession is used (pages 81–90 below).
The president prays for forgiveness using an authorized Absolution in the
'us' form.

The Confession at **St Bartholomew's** during Holy Communion is said after
the Prayers of Intercession. The priest invites the people to sit or kneel and,
after a pause, reads a seasonal sentence calling the people to repentance and
to make their confession. A responsive song is used to give space for
reflection and to set the mood before the Confession is said. As it is Lent,
the responsive seasonal Confession, 'Lord Jesus Christ we confess we have
failed you …', is used, the priest first reminding the congregation of the
response: Lord, forgive us: Christ have mercy. After the Confession, the
priest pronounces the Absolution.

The congregation at **St Christopher's** remain standing for the Confession,
which takes place immediately after the introduction to worship. The Prayers
of Penitence are introduced with the Summary of the Law, followed by a
Kyrie Confession, with appropriate insertions (see pages 91–94). At the
Absolution, the sign of the cross is made by all, signalling their acceptance
of God's forgiveness in Christ.

At **St Dodo's** it is the monthly 'Family Service' and the minister has
decided to use the Confession at the top of page 129 in *Common Worship*.
No indication is given as to whether the congregation should sit or kneel,
so there is confusion as people look around to see what to do. After a
pause while the minister finds the service sheet, the people are asked to
find their sheets on which is printed the Confession. The minister invites
the congregation to be quiet and remember their sins before God in silence,
but without waiting begins to list in a rather harsh tone a number of sins on
which the people may care to reflect and starts the Confession, inserting
these sins into it. The Absolution is mumbled inaudibly while the minister
continues to kneel in the stall.

How can the penitential prayers have more impact on the congregation?

At **St Ann's** they have been having some teaching about sin and forgiveness. One of the results has been exploration of other ways of bringing home the reality of sin and the power of God's forgiveness. Among other things, they have tried:

✳ The use of images, objects, or simple drama related to the Confession.

✳ A Kyrie Confession led by two people standing with their backs to each other, each offering a bidding in turn.

✳ Changing posture, so that the congregation kneels for the Confession and stands for the Absolution. They have found that this not only reflects, but creates, an inner attitude.

✳ The use of dim lighting to create a penitential atmosphere. They found this could be achieved very simply by lowering or switching off the lighting after the introduction, and switching it on again at the absolution.

✳ The burning of incense or aromatic oils to make the congregation smell 'sweeter', and the sprinkling of water over the people as a sign of cleansing.

Where is the best place in a service for confession?

At **St Christopher's** several weeks are being devoted to teaching on repentance, confession and forgiveness. As a result the worship group has recommended that the Confession be used at different points in the service:

✳ In both A Service of the Word and Order One Holy Communion, the usual place for the Prayers of Penitence is going to be – as in the *Common Worship* books – after the Greeting (and Prayer of Preparation, if it is used) in the Gathering part of the service. But as it is also possible for it to come later in the service, those who plan the worship will pick up when there is a need, for example, to respond to a sermon with penitence, and put the Confession after the sermon or with the intercessions.

✳ A Service of the Word opens up the possibility of Penitence coming towards the end of the service, as its climax. There might be some occasions in the traditionally penitential seasons of Lent or Advent when this might work well.

✳ The worship planning group will also look for occasional opportunities for using material for corporate preparation for confession. This might be done in silence; whilst sentences or passages of Scripture are read aloud; or by the singing of a suitable hymn or song, either corporately or by a solo voice. The material in A Form of Preparation on pages 161–165 of *Common Worship* will also provide a resource for this.

The minister at **St Dodo's** had been on a diocesan day on 'Preparing for Worship in Advent' but ignored all the points made there about the importance of introducing the Confession properly. As the handout said:

✳ The purpose of the Invitation to Confession is to encourage people to call their sins to mind and to give them space to do so.

✳ There should be time for silent reflection between the Invitation and the Confession. This may be a significant period of silence, with a structure indicated by the leader.

✳ Words for the Invitation to Confession are provided for each part of the year in the Seasonal Provisions pages in *Common Worship* (page 300ff.), but any suitable words may be used, and other options are provided in *New Patterns for Worship*. Looking at the examples there will help those constructing their own invitations.

✳ Words taken from one of the readings may be suitable, but care needs to be taken that the words will not be misunderstood when heard outside their biblical context. This is one example, using Matthew 1.21 as the inspiration for a Christmas invitation to confession:

> Hear the words of the angel to Joseph:
> 'You shall call his name Jesus,
> for he will save his people from their sins.'
> Therefore let us [*kneel/stand* and] seek the forgiveness of God
> through Jesus the Saviour of the world.

Can forms of confession and absolution be written for special occasions?

Only forms of confession and absolution which have been authorized may be used. This includes all those in the Holy Communion services and in the Confession and Absolution section of *Common Worship* (page 122f.), as well as the forms in *The Book of Common Prayer*. The reason for this is that the issue of penitence and reconciliation is a controversial one in the Church of England. Limiting the options in controversial areas such as this is intended to promote unity and avoid unnecessary division. The best way to incorporate words designed for a particular occasion, if one of the seasonal thematic confessions is not suitable, is to use the Kyrie option, which provides for the insertion of 'short penitential sentences' between the petitions of the Kyrie.

The note at the top of page 133 in *Common Worship* indicates that the Kyries may replace any form of confession, provided that the sentences inserted between the petitions are of a penitential character. Examples are given on page 133f. and pages 277–278 of *Common Worship*, and more can be found here. The appointed psalms and readings might be the first place to look for suitable sentences from the Bible. The use of a concordance, in book or electronic form, may be useful in leading to other biblical sentences, though it should be noted that the sentences do not have to come from the Bible. The sentences should not be too long, and the three should match each other in length and pattern. As the rubric in *Common Worship*, page 170, makes clear, if the Kyrie has been used as the confession, it should not be used again before or after the absolution.

Here is an example of a Kyrie Confession for Holy Week, which is clearly linked to a particular passage of Scripture:

> We watch at a distance,
> and are slow to follow Christ in the way of the cross.
> Lord, have mercy.
> **Lord, have mercy.**
>
> We warm our hands by the fire,
> and are afraid to be counted among his disciples.
> Christ, have mercy.
> **Christ, have mercy.**
>
> We run away,
> and fail to share the pain of Christ's suffering.
> Lord, have mercy.
> **Lord, have mercy.**

Does it matter which absolution is used?

If possible, an absolution should be chosen which reflects the style (in language, length and theme) of the confession, and also of the occasion or season. A penitential service, in Advent or Lent, for instance, may need the kind of confession and absolution which gives people more space for reflection. In this section, absolutions are suggested for each confession to assist in this choice, but any authorized absolution may be used. The printing of any of these absolutions in either the 'you' or 'us' form has no doctrinal or other significance. In each case, either a 'you' or 'us' form can be used (though those not ordained priest should use the 'us' form). Words in italics indicate the points where changes may be necessary.

Invitations to confession

General
B1

Jesus says, 'Repent, for the kingdom of heaven is close at hand.'
So let us turn away from sin and turn to the Lord,
confessing our sins in penitence and faith.

cf Matthew 4.17

General
B2

Brothers and sisters,
as we prepare to celebrate,
let us call to mind our sins.

General
B3

The gospel calls us to turn away from sin
and be faithful to Christ.
As we offer ourselves to him in penitence and faith,
we renew our confidence and trust in his mercy.

Father, Son and Spirit
Lament
B4

'Holy, holy, holy is the Lord God Almighty.'
We long for the fire of God's cleansing
to touch our unclean lips,
for our guilt to be removed and our sin wiped out.
So we meet Father, Son and Holy Spirit
with repentance in our hearts.

cf Isaiah 6 and Revelation 4

Father, Son and Spirit
B5

St Paul says
'Be imitators of God;
love as Christ loved;
do not grieve the Holy Spirit;
put away all anger and bitterness,
all slander and malice.'
So let us confess our sins to God,
who forgives us in Christ.

cf Ephesians 4.30 – 5.1

God in creation
Lament
B6

Human sin disfigures the whole creation,
which groans with eager longing for God's redemption.
We confess our sin in penitence and faith.

cf Romans 8.22,23

Christ's coming
Lament
B7

When the Lord comes,
he will bring to light the things now hidden in darkness,
and will disclose the purposes of the heart.
Therefore in the light of Christ let us confess our sins.

Christ's coming
B8

Christ the light of the world has come to dispel
the darkness of our hearts.
In his light let us examine ourselves and confess our sins.

Incarnation **B**9	Hear the words of the angel to Joseph: 'You shall call his name Jesus, for he will save his people from their sins.' Therefore let us seek the forgiveness of God through Jesus the Saviour of the world. *cf Matthew 1.21*
Incarnation **B**10	As we kneel with the shepherds before the newborn Christ child, we open our hearts in penitence and faith.
Incarnation **B**11	The grace of God has dawned upon the world through our Saviour Jesus Christ, who sacrificed himself for us to purify a people as his own. Let us confess our sins. *cf Titus 2.11-14*
Cross **B**12	God shows his love for us in that, while we were still sinners, Christ died for us. Let us then show our love for him by confessing our sins in penitence and faith. *cf Romans 5.8*
Resurrection **B**13	Christ our passover lamb has been sacrificed for us. Let us therefore rejoice by putting away all malice and evil and confessing our sins with a sincere and true heart. *cf 1 Corinthians 5.7,8*
Ascension **B**14	Jesus is our high priest, tempted like us, yet without sin. He lives for ever in heaven to intercede for us. Through him we approach the throne of grace with confidence, and confess our sins. *cf Hebrews 4.15,16*
Ascension **B**15	Seeing we have a great high priest who has passed into the heavens, Jesus the Son of God, let us draw near with a true heart, in full assurance of faith, and make our confession to our heavenly Father.
Holy Spirit **B**16	The Spirit of truth will convict the world of guilt about sin, righteousness and judgement. We have grieved the Holy Spirit. In sorrow we confess our sins. *cf John 16.8*

Holy Spirit **B**17	What God has prepared for those who love him, he has revealed to us through the Spirit; for the Spirit searches everything. Therefore, let us in penitence open our hearts to the Lord, who has prepared good things for those who love him. *cf 1 Corinthians 2.9*
Holy Spirit **B**18	The Spirit of the Lord fills the world and knows our every word and deed. Let us then open ourselves to the Lord and confess our sins in penitence and faith.
Word **B**19	The word of God is living and active. It judges the thoughts and intentions of the heart. All is open and laid bare before the eyes of him to whom we give account. We confess our sins in penitence and faith. *cf Hebrews 4.12*
Lament **B**20	The sacrifice acceptable to God is a broken spirit; a broken and contrite heart God will not despise. Our sins accuse us. We confess them to God. *cf Psalm 51.17*
Lament **B**21	The sacrifice of God is a broken spirit; a broken and contrite heart God will not despise. Let us come to the Lord, who is full of compassion, and acknowledge our transgressions in penitence and faith. *Psalm 51.17*
Lament **B**22	Compassion and forgiveness belong to the Lord our God, though we have rebelled against him. Let us then renounce our wilfulness and ask his mercy by confessing our sins in penitence and faith. *cf Daniel 9.9*
Relationships and healing *Lament* **B**23	Christ himself bore our sins in his body on the cross so that, free from sin, we might live for righteousness; by his wounds we have been healed. Let us confess our sins. *cf 1 Peter 2.24*
Relationships and healing *Incarnation* **B**24	The sun of righteousness has dawned with healing in his wings. Let us come to the light of Christ, confessing our sins in penitence and faith. *cf Malachi 4.2*

Relationships and healing **B**25	Jesus said, 'Before you offer your gift, go and be reconciled.' As sisters and brothers in God's family, we come together to ask our Father for forgiveness. <div align="right">*Matthew 5.24*</div>
Relationships and healing **B**26	We come to God as one from whom no secrets are hidden, to ask for his forgiveness and peace.
Relationships and healing **B**27	The grace of God has dawned upon the world with healing for all. Let us come to him, in sorrow for our sins, seeking healing and salvation. <div align="right">*cf Titus 2.11*</div>
Living in the world **B**28	Jesus saw the city and wept over it, because it did not recognize the time of God's coming. We confess our part in the self-centredness, blindness and sin of the life of our *city/community*. <div align="right">*cf Luke 19.41*</div>
Holy Communion **B**29	Brothers and sisters in Christ, as we gather at the Lord's table we must recall the promises and warnings given to us in the Scriptures. Let us therefore examine ourselves and repent of our sins.
Heaven **B**30	Christ calls us to share the heavenly banquet of his love with all the saints in earth and heaven. Knowing our unworthiness and sin, let us ask from him both mercy and forgiveness.
Heaven **B**31	Since we are surrounded by a great cloud of witnesses, let us also lay aside every weight and the sin that clings so closely, looking to Jesus in penitence and faith. <div align="right">*cf Hebrews 12.1*</div>
Heaven **B**32	The saints were faithful unto death and now dwell in the heavenly kingdom for ever. As we celebrate their joy, let us bring to the Lord our sins and weaknesses, and ask for his mercy.

Confessions

Where absolutions are suggested, these are designed to match the Confession with an absolution of similar style or which picks up similar themes or which is appropriate for the same season. They are suggestions only – other absolutions may be more appropriate for particular situations.

General
B33

Father eternal, giver of light and grace,
we have sinned against you and against our neighbour,
in what we have thought,
in what we have said and done,
through ignorance, through weakness,
through our own deliberate fault.
We have wounded your love,
and marred your image in us.
We are sorry and ashamed,
and repent of all our sins.
For the sake of your Son Jesus Christ,
who died for us,
forgive us all that is past;
and lead us out from darkness
to walk as children of light.
Amen.

Suggested absolution: B78

General
B34

Almighty and most merciful Father,
we have wandered and strayed from your ways
   like lost sheep.
We have followed too much the devices and desires
   of our own hearts.
We have offended against your holy laws.
We have left undone those things
   that we ought to have done;
and we have done those things
   that we ought not to have done;
and there is no health in us.
But you, O Lord, have mercy upon us sinners.
Spare those who confess their faults.
Restore those who are penitent,
according to your promises declared to mankind
   in Christ Jesus our Lord.
And grant, O most merciful Father, for his sake,
that we may live a disciplined, righteous and godly life,
to the glory of your holy name.
Amen.

Suggested absolution: B80

Almighty God,
Father of our Lord Jesus Christ,
maker of all things, judge of all people,
we acknowledge and lament our many sins
and the wickedness we have committed time after time,
by thought, word and deed against your divine majesty.
We have provoked your righteous anger
and your indignation against us.
We earnestly repent,
and are deeply sorry for these our wrongdoings;
the memory of them weighs us down,
the burden of them is too great for us to bear.
Have mercy upon us,
have mercy upon us, most merciful Father.
For your Son our Lord Jesus Christ's sake,
forgive us all that is past;
and grant that from this time forward
we may always serve and please you in newness of life,
to the honour and glory of your name;
through Jesus Christ our Lord.
Amen.

Suggested absolution: B76

Almighty God,
Father of our Lord Jesus Christ,
maker of all things, judge of all people,
we acknowledge and confess
   the grievous sins and wickedness
which we have so often committed
by thought, word and deed
against your divine majesty,
provoking most justly your anger
   and indignation against us.
We earnestly repent,
and are deeply sorry for these our wrongdoings;
the memory of them weighs us down,
the burden of them is too great for us to bear.
Have mercy upon us,
have mercy upon us, most merciful Father,
for your Son our Lord Jesus Christ's sake,
forgive us all that is past;
and grant that from this time onwards
we may always serve and please you
   in newness of life,
to the honour and glory of your name,
through Jesus Christ our Lord.
Amen.

Suggested absolution: B76

General
B37

Most merciful God,
Father of our Lord Jesus Christ,
we confess that we have sinned
in thought, word and deed.
We have not loved you with our whole heart.
We have not loved our neighbours as ourselves.
In your mercy
forgive what we have been,
help us to amend what we are,
and direct what we shall be;
that we may do justly,
love mercy,
and walk humbly with you, our God.
Amen.

Suggested absolution: B80

General
B*38*

Almighty God, our heavenly Father,
we have sinned against you
and against our neighbour
in thought and word and deed,
through negligence, through weakness,
through our own deliberate fault.
We are truly sorry
and repent of all our sins.
For the sake of your Son Jesus Christ,
who died for us,
forgive us all that is past
and grant that we may serve you in newness of life
to the glory of your name.
Amen.

Suggested absolution: B70

General
B*39*

Almighty God, our heavenly Father,
we have sinned against you,
through our own fault,
in thought, and word, and deed,
and in what we have left undone.
We are heartily sorry,
and repent of all our sins.
For your Son our Lord Jesus Christ's sake,
forgive us all that is past;
and grant that we may serve you in newness of life
to the glory of your name.
Amen.

Suggested absolution: B74

God of mercy,
we acknowledge that we are all sinners.
We turn from the wrong that we have thought and said
    and done,
and are mindful of all that we have failed to do.
For the sake of Jesus, who died for us,
forgive us for all that is past,
and help us to live each day
in the light of Christ our Lord.
Amen.

Suggested absolution: B84

Father, Son
    and Spirit
Ascension
Word
B41

O King enthroned on high,
filling the earth with your glory:
holy is your name,
Lord God almighty.
In our sinfulness we cry to you
to take our guilt away,
and to cleanse our lips to speak your word,
through Jesus Christ our Lord.
Amen.

cf Isaiah 6
Suggested absolutions: B77, B80

God in creation
B42

[We confess our sin, and the sins of our society,
in the misuse of God's creation.]

God our Father, we are sorry
for the times when we have used your gifts carelessly,
and acted ungratefully.
Hear our prayer, and in your mercy:
forgive us and help us.

We enjoy the fruits of the harvest,
but sometimes forget that you have given them to us.
Father, in your mercy:
forgive us and help us.

We belong to a people who are full and satisfied,
but ignore the cry of the hungry.
Father, in your mercy:
forgive us and help us.

We are thoughtless,
and do not care enough for the world you have made.
Father, in your mercy:
forgive us and help us.

We store up goods for ourselves alone,
as if there were no God and no heaven.
Father, in your mercy:
forgive us and help us.

Suggested absolution: B72

Christ's coming
B43

[Come, let us return to the Lord and say:]

Lord our God,
in our sin we have avoided your call.
Our love for you is like a morning cloud,
like the dew that goes away early.
Have mercy on us;
deliver us from judgement;
bind up our wounds and revive us;
in Jesus Christ our Lord.
Amen.

cf Hosea 6
Suggested absolution: B73

Incarnation
B44

[Christ the light of the world has come to dispel the
darkness of our hearts. In his light let us examine ourselves and
confess our sins.]

Silence is kept.

Lord of grace and truth,
we confess our unworthiness
to stand in your presence as your children.
We have sinned:
forgive and heal us.

The Virgin Mary accepted your call
to be the mother of Jesus.
Forgive our disobedience to your will.
We have sinned:
forgive and heal us.

Your Son our Saviour
was born in poverty in a manger.
Forgive our greed and rejection of your ways.
We have sinned:
forgive and heal us.

The shepherds left their flocks
to go to Bethlehem.
Forgive our self-interest and lack of vision.
We have sinned:
forgive and heal us.

The wise men followed the star
to find Jesus the King.
Forgive our reluctance to seek you.
We have sinned:
forgive and heal us.

Suggested absolution: B79

Cross
B45

Lord Jesus Christ,
we confess we have failed you as did your first disciples.
We ask for your mercy and your help.

Our selfishness betrays you:
Lord, forgive us.
Christ have mercy.

We fail to share the pain of your suffering:
Lord, forgive us.
Christ have mercy.

We run away from those who abuse you:
Lord, forgive us.
Christ have mercy.

We are afraid of being known to belong to you:
Lord, forgive us.
Christ have mercy.

Suggested absolution: B78

Resurrection
Heaven
B46

Jesus Christ, risen master and triumphant Lord,
we come to you in sorrow for our sins,
and confess to you our weakness and unbelief.

We have lived by our own strength,
and not by the power of your resurrection.
In your mercy, forgive us.
Lord, hear us and help us.

We have lived by the light of our own eyes,
as faithless and not believing.
In your mercy, forgive us.
Lord, hear us and help us.

We have lived for this world alone,
and doubted our home in heaven.
In your mercy, forgive us.
Lord, hear us and help us.

Suggested absolution: B80

Christian
beginnings
B47

God our Father,
long-suffering, full of grace and truth,
you create us from nothing and give us life.
You give your faithful people new life in the water
of baptism.
You do not turn your face from us,
nor cast us aside.
We confess that we have sinned
against you and our neighbour.
We have wounded your love and marred your image in us.

Restore us for the sake of your Son,
and bring us to heavenly joy,
in Jesus Christ our Lord.
Amen.

Suggested absolution: B81

Lament
B*48*

[Let us admit to God the sin which always confronts us.]

Lord God,
we have sinned against you;
we have done evil in your sight.
We are sorry and repent.
Have mercy on us according to your love.
Wash away our wrongdoing and cleanse us from our sin.
Renew a right spirit within us
and restore us to the joy of your salvation,
through Jesus Christ our Lord.
Amen.

cf Psalm 51
Suggested absolution: B71

Lament
B*49*

God our Father,
we come to you in sorrow for our sins.

For turning away from you,
and ignoring your will for our lives;
Father, forgive us:
save us and help us.

For behaving just as we wish,
without thinking of you;
Father, forgive us:
save us and help us.

For failing you by what we do,
and think and say;
Father, forgive us:
save us and help us.

For letting ourselves be drawn away from you
by temptations in the world about us;
Father, forgive us:
save us and help us.

For living as if we were ashamed
to belong to your Son;
Father, forgive us:
save us and help us.

Suggested absolution: B69

Almighty God,
long-suffering and of great goodness:
I confess to you,
I confess with my whole heart
my neglect and forgetfulness of your commandments,
my wrong doing, thinking, and speaking;
the hurts I have done to others,
and the good I have left undone.
O God, forgive me, for I have sinned against you;
and raise me to newness of life;
through Jesus Christ our Lord.
Amen.

Suggested absolution: B76

My God, for love of you
I desire to hate and forsake all sins
by which I have ever displeased you;
and I resolve by the help of your grace
to commit them no more;
and to avoid all opportunities of sin.
Help me to do this,
through Jesus Christ our Lord.
Amen.

Suggested absolution: B70

[Let us return to the Lord our God and say to him:]

Father,
we have sinned against heaven and against you.
We are not worthy to be called your children.
We turn to you again.
Have mercy on us,
bring us back to yourself
as those who once were dead
but now have life through Christ our Lord.
Amen.

cf Luke 15
Suggested absolution: B83

Living in the world
God in creation
Church and
  mission
B53

Lord God, our maker and our redeemer,
this is your world and we are your people:
come among us and save us.

We have wilfully misused your gifts of creation;
Lord, be merciful:
forgive us our sin.

We have seen the ill-treatment of others
and have not gone to their aid;
Lord, be merciful:
forgive us our sin.

We have condoned evil and dishonesty
and failed to strive for justice;
Lord, be merciful:
forgive us our sin.

We have heard the good news of Christ,
but have failed to share it with others;
Lord, be merciful:
forgive us our sin.

We have not loved you with all our heart,
nor our neighbours as ourselves;
Lord, be merciful:
forgive us our sin.

Suggested absolution: B82

Heaven
B54

Man born of woman has but a short time to live.*
We have our fill of sorrow.
We blossom like a flower and wither away.
We slip away like a shadow and do not stay.
Holy God,
holy and strong,
holy and immortal,
have mercy upon us.

In the midst of life we are in death;
where can we turn for help?
Only to you, Lord,
who are justly angered by our sins.
Holy God,
holy and strong,
holy and immortal,
have mercy upon us.

Shut not your ears to our prayers,
but spare us, O Lord.
Holy God,
holy and strong,
holy and immortal,
have mercy upon us.

You know the secrets of our hearts;
forgive us our sins.
Holy God,
holy and strong,
holy and immortal,
have mercy upon us.

Eternal and merciful judge,
both in life and when we come to die,
let us not fall away from you.
Holy God,
holy and mighty,
holy and merciful Saviour,
do not abandon us to the bitterness of eternal death.

Alternative text:
Those born of women have but a short time to live.

Suggested absolution: B82

Kyrie Confessions

Short sentences may be inserted between the petitions of the Kyrie, suitable for particular seasons or themes. The insertion of such sentences may replace any form of confession, provided that the sentences are of a penitential character, and are followed by an authorized form of absolution. The forms of Kyrie Confession which follow are examples only.

Father, Son and Spirit
B55

We have not always worshipped God, our creator.
Lord, have mercy.
Lord, have mercy.

We have not always followed Christ, our Saviour.
Christ, have mercy.
Christ, have mercy.

We have not always trusted in the Spirit, our guide.
Lord, have mercy.
Lord, have mercy.

God in creation
B56

We confess to you
our lack of care for the world you have given us.
Lord, have mercy.
Lord, have mercy.

We confess to you
our selfishness in not sharing the earth's bounty fairly.
Christ, have mercy.
Christ, have mercy.

We confess to you
our failure to protect resources for others.
Lord, have mercy.
Lord, have mercy.

Incarnation
B57

Christ came in humility to share our lives:
forgive our pride.
Lord, have mercy.
Lord, have mercy.

Christ came with good news for all people:
forgive our silence.
Christ, have mercy.
Christ, have mercy.

Christ came in love to a world of suffering:
forgive our self-centredness.
Lord, have mercy.
Lord, have mercy.

Cross
B58

We are often slow to follow the example of Christ.
Lord, have mercy.
Lord, have mercy.

We often fail to be known as Christ's disciples.
Christ, have mercy.
Christ, have mercy.

We often fail to walk the way of the cross.
Lord, have mercy.
Lord, have mercy.

Resurrection
B59

Like Mary at the empty tomb,
we fail to grasp the wonder of your presence.
Lord, have mercy.
Lord, have mercy.

Like the disciples behind locked doors,
we are afraid to be seen as your followers.
Christ, have mercy.
Christ, have mercy.

Like Thomas in the upper room,
we are slow to believe.
Lord, have mercy.
Lord, have mercy.

Holy Spirit
Church and mission
B60

We confess to you our selfishness and lack of love:
fill us with your Spirit.
Lord, have mercy.
Lord, have mercy.

We confess to you our fear and failure in sharing our faith:
fill us with your Spirit.
Christ, have mercy.
Christ, have mercy.

We confess to you our stubbornness and lack of trust:
fill us with your Spirit.
Lord, have mercy.
Lord, have mercy.

Holy Spirit
Relationships and healing
B61

You raise the dead to life in the Spirit.
Lord, have mercy.
Lord, have mercy.

You bring pardon and peace to the broken in heart.
Christ, have mercy.
Christ, have mercy.

You make one by your Spirit the torn and divided.
Lord, have mercy.
Lord, have mercy.

Word
B62

May your loving mercy come to me, O Lord,
and your salvation according to your word:
Lord, have mercy.
Lord, have mercy.

Your word is a lantern to my feet and a light to my path:
Christ, have mercy.
Christ, have mercy.

O let your mercy come to me that I may live,
for your law is my delight:
Lord, have mercy.
Lord, have mercy.

Lament
B63

Wash away all my iniquity
and cleanse me from my sin.
Lord, have mercy.
Lord, have mercy.

Against you, you only have I sinned
and done what is evil in your sight.
Christ, have mercy.
Christ, have mercy.

Create in me a pure heart, O God,
and renew a steadfast spirit within me.
Lord, have mercy.
Lord, have mercy.

cf Psalm 51

Church and mission
Living in the world
B64

In a dark and disfigured world
we have not held out the light of life:
Lord, have mercy.
Lord, have mercy.

In a hungry and despairing world
we have failed to share our bread:
Christ, have mercy.
Christ, have mercy.

In a cold and loveless world
we have kept the love of God to ourselves:
Lord, have mercy.
Lord, have mercy.

Relationships and healing
B65

Friend of sinners, you bring hope in our despair.
Lord, have mercy.
Lord, have mercy.

Healer of the sick, you give strength in our weakness.
Christ, have mercy.
Christ, have mercy.

Destroyer of evil, you bring life in our dying.
Lord, have mercy.
Lord, have mercy.

Living in the world
B66

God be gracious to us and bless us,
and make your face shine upon us:
Lord, have mercy.
Lord, have mercy.

May your ways be known on the earth,
your saving power among the nations:
Christ, have mercy.
Christ, have mercy.

You, Lord, have made known your salvation,
and reveal your justice in the sight of the nations:
Lord, have mercy.
Lord, have mercy.

Living in the world
B67

Lord Jesus, you wept over the sins of your city.
On our city: Lord, have mercy.
Lord, have mercy.

Lord Jesus, you heal the wounds of sin and division,
        jealousy and bitterness.
On us: Christ, have mercy.
Christ, have mercy.

Lord Jesus, you bring pardon and peace to the sinner.
Grant us peace: Lord, have mercy.
Lord, have mercy.

Living in the world
B68

You made us to be one family,
yet we have divided humanity.
Lord, have mercy.
Lord, have mercy.

You were born a Jew to reconcile all people,
yet we have brought disharmony amongst races.
Christ, have mercy.
Christ, have mercy.

You rejoice in our differences,
yet we make them a cause of enmity.
Lord, have mercy.
Lord, have mercy.

Absolutions

All of these absolutions are authorized for use with any authorized Confession. Indications of themes and seasons should be understood as suggestions only.

The printing of any of these absolutions in either the 'you' or the 'us' form has no doctrinal or other significance. In most cases, either a 'you' or an 'us' form can be used (though those not ordained priest should use the 'us' form). Words in italics indicate the points where changes may be necessary. Absolution B75 is intended for use by those ordained priest.

General
B69

The almighty and merciful Lord
grant *you* pardon and forgiveness of all *your* sins,
time for amendment of life,
and the grace and strength of the Holy Spirit.
Amen.

General
B70

Almighty God,
who forgives all who truly repent,
have mercy upon *you*,
pardon and deliver *you* from all *your* sins,
confirm and strengthen *you* in all goodness,
and keep *you* in life eternal;
through Jesus Christ our Lord.
Amen.

General
B71

May almighty God,
who sent his Son into the world to save sinners,
bring *you* his pardon and peace, now and for ever.
Amen.

General
B72

The Lord enrich *you* with his grace,
and nourish *you* with his blessing;
the Lord defend *you* in trouble and keep *you* from all evil;
the Lord accept *your* prayers,
and absolve *you* from *your* offences,
for the sake of Jesus Christ, our Saviour.
Amen.

General
B73

May the God of love
bring *us* back to himself,
forgive *us* *our* sins,
and assure *us* of his eternal love
in Jesus Christ our Lord.
Amen.

General

B74

May almighty God have mercy on *us*,
forgive *us* *our* sins,
and bring *us* to everlasting life,
through Jesus Christ our Lord.
Amen.

General

B75

God, the Father of mercies,
has reconciled the world to himself
through the death and resurrection of his Son, Jesus Christ,
not counting our trespasses against us,
but sending his Holy Spirit
to shed abroad his love among us.
By the ministry of reconciliation
entrusted by Christ to his Church,
receive his pardon and peace
to stand before him in his strength alone,
this day and evermore.
Amen.

General

B76

Almighty God, our heavenly Father,
who in his great mercy
has promised forgiveness of sins
to all those who with heartfelt repentance and true faith
        turn to him:
have mercy on *you*,
pardon and deliver *you* from all *your* sins,
confirm and strengthen *you* in all goodness,
and bring *you* to everlasting life,
through Jesus Christ our Lord.
Amen.

Father, Son and Spirit
Cross
Holy Spirit

B77

May the Father forgive *us*
by the death of his Son
and strengthen *us*
to live in the power of the Spirit
all *our* days.
Amen.

Resurrection

B78

May the Father of all mercies
cleanse *us* from *our* sins,
and restore *us* in his image
to the praise and glory of his name,
through Jesus Christ our Lord.
Amen.

Relationships and healing
Incarnation
B79

May the God of all healing and forgiveness
draw *us* to himself
and cleanse *us* from all *our* sins,
that *we* may behold the glory of his Son,
the Word made flesh,
Jesus Christ our Lord.
Amen.

Relationships and healing
B80

May the God of love and power
forgive *you* and free *you* from *your* sins,
heal and strengthen *you* by his Spirit,
and raise *you* to new life in Christ our Lord.
Amen.

Living in the world
B81

Almighty God,
who in Jesus Christ has given us
a kingdom that cannot be destroyed,
forgive *us our* sins,
open *our* eyes to God's truth,
strengthen *us* to do God's will
and give *us* the joy of his kingdom,
through Jesus Christ our Lord.
Amen.

Living in the world
B82

May God who loved the world so much
that he sent his Son to be our Saviour
forgive *us our* sins
and make *us* holy to serve him in the world,
through Jesus Christ our Lord.
Amen.

Heaven
Holy Communion
B83

May God our Father forgive *us our* sins,
and bring *us* to the fellowship of his table
with his saints for ever.
Amen.

Heaven
B84

May God our Father forgive *us our* sins
and bring *us* to the eternal joy of his kingdom,
where dust and ashes have no dominion.
Amen.

liturgy of the word

c

Liturgy of the Word

Stories from the four churches

At **St Ann's** they are having an adult teaching series on Romans, using the lectionary material in Module 37 below. The response 'The same Lord is Lord of all …' is used as part of the Gathering and Greeting, at the Gospel alleluia, and in a response after the sermon. They have decided not to use the Gospel reading provided in that module, but to continue with the Gospel reading set in the *Common Worship* Principal Service Lectionary. This is because they have discovered teaching material for children which is based on the lectionary.

The children usually depart before the Gospel, and might not follow the long reading from Romans, so the Gospel today comes immediately after the Collect. Everyone remains standing and the children go out after the psalm that follows. The Gospel is the story of the breakfast on the seashore after the resurrection. It is read dramatically from different parts of the building – the narrator at the lectern, Jesus by the communion table, and the disciples coming forward from the middle of the congregation.

For the sermon time, which lasts just over half an hour, the adults at St Ann's have a choice. Some go out to a discussion Bible study on Romans, others to a well-structured adult education session on the Church and politics (linking up with Romans 13). The rest stay in church for a sermon on the same passage, with visuals on an overhead projector and questions at the end.

The four people who share the responsibility for reading at **St Bartholomew's** have recently been on a deanery training day for those who read. They have returned with some good ideas for varying the usual pattern and are much more confident. There is a card on the lectern reminding the reader how to announce the reading. She introduces the reading with the paragraph heading and the page number from the pew Bible. After the reading she leaves space for some reflective silence before saying, 'This is the word of the Lord.'

At **St Christopher's** the worship committee has asked one or two artistic people in the church to produce something based on this Sunday's Gospel. As a result there is a throw-over frontal on the altar, picking up the bread and fishes theme. Today the Gospel procession, with the deacon carrying the book of the Gospels, preceded by acolytes and crucifer, comes only to the front row of the congregation, rather than taking up its normal position halfway up the centre aisle of the nave. This is to allow the people to remain facing towards the front, where on a screen behind the lectern there is a beautiful sequence of slides of Galilee, fishermen, bread and fishes. The sermon is about ten minutes long, and ends with some guided meditation inviting people to imagine themselves playing a part in the Gospel story.

At **St Dodo's** no one comes forward to read the first reading so the president glares at the churchwarden, moves to the lectern and intones the lesson in a voice betraying boredom. There is a bit of excitement, though, as – inevitably – two people come forward to read the second reading and look like having a punch up. The one who wins fails to announce where the reading comes from, which is a pity, as it seems to have been changed from what is on the notice sheet. It would have helped to be able to follow the reading, as he was speaking very quietly, on the mistaken assumption that the microphone was amplifying all he said. But no one had adjusted the height of it since one of the children read last Sunday.

Making it live

St Ann's worship group plans how the readings are done, usually a month at a time to make sure that there is variety and that the 'unusual' element is not overdone. Different methods they have used include:
* gentle musical backing to the reading, on tape or live;
* mime to the reading;
* especially at an all-age service, having the reading interrupted by someone asking questions, and putting in mistakes and asking the children to spot them;
* memorizing a Gospel reading and telling it as a story;
* a dramatic reading using different parts of the building;
* putting out all lights apart from a spotlight on the reader;
* breaking up long story reading with songs or choruses.

The sermon: what and where?

Note 7 in A Service of the Word and Note 13 in Holy Communion in *Common Worship* redefine the sermon. There are a number of possibilities:
* the use of drama, interviews, discussion and audio-visuals;
* having more than one person taking part;
* dividing the congregation into groups for all (as at St Ann's here), or for part of the time (for example, getting people talking to those near them about how what is being said applies to them);
* preaching the sermon in, say, two parts at different points in the service;
* time for silent – or guided – reflection or meditation after the sermon.

Add to this some further things to consider:

* the use of handouts, either outlining the whole sermon or giving points for action;
* using data projector or overhead projector visuals in an integrated way, with pictures taking the application or story further, rather than merely summarizing the sermon in words;
* sermons with deliberate interruptions and questions, or with pauses to pray or worship and sing;
* the use of drama, again as an integral part of the sermon.

Discussing these ideas should open some new possibilities and also begin to answer the question 'Where?' Clearly not all of these sermon activities are suitable for the pulpit. Different areas of the church may be used. And even with a more traditional sermon there may be a case for leaving the pulpit, moving nearer a small congregation at the back, or moving to and speaking from different points in the church, for example from the lectern where the word has been read, or from under a window whose stained glass enshrines the story.

Responding to the readings

St Bartholomew's have been making a list of possible ways the congregation might respond to the readings:

* more pauses for meditation;
* responses which reflect the nature of the reading (such as those in the modular material in this resource section);
* short prayers or a verse of a psalm after the reading;
* involving the congregation in drama and dialogue readings;
* physical action, such as the stamping of feet in the synagogue when the story of Haman in the book of Esther is read!

Discussion starter: improving Bible reading in our worship

1   **Make a list of the problems with reading the Bible, for example:**

* The readings sound boring and are simply something to get through as a duty, and not as part of the worship.
* They are too long.
* Bad introductions impose partial or unhelpful meanings on the readings, or fail to raise expectations. This might lead into some discussion about how the readings should be introduced.
* Failure to use the lectionary provision can result in a narrower overall diet of Scripture: sometimes only a few verses are read, to be used as the sermon text, determined by the particular interests of the minister.
* People are not used to listening to large amounts of prose being read, so those who read need training and may need time to prepare. There might

be some discussion about the pros and cons of having children reading in all-age services, and whether the advantages of involving them outweigh the possible disadvantages of inaudibility or lack of understanding.

* Nowadays people think in visual terms, and many readings do not conjure up pictures in people's minds.
* People don't know why the Bible is being read.
* No response is expected.

2   **Working in pairs, put the following reasons for reading the Bible in church in order of importance, and then discuss the results with everyone else:**

* To teach and instruct;
* to link us firmly with the tradition;
* to ensure that we listen to the whole counsel of God;
* to deliver us from the personal whim or interest of the preacher or worship leader;
* to allow one part of Scripture to throw kaleidoscopic light on another;
* to identify ourselves again as the people to whom God is speaking.

By publicly rehearsing its corporate story the community is proclaiming its identity as the people of God. Shared stories bind people together. Story is important because

* it is easy to listen to, identify with, remember and re-tell;
* it links the community clearly with the tradition of God's saving action;
* in worship, it can more easily be used to stimulate praise, as we hear what God has done, rather than receive instruction;
* it is important for children: action stories keep things moving, add a sense of excitement and humanity.

3   **How can we get the whole congregation to 'own' the readings?**

Discuss the ideas in the section 'Responding to the readings' on page 101. Are there other ideas, or some other things in the St Ann's section 'Making it live' on page 100, which we could put into practice in our church?

Liturgy of the Word:
modular lectionary material

The use of one of the authorized lectionaries (from *Common Worship* or *The Book of Common Prayer*) around the main festivals serves to foster the sense that different worshipping communities are all 'telling the same story'. This is more possible than ever since the advent of the three-year *Common Worship* lectionary which shares so much in common with the versions of the three-year lectionary in use in other churches.

Some parts of the early Church used this principle of thematic reading for festivals, and we can see this reflected in the traditional readings for Lent and Easter, Advent, Christmas and Epiphany.

Outside that time, in Ordinary Time, the particular needs of different congregations may be met by different patterns of readings. A particular event in the life of the church (for instance, a new building project, a new phase in the life of the church, a disastrous fire, or a traumatic pastoral situation) might be the trigger for such a pattern. The reason might equally be the more mundane desire to match the Sunday preaching to the material being studied in small groups, such as home groups or cell groups, during the week. There will be times when the small groups will follow the lead given by the Sunday readings, but there might be other times when the lead is given by the small group materials.

Common Worship makes provision in two places for just such flexibility:

1 The Lectionary

During the period from the First Sunday of Advent to the Presentation of Christ in the Temple, during the period from Ash Wednesday to Trinity Sunday, and on All Saints' Day, the readings shall come from an authorized lectionary. During Ordinary Time (i.e. between the Presentation and Ash Wednesday and between Trinity Sunday and Advent Sunday), authorized lectionary provision remains the norm but, after due consultation with the Parochial Church Council, the minister may, from time to time, depart from the lectionary provision for pastoral reasons or preaching or teaching purposes.

Rule 7, Common Worship, page 540

2 A Service of the Word

There should preferably be at least two readings from the Bible, but it is recognized that if occasion demands there may be only one reading. It may be dramatized, sung or read responsively. The readings are taken from an authorized lectionary during the period from the Third Sunday of Advent to the Baptism of Christ, and from Palm Sunday to Trinity Sunday. When A Service of the Word is combined with Holy Communion on Sundays and Principal Holy Days, the readings of the day are normally used.

Note 5, A Service of the Word

This means that there are periods during which one of the authorized lectionaries is to be followed. The Note indicates that normally these periods are longer in the case of services of Holy Communion than in the case of non-eucharistic services.

Services of Holy Communion

Non-eucharistic services

The modular lectionary provision

The lectionary modules provided here are designed as replacements for the authorized readings during parts of the remaining periods of the year.

They illustrate how provision can be made for the semi-continuous reading of Scripture in short units comprising several weeks. They also provide examples of thematic and story material suitable both for all-age services and for adult worship.

These modules are samples only. The local church is at liberty to amend these, or other provision, or to produce its own material, as long as the requirements of Note 6 below are fulfilled.

Verse numbers for Bible readings have been taken from the New Revised Standard Version, except for the Psalms, where the numbering used in the *Common Worship* psalter has been followed.

Notes to the resources

1 Controlling reading

The controlling reading, in bold, must always be used in some form.
For some modules (mainly those in which the controlling reading takes
the form of a narrative) the controlling reading is given a brief 'title'. This
is designed to aid planning, and it should not be taken as the only way of
summarizing the reading.

2 Adapting the length of modules

It is important to plan ahead. Where necessary, the modules may be
shortened or amended, to fit the number of weeks available. Square brackets
[ ] around the week number in the lectionary charts indicate suggested
weeks to omit where necessary. This may also occasionally be necessary in
order to avoid having the same or similar readings at the point at which the
local church moves from one of these modules to another, or between these
(or other local provision) and an authorized lectionary.

When omitting part of the module in this way, care should be taken to
preserve the balance of the readings.

3 Editing and adapting the length of readings

Where verses have been bracketed or omitted to shorten the reading, a
longer version may be used if appropriate. Long readings may be broken up
by teaching or songs. Care should be taken in the selection of the translation
to be used at the service, and in any editing of the passages, to ensure that
the reading makes sense. Particular care is needed in identifying speakers in
the passage and making clear to whom pronouns refer.

4 Collects and other prayers

The *Common Worship* collects, especially in Ordinary Time, do not relate
particularly to the readings and so will be just as appropriate with these
readings as with the authorized lectionary readings. If a thematic prayer
is required, this may be sought from other sources or devised locally.

5 Use of responses

Each module below is provided with a verse and response. This could be
used in one or more of the following places:
* at the start of the service, following the greeting;
* as a refrain for the psalm (perhaps in an adapted form);
* before the reading;
* after the reading;
* after the sermon, or other teaching, as part of the response;
* after the Creed or Affirmation of Faith;
* as part of the conclusion of the service;
* as part of worship in small groups (such as cell groups, home groups
  or all-age worship) taking place during the week.

6   Local provision
     Churches may design their own reading scheme for parts of the church year,
     in accordance with the Notes in *Common Worship* and A Service of the
     Word. Where they do so they should ensure that an adequate amount of
     Scripture is chosen; that justice is done to the balance of the book and to the
     general teaching of Scripture; that appropriate Gospel passages are included
     if the services include Holy Communion; and that the PCC or an appropriate
     lay group is involved in the decisions.

7   Appropriate times for the use of modules
     In some cases, a particular time (or times) of the year may suggest itself for
     the use of a particular module. Some modules could appropriately be used in
     more than one season.

8   Interruptions to the modules
     The modules do not have to be used for a series of consecutive Sundays.
     It may sometimes be necessary to interrupt a module for a special service
     or celebration (such as Harvest Festival).

     Further, a module could be spread over a number of months, being used only
     for certain sorts of services (such as all-age services). Where this is the case,
     the provision of readings for the other Sundays will need to take account of
     this. One way of tackling this sort of situation would be to have two modular
     sets of readings operating in parallel: one for all-age services and one for
     other services.

Sample modules

Week	Old Testament	Psalm	New Testament	Gospel

1 God and the world

God is not far from each one of us;
in him we live and move and have our being.
cf Acts 17.27-28

Week	Old Testament	Psalm	New Testament	Gospel
1	**Genesis 1.1, 2; 1.24 – 2.3** (Creation)	33.1-9	Colossians 1.15-20	Matthew 6.25-30
2	**Genesis 2.4-9 (10-14); 15-end** (Creation of humankind)	104.15-25	Romans 5.12-19	Matthew 19.3-5
3	**Genesis 3.1-19** (Adam and Eve disobey God)	139.1-11	Romans 7.7-13	John 8.31-36
4	**Genesis 4.2b-16** (Cain and Abel)	6	1 John 3.9-18	Matthew 5.21-24
5	**Genesis 5.1-4; 6.9-14, 22** (The world and Noah)	53	1 John 4.1-6	Luke 12.16-20
6	**Genesis 11.1-9** (The Tower of Babel)	87	Romans 8.14-17	Matthew 8.5-13

2 Noah

Sowing and harvest, cold and heat, summer and winter, day and night;
as long as the earth endures, these shall never cease.
cf Genesis 8.22

Week	Old Testament	Psalm	New Testament	Gospel
1	**Genesis 6.5-22** (The wickedness of humankind)	26	2 Peter 2.4-9	Mark 7.14-23
2	**Genesis 7.11-24** (The flood)	29	1 Peter 3.18-22	Matthew 24.36-42
3	**Genesis 8.13, 20-22; 9.1-13** (After the flood)	24.1-6	2 Corinthians 1.18-22	Mark 14.22-25

3 Abraham

Abraham believed God;
God treated his faith as righteousness.
cf Genesis 15.6

Week	Old Testament	Psalm	New Testament	Gospel
1	**Genesis 11.31 – 12.7** (The call of Abram)	22.27-31	Hebrews 11.8-10	Mark 1.16-20
[2]	**Genesis 13** (Abram and Lot separate)	131	James 3.13-18	Matthew 20.20-23
3	**Genesis 17.1-7 (8-14) 15-22** (A son is promised)	105.7-15	Galatians 3.(1-5) 6-14	John 8.51-59

4	**Genesis 18.1-15** (The three visitors)	105.1-6	2 Corinthians 12.1-6 (7-10)	Luke 24.28-31
5	**Genesis 18.17-33** (Abraham pleads for Sodom)	145.13-22	James 5.13-20	John 15.14-16
[6]	**Genesis 20** (Abraham lies to Abimelech)	118.1-9	Acts 5.1-11	Luke 12.1-7

4 Sarah, Hagar and Rebekah

Cast your cares upon God.
Know that the Lord cares for you.
cf 1 Peter 5.7

1	**Genesis 16** (Sarah and Hagar)	13	Romans 4.13-22	John 7.1-9
2	**Genesis 18.9-15; 21.1-7** (God's promise to Sarah)	98	Romans 9.6-9	John 12.44-50
3	**Genesis 21.9-21** (God's promise to Hagar)	30	Galatians 4.21-26	John 10.14-16
4	**Genesis 24.42-end** (Rebekah meets Isaac)	32.8-12	1 Corinthians 7.1-9	John 14.1-6
5	**Genesis 25.19-28** (Rebekah gives birth to Esau and Jacob)	113	Romans 9.10-13	Luke 16.20-24
6	**Genesis 27.1-17** (Rebekah and Jacob deceive Isaac)	37.3-8	Hebrews 11.17-21	Luke 6.12-16

5 Jacob

Happy are those who have the God of Jacob for their help,
whose hope is in the Lord their God.
cf Psalm 146.5

1	**Genesis 25.19-34** (Jacob and Esau 1)	105.4-11	Romans 9.10-16	Luke 1.26-33
2	**Genesis 27.11-19 (1-45)** (Jacob and Esau 2)	50.16-end	2 Timothy 1.3-7	Mark 3.31-35
3	**Genesis 28.10-22 (27.46 – 28.22)** (Jacob's journey to Bethel)	119.17-24	Revelation 7.9-12	John 1.47-51
4	**Genesis 29.15-30 (29.1-30)** (Jacob marries)	146	Ephesians 5.25-33	Luke 15.11-14
5	**Genesis 32.22-33 (32.3 – 33.16)** (Reconciliation)	34.1-10	2 Corinthians 5.16-20	Matthew 5.3-9

6 Leah and Rachel

The Lord looks with favour on the righteous.
He rescues them from all their troubles.
cf Psalm 34.15

1	**Genesis 29.31 – 30.24**	120	Ephesians 5.21-33	Luke 1.36-38
2	**Genesis 35.9-20**	17.8-16	Acts 9.36-43	Luke 20.34-38

7 Joseph

All things work together for good for those who love God,
for those who are called according to his purpose.
cf Romans 8.28

1	**Genesis 37.3-13, 18-24 (37.1-end)** (An unhappy family)	57.1-7	Romans 8.28-32	John 7.1-6
2	**Genesis 39.1-15, 20-end (39; 40.1-14)** (Joseph in trouble)	138	Romans 8.33-end	Matthew 5.27-30
3	**Genesis 41.15-25, 29-40 (41)** (Joseph, Governor of Egypt)	105.16-22	Romans 12.6-13	Luke 12.27-31
4	**Genesis 42.6-25, 29, 30, 35, 36 (42; 43)** (Joseph meets his brothers)	103.1-12	Romans 13.1-5	Matthew 21.28-32
5	**Genesis 44.1-4, 14-18, 24 – 45.9 (44; 45)** (Joseph reveals who he is)	32	Romans 13.8-11	Matthew 5.23-26
6	**Genesis 46.1-7, 28-30; 47.7-11 (46.1-7, 28-34; 47.1-12)** (A reunited family)	126	Romans 15.1-6	Matthew 6.25-27
7	**Genesis 50.1-15** (The death of Jacob)	128	Romans 16.25-27	Luke 10.23-24

8 Women in the messianic line

Who are those who fear the Lord?
He will teach them the way that they should choose.
cf Psalm 25.12

1	**Genesis 38.11-27** (Tamar)	63.1-9	1 Corinthians 5.1-5	Mark 7.25-30
2	**Joshua 2.1-21** (Rahab)	25.1-9	Hebrews 11.29-31	John 10.7-9
3	**Ruth 1.1-18** (Ruth)	68.4-10	1 Corinthians 13.1-7	Mark 10.28-31
4	**1 Kings 1.15-31** (Bathsheba)	51.1-17	1 Corinthians 7.1-4	Mark 2.13-17
5	Deuteronomy 22.13-21	40.1-10	Revelation 12.1-6	**Matthew 1.18-25** (Mary)

9 Moses

Declare God's glory among the nations;
his wonders among all peoples.
cf Psalm 96.3

1	**Exodus 1.6 – 2.10** (Birth of Moses)	64	Ephesians 2.1-5	Luke 1.67-75
2	**Exodus 2.11-25** (Moses flees to Midian)	142	Hebrews 11.24-27	Matthew 3.13-17
3	**Exodus 3.1-15** (The burning bush)	96	Galatians 1.11-17	John 8.52-59
4	**Exodus 3.16 – 4.17** (God calls Moses)	146	Hebrews 5.1-10	John 14.8-14
5	**Exodus 5.22 – 6.12; 7.1-7** (Moses sent to Pharaoh)	121	1 Peter 3.13-18	Mark 13.5-13
6	**Exodus 11** (Warning of a final plague)	33.1-17	2 Thessalonians 1.5-10	Luke 16.19-31

10 Passover and deliverance

Who among the gods is like you, O Lord?
Majestic in holiness, awesome in glory, working wonders?
cf Exodus 15.11

1	**Exodus 12.1-13** (Passover instructions)	138	1 Cor. 11.23-32	Luke 22.7-13
2	**Exodus 12.14-28** (Passover for future generations)	16	1 Peter 1.18-23	Luke 22.14-23
3	**Exodus 12.29-42** (The Israelites escape)	116.1-8	Acts 2.22-24, 32-36	Luke 22.24-30
4	**Exodus 13.17 – 14.12** (Pharaoh pursues the Israelites)	3	Hebrews 11.28, 29	Luke 22.31-37
5	**Exodus 14.13-31** (Crossing the Red Sea)	115	1 Corinthians 10.1-4	Luke 22.39-46
6	**Exodus 15.1-21** (The song of the Israelites)	9.1-10	Hebrews 3.1-6	Luke 22.63-71

11 Ruth

I will sing of the loving-kindness of the Lord;
my mouth will proclaim your faithfulness to every generation.
cf Psalm 89.1

1	**Ruth 1.1-22** (Ruth returns with Naomi)	88.1-11	Romans 8.28-39	Mark 3.31-35
2	**Ruth 2.1-23** (Ruth meets Boaz)	23	Ephesians 2.11-20	Luke 1.46-55

| 3 | **Ruth 3.1-18**
(Boaz agrees to help) | 138 | I Corinthians 4.1-5 | Matthew 6.25-34 |
| 4 | **Ruth 4.1-17**
(Ruth and Boaz marry) | 89.1-4 | James 5.7-11 | John 16.16-24 |

12   David

I love you, O Lord my strength:
the Lord is my rock, my fortress and my deliverer.
cf Psalm 18.1,2

1	**I Samuel 16.1-13**	2.6-11	2 Timothy 1.3-7	Mark 1.9-11
2	**I Samuel 17.17-49**	18.33-39	Acts 16.22-34	Matthew 17.18-20
[3]	**I Samuel 17.57 – 18.16**	23	I Corinthians 1.1-17	Mark 1.35-38
4	**2 Samuel 1.1-27**	62.1-8	Romans 7.14-25a	John 11.32-36
5	**2 Samuel 5.1-10**	48 *or* 132.13-18	Revelation 21.1-5	Luke 13.31-35
6	**2 Samuel 7.1-17**	89.1-4 *or* 89.29-38	2 Corinthians 3.7-18	Matthew 22.41-46
7	**2 Samuel 11.1-15; 12.1-7a**	51.1-17	I Corinthians 5	Matthew 5.27-30
[8]	**2 Samuel 15.7-22**	57	2 Timothy 4.9-18	John 11.5-16

13   I Chronicles

Yours, Lord, is the greatness, the power, the glory, the splendour, and the majesty;
for everything in heaven and on earth is yours.
cf I Chronicles 29.11

1	**I Chronicles 10.13–11.9**	89.19-29	Acts 13.16-23	Mark 11.1-11
2	**I Chronicles 13.5-12; 15.13-16, 28, 29; 16.1**	132.1-9	I Cor. 11.23-34	John 4.19-24
3	**I Chronicles 17.16-27**	132.11-18	Ephesians 1.3-14	Luke 1.46-55
4	**I Chronicles 21.15-30**	51.1-12	Hebrews 9.11-15	Mark 15.33-39
5	**I Chronicles 28.2-10, 20**	72.1-7	I Corinthians 3.5-15	John 15.5-11
6	**I Chronicles 29.10-20**	96.1-9	2 Corinthians 9.6-15	Matthew 25.14-30

14 2 Chronicles

If my people will humble themselves and pray and seek my face
I will forgive their sin and heal their land.
cf 2 Chronicles 7.14

1	**2 Chronicles 6.12-21**	143	1 Timothy 2.1-8	Matthew 6.9-13
2	**2 Chronicles 9.1-12**	72.8-19	Revelation 7.9-17	Luke 11.29-32
3	**2 Chronicles 20.1-12**	70	Acts 4.23-31	Mark 4.35-41
4	**2 Chronicles 26.1-5, 16-23**	18.25-30	1 Corinthians 10.1-13	Mark 9.33-37
5	**2 Chronicles 29.1-11, 15**	24	Hebrews 10.19-25	John 2.13-17
6	**2 Chronicles 33.1-6, 10-13**	107.10-16	1 Timothy 1.12-17	Luke 15.1-7

15 Job

Christ himself carried our sins in his body on the cross.
By his wounds we have been healed.
cf 1 Peter 2.24

1	**Job 2.3-end**	73.1-20	Revelation 3.14-22	John 12.1-11
2	**Job 4; 6.1-11**	62	2 Corinthians 1.3-11a	John 11.45-54
3	**Job 18.1–19.12**	144.1-10	2 Corinthians 12.7-10	John 14.27-end
4	**Job 24.19-24; 29.1-8**	94.1-11	1 Peter 4.12-19	John 15.18-21
5	**Job 36.22-end; 38.1-13**	93	Ephesians 3.16-21	John 15.1-6
6	**Job 42.1-10a**	145.1-13	2 Corinthians 7.5-10	John 16.19-28

16 Isaiah – part 1

Come, O house of Jacob,
let us walk in the light of the Lord.
cf Isaiah 2.5

1	**Isaiah 1.1-4, 9-20**	50.7-15	Romans 9.27 – 10.4	Matthew 15.4-11
[2]	**Isaiah 5.1-10, 18-23**	80.8-15	2 Peter 2.1-10	Luke 16.10-15
3	**Isaiah 6**	93	Romans 11.1-10	John 12.36-41
4	**Isaiah 8.9 – 9.7**	119.81-88	Ephesians 5.8-14	Matthew 4.12-17
5	**Isaiah 11.1-11**	72.1-11	Romans 15.5-13	John 12.31-33

17 Isaiah – part 2

You shall go out in joy,
and be led forth in peace.
cf Isaiah 55.12

I	**Isaiah 40.1-17, 27-end**	102.12-22	I Peter 1.22 – 2.3	Mark 1.1-4
2	**Isaiah 42.1-12(-17)**	110	I Peter 2.20-25	Matthew 12.9-23
[3]	**Isaiah 43.1-13(-19)**	111	I Peter 5.6-11	Luke 24.44-49
4	**Isaiah 52**	122	I Peter 1.8-12	Mark 1.14-15
5	**Isaiah 55**	21.1-6	I Peter 1.3-7	John 4.13-15

18 Isaiah – part 3

The spirit of the Lord is upon me;
he has sent me to bring good news to the oppressed.
cf Isaiah 61.1

I	**Isaiah 56.1-8**	84	Hebrews 4.12-16	Matthew 21.12-16
2	**Isaiah 58**	41.1-4, 11-13	James 1.22-27	Matthew 25.34-40
3	**Isaiah 60.1-6, 10-end**	138	Hebrews 12.18-24	Matthew 2.1-11
4	**Isaiah 61.10 – 62.7**	45.1-9	Hebrews 13.11-16	Matthew 9.35-38
[5]	**Isaiah 65.17-end**	45.10-17	Revelation 21.1-4	Mark 10.28-31

19 Jeremiah – series A

Sing to the Lord; give praise to the Lord!
He rescues the oppressed from the hands of the wicked.
cf Jeremiah 20.13

I	**Jeremiah 1**	119.9-16	I Corinthians 1.26-31	Matthew 10.16-20
[2]	**Jeremiah 16.1-18**	119.33-40	I Peter 4.12-19	Matthew 19.8-12
3	**Jeremiah 20.7-18**	119.25-32	I Timothy 4. 9-16	Mark 10.35-40
[4]	**Jeremiah 28**	119.41-48	2 John 7-11	Luke 10.13-16
5	**Jeremiah 36.1-10, 14-28**	119.49-56	2 Corinthians 2.14-17	Matthew 5.14-18
6	**Jeremiah 38.1-23**	119.17-24	Romans 2.1-16	Matthew 10.41-42

20   Jeremiah – series B

Heal us, Lord, and we shall be healed;
save us, and we shall be saved.
cf Jeremiah 17.14

I	**Jeremiah 2.1-13**	78.33-40	Revelation 2.1-7	Mark 2.18-19
2	**Jeremiah 8.8 – 9.3**	19.7-end	I Corinthians 2.20-25	Matthew 15.12-14
3	**Jeremiah 18.1-17**	28.1-5	Romans 9.14-26	Matthew 12.33-37
4	**Jeremiah 23.16-32**	74.9-12	I John 4.1-6	John 5.37-44
5	**Jeremiah 29.1, 4-14**	137.1-6	I Timothy 2.1-7	Luke 11.9-13
[6]	**Jeremiah 31.31-37**	51.8-13	Hebrews 10.11-18	Mark 14.22-25

21   Ezekiel

O dry bones, hear the word of the Lord.
Then you shall know that the Lord is God.
cf Ezekiel 37.4,7

I	**Ezekiel 1.1-4, 22-end**	29	Revelation 4.2-11	John 1.14-18
[2]	**Ezekiel 8.1-18**	101	Revelation 2.18-29	Mark 9.43-47
3	**Ezekiel 33.7-20**	32	Romans 3.21-26	Matthew 20.1-16
4	**Ezekiel 34.1-24**	23	I Peter 2.18-25	John 10.11-18
5	**Ezekiel 36.16-32**	51.10-14	Titus 3.3-8	John 7.37-39
[6]	**Ezekiel 47.1-12**	46	Revelation 22.1-6	John 17.20-23

22   Daniel

Blessed be the name of God for ever;
wisdom and power belong to him.
cf Daniel 2.20

I	**Daniel 1.1-20**	101.1-8	I Timothy 6.11-16	Matthew 5.13-16
2	**Daniel 2.1-6, 25-35, 37-47**	96.1-10	I Corinthians 2.6-10	Matthew 16.15-18
[3]	**Daniel 3.3, 8-12, 16-25**	16	2 Timothy 4.1-8	Luke 12.4-12
4	**Daniel 5.1, 5-8, 17-30**	75	Acts 12.19a-24	Matthew 6.19-23
5	**Daniel 6.4-23**	27.1-8	Hebrews 11.32-40	Matthew 5.10-12

23 Visions of Daniel

O Lord, hear; O Lord, forgive;
O Lord, listen and do not delay.
cf Daniel 9.19

1	**Daniel 7.2-18**	80.14-end	Revelation 1.4-8	Luke 22.66-70
2	**Daniel 9.1-7, 17-23(-27)**	122	James 4.4-10	Matthew 24.15-31
3	**Daniel 10.2-20**	34.1-9	Revelation 1.12-18	John 14.25-31
4	**Daniel 12**	44.21-end	Philippians 2.12-18	John 16.29-33

24 Hosea

Come, let us return to the Lord;
for he has torn us that he may heal us.
cf Hosea 6.1

1	**Hosea 1.1 – 2.1**	95.6-11	Romans 9.22-28	Matthew 23.37-39
2	**Hosea 4.1-14**	81.10-16	Romans 1.18-23	Luke 6.43-45
3	**Hosea 5.13 – 6.6**	80.1-7	Romans 13.10-14	Matthew 11.25-30
[4]	**Hosea 8**	115.2-8	Romans 3.9-20	Mark 12.1-9
5	**Hosea 11.1-11**	81.1-9	Romans 11.25-32	John 13.1-9
[6]	**Hosea 14**	37.27-35	Romans 12.1-2	Luke 15.3-7

25 Amos

Let justice roll down like a river;
let righteousness flow like a stream.
cf Amos 5.24

1	**Amos 1.1-10**	82	2 Thessalonians 1.5-10	Luke 4.22-28
2	**Amos 2.1 – 3.2**	10	1 Peter 4.12-19	Luke 19.1-10
3	**Amos 4.1-13**	123	1 Timothy 5.3-10	Luke 8.1-3
4	**Amos 6.1-12**	49	Revelation 3.14-22	Luke 6.20-26
5	**Amos 7.(1-9) 10-17**	52	Acts 13.4-12	Luke 13.31-35
[6]	**Amos 8.1-12**	119.25-32	Revelation 20.11-15	Luke 16.19-31

26 Jonah

As Jonah was a sign to the people of Nineveh,
so will the Son of Man be to this generation.
cf Luke 11.30

1	**Jonah 1** (Jonah runs away)	139.1-11 *or* Jonah 2.2-9	1 Timothy 1.15-20	Luke 9.7-62
2	**Jonah 2.10 – 3.10** (Jonah's preaching in Nineveh)	2.6-11	Ephesians 2.1-10	Luke 11.29-32
3	**Jonah 4** (Jonah sulks)	8	Colossians 4.2-6	Matthew 9.10-13

27 Habakkuk

The Lord is in his holy temple;
let all the earth be silent before him.
cf Habakkuk 2.20

1	**Habakkuk 1.1 – 2.1**	6	Jude 17-25	Mark 13.28-37
2	**Habakkuk 2.2-20**	7.1-10	2 Timothy 3.1-9	Luke 12.13-21
3	**Habakkuk 3.1-19a**	9.1-10	Revelation 1.12-19	John 1.14-18

28 Haggai

The Lord of hosts is with us;
the God of Jacob is our stronghold.
cf Psalm 46.7

1	**Haggai 1.1-15**	132.1-10	Revelation 2.1-7	Matthew 6.25-34
2	**Haggai 2.1-9**	46.4-11	2 Corinthians 3.7-18	John 2.13-22
3	**Haggai 2.10-19**	85.1-7	Titus 1.10 – 2.1	Matthew 6.19-24
4	**Haggai 2.20-23**	97.1-6	Hebrews 12.25-29	Mark 13.24-31

29 Malachi

God's saving power will rise like the sun.
He will bring healing like the sun's rays.
cf Malachi 4.2

1	**Malachi 1.1-14**	75	1 Cor. 11.17-34	Luke 18.9-14
2	**Malachi 2.1-16**	25.1-9	2 Timothy 3.10 – 4.5	John 5.39-47
3	**Malachi 2.17 – 3.12**	65	1 Corinthians 3.10-21	Matthew 3.1-12
4	**Malachi 3.13 – 4.6**	66	Romans 1.18-32	Matthew 11.2-15

30 People Jesus met

For there is no distinction; the same Lord is Lord of all and generous to all who call on him.
Everyone who calls on the name of the Lord shall be saved.
cf Romans 10.13

1	Numbers 21.4-9	1	1 Cor. 2.11-16	**John 3.1-15** (Nicodemus)
2	Amos 8.11-13	65	Revelation 22.1,2	**John 4.5-26(-34)** (The Samaritan woman)
3	Hosea 2.19-end	103.6-18	James 2.1-4	**Luke 7.36-50** (Simon the Pharisee)
4	Ezekiel 3.1-3	84	2 Timothy 3.14-end	**Luke 10.38-42** (Martha and Mary)
5	Jonah 2.2-9	41	James 5.13-15	**John 5.1-18** (The man at the pool)
6	Leviticus 24.10-16	2	1 Cor. 1.18-25	**John 18.28 – 19.11** (Pilate)
[7]	Joshua 24.14-18	22.1-8	Revelation 21.1-8	**Luke 23.32-43** (The two criminals)

31 Time for a feast

Taste and see that the Lord is good!
Blessed are those who trust in him.
cf Psalm 34.8

1	Isaiah 55.1, 2, 10, 11	49	Romans 5.6-11	**Luke 5.27-32(-35)** (Matthew holds a party)
2	Exodus 16.12-18	104.26-32	2 Cor. 9.6-10	**Luke 9.10-17** (Feeding of the 5000)
3	Proverbs 25.6,7	113	1 Peter 5.5-7	**Luke 14.1-14** (Dinner at a Pharisee's house)
4	Proverbs 9.1-6	23	Philippians 3.18-end	**Luke 14.15-24** (God's great feast)
5	Genesis 3.2-6	32.1-8	Acts 16.25-34	**Luke 19.1-10** (Tea with Zaccheus)
6	Exodus 12.21-28	69.13-23	1 Cor. 10.16,17	**Luke 22.7-20** (The last supper)

Five parables from Matthew

O Lord, your word is everlasting;
it stands firm for ever in the heavens.
cf Psalm 119.89

1	2 Samuel 22.2-7	127	1 Peter 2.4-8	**Matthew 7.24-27** (Two house-builders)
2	Isaiah 5.1-7	119.33-40	Galatians 5.22-23; 6.7-10	**Matthew 13.1-9** (The sower)
3	Genesis 41.46-57	145.8-13	1 Peter 4.7-11	**Matthew 25.14-30** (The talents)
4	Ezekiel 34.1-6,11-16	23	1 Peter 2.21-25	**Matthew 18.10-14** (The lost sheep)
5	Isaiah 55.1-7	37.1-9	Ephesians 2.4-9	**Matthew 20.1-16** (The labourers in the vineyard)

33 **Five parables from Luke**

O Lord, your word is everlasting;
it stands firm for ever in the heavens.
cf Psalm 119.89

1	Leviticus 19.9-18	25.1-10	1 John 3.13-18	**Luke 10.25-37** (The good Samaritan)
2	Jeremiah 31.31-34	51.1-11	Romans 8.12-17	**Luke 15.11-32** (The prodigal son)
3	Ecclesiastes 5.10-15	49.1-12	James 4.13 – 5.6	**Luke 12.13-21** (The rich fool)
4	Isaiah 58.1-11	112.1-9	1 Cor. 1.26-31	**Luke 18.9-14** (The Pharisee and the tax collector)
5	Exodus 19.1-8	150	Revelation 19.5-9	**Luke 14.15-24** (The great banquet)

34 **Eight miracles of Jesus**

The Lord heals the brokenhearted;
he binds up all their wounds.
cf Psalm 147.3

1	Judges 15.9-17	147.1-11	Acts 19.11-20	**Matthew 12.22-37** (Casting out an evil spirit)
2	2 Kings 5.8-15a	103.1-12	1 John 1.5 – 2.2	**Mark 2.1-12** (Healing a paralysed man)

3	2 Kings 4.27-37	73.21-28	Acts 14.19-23	**Luke 7.11-17** (Raising the widow's son)
4	Exodus 17.1-17	67	I John 5.13-15	**John 2.1-11** (Turning water into wine)
5	Isaiah 55.8-13	63.1-8	Galatians 3.26-29	**Matthew 8.5-13** (Healing the centurion's servant)
6	Isaiah 43.1-17	107.23-32	Colossians 1.15-20	**Mark 6.45-52** (Jesus walks on the lake)
7	I Samuel 17.41-50	107.10-16	Revelation 4.6b-11	**Luke 8.26-39** (Freeing a man with many evil spirits)
8	Isaiah 35	25.1-6	I John 1.5-10	**John 9.1-12, 35-41** (Healing a blind man)

35   The road to Emmaus

Why look for the living among the dead?
Christ is not among the dead: he has risen. Alleluia.
cf Luke 24.5

1	Isaiah 42.5-8	62	Acts 13.16-30	**Luke 24.13-24**
2	Isaiah 43.1-7	2	Acts 8.26-37	**Luke 24.25-27**
3	Isaiah 63.7-9	92.1-5	2 Timothy 3.14-17	**Luke 24.28-35**

36   Romans – part I

I am not ashamed of the gospel;
it is the power of God for salvation.
cf Romans 1.16

1	Habakkuk 2.1-4a	106.20-24	**Romans 1.13-25; 2.12-16**	Matthew 3.4-12
2	Isaiah 59.1-8	72.1-7	**Romans 3.9-end**	Mark 10.17-21
3	Job 8.20 – 9.13	103.8-14	**Romans 5.1-17**	Mark 10.42-45
4	Ezekiel 36.24-29a	32	**Romans 6.1-4, 12-end**	John 8.2-11
[5]	Isaiah 44.1-5	98	**Romans 8.1-4, 9-11, 18-27**	Matthew 19.23-29
[6]	Deuteronomy 7.7-11	84	**Romans 8.28-end**	John 10.27-29

37 Romans – part 2

The same Lord is lord of all;
he bestows his riches on all who call upon him.
cf Romans 10.12

1	Isaiah 59.19-21	107.1-9	**Romans 11.1-6, 11-24**	Matthew 15.21-28
2	Proverbs 3.5-12	116.1-9	**Romans 12**	Luke 6.27-36
[3]	Leviticus 19.1, 2, 9-18	94.14-23	**Romans 13**	Luke 20.19-25
4	Ezekiel 34.11-16	133	**Romans 14.1-6, 13-23**	Matthew 7.1-5
5	Isaiah 49.5-6	117	**Romans 15.7-21**	John 17.20-23

38 The Church in the world: 1 Corinthians 1 to 13

The message of the cross is a stumbling block to some;
we proclaim it as the power and wisdom of God.
cf 1 Corinthians 1.23-25

1	Isaiah 29.13-16	111	**1 Cor. 1.18 – 2.5**	Matthew 11.25-30
2	1 Kings 8.22-27	27.1-8	**1 Cor. 3.1-17**	John 2.13-22
3	Hosea 2.16-20	128	**1 Cor. 7.1-20**	Matthew 19.1-12
4	Isaiah 49.1-6	34.1-10	**1 Cor. 9.13-27**	John 4.5-9, 27-42
5	Isaiah 1.10-20	133	**1 Cor. 11.17-34**	Luke 22.14-27
6	Jeremiah 31.1-6	31.14-24	**1 Cor. 13**	John 15.9-17

39 Christ's resurrection and ours: 1 Corinthians 15

Christ has been raised from the dead,
the first fruits of those who have died.
cf 1 Corinthians 15.20

1	Daniel 7.7-14	16	**1 Cor. 15.1-11**	Luke 24.36-49
2	Isaiah 40.25-31	81	**1 Cor. 15.12-20**	John 20.24-31
3	Isaiah 45.18-25	98	**1 Cor. 15.20-34**	Mark 13.24-37
4	2 Samuel 12.15-23	73.21-28	**1 Cor. 15.35-49**	Mark 12.18-27
5	1 Chronicles 29.10-20	150	**1 Cor. 15.50-58**	Matthew 28.16-20

40 Ephesians

Once we were darkness;
but now in the Lord we are light.
cf Ephesians 5.8

1	Exodus 19.1-6	145.1-9	**Ephesians 1.1-14 (15-23)**	John 1.14-16
2	Deuteronomy 4.25-31	116.1-9	**Ephesians 2.1-10**	Luke 23.39-43
3	Isaiah 65.1-5	87	**Ephesians 2.11-22; 3.8-13**	Matthew 28.16-end
[4]	Deuteronomy 6.1-5	133	**Ephesians 4.1-16**	Matthew 16.13-18
5	Deuteronomy 10.12-21	5.1-7	**Ephesians 4.22– 5.14**	Matthew 6.19-23
[6]	Isaiah 59.16b-19	44.5-9	**Ephesians 6.10-20**	Luke 10.17-20

41 1 Thessalonians

This is the will of God for us, in Christ Jesus:
rejoice always, pray without ceasing, give thanks in all circumstances.
cf 1 Thessalonians 5.16-18

1	Isaiah 62.1-5	115.1-8	**1 Thess. 1**	Matthew 13.45-46
2	Isaiah 55.9-13	34.11-end	**1 Thess. 2.1-13**	Matthew 23.1-12
[3]	Isaiah 8.11-18	15	**1 Thess. 3.12 – 4.12**	Luke 19.11-27
4	Isaiah 64.1-7	98	**1 Thess. 4.13 – 5.11**	John 3.17-21
[5]	Proverbs 3.1-6	105.1-8	**1 Thess. 5.12-end**	John 17.11-18

42 2 Thessalonians

May our Lord Jesus Christ comfort our hearts;
may he strengthen us in every good work and word.
cf 2 Thessalonians 2.16, 17

1	Isaiah 24.1-5	95	**2 Thess. 1**	Matthew 22.1-14
2	Isaiah 24.20-23	97	**2 Thess. 2.1-15**	Matthew 24.23-27
3	Isaiah 26.1-7	98	**2 Thess. 3**	Mark 4.2-9

43 Hebrews

Let us approach the throne of grace with boldness;
there we receive mercy and grace in our time of need.
cf Hebrews 4.16

1	1 Kings 19.9b-12	45.1-7	**Hebrews 1.1 – 2.4**	John 17.1-5
2	Ecclesiastes 9.1-6	8	**Hebrews 2.5-18**	Mark 3.31-34
3	Numbers 12.1-9	95	**Hebrews 3.1-14**	Matthew 17.1-8
4	Genesis 1.31 – 2.3	33.8-17	**Hebrews 4.1-13**	Matthew 10.24-31
5	Genesis 14.17-20	130	**Hebrews 4.14 – 5.10**	Luke 22.39-46
6	Jeremiah 31.31-34	40.1-10	**Hebrews 9.1-5, 11-15**	Mark 10.35-45
7	Acts 5.1-11	95	**Hebrews 10.19-31**	Luke 12.35-40
8	Philippians 3.7-16	119.65-72	**Hebrews 12.1-11**	Mark 9.2-13

44 1 John

God is light;
in him is no darkness at all.
cf 1 John 1.5

1	Deuteronomy 30.11-20	36	**1 John 1.1 – 2.6**	John 3.19-21
2	Jeremiah 8.8-12	1	**1 John 2.18 – 3.3**	John 1.9-13
3	Jeremiah 31.31-37	43	**1 John 3.4-10; 3.19 – 4.6**	John 8.42-47
4	Song of Solomon 2.8-13	67	**1 John 4.7 – 5.5**	John 1.14-18
[5]	Deuteronomy 6.1-12	2.6-end	**1 John 5.6-end**	John 16.7-15

45 Revelation – series A

Blessed is the one who reads the words of this prophecy;
and blessed are those who hear it and take it to heart.
cf Revelation 1.3

1	Daniel 10:4-19	45.1-9	**Rev. 1.4-end**	Matthew 17.1-8
2	Joshua 24.14-24	7.9-end	**Rev. 3**	Matthew 16.15-18
3	Job 1.1-12	47	**Rev. 12**	John 12.31-36
4	Ezekiel 42.15 – 43.7	45.10-17	**Rev. 21.1-14**	John 6.35-40

Holy, holy, holy is the Lord God Almighty;
who was, and is, and is to come.
cf Revelation 4.8

1	Daniel 7.1-10	118.19-26	**Rev. 4.1-2; 5**	John 1.25-29
2	Amos 4.6-13	44.19-27	**Rev. 6**	Mark 13.5-13
3	2 Kings 19.20-28	52	**Rev. 13**	John 15.19-25
4	Zephaniah 3.9-20	49.12-21	**Rev. 18.21 – 19.9**	Luke 6.20-26
5	Ezekiel 48.30-35	66.1-8	**Rev. 21.10-14; 21.22 – 22.5**	Matthew 25.1-13

psalms and canticles

D Psalms and Canticles

Stories from the four churches

At **St Ann's** the worship planning group have been giving some thought to the fact that theirs is one of many churches where people are reluctant to sing psalms to traditional Anglican chant because they want the worship to be accessible and 'user-friendly', especially to those unfamiliar with traditional worship. At one stage they hadn't the musical resources anyway. They went for a couple of years without using the psalms in any regular way at all, and were in danger of becoming unfamiliar with the riches they contain. So they explored the ways in which other churches are using the psalms musically today, ways which are adaptable to different levels of musical expertise and resourcing. As a result, they're using a metrical psalm in today's Sunday service. Metrical psalms have been popular since the sixteenth century, and many have been written recently, including many worship songs based on psalms. Any congregation that finds hymn singing valuable can sing psalms in this way, though hymns and songs vary considerably in how closely they stick to the written text of the psalm itself.

Today **St Bartholomew's** are using Psalm 66 from this section of *New Patterns for Worship*. The two sides of the congregation are saying alternate verses of the psalm. They have not much in the way of musical resources, and so have been studying a variety of ways of saying the psalms (see page 126). They have tried some of these approaches with the canticles too, but have realized that some of them are different from the psalms, in that they do not necessarily follow the parallelism of Hebrew poetry. Therefore the verses don't have to be said alternately, which sometimes destroys the sense. Some canticles are best said all together. Some might be sung by a cantor with responses.

At **St Christopher's** there is a cantor (someone with a strong voice who can give a lead and sing solo) who sings the text of the psalm to a simple 'tone' or melody. The congregation then sing a simple response, which can begin and conclude the psalm, or be repeated after each verse or group of verses. This works well unaccompanied but today the organ is used; other instrumental accompaniments are also used. There are many books available which contain this sort of simple chant. Some use a similar approach but with a more 'worship-song' style of melody for the response. Another approach they have tried at St Christopher's is to speak the words of a psalm over a background of quiet instrumental music, using either suitable pieces of music found by the organist, or published resources specifically designed for this.

The board outside **St Dodo's** advertises Choral Evensong. For a while, when they had no organist, they set up a gramophone (as they called it) on the chancel steps and had the choir singing along to a record of a famous cathedral choir while everyone listened. This evening there is an organist and a robed choir of five people, and they sing the psalms to the *New Cathedral Psalter*, but to an unfamiliar chant pitched very high and too irregular for anyone else to join in. It is difficult to hear the words, which are different from those in the *Common Worship* books, because the organ is so loud it is drowning out their voices, which is perhaps as well, because it sounds as if they are having a competition to see how many words they can get on to one note …

Saying the Psalms: what St Bartholomew's considered

Saying the Psalms is perfectly acceptable, and not necessarily a poor substitute for singing them. Here are some approaches to consider:

* solo voice for the main text, with an unvarying congregational response after each verse or after a group of verses (see, for example, Psalm 8 below);
* splitting the congregation into two parts (two sides of the building; men and women; adults and children; or whatever is appropriate) and having each part take alternate verses of the psalm; alternatively, give the groups half of each verse – this is especially effective if the psalm utilizes the technique of 'parallelism', where each verse contains the same idea articulated in two different ways (Psalm 66, below, could work in this way);
* using the same approach, but splitting the psalm between leader and congregation (see, for example, Psalm 141 below);
* saying the whole psalm together congregationally (see, for example, Psalm 118a below);
* listening while the psalm is read by one or more solo voices (see, for instance, Psalm 70 below), perhaps with a quiet, reflective instrumental accompaniment on a flute, acoustic guitar or soft keyboard at a distance.

In each case it will be important to consider the particular style and genre of the psalm in question to determine the most appropriate way of using it. Such considerations will also have implications for the manner in which the psalm is recited:

* shouted loudly, by a standing congregation, for a psalm which is an act of praise to God;
* recited quietly, slowly and reflectively, with the congregation kneeling or seated, for a psalm of lament;
* proclaimed loudly from one part of the congregation to another for a psalm which is a call to worship;
* listened to quietly, followed by silence, for a psalm which articulates the psalmist's anger and frustration etc.

As the Introduction to the Psalter in *Common Worship: Daily Prayer* says, 'some psalms, or parts of psalms, lend themselves to one method rather than another, and those leading worship should consider carefully which will be best in each instance'.

Singing the Psalms

Psalm and canticle texts can be sung in four different ways:

* by everyone;
* in dialogue between two groups, or between soloist and everyone else;
* by a soloist (or choral group) with refrain for everyone else;
* by a soloist or choral group, with everyone else listening.

The nature of the music will depend whether the text is metrical or irregular prose. Metrical texts can have hymn- or song-style music; irregular prose texts need some form of repeated melody that can be adapted to irregular patterns of words.

As with saying psalms, some ways of singing them may be more appropriate for different churches, for different contexts of worship, or for different psalm texts. There are many permutations and possibilities, and a whole range of musical styles.

Here are some options.

Psalm and canticle paraphrases (metrical psalms)

Hymn style, sung by everyone (or shared alternate verses).
Song style, sung by everyone (or shared alternate verses).
Song style, with solo or choral verses, and refrain for everyone.
Song style, sung by a cantor or choral group.

Psalm and canticle texts

Stressed prose (e.g. the Grail Psalter)

* Sung to a simple chant by a cantor, or choral group, or by all, with or without refrain for everyone (these include the psalms and canticles set by Joseph Gelineau).

Unstressed prose (e.g. *Common Worship* Psalter, ICEL Psalter, *Book of Common Prayer* Psalter)

* Sung by a cantor, or choral group, or by all, to a simple, modern chant, with or without refrain for everyone.
* Sung to a plainsong tone by a cantor, or choral group, or by all, with or without refrain for everyone.
* Sung to Anglican chant by a cantor, or choral group, or by all, with or without refrain for everyone.

In all these examples, the refrain can be sung in the style of a chant, or can be a hymn- or song-style setting.

Psalm or canticle settings (paraphrase or prose)

* Intended for singing by a soloist or choir, and to be heard by everyone else.

A sung repertory of psalms and canticles needs to be built slowly, so that everyone is comfortable and confident.

The large range of psalms specified in the lectionary means that it may not always be possible to sing the psalm specified as part of the Liturgy of the Word. There are, however, opportunities to use a psalm text in other parts of the service where there is singing.

It's often easier to sing psalm paraphrases (metrical psalms) to familiar hymn and song melodies. However, prose psalms and canticles can become part of the musical repertory of a congregation, particularly if the number of psalm or canticle texts and chants used is reasonably small.

How to construct a psalm or canticle response

Both here in this section, and in the Psalms and Canticles in *Common Worship: Daily Prayer*, some responses are provided for the congregation, but alternative responses may be used for particular occasions, for instance to fit with a particular season or theme.

* A verse or half-verse from within the psalm or canticle may be appropriate, or a text from elsewhere may be chosen.
* Remember that the main aim of the response is to provide an opportunity for reflecting on the theme.
* Responses should be short, memorable, and capable of repetition.
* The response should support and not interrupt the flow of the psalm or canticle, either in its rhythm or in its sequence of thought.

Notes to the resources

1. The note on Psalms from A Service of the Word (Note 6) gives considerable scope for variety and flexibility in the use of psalms. It permits:
   * saying or singing the psalms in traditional ways;
   * using a metrical version (that is, a hymn or song based on a psalm);
   * using a responsive form, or a paraphrase.

   In addition, permission is given for the use (on occasions) of a song or canticle taken directly from another part of Scripture to replace the psalm.

2. In this section we have provided a small selection of material taken from, or based on, psalms and canticles. There is a variety of style and presentation, and we have tried to consider the needs of a congregation saying the psalms as well as singing them. One of these examples might replace the psalm set in the lectionary on suitable occasions. Each of them could be further adapted, and they are intended to encourage local creativity.

3. These examples, apart from one instance, do not follow the *Common Worship* Psalter. They are drawn and adapted from a variety of translations of the Bible. Some are much closer to paraphrase than translation. In doing this we have tried to keep in mind the needs of children and of worshippers who are familiar neither with church, nor with echoes of traditional translations or biblical passages.

4. For one of the psalms (Psalm 34) and some of the canticles (Venite, Jubilate, Magnificat) we have deliberately included a number of alternatives, to demonstrate the wide range of styles in which psalms and canticles can be spoken or sung. Metrical versions may of course be spoken as well as sung.

5. We have tried to provide psalms which connect with particular 'moods' (such as joy, thanks, lament, struggle, praise, anger, reflection, questioning, etc.) as well as with particular seasons.

Psalms and verses from psalms

Verses from Psalm 8
D *1*

The ICEL (International Commission on English in the Liturgy) translation, with a response.

Lord our God,
the whole world tells the greatness of your name.
Your glory reaches beyond the stars.

Even the babble of infants
declares your strength,
your power to halt the enemy and avenger.
Your glory reaches beyond the stars.

I see your handiwork in the heavens:
the moon and the stars you set in place.
Your glory reaches beyond the stars.

What is humankind that you remember them,
the human race that you care for them?
Your glory reaches beyond the stars.

You treat them like gods,
dressing them in glory and splendour.
You give them charge of the earth, laying all at their feet:
cattle and sheep, wild beasts,
birds of the sky, fish of the sea, every swimming creature.
Your glory reaches beyond the stars.

Lord our God,
the whole world tells the greatness of your name.
Your glory reaches beyond the stars.

Psalm 34
D2

Common Worship: Daily Prayer *contains responsive versions of all the psalms, with psalm prayers for each one. One of these, Psalm 34, is included here as an example.*

This is followed by two versions of verses from Psalm 34, turned into a responsive acclamation. The first of these two versions uses the Common Worship *translation of the psalm; the second is based loosely on the CEV (Contemporary English Version of the Bible).*

There are a number of metrical and sung versions of Psalm 34 easily available in hymn books, such as:

✳ *'Tell his praise in song and story' (8787 D) – T. Dudley Smith*
✳ *'Through all the changing scenes of life' (8686 CM) – Tate and Brady*
✳ *'Praise to the Lord' (Songs from the Psalms © Make Way Music) – Graham Kendrick*

Two further singable versions are also included here, by Teresa Brown and Paul Wigmore.

Refrain:

1   *I will bless the Lord at all times;* ♦
   his praise shall ever be in my mouth.

2   My soul shall glory in the Lord; ♦
   let the humble hear and be glad.

3   O magnify the Lord with me; ♦
   let us exalt his name together.

4   I sought the Lord and he answered me ♦
   and delivered me from all my fears.

5   Look upon him and be radiant ♦
   and your faces shall not be ashamed.

6   This poor soul cried, and the Lord heard me ♦
   and saved me from all my troubles. ℞

7   The angel of the Lord encamps around those
      who fear him ♦
   and delivers them.

8   O taste and see that the Lord is gracious; ♦
   blessed is the one who trusts in him.

9   Fear the Lord, all you his holy ones, ♦
   for those who fear him lack nothing.

10   Lions may lack and suffer hunger, ♦
   but those who seek the Lord
      lack nothing that is good. ℞

11   Come, my children, and listen to me; ♦
   I will teach you the fear of the Lord.

12   Who is there who delights in life ♦
   and longs for days to enjoy good things?

13   Keep your tongue from evil ♦
   and your lips from lying words.

14   Turn from evil and do good; ♦
   seek peace and pursue it. ℞

15   The eyes of the Lord are upon the righteous ♦
   and his ears are open to their cry.

16   The face of the Lord is against those who do evil, ♦
   to root out the remembrance of them from the earth.

17   The righteous cry and the Lord hears them ♦
   and delivers them out of all their troubles.

18   The Lord is near to the brokenhearted ♦
   and will save those who are crushed in spirit. ℞

19 Many are the troubles of the righteous; ◆
from them all will the Lord deliver them.

20 He keeps all their bones, ◆
so that not one of them is broken.

21 But evil shall slay the wicked ◆
and those who hate the righteous will be condemned.

22 The Lord ransoms the life of his servants ◆
and will condemn none who seek refuge in him. ℟

Verses from Psalm 34
D3

O magnify the Lord with me;
let us exalt his name together.
O magnify the Lord with me;
let us exalt his name together.

I sought the Lord and he answered me;
he delivered me from all my fears.
O magnify the Lord with me.

In my weakness I cried to the Lord;
he heard me and saved me from my troubles.
Let us exalt his name together.

Glory to the Father and to the Son
and to the Holy Spirit.
O magnify the Lord with me;
let us exalt his name together.

Verses from Psalm 34
D4

Honour the Lord with me!
Celebrate his great name.
Honour the Lord with me!
Celebrate his great name.

I asked the Lord for help
and he saved me from all my fears.
Honour the Lord with me.

I was a nobody, but I prayed,
and the Lord saved me from all my troubles.
Celebrate his great name.

Glory to the Father and to the Son
and to the Holy Spirit.
Honour the Lord with me.
Celebrate his great name.

The Lord is close
to the brokenhearted
D5

Refrain:
The Lord is close to the brokenhearted;
blessed be the Lord.

Cantor/Choir
I will bless the Lord at all times,
    God's praise always on my lips;
glorify the Lord with me,
    together let us praise God's name. ℞

I sought the Lord and was heard;
    from all my terrors set free.
When the poor cry out the Lord hears them
    and rescues them from all their distress. ℞

The Lord is close to the brokenhearted;
    those whose spirit is crushed God will save.
Many are the trials of the upright
    but the Lord will come to rescue them. ℞

I'll praise the Lord for ever
D6

Refrain:
Glorify the Lord with me; exalt his name, for great is he!
I'll praise the Lord for ever and ever.

I'll praise the Lord for ever and ever,
my soul shall boast of his wonderful name: ℞

I sought the Lord, he answered my calling,
delivered me from my innermost fears: ℞

O taste and see how gracious the Lord is –
secure are they who take refuge in him: ℞

The Lord redeems the faithful who serve him,
and those who trust him he never condemns: ℞

Verses from Psalm 40
D7

A paraphrase of some verses from the psalm, with a response.

You put a new song in my mouth:
a song of praise to you, my God.
You put a new song in my mouth:
a song of praise to you, my God.

I waited patiently for you, Lord;
you bent down to me and heard my cry for help.
You put a new song in my mouth.

Many shall see, and stand amazed,
and put their trust in you, Lord.
You put a new song in my mouth.

I love to do your will, Lord God;
your law is deep in my heart.
You put a new song in my mouth.

I proclaimed your righteousness in the gathering of
    God's people;
I did not hold back from speaking out.
You put a new song in my mouth.

Glory to the Father, and to the Son, and to the Holy Spirit.
You put a new song in my mouth:
a song of praise to you, my God.

cf Psalm 40.1-3,9,10

Verses from Psalm 46
D8

Verses from the psalm, with a response.

The Lord is with us, he is our stronghold;
God will help at the break of day.
The Lord is with us, he is our stronghold;
God will help at the break of day.

God is our refuge and strength,
ready to help whenever we are in trouble:
God will help at the break of day.

We will not fear, even if the earth shakes,
and the mountains topple into the sea:
God will help at the break of day.

Come now and look at the works of the Lord,
the awesome things he has done on earth:
God will help at the break of day.

Be still and know that I am God;
I will be exalted among the nations;
I will be exalted in the earth:
God will help at the break of day.

Glory to the Father, and to the Son, and to the Holy Spirit.
The Lord is with us, he is our stronghold:
God will help at the break of day.

Psalm 46.1-3,8,10

Verses from Psalm 66
D9

A psalm used by the congregation in two parts, A and B.

Leader   Let the praises of God ring out.
All   **He is the source of our life.**

A   Let all creation rejoice in God;
B   *sing the glory of his name.*

A   Come and see the work of God,
B   *how wonderful he is to all people.*

A   He turned the sea into dry land,
B   *so his people went through the water on foot.*

A   There we rejoiced in him.
B   *In his might he rules for ever.*

Leader	Glory to the Father, and to the Son, and to the Holy Spirit.
All	**Let the praises of God ring out.**
	He is the source of our life.

cf Psalm 66.4-8

Psalm 70
D10

This is the ICEL translation, probably best spoken by a single voice.

Help me, God.
Lord, be quick to save me.
People are plotting to kill me;
humble them, shame them.

They want to ruin me;
ruin and disgrace them.
Let those who jeer at me
swallow their shameful taunts.

But those who seek you
and trust your saving love
rejoice and always sing,
'God is great.'

I am poor and helpless,
O God, hurry to my side!
Lord, my help, my rescue,
do not delay.

Verses from Psalm 95
D11

This is a very free paraphrase of selected verses from the psalm, intended to convey the mood of the psalm and not just its content.

Come, let us sing to the Lord our God;
raise the roof to the Rock of rescue.

Come into the presence of the Lord with thanks;
raise the rafters with songs of praise.

The Lord is the great God, over all;
greater than every other power.

He holds the depths of the earth in his hands,
and the mountain peaks belong to him.

The ocean is the Lord's: it was made by God;
the land was formed by his own hands.

Come, let us bow before the Lord our maker;
with humble hearts we worship God.

The Lord is God and we are his;
we are the Shepherd's very own flock.

cf Psalm 95.1-7

Verses from Psalm 102
D12

Selected verses from the psalm, turned into a responsive acclamation.

Turn your ear to me;
be swift to answer when I call.
Turn your ear to me;
be swift to answer when I call.

Lord, hear my prayer,
and let my cry come before you:
be swift to answer when I call.

Do not hide your face from me
in the day of my trouble:
be swift to answer when I call.

You, Lord, endure for ever,
and your name from age to age:
be swift to answer when I call.

You will be moved to have compassion on Zion,
for it is time to have pity on her:
be swift to answer when I call.

Glory to the Father, and to the Son, and to the Holy Spirit.
Turn your ear to me;
be swift to answer when I call.

Psalm 102.1,2,12,13

Verses from Psalm 118 (a)
D13

A selection of verses, in a contemporary translation, designed for the congregation to say together.

When I was really going through it, I prayed to the Lord.
He answered my prayer, and set me free.

The Lord is on my side,
I am not afraid of what others can do to me.

With the Lord on my side
I will defeat all my enemies.

It is best to trust the Lord for protection.
Don't put your trust in anyone else.

cf Psalm 118.5-8

Verses from Psalm 118 (b)
D14

A further selection of verses from Psalm 118, this time set out as a dialogue between leader and congregation.

Open the gates of justice!
I will enter and tell the Lord how thankful I am.

Here is the gate of the Lord!
All who do right may enter this gate.
I praise the Lord for answering my prayers and
saving me.

The stone the builders rejected has now become
the most important stone.
The Lord has done this, and it is amazing to us.

This is a day that belongs to the Lord!
Let us rejoice and be glad today.

We'll ask the Lord to save us.
We'll ask the Lord to let us succeed.

God bless the one who comes in the name of the Lord.
We bless you from here, in the house of the Lord.

The Lord is God; he has given us light.
**Let us join the joyful procession to the
altar of the Lord.**

The Lord is my God.
I will praise him and tell him how thankful I am.

Tell the Lord how thankful you are
because he is kind and always merciful.

cf Psalm 118.19-29

Verses from Psalm 119
D*15*

*A selection of verses, based on a contemporary translation and
set out as a dialogue between leader and congregation.*

Treat me with kindness, Lord
so that I may live and do what you say.
**Open my mind:
let me discover the wonders of your law.**

Your laws are my greatest joy!
I do what they say.

I am at the point of death.
**Breathe new life into me, as your word
has promised.**

When I told you my troubles, you answered my prayers.
Now teach me your laws.
**Help me to understand your teachings,
and I will think about your marvellous deeds.**

I am overcome with sorrow.
Strengthen me, as you have promised.
**I am eager to do all that you want.
Help me to understand more and more.**

cf Psalm 119.17,18,24-28,32

A selection of verses with the same response between each block of text, allowing the psalm to be used without a text for the congregation.

Out of the depths I have called to you, Lord.
Let your ears be open to hear my voice.
My hope is in God's word.

If you recorded all our sins
who could come before you?
My hope is in God's word.

There is forgiveness with you:
therefore you shall be feared.
My hope is in God's word.

My soul is longing for the Lord,
more than those who watch for daybreak.
My hope is in God's word.

O Israel, wait for the Lord,
for with the Lord there is mercy.
My hope is in God's word.

Glory to the Father, and to the Son, and to the Holy Spirit.
My hope is in God's word.

A selection of verses, set out as a dialogue between leader and congregation.

O Lord, we call to you: come to us quickly.
Hear us when we cry to you.
**Let our prayers rise up before you like incense:
let our lifted hands be like an evening sacrifice.**

Put a guard on our mouths, O Lord;
keep watch over our lips.
**Turn our hearts from evil desires,
and keep us from doing wrong.**

Glory to the Father and to the Son
and to the Holy Spirit;
**as it was in the beginning is now
and shall be for ever. Amen.**

cf Psalm 141.1-4

A selection of verses, set out as a dialogue between leader and congregation.

Great is the Lord and greatly to be praised:
there is no end to his greatness.
**One generation shall praise your works to another,
and shall declare your power.**

All creation praises you, Lord,
and your faithful servants bless you.
**They declare the glory of your kingdom
and tell of your mighty power.**

My mouth shall proclaim the praise of the Lord.
**Let every living thing bless his holy name
    for ever and ever.**

cf Psalm 145.3, 4, 10, 11, 12, 21

Canticles

Te Deum Laudamus

We praise you, O God,
we acclaim you as the Lord;
all creation worships you,
the Father everlasting.
To you all angels, all the powers of heaven,
the cherubim and seraphim, sing in endless praise:
Holy, holy, holy Lord, God of power and might,
heaven and earth are full of your glory.
The glorious company of apostles praise you.
The noble fellowship of prophets praise you.
The white-robed army of martyrs praise you.
Throughout the world the holy Church acclaims you:
Father, of majesty unbounded,
your true and only Son, worthy of all praise,
the Holy Spirit, advocate and guide.

You, Christ, are the King of glory,
the eternal Son of the Father.
When you took our flesh to set us free
you humbly chose the Virgin's womb.
You overcame the sting of death
and opened the kingdom of heaven to all believers.
You are seated at God's right hand in glory.
We believe that you will come and be our judge.
Come then, Lord, and help your people,
bought with the price of your own blood,
and bring us with your saints
to glory everlasting.

[Save your people, Lord, and bless your inheritance.
Govern and uphold them now and always.

Day by day we bless you.
We praise your name for ever.

Keep us today, Lord, from all sin.
Have mercy on us, Lord, have mercy.

Lord, show us your love and mercy,
for we have put our trust in you.

In you, Lord, is our hope:
let us never be put to shame.]

Te Deum Laudamus (God, we praise you)

God, we praise you, God, we bless you,
God, we name you sovereign Lord!
Mighty king whom angels worship,
Father, by your Church adored:
All creation shows your glory,
Heaven and earth draw near your throne
Singing 'Holy, holy, holy,'
Lord of hosts, and God alone.

True apostles, faithful prophets,
Saints who set their world ablaze,
Martyrs, once unknown, unheeded,
Join one growing song of praise,
While your Church on earth confesses
One majestic Trinity:
Father, Son, and Holy Spirit,
God, our hope eternally.

Jesus Christ, the King of glory,
Everlasting Son of God,
Humble was your virgin mother,
Hard the lonely path you trod:
By your cross is sin defeated,
Hell confronted face to face,
Heaven opened to believers,
Sinners justified by grace.

Christ, at God's right hand victorious,
You will judge the world you made;
Lord, in mercy help your servants
For whose freedom you have paid:
Raise us up from dust to glory,
Guard us from all sin today;
King enthroned above all praises,
Save your people, God, we pray.

8.7.8.7.D

Te Deum with Celtic Alleluia

Refrain:
Alleluia, alleluia. Alleluia, alleluia.

Father, we praise you as Lord,
all of the earth gives you worship,
for your majesty fills the heavens, fills the earth. R

Blessed apostles sing praise;
prophets and martyrs give glory:
'for your majesty praise the Spirit, praise the Son!' R

You are the Christ everlasting
born for us all of a virgin,
you have conquered death, opened heaven to all believers. ℞

Help those you saved by your blood,
raise them to life with your martyrs.
Save your people, Lord, as their ruler raise them up. ℞

Father, Son and Spirit
Approach to worship
D22

Venite – a Song of Triumph

1   O come, let us sing to the Lord; ♦
    let us heartily rejoice in the rock of our salvation.

2   Let us come into his presence with thanksgiving ♦
    and be glad in him with psalms.

3   For the Lord is a great God ♦
    and a great king above all gods.

4   In his hand are the depths of the earth ♦
    and the heights of the mountains are his also.

5   The sea is his, for he made it, ♦
    and his hands have moulded the dry land.

6   Come, let us worship and bow down ♦
    and kneel before the Lord our Maker.

7   For he is our God; ♦
    we are the people of his pasture and the sheep of his hand.

    Glory to the Father and to the Son
    and to the Holy Spirit;
    as it was in the beginning is now
    and shall be for ever. Amen.

                                        cf Psalm 95

Father, Son and Spirit
Approach to worship
D23

Venite – a metrical version

Come, worship God who is worthy of honour,
Enter his presence with thanks and a song!
He is the rock of his people's salvation,
To whom our jubilant praises belong.

Ruled by his might are the heights of the mountains,
Held in his hands are the depths of the earth;
His is the sea, his the land for he made them,
King above all gods, who gave us our birth.

We are his people, the sheep of his pasture,
He is our maker and to him we pray;
Gladly we kneel in obedience before him –
Great is the God whom we worship this day!

Now let us listen, for God speaks among us,
Open our hearts and receive what he says:
Peace be to all who remember his goodness,
Trust in his word and rejoice in his ways!

11.10.11.10.

Father, Son and Spirit
Approach to worship
D24

Jubilate – a Song of Joy

1   O be joyful in the Lord, all the earth; ♦
serve the Lord with gladness
       and come before his presence with a song.

2   Know that the Lord is God; ♦
it is he that has made us and we are his;
       we are his people and the sheep of his pasture.

3   Enter his gates with thanksgiving
       and his courts with praise; ♦
give thanks to him and bless his name.

4   For the Lord is gracious; his steadfast love is everlasting ♦
and his faithfulness endures from generation to generation.

Glory to the Father and to the Son
and to the Holy Spirit;
as it was in the beginning is now
and shall be for ever. Amen.

Psalm 100

Father, Son and Spirit
Approach to worship
D25

Jubilate, ev'rybody (from Psalm 100)

Jubilate, ev'rybody,
serve the Lord in all your ways,
and come before his presence singing:
enter now his courts with praise.
For the Lord our God is gracious,
and his mercy everlasting,
Jubilate, Jubilate, Jubilate Deo!

Come, rejoice before your maker (from Psalm 100)

Come, rejoice before your maker
All you peoples of the earth;
Serve the Lord your God with gladness,
Come before him with a song!

Know for certain that Jehovah
Is the true and only God:
We are his, for he has made us;
We are sheep within his fold.

Come with grateful hearts before him,
Enter now his courts with praise;
Show your thankfulness towards him,
Give due honour to his name.

For the Lord our God is gracious,
Everlasting in his love;
And to every generation
His great faithfulness endures.

8.7.8.7.

Jubilate (Laudate Dominum)

Refrain:
Laudate Dominum, laudate Dominum,
Omnes gentes, alleluia!

(Sing, praise and bless the Lord, sing, praise and bless the Lord,
Peoples! Nations! Alleluia!)

Cantor:
We come before you with joyful songs, alleluia, alleluia.
You are our God, you have made us,
        alleluia, alleluia, ℟

You are our God, we belong to you, alleluia, alleluia,
We are your people, the sheep of your flock,
        alleluia, alleluia, ℟

Let us then enter your gates with thanksgiving,
        alleluia, alleluia,
Let us give thanks and praise your name, alleluia, alleluia, ℟

For you are good and your love lasts for ever,
        alleluia, alleluia,
Your faithfulness lasts from age to age, alleluia, alleluia, ℟

Father, Son and Spirit
Approach to worship
D28

Jubilate (Sing all creation)

Sing all creation, sing to God in gladness!
Joyously serve him, singing hymns of homage!
Chanting his praises, come before his presence!
Praise the Almighty!

Know that our God is Lord of all the ages!
He is our maker, we are all his creatures,
people he fashioned, sheep he leads to pasture!
Praise the Almighty!

Enter his temple, ringing out his praises!
Sing in thanksgiving as you come before him!
Blessing his bounty, glorify his greatness!
Praise the Almighty!

Great in his goodness is the Lord we worship;
steadfast his kindness, love that knows no ending!
Faithful his word is, changeless, everlasting!
Praise the Almighty!

11.11.11.5.

God in creation
D29

Benedicite – a Song of Creation (shorter version)

1   Bless the Lord all you works of the Lord: ♦
    sing his praise and exalt him for ever.

2   Bless the Lord you heavens: ♦
    sing his praise and exalt him for ever.

3   Bless the Lord you angels of the Lord: ♦
    sing his praise and exalt him for ever.

4   Bless the Lord all people on earth: ♦
    sing his praise and exalt him for ever.

5   O people of God bless the Lord: ♦
    sing his praise and exalt him for ever.

6   Bless the Lord you priests of the Lord: ♦
    sing his praise and exalt him for ever.

7   Bless the Lord you servants of the Lord: ♦
    sing his praise and exalt him for ever.

8   Bless the Lord all you of upright spirit: ♦
    bless the Lord you that are holy and humble in heart;

    bless the Father, the Son and the Holy Spirit: ♦
    sing his praise and exalt him for ever.

Benedicite (Glory to God above)

Refrain:
O sing hallelujah
and praise God for evermore!

Glory to God above!
Heavens declare his love;
praise him, you angels,
praise him all you high and heavenly host.
Worship him, sun and moon;
stars, complement their tune:
grounded in God's good purpose
let his grace become your boast. ℟

Glory to God below
let depths of ocean show;
lightning and hail, snow,
wind and cloud perform at his command!
Let every mountain range,
forest and grove and grange,
creatures of earth and air and sea
praise God in every land. ℟

'Glory to God!' now sing
commoner, queen and king;
women and men of every age
unite to praise the Lord.
Worship God's holy name
and let your lives proclaim
God's saving power extends to those
who love and serve his word. ℟

Benedicite (Let us sing to the Lord)

Refrain:
Let us sing to the Lord, let us sing to the Lord!
Let us sing to the Lord, let us sing to the Lord!

Cantor:
All creation bless the Lord;
and you, angels of the Lord,
praise and glorify the Lord. ℟

Sun and moon, bless the Lord;
and you, night and day, bless the Lord,
and you, light and darkness, bless the Lord. ℟

Praise the Lord all the earth.
Birds of the air, bless the Lord,
all creatures of the sea, bless the Lord. ℟

Fire and hail, bless the Lord.
Snow and frost, bless the Lord,
mountains and hills, bless the Lord. ℟

Praised be Christ, he is our hope,
he is the joy of our hearts.
Compassionate and gracious is our God. ℟

The Lord opens up a way,
and leads us on paths of life,
the earth is full of God's love. ℟

The glory of the Lord fills the earth.
Let all peoples bless God's name,
Let everything that breathes bless the Lord. ℟

Christ's coming
D32

Benedictus (The Song of Zechariah)

Refrain:
You have raised up for us a mighty Saviour,
born of the house of your servant David.

1   Blessed be the Lord the God of Israel, ♦
     who has come to his people and set them free.

2   He has raised up for us a mighty Saviour, ♦
     born of the house of his servant David.

3   Through his holy prophets God promised of old ♦
     to save us from our enemies,
         from the hands of all that hate us,

4   To show mercy to our ancestors, ♦
     and to remember his holy covenant.

5   This was the oath God swore to our father Abraham: ♦
     to set us free from the hands of our enemies,

6   Free to worship him without fear, ♦
     holy and righteous in his sight
         all the days of our life.

7   And you, child, shall be called the prophet
         of the Most High, ♦
     for you will go before the Lord to prepare his way,

8   To give his people knowledge of salvation ♦
     by the forgiveness of all their sins.

9   In the tender compassion of our God ♦
     the dawn from on high shall break upon us,

10   To shine on those who dwell in darkness
         and the shadow of death, ♦
     and to guide our feet into the way of peace.

Luke 1.68-79

Glory to the Father and to the Son
and to the Holy Spirit;
as it was in the beginning is now
and shall be for ever. Amen.

You have raised up for us a mighty Saviour,
born of the house of your servant David.

Christ's coming
D33

Benedictus (Now bless the God of Israel)

Now bless the God of Israel
who comes in love and power,
who raises from the royal house
deliv'rance in this hour.
Through holy prophets God has sworn
to free us from alarm,
to save us from the heavy hand
of all who wish us harm.

Remembering the covenant,
God rescues us from fear,
that we might serve in holiness
and peace from year to year.
And you, my child, shall go before,
to preach, to prophesy,
that all may know the tender love,
the grace of God most high.

In tender mercy, God will send
the dayspring from on high,
Our rising sun, the light of life
for those who sit and sigh.
God comes to guide our way to peace,
that death shall reign no more.
Sing praises to the Holy One,
O worship and adore.

C.M.

Incarnation
D34

Benedictus (O bless the God of Israel)

O bless the God of Israel,
who comes to set us free,
who visits and redeems us
and grants us liberty.
The prophets spoke of mercy,
of rescue and release;
God shall fulfil the promise
to bring our people peace.

Now from the house of David
a child of grace is given;
a Saviour comes among us
to raise us up to heaven.
Before him goes the herald,
forerunner in the way,
the prophet of salvation,
the messenger of Day.

Where once were fear and darkness
the sun begins to rise –
the dawning of forgiveness
upon the sinner's eyes,
to guide the feet of pilgrims
along the paths of peace:
O bless our God and Saviour,
with songs that never cease!

7.6.7.6.D

Incarnation
D35

Benedictus (Blest be the Lord)

Blest be the Lord, the God of Israel,
Who brings the dawn and darkest night dispels,
Who raises up a mighty Saviour from the earth,
Of David's line, a son of royal birth.

The prophets tell a story just begun
Of vanquished foe and glorious victory won,
Of promise made to all who keep the law as guide:
God's faithful love and mercy will abide.

Men:

This is the oath once sworn to Abraham:
All shall be free to dwell upon the land,
Free now to praise, unharmed by the oppressor's rod,
Holy and righteous in the sight of God.

Women:

And you, my child, this day you shall be called
The promised one, the prophet of our God,
For you will go before the Lord to clear the way,
And shepherd all into the light of day.

The tender love God promised from our birth
Is soon to shine upon this shadowed earth,
To shine on those whose sorrows seem to never cease,
To guide our feet into the path of peace.

10.10.12.10.

Magnificat (The Song of Mary)

Refrain:
You have done great things, O God,
and holy is your name.

1   My soul proclaims the greatness of the Lord,
        my spirit rejoices in God my Saviour; ◆
    he has looked with favour on his lowly servant.

2   From this day all generations will call me blessed; ◆
    the Almighty has done great things for me
        and holy is his name.

3   He has mercy on those who fear him, ◆
    from generation to generation.

4   He has shown strength with his arm ◆
    and has scattered the proud in their conceit,

5   Casting down the mighty from their thrones ◆
    and lifting up the lowly.

6   He has filled the hungry with good things ◆
    and sent the rich away empty.

7   He has come to the aid of his servant Israel, ◆
    to remember his promise of mercy,

8   The promise made to our ancestors, ◆
    to Abraham and his children for ever.

Luke 1.46-55

Glory to the Father and to the Son
and to the Holy Spirit;
as it was in the beginning is now
and shall be for ever. Amen.

You have done great things, O God,
and holy is your name.

Magnificat (The Song of Mary)

With Mary let my soul rejoice,
And praise God's holy name –
His saving love from first to last,
From age to age the same!

How strong his arm, how great his power!
The proud he will disown;
The meek and humble he exalts
To share his glorious throne.

The rich our God will send away
And feed the hungry poor
The arms of love remain outstretched
At mercy's open door.

So shall God's promise be fulfilled,
To Israel firmly made:
A child is born, a Son is given
Whose crown will never fade.

All glory to the Father, Son
And Spirit now proclaim;
With Mary let the world rejoice
And praise God's holy name!

C.M.

Magnificat (Holy is his name)

Refrain:
And holy is his name through all generations!
Everlasting is his mercy to the people he has chosen,
and holy is his name!

My soul is filled with joy as I sing to God my Saviour:
he has looked upon his servant, he has visited his people.℞

I am lowly as a child, but I know from this day forward
that my name will be remembered, for the world will call
    me blessed. ℞

I proclaim the pow'r of God! He does marvels for
    his servants;
though he scatters the proud-hearted and destroys
    the might of princes. ℞

To the hungry he gives food, sends the rich away empty.
In his mercy he is mindful of the people he has chosen. ℞

In his love he now fulfils what he promised to our fathers.
I will praise the Lord, my Saviour. Everlasting is his mercy. ℞

Magnificat (The Song of Mary)

Great is the Lord my soul proclaims,
  in him my spirit sings for joy;
for he who saves has looked on me
  with boundless love to raise me high.

Ages to come shall know that I am blessed and favoured
  by the Lord:
his name is holy, mighty God;
  his wondrous power on me is poured.

All those who fear him find his love, in ev'ry age,
  in ev'ry land.
His strong right arm puts down the proud,
  disperses them like grains of sand.

Down from their thrones he casts the strong,
  and raises up the meek of heart.
He gives the hungry choicest food;
  in emptiness the rich depart.

Israel, his servant, knows his help in keeping
  with the promise sworn
to Abraham and all his race:
  God's love will never be withdrawn.

Glory to God: the Father, Son, and Spirit, Trinity sublime.
All honour, thanks and praise be theirs across
  the spans of endless time.

L.M.

Magnificat (The Song of Mary)

Refrain:
The Almighty works marvels for me.
Holy his name, holy his name.

Verses (Cantor):
My soul glorifies the Lord.
My spirit rejoices in God my Saviour.
He looks on his servant in her lowliness;
henceforth all ages will call me blessed. ℟

His mercy is from age to age;
on those who fear him, on those who fear him
he puts forth his arm in strength
and scatters the proud-hearted;
he casts the mighty down and raises the lowly. ℟

He protects Israel, rememb'ring his mercy,
as he promised to our fathers,
to Abraham and his children for ever.
Alleluia. ℟

Incarnation
Living in the world
D*41*

Magnificat (The Song of Mary)

My soul proclaims the greatness of the Lord.
My spirit sings to God, my saving God,
Who on this day above all others favoured me
And raised me up, a light for all to see.

Through me great deeds will God make manifest,
And all the earth will come to call me blest.
Unbounded love and mercy sure will I proclaim
For all who know and praise God's holy name.

God's mighty arm, protector of the just,
Will guard the weak and raise them from the dust.
But mighty kings will swiftly fall from thrones corrupt.
The strong brought low, the lowly lifted up.

Soon will the poor and hungry of the earth
Be richly blest, be given greater worth.
And Israel, as once foretold to Abraham,
Will live in peace throughout the promised land.

All glory be to God, Creator blest,
To Jesus Christ, God's love made manifest,
And to the Holy Spirit, gentle Comforter,
All glory be, both now and evermore.

10.10.12.10.

Other metrical settings are available,
e.g. 'Tell out, my soul' by T. Dudley Smith

The Easter Anthems

1   Christ our passover has been sacrificed for us: ◆
    so let us celebrate the feast,

2   not with the old leaven of corruption and wickedness: ◆
    but with the unleavened bread of sincerity and truth.

                                        I Corinthians 5.7b,8

3   Christ once raised from the dead dies no more: ◆
    death has no more dominion over him.

4   In dying he died to sin once for all: ◆
    in living he lives to God.

5   See yourselves therefore as dead to sin: ◆
    and alive to God in Jesus Christ our Lord.

                                        Romans 6.9-11

6   Christ has been raised from the dead: ◆
    the first fruits of those who sleep.

7   For as by man came death: ◆
    by man has come also the resurrection of the dead;

8   for as in Adam all die: ◆
    even so in Christ shall all be made alive.

                                        I Corinthians 15.20-22

    Glory to the Father and to the Son
    and to the Holy Spirit;
    as it was in the beginning is now
    and shall be for ever. Amen.

Nunc dimittis (The Song of Simeon)

1   Now, Lord, you let your servant go in peace: ◆
    your word has been fulfilled.

2   My own eyes have seen the salvation ◆
    which you have prepared in the sight of every people;

3   A light to reveal you to the nations ◆
    and the glory of your people Israel.

                                        Luke 2.29-32

    Glory to the Father and to the Son
    and to the Holy Spirit;
    as it was in the beginning is now
    and shall be for ever. Amen.

Nunc dimittis (Lord, now let your servant)

Lord, now let your servant
Go his way in peace.
Your great love has brought me
Joy that will not cease:

For my eyes have seen him
Promised from of old,
Saviour of all people,
Shepherd of one fold.

Light of revelation
To the gentiles shown,
Light of Israel's glory
To the world made known.

6.5.6.5.

Nunc dimittis (Jesus, hope of every nation)

Jesus, hope of every nation,
Light of heaven upon our way;
Promise of the world's salvation,
Spring of life's eternal day!

Saints by faith on God depending
Wait to see Messiah born;
Sin's oppressive night is ending
In the glory of the dawn!

Look, he comes! – the long-awaited
Christ, redeemer, living Word;
Hope and faith are vindicated
As with joy we greet the Lord.

Glory in the highest heaven
To the Father, Spirit, Son;
And on earth let praise be given
To our God, the Three-in-One!

8.7.8.7.

Phos hilaron — a Song of the Light

O gladdening light,
of the holy glory of the immortal Father
heavenly, holy, blessed,
O Jesus Christ.

Now that we have come to the setting of the sun
and see the evening light
we give praise to God,
Father, Son and Holy Spirit.

Worthy are you at all times
to be worshipped with holy voices,
O Son of God and giver of life:
therefore all the world glorifies you.

Light of gladness, Lord of glory

Light of gladness, Lord of glory,
Jesus Christ our king most holy,
Shine among us in your mercy:
Earth and heaven join their hymn.

Let us sing at sun's descending
As we see the lights of evening,
Father, Son and Spirit praising
With the holy seraphim.

Son of God, through all the ages
Worthy of our holiest praises,
Yours the life that never ceases,
Light which never shall grow dim.

8.8.8.7.

creeds and authorized affirmations of faith

E Creeds and Authorized Affirmations of Faith

Stories from the four churches

At **St Ann's**, after the sermon, the preacher announces a reflective song, and encourages people to use it to make their response to the preaching. She then introduces the Creed as the second part of the response to the sermon. She uses the interrogative form of the Creed from page 143 in *Common Worship*, pointing out that the sermon was asking direct questions about their faith.

The sermon in **St Bartholomew's** mentions using the Creed as a symbol of our unity in faith with the worldwide Church through the ages. After a period of silence the president stands and begins the Nicene Creed simply by saying 'We believe in God'. There is no explicit reference back to the sermon, but the intended link is clear.

St Christopher's have recently had some teaching on the Creed. They have used one or two of the seasonal Affirmations of Faith from *Common Worship* to fit with the teaching subject. One of the points that has been highlighted is the 'doxological' use of the Creed in Eastern churches, to gather together the praise of the congregation. So today the Creed is postponed until after the intercessions, when the choir lead an outburst of praise in a glorious setting of the Nicene Creed.

Meanwhile, in **St Dodo's** they all sing Merbecke's setting of the Nicene Creed. Unfortunately the choir copies have not been revised, so they sing the original Prayer Book text. The congregation wonder whether they should join in, but are not sure how the melody fits the words. It is marginally better than last Sunday, when the choir had a go at singing the Creed from Schubert's Mass in G. They came a cropper and had to start again – not surprising since some faced east, some sang it as a 'piece' to the congregation, and the remainder looked to one another to try to keep time. On neither occasion could the Creed be said to have fulfilled its function of uniting the church in the faith.

Which creed?

St Christopher's have had a debate about whether to use the Nicene Creed or the Apostles' Creed.

✳ The Nicene Creed is traditional in celebrations of Holy Communion and, in contemporary versions, emphasizes the corporate: 'We believe …';

✳ The Apostles' Creed has an individual emphasis, is shorter, and in easier language.

Both **St Ann's** and **St Bartholomew's** use the Corporate Renewal of Baptismal Vows (pages 167–169), with the interrogative form of the Apostles' Creed, at Easter and sometimes at New Year. In previous years, the popularity of the corporate renewal of baptismal vows prompted the clergy at St Bartholomew's to use it at almost every opportunity. This led to some objections that it was becoming meaningless, and the more regular pattern of using it only once or twice a year, with appropriate warning and chance for preparation, has left the congregation feeling much happier and valuing it even more.

Suggestions about when Affirmations might be used

✳ Affirmation 4 for the Incarnation and Lent.
✳ Affirmation 5 for the Resurrection and memorial services.
✳ Affirmation 6 for Advent, Trinity and Heaven.
✳ Affirmation 2 for the Incarnation and Trinity.

The role of creeds

It is important for our unity in the catholic faith that any creeds used are not private or local compositions, but ones that are recognized by the wider Church. However, in Morning and Evening Prayer and in both Order One and Order Two Holy Communion the Creed may be omitted on weekdays, so omitting it clearly does not make the service invalid in some way! Public recitation of the Creed has not always been an essential part of the Church's worship. A Service of the Word allows for the occasional substitution of one of the Affirmations of Faith (pages 163–166) for the Creed. Some of these are already set to music, and one of them is the specially-commissioned hymn paraphrase of the Apostles' Creed, 'We believe in God the Father' by Timothy Dudley-Smith. There is no provision for the use of any other credal hymn as a substitute, and where one is used on a Sunday it might well follow one of the shorter Affirmations of Faith.

¶ Creeds

At a celebration of Holy Communion, the Apostles' Creed or the
Athanasian Creed in an authorized form may be used in place of the
Nicene Creed, or an authorized Affirmation of Faith may be used.
Suitable words of introduction or conclusion (such as 'Let us declare our
faith in God, Father, Son and Holy Spirit') to the Creed or Affirmation
of Faith may be used.

The Nicene Creed

E1   All   **We believe in one God,
the Father, the Almighty,
maker of heaven and earth,
of all that is,
seen and unseen.**

**We believe in one Lord, Jesus Christ,
the only Son of God,
eternally begotten of the Father,
God from God, Light from Light,
true God from true God,
begotten, not made,
of one Being with the Father;
through him all things were made.
For us and for our salvation he came down from heaven,
was incarnate from the Holy Spirit and the Virgin Mary
and was made man.
For our sake he was crucified under Pontius Pilate;
he suffered death and was buried.
On the third day he rose again
in accordance with the Scriptures;
he ascended into heaven
and is seated at the right hand of the Father.
He will come again in glory to judge the living and the dead,
and his kingdom will have no end.**

**We believe in the Holy Spirit,
the Lord, the giver of life,
who proceeds from the Father and the Son,
who with the Father and the Son is worshipped and glorified,
who has spoken through the prophets.
We believe in one holy catholic and apostolic Church.
We acknowledge one baptism for the forgiveness of sins.
We look for the resurrection of the dead,
and the life of the world to come.
Amen.**

E2 We believe in one God,
the Father, the Almighty,

All **maker of heaven and earth,**
of all that is,
seen and unseen.

We believe in one Lord, Jesus Christ,
the only Son of God,
eternally begotten of the Father,

All **God from God, Light from Light,**
true God from true God,
begotten, not made,
of one Being with the Father.

All **Through him all things were made.**
For us and for our salvation he came down from heaven,
was incarnate from the Holy Spirit and the Virgin Mary,
and was made man.

All **For our sake he was crucified under Pontius Pilate;**
he suffered death and was buried.
On the third day he rose again
in accordance with the Scriptures;

All **he ascended into heaven**
and is seated at the right hand of the Father.
He will come again in glory to judge the living and the dead,
and his kingdom will have no end.

We believe in the Holy Spirit,

All **the Lord, the giver of life,**
who proceeds from the Father and the Son.

All **With the Father and the Son he is worshipped and glorified.**
He has spoken through the prophets.

All **We believe in one holy, catholic and apostolic Church.**
We acknowledge one baptism for the forgiveness of sins.

All **We look for the resurrection of the dead,**
and the life of the world to come. Amen.

The text of the Nicene Creed which omits the phrase 'and the Son'
in the third paragraph may be used on suitable ecumenical occasions.
See Common Worship, page 140.

The other authorized texts of the Nicene Creed are printed in the
Order for the Celebration of Holy Communion – Order One (Traditional
Language) and Order Two (Common Worship, pages 213 and 234).

The Apostles' Creed

The origin of the Apostles' Creed is the profession of faith made at baptism. This association may have implications for the occasion when it is used at Holy Communion.

E3   *All*   **I believe in God, the Father almighty,**
creator of heaven and earth.

I believe in Jesus Christ, his only Son, our Lord,
who was conceived by the Holy Spirit,
born of the Virgin Mary,
suffered under Pontius Pilate,
was crucified, died, and was buried;
he descended to the dead.
On the third day he rose again;
he ascended into heaven,
he is seated at the right hand of the Father,
and he will come to judge the living and the dead.

I believe in the Holy Spirit,
the holy catholic Church,
the communion of saints,
the forgiveness of sins,
the resurrection of the body,
and the life everlasting.
Amen.

(or)

E4   *All*   **I believe in God the Father almighty,**
maker of heaven and earth:

And in Jesus Christ his only Son our Lord,
who was conceived by the Holy Ghost,
born of the Virgin Mary,
suffered under Pontius Pilate,
was crucified, dead and buried.
He descended into hell;
the third day he rose again from the dead;
he ascended into heaven,
and sitteth on the right hand of God the Father almighty;
from thence he shall come to judge the quick and the dead.

I believe in the Holy Ghost;
the holy catholic Church;
the communion of saints;
the forgiveness of sins;
the resurrection of the body,
and the life everlasting.
Amen.

The Apostles' Creed may also be used in the following form

E5   Do you believe and trust in God the Father?

All   **I believe in God, the Father almighty,**
creator of heaven and earth.

Do you believe and trust in his Son Jesus Christ?

All   **I believe in Jesus Christ, his only Son, our Lord,**
who was conceived by the Holy Spirit,
born of the Virgin Mary,
suffered under Pontius Pilate,
was crucified, died, and was buried;
he descended to the dead.
On the third day he rose again;
he ascended into heaven,
he is seated at the right hand of the Father,
and he will come to judge the living and the dead.

Do you believe and trust in the Holy Spirit?

All   **I believe in the Holy Spirit,**
the holy catholic Church,
the communion of saints,
the forgiveness of sins,
the resurrection of the body,
and the life everlasting.
Amen.

The Athanasian Creed

The authorized form of the Athanasian Creed is that contained in
The Book of Common Prayer.

¶ *Authorized Affirmations of Faith*

In addition to the Nicene Creed, the Apostles' Creed and the
Athanasian Creed, these Affirmations of Faith are also authorized.

1

E6   Do you believe and trust in God the Father,
source of all being and life,
the one for whom we exist?

All   **We believe and trust in him.**

Do you believe and trust in God the Son,
who took our human nature,
died for us and rose again?

All   **We believe and trust in him.**

Do you believe and trust in God the Holy Spirit,
who gives life to the people of God
and makes Christ known in the world?

All **We believe and trust in him.**

This is the faith of the Church.

All **This is our faith.**
We believe and trust in one God,
Father, Son and Holy Spirit.
Amen.

2

E7 We proclaim the Church's faith in Jesus Christ.

All **We believe and declare that our Lord Jesus Christ,**
the Son of God, is both divine and human.

God, of the being of the Father,
the only Son from before time began;
human from the being of his mother, born in the world;

All **fully God and fully human;**
human in both mind and body.

As God he is equal to the Father,
as human he is less than the Father.

All **Although he is both divine and human**
he is not two beings but one Christ.

One, not by turning God into flesh,
but by taking humanity into God;

All **truly one, not by mixing humanity with Godhead,**
but by being one person.

For as mind and body form one human being
so the one Christ is both divine and human.

All **The Word became flesh and lived among us;**
we have seen his glory,
the glory of the only Son from the Father,
full of grace and truth.   *from the Athanasian Creed*

3

E8 *All* **We believe in God the Father,**
God almighty, by whose plan
earth and heaven sprang to being,
all created things began.
We believe in Christ the Saviour,
Son of God in human frame,
virgin-born, the child of Mary
upon whom the Spirit came.

Christ, who on the cross forsaken,
like a lamb to slaughter led,

suffered under Pontius Pilate,
he descended to the dead.
We believe in Jesus risen,
heaven's king to rule and reign,
to the Father's side ascended
till as judge he comes again.

We believe in God the Spirit;
in one Church, below, above:
saints of God in one communion,
one in holiness and love.
So by faith, our sins forgiven,
Christ our Saviour, Lord and friend,
we shall rise with him in glory
to the life that knows no end.

(May be sung to any 87.87. or 87.87D. tune.)

4

E9   Let us affirm our faith in Jesus Christ the Son of God.

All   **Though he was divine,**
he did not cling to equality with God,
but made himself nothing.
Taking the form of a slave,
he was born in human likeness.
He humbled himself
and was obedient to death,
even the death of the cross.
Therefore God has raised him on high,
and given him the name above every name:
that at the name of Jesus
every knee should bow,
and every voice proclaim that Jesus Christ is Lord,
to the glory of God the Father.   *cf Philippians 2.6-11*
Amen.

5

E10   Let us declare our faith
in the resurrection of our Lord Jesus Christ.

All   **Christ died for our sins**
in accordance with the Scriptures;
he was buried;
he was raised to life on the third day
in accordance with the Scriptures;
afterwards he appeared to his followers,
and to all the apostles:
this we have received,
and this we believe.   *cf 1 Corinthians 15.3-7*
Amen.

6

E11   We say together in faith

All   **Holy, holy, holy**
is the Lord God almighty,
who was, and is, and is to come.

We believe in God the Father,
who created all things:
All   **for by his will they were created**
and have their being.

We believe in God the Son,
who was slain:
All   **for with his blood,**
he purchased us for God,
from every tribe and language,
from every people and nation.

We believe in God the Holy Spirit:
All   **the Spirit and the Bride say, 'Come!'**
Even so come, Lord Jesus!   *cf Revelation 4.8, 11; 5.9; 22.17, 20*
Amen.

7

E12   Let us declare our faith in God.

All   **We believe in God the Father,**
from whom every family
in heaven and on earth is named.

We believe in God the Son,
who lives in our hearts through faith,
and fills us with his love.

We believe in God the Holy Spirit,
who strengthens us
with power from on high.

We believe in one God;
Father, Son and Holy Spirit.   *cf Ephesians 3*
Amen.

¶ *A Form for the Corporate Renewal of Baptismal Vows*

when celebrated within a service other than Baptism or Confirmation

Notes

1   This form should be used only when there has been due notice and proper preparation. It is recommended that it is used no more than once or twice in any one year. Suitable opportunities include Easter, Pentecost, the Baptism of Christ in Epiphany, and the inauguration of a new ministry.

2   This form is a corporate affirmation for use within a service. When it is used it replaces the Creed or other Affirmation of Faith.

3   Where it is customary for the assembly to be sprinkled with water from the font or to sign themselves with water from the font, this may take place immediately after the Profession of Faith or during a hymn, canticle or song at the conclusion of this form.

A Corporate Renewal of Baptismal Vows

E13   *The president may use words of introduction to this part of the service.*

A large candle may be lit. The president may address the congregation as follows

In baptism, God calls us out of darkness into his marvellous light.
To follow Christ means dying to sin and rising to new life with him.
Therefore I ask:

Do you reject the devil and all rebellion against God?

All   **I reject them.**

Do you renounce the deceit and corruption of evil?

All   **I renounce them.**

Do you repent of the sins that separate us from God and neighbour?

All   **I repent of them.**

Do you turn to Christ as Saviour?

All   **I turn to Christ.**

Do you submit to Christ as Lord?

All   **I submit to Christ.**

Do you come to Christ, the way, the truth and the life?

All   **I come to Christ.**

The president may say

May almighty God who has given you the desire to follow Christ
give you the strength to continue in the way.

The Profession of Faith

The president addresses the congregation

Brothers and sisters, I ask you to profess the faith of the Church.

Do you believe and trust in God the Father?

All **I believe in God, the Father almighty,
creator of heaven and earth.**

Do you believe and trust in his Son Jesus Christ?

All **I believe in Jesus Christ, his only Son, our Lord,
who was conceived by the Holy Spirit,
born of the Virgin Mary,
suffered under Pontius Pilate,
was crucified, died, and was buried;
he descended to the dead.
On the third day he rose again;
he ascended into heaven,
he is seated at the right hand of the Father,
and he will come to judge the living and the dead.**

Do you believe and trust in the Holy Spirit?

All **I believe in the Holy Spirit,
the holy catholic Church,
the communion of saints,
the forgiveness of sins,
the resurrection of the body,
and the life everlasting.
Amen.**

The president says

Almighty God,
we thank you for our fellowship in the household of faith
with all who have been baptized into your name.
Keep us faithful to our baptism,
and so make us ready for that day
when the whole creation shall be made perfect in your Son,
our Saviour Jesus Christ.

All **Amen.**

The president may use the Affirmation of Commitment (E14).

The president concludes the Renewal of Vows saying

May Christ dwell in your hearts through faith,
that you may be rooted and grounded in love
and bring forth the fruit of the Spirit.

All **Amen.**

¶ *Affirmation of Commitment*

E14   *This Affirmation of Commitment may be used after an authorized Creed*
or Affirmation of Faith

Will you continue in the apostles' teaching and fellowship,
in the breaking of bread, and in the prayers?

All **With the help of God, I will.**

Will you persevere in resisting evil and,
whenever you fall into sin, repent and return to the Lord?

All **With the help of God, I will.**

Will you proclaim by word and example
the good news of God in Christ?

All **With the help of God, I will.**

Will you seek and serve Christ in all people,
loving your neighbour as yourself?

All **With the help of God, I will.**

Will you acknowledge Christ's authority over human society,
by prayer for the world and its leaders,
by defending the weak, and by seeking peace and justice?

All **With the help of God, I will.**

prayers

F Prayers

Stories from the four churches

At **St Ann's** one of the church leaders comes forward to lead the intercessions, and asks the congregation to mention things to pray for. A series of people say 'Can we pray for …', usually mentioning things of a fairly personal and practical nature. The leader fits this list of requests into the litany prepared before the service. From the intercession that follows, it is clear that the leader has been awake during the notices and sermon. Both the sermon and the Bible reading on which it was based are clearly reflected in the prayers. St Ann's have tried other variations for the intercessions, and at the all-age service these are sometimes led by a family together (using the microphone for all of them). Once or twice for a special occasion they have used visuals – photographs, video clips and drawings (but with few words) on the data projector – inviting people to have their eyes open as they pray. Occasionally they pray in small groups, which they find a good way of including children in the intercessions. Some have suggested using extempore prayer with the whole congregation free to join in, but the severe difficulties with audibility have ruled this out.

A small group from **St Bartholomew's** went to a deanery course on praying in public and in private, and came back with a checklist of do's and don'ts (see pages 173–174). Intercessions at Evensong, where the congregation is small, are usually led by the preacher, who can most easily relate the contents of the prayers to the sermon. Recently in the mornings they have been following a pattern using traditional collects, each introduced with a bidding from a different person, followed by silence before the collect. Today, the intercession is based on the Lord's Prayer (in its traditional form), with a pause after each petition, into which another person (with a contrasting voice) inserts appropriate intercessions relating to the petition. Next week they are going to do the same sort of thing with the lesser litany in Evening Prayer. Some of the topics come from the Anglican Cycle of Prayer, so that they get a wider – and international – view of the Church. Since going on the deanery course they have adopted the practice of the intercession leader joining the preacher and whoever is leading the worship in the vestry for prayer before the service.

As you enter **St Christopher's** today, there are display boards with some posters, newspaper cuttings and pictures which indicate the theme and some of the contents of the intercession. The person leading the intercessions is well prepared, and has arrived in time to look at the requests for prayer pinned on the board by the votive candle stand, and decide how many of these can be included within the Sunday intercessions – not all are suitable! The prayers are led from the centre of the church, among the people.

The standard form of response to the intercessions, from *New Patterns for Worship*, is sung to a Taizé-style chant. The congregation picks up the note and hums it while the intercession leader continues to the next response. This didn't work very well the first time they tried it, but they soon got used to it.

At **St Dodo's**, the person leading the intercessions says 'Let us pray', but hasn't found the right text, so we hear the pages of *New Patterns for Worship* turning during the ensuing silence. He begins the responsive intercession for Creation, which unfortunately fits neither the readings nor the mood of the congregation. He forgets to rehearse the response at the start and so has to stop at the first break and say 'When I say ... you should say ...' in a voice which implies that the congregation should have known this all along. He keeps switching between addressing God and addressing the congregation throughout the prayers: 'We really ought to pray for Ann ('Who is she?' half the congregation wonder) especially today because ...' – and more of his views of the circumstances of members of the community follow.

Constructing prayers of intercession

The standard *Common Worship* pattern, both in Order One and in Order Two (Contemporary), provides a helpful outline covering five areas:

The prayers usually include these concerns and may follow this sequence:
* The Church of Christ
* Creation, human society, the Sovereign and those in authority
* The local community
* Those who suffer
* The communion of saints

As Note 15 to *Common Worship* Holy Communion says, 'Several forms of intercession are provided' (pages 281–287 in *Common Worship*), but 'other suitable forms may be used. They need not always conform to the sequence indicated.' The forms of intercession in this section are designed as further alternatives to the options in *Common Worship*, and are also intended as models for those constructing their own prayers. It may help to note the pattern for the response most commonly used here, which is designed to help the congregation to know when to make their response, without needing to have the full text of the prayers in front of them. Two things are of particular help to a congregation:
* First, making the response unvarying, short and memorable, introduced each time with the same 'cue line'.

* Second, taking care over how the response and its cue line are introduced to the congregation at the beginning of the prayers. This may be done by saying 'Each section of the prayer concludes [the words of the cue], and the response is [the words of the response].' For example:

> Each section of the prayer concludes 'Lord in your mercy,' and the response is 'hear our prayer':
>> We pray for all people everywhere.
>> Lord, in your mercy
>> **hear our prayer.**

Another perfectly acceptable way of constructing the prayers is to use a series of short prayers or biddings, followed by silence and one of the congregational endings.

A variety of patterns can be used, for example:
* bidding – silence – collect or own prayer
* bidding – set words of one of the litanies – silence – response
* series of biddings with silences – longer prayer such as that on page 282 of *Common Worship*.

Whatever pattern is used should be used throughout the Prayers of Intercession. It is important to keep the distinction between biddings (addressed to the congregation) and prayer (addressed directly to God and not referring to him in the third person) and not to slide from one to the other without realizing it.

Other points to note:
* In planning the prayers section of A Service of the Word, remember that the outline requires that the service should include thanksgiving (and the Lord's Prayer) as well as intercession. Suitable material is provided in Resource Section G on pages 234–257.
* In some circumstances it may be appropriate for the president to say both the opening invitation and the concluding words such as the collect or other endings.

St Bartholomew's checklist: how to lead the prayers

* DO read the readings. Sometimes they might be used as a basis for prayer ('Father, thank you for … [what the verse says]; now please help us to …).
* DO discover the main theme of the service: is it based on the readings, the season or day? Ask the preacher if there is something specific to pray for if the prayers follow the preaching.
* DO find out about particular needs, who is ill or what church meetings or organizations need prayer this week. Watch the news, and vary the way in which international topics are prayed for; DON'T be out of date! But remember also the need for balance and breadth. As Note 15 to *Common Worship* Holy Communion says, 'the prayers of intercession are normally broadly based, expressing a concern for the whole of God's world and the ministry of the whole Church'.
* DO be aware of special events like baptisms or when there are large numbers of children or the Town Council present. DON'T focus on them (for example, a group of bereaved people the week after a funeral) in a way which will embarrass them.

* DO remember what was prayed for last week: should there be thanksgiving for prayer being answered? What other thanksgiving should there be? Again, as Note 15 says, 'intercession frequently arises out of thanksgiving'.
* DO decide what pattern of intercessions will be best, given what has been discovered and the pattern of the rest of the service (see the section on constructing the prayers of intercession on pages 172–173).
* DON'T cram so much in that you have to rush.
* DON'T forget about the need for silences, and how and whether to introduce them.
* DON'T preach at people ('We pray we may all give generously at Gift Day').
* DO pray the intercessions out loud before the service, especially if they are home-grown. Watch the speed: will the congregation have time to pray, or be overwhelmed by the variety of images and topics? Will they know when to come in with the response? Is it short enough to remember? Look at the examples in this section.

Collects: stories from the four churches

Today, **St Ann's** are using A Service of the Word with a Celebration of Holy Communion. They have seen that the rubric in the service shows that they can use the Collect as a summing up prayer which draws together the intercessions and thanksgivings before the service moves on into the Holy Communion. This means that it need not be particularly linked with the readings or the Liturgy of the Word. They have recently been printing it on the notice sheet, so that members of the church can use it at home during the week.

Children in the church school at **St Bartholomew's** have been learning this week how to write collects. They have used a very simple formula (see page 176) which shows them how to take a verse of Scripture, thank God for something about himself and then pray for something connected with that aspect of God's character. The teacher hopes it will help them in making up their own prayers at home (and the vicar secretly thinks some of the adults would find this a help too!). He recently preached on the prayer of the believers in Acts 4.24-31, pointing out how many lines of the prayer were taken up with telling God how great he was and what he had done, using that as the reason why God should take notice of their request, which was to result in 'wonders and miracles … through the name of Jesus'. Compare this with the pattern in the 'Collect construction' section on page 176. Four of the children's collects are going to be used in the worship this month.

The vicar and Reader at **St Christopher's** have been particularly struck recently by how good some of the BCP Collects still sound. They have been using them in less formal settings, in small groups and to open or close meetings, following the pattern: 'Let us pray (for …)' – silence – collect. They have also used them, where they fit the theme or season of the year, before the final prayer at the Eucharist. The congregation already know three alternative post-communion prayers by heart, so that they can join in from the first phrase of the prayer.

At **St Dodo's**, the vicar announces the Collect on page 498 of *Common Worship* as if he intends people to join in with him. He realizes with dismay that this is the traditional version and he had intended to use the modern version. There is quite a silence before the Collect (which is unusual for them) as he gets almost to the right page but then, despite blowing hard at the pages to try to separate them, he gives up the struggle and prays the Collect one page earlier instead, which one or two remember from last week. He also announces that as it is 'St William Tyndale's day' tomorrow, he is going to pray that prayer too. There is another suitably long silence while he fumbles for the page in another book. The congregation are left with the impression that the Collect is just a bit of mumbo jumbo to be got through, rather than contributing to the movement of the worship.

Collect construction

Ash Wednesday

I	**Address:** *God, you are ...* *you say ...* *you do ... / have done ...*	Almighty and everlasting God, you hate nothing that you have made and forgive the sins of all those who are penitent:
2	**Petition or request:** *Therefore, Lord, please ...*	create and make in us new and contrite hearts
3	**Result or reason:** *So that ...*	that we, worthily lamenting our sins and acknowledging our wretchedness, may receive from you, the God of all mercy, perfect remission and forgiveness;
4	**Ending:**	through Jesus Christ your Son our Lord,

Guidelines on language

These guidelines may help those writing their own material, for collects or intercessions for example, to be on the same level of language as the new writing in *New Patterns*.

* Use concrete visual images rather than language which is conceptual and full of ideas.
* Avoid complicated sentence constructions.
* If there is a choice, prefer the word with fewer syllables.
* Address God as 'you'.
* Keep sentences as short as possible. Use full stops rather than semicolons.
* Use language which includes women as well as men, black as well as white.
* Watch the rhythm. The language should be rhythmic and flow easily, but take care not to have a repetitive 'dum-de-dum'.
* Liturgical language should not be stark or empty. It is not wrong to repeat ideas or say the same thing twice in different words. Cranmer recognized that people need time and repetition to make the liturgy their own: we need to do it without a string of dependent clauses.
* Be prepared to throw it away after using it, and to do it differently next time.

Notes to the resources

This section includes:
* Responses for use in prayers of intercession;
* Alternative endings for the intercessions;
* Introductions for the Lord's Prayer;
* Responsive forms of intercession and litanies.

The forms of intercession in this section may replace the intercessions in the Holy Communion, or be used in the prayer section of A Service of the Word, or after the third collect in Morning or Evening Prayer (*The Book of Common Prayer*) or after the Creed in Morning or Evening Prayer on Sundays. They may also be used at eucharistic or non-eucharistic services on weekdays.

Responses for prayers of intercession

Any suitable response may be used. A selection follows, and more, including some seasonal ones, can be found in *Common Worship: Daily Prayer*, on page 326. Care should be taken that the response is appropriate for the form of prayer being used and for the concluding prayer (such as, 'Merciful Father, accept these prayers …'). For instance, if the intercessions address the Father, make sure that the response does not address the Son, and so on.

Responses

F1
Lord, have mercy.
Lord, have mercy.

F2
Lord, in your mercy
hear our prayer.

F3
Hear us,
hear us, good Lord.

F4
Lord, hear us.
Lord, graciously hear us.

F5
In faith we pray
we pray to you our God.

F6
Lord, hear your people
and answer our prayers.

F7
God of love
hear our prayer.

F8
We pray to the Father.
Hear our prayer.

F9
Lord, meet us in the silence
and hear our prayer.

F10
Jesus [or 'Father'], Lord of …
(life, creation, … a phrase which can be varied)
in your mercy, hear us.

F11
Loving God, we look to you.
Receive our prayer.

F12
Generous God
pour out your love.

F13
Your kingdom come
your will be done.

Sung responses

It can be effective to use a simple sung response during the intercessions.
Musicians might be able to set any of the above to music. Examples follow:

F14

F15

♩ = 92

Em D G D Em C Am B

O - cu - li nos - tri ad Do - mi - num Je - sum,
Our eyes are turned to the Lord Je - sus Christ,___

Em D G D Em C Am6 B Em

o - cu - li nos - tri ad Do - mi - num nos - trum.
Our eyes are turned to the Lord God, our Sav - iour.

Watch, watch and pray_____

Je - sus will keep to his word._____

Je - sus keeps to his word.

Je - sus keeps to his word.

(SOLO)

Je - sus Christ, Son of God, have

mer - cy up - on us.

(ALL)

Je - sus Christ, Son of God, have

Mer - cy up - on us.

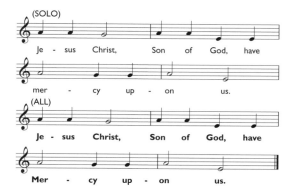

180 *Prayers*

Endings for the intercessions

The section about the communion of saints

In any service which includes Holy Communion, the section of the intercessions concerned with the communion of saints may be replaced by one of the following, which provide a weightier ending and point ahead to the communion.

F19   Almighty God,
by your Holy Spirit you have made us one
    with your saints in heaven and on earth:
grant that in our earthly pilgrimage
we may ever be supported by this fellowship
    of love and prayer,
and know ourselves surrounded by their witness to your
    power and mercy;
through Jesus Christ our Lord.
Amen.

F20   Bring us all to your heavenly city,
to the joyful gathering of thousands of angels,
to the assembly of your firstborn,
to the spirits of good people made perfect,
to Jesus the mediator of the new covenant
and to the sprinkled blood that promises peace.
Merciful Father ...

cf Hebrews 12.22-24

F21   Hasten, Lord, the day
when people will come from east and west,
from north and south,
and sit at table in your kingdom
and we shall see your Son in his glory.
Merciful Father ...

cf Luke 13.29

F22   Lord and judge of all, grant to us
and to all those who long for your appearing
the crown of righteousness on the great day
    of your coming.
Merciful Father ...

F23   Fill our hunger with the food that lasts,
the bread of God which comes down from heaven
and gives life to the world.
Merciful Father …

cf John 6.33

The congregational ending

The congregational ending for the *Common Worship* Holy Communion
intercessions ('Merciful Father …') may be replaced by one of the
following endings. Further endings may be found at sections 1–4 and 8
on pages 288–9 of *Common Worship*.

F24   Lord of the Church,
**hear our prayer,
and make us one in heart and mind
to serve you with joy for ever.
Amen.**

F25   God of mercy,
**you know us and love us
and hear our prayer:
keep us in the eternal fellowship of
Jesus Christ our Saviour.
Amen.**

Introductions to the Lord's Prayer

Whenever the Lord's Prayer is introduced it needs to be clear to the congregation which version is to be used. A full printed text is one way to make this clear. In *Common Worship*, the modified traditional and modern forms each have a distinctive introduction, to help the congregation to know which one to expect, as follows:

> As our Saviour has taught us, so we pray:
> **Our Father in heaven,** *(the modern English version)*
>
> *(or)*
>
> Let us pray with confidence as our Saviour has taught us:
> **Our Father who art in heaven,** *(the modified traditional version)*

> *Seasonal and thematic prefaces may be added to these introductions, such as*

Christ's coming **F**26	Awaiting his coming in glory,
Incarnation **F**27	Rejoicing in the presence of God here among us,
Church and mission **F**28	Seeking the salvation of the world,
Lament **F**29	Trusting in the compassion of God,
Cross **F**30	Standing at the foot of the cross,
Resurrection **F**31	Rejoicing in God's new creation,
Holy Spirit **F**32	Being made one by the power of the Spirit,

> *The introductions which follow here may be used with any form of the Lord's Prayer. If they are used without a full printed text, care should be taken to ensure that the congregation is clear about which form of the Lord's Prayer is to follow.*

General **F**33	Jesus taught us to call God our Father, so in faith and trust we pray …

General *(not at Holy Communion)* **F**34	Gathering our prayers and praises into one, let us pray as our Saviour taught us.
General **F**35	We praise the Father, and pray in the words of Christ himself.
Christ's coming *General* **F**36	Let us pray for the coming of God's kingdom in the words our Saviour taught us.
Holy Spirit *Father, Son and Spirit* *General* **F**37	As God's children, and heirs with Christ we cry in the Spirit, 'Abba', Father.
Heaven *Cross* *General* **F**38	Lord, remember us in your kingdom, as we pray in the words you gave us.

Responsive forms of intercession and litanies

[Let us pray to the Lord.
Lord, have mercy.]

For the peace that comes from God alone,
for the unity of all peoples,
and for our salvation,
let us pray to the Lord.
Lord, have mercy.

For the Church of Christ, for *N* our Bishop, [*for …*]
and for the whole people of God,
let us pray to the Lord.
Lord, have mercy.

For the nations of the world, [*for …,*]
for Elizabeth our Queen and for all in authority,
let us pray to the Lord.
Lord, have mercy.

For this city (*or town or village or community*), [*for …,*]
for our neighbours and our friends,
let us pray to the Lord.
Lord, have mercy.

For the good earth which God has given us,
and for the wisdom and will to conserve it,
let us pray to the Lord.
Lord, have mercy.

For the aged and infirm,
for the widowed and orphans,
for the sick and suffering,
[*for …*] and for all in any need,
let us pray to the Lord.
Lord, have mercy.

For the poor and the oppressed,
for the unemployed and the destitute,
for prisoners and captives,
and for all who remember and care for them,
let us pray to the Lord.
Lord, have mercy.

[*For …* let us pray to the Lord.
Lord, have mercy.]

For the dying, for those who mourn [*the death of …*],
for the faithful whom we entrust to the Lord in hope,
as we look forward to the day when we share
    the fullness of the resurrection,
let us pray to the Lord.
Lord, have mercy.

Rejoicing in the communion of [... *and of all*] the saints,
let us commend ourselves, and one another,
and all our life, to God.

Silence is kept.

For yours is the majesty,
Father, Son, and Holy Spirit;
yours is the kingdom and the power and the glory,
now and for ever.
Amen.

*The following prayers are in versicle and response form.
Some of the acclamations in Resource Section G may
also be suitable. Further examples may be found in
Common Worship: Daily Prayer.*

General
F*40*

Make your ways known upon earth, Lord God,
your saving power among all peoples.

Renew your Church in holiness
and help us to serve you with joy.

Guide the leaders of this and every nation,
that justice may prevail throughout the world.

Let not the needy be forgotten,
nor the hope of the poor be taken away.

Make us instruments of your peace
and let your glory be over all the earth.

General
F*41*

Blessed are you, eternal God,
to be praised and glorified for ever.

Hear us as we pray for your holy catholic Church:
make us all one, that the world may believe.

Grant that every member of the Church
may truly and humbly serve you:
that the life of Christ may be revealed in us.

Strengthen all who minister in Christ's name:
give them courage to proclaim your Gospel.

Inspire and lead those who hold authority
in the nations of the world:
guide them in the ways of justice and peace.

Make us alive to the needs of our community:
help us to share each other's joys and burdens.

Look with kindness on our homes and families:
grant that your love may grow in our hearts.

Deepen our compassion for all who suffer from sickness,
grief or trouble:
in your presence may they find their strength.

We remember those who have died:
Father, into your hands we commend them.

We praise you for all your saints who have entered
your eternal glory:
bring us all to share in your heavenly kingdom.

*General
Word
F42*

In your glory, Lord, protect us by the power of your name,
that we may be one as you are one.

We are in the world but not of it.
Protect us from the evil one.

Give us your word and the full measure of your joy.
Sanctify us by your truth.

May your Spirit unite us in the love and glory of
Father and Son.
May we be one that the world may believe.

As you sent your Son into the world
so send us, to make your glory known.

cf John 17.11-18

*General
Word
F43*

[We pray for strength to follow Jesus.
Saviour, we hear your call.
Help us to follow.]

Jesus said: 'Whoever wishes to be great among you
must be your servant.'
Saviour, we hear your call.
Help us to follow.

Jesus said: 'Unless you change
and become humble like little children,
you can never enter the kingdom of heaven.'
Saviour, we hear your call.
Help us to follow.

Jesus said: 'Happy are the humble;
they will receive what God has promised.'
Saviour, we hear your call.
Help us to follow.

Jesus said: 'Be merciful as your Father is merciful;
love your enemies and do good to them.'
Saviour, we hear your call.
Help us to follow.

Jesus said: 'Love one another, as I love you;
there is no greater love than this,
to lay down your life for your friends.'
Saviour, we hear your call.
Help us to follow.

Jesus said: 'Go to people everywhere
and make them my disciples,
and I will be with you always, to the end of time.'
Saviour, we hear your call.
Help us to follow.

God of mercy,
you know us and love us
and hear our prayer:
keep us in the eternal fellowship of
 Jesus Christ our Saviour.
Amen.

General
Church and mission
F44

Gracious God, fountain of all wisdom,
we pray for all Christian people;
for Bishop *N*, for all Christian leaders,
and for those who teach and guard the faith ...
May the word of Christ dwell richly in our hearts,
and knit us together in the bond of your love.
Hear us.
Hear us, good Lord.

We pray for the leaders of the nations,
and for those in authority under them ...
Give them the gift of your wisdom,
and a right discernment in all things.
Hear us.
Hear us, good Lord.

We pray for our ... (*city/town/village/community*);
for those who live and work here,
and for those who visit this place ...
Speak your word of peace in our midst,
and help us to serve one another as Christ has served us.
Hear us.
Hear us, good Lord.

We pray for those who do not believe,
and yet who long to know you, the very Word of life ...
Open their ears to hear your voice,
and open their hearts to the knowledge
 of your love in Christ.
Hear us.
Hear us, good Lord.

We pray for those bowed down with grief,
    fear or sickness,
especially ...
May your living Word bring comfort and healing
    to all those in need.
Hear us.
Hear us, good Lord.

We give thanks for all those who have died in the
    faith of Christ
and we rejoice with [*N and*] all your saints,
trusting in the promise of your word fulfilled.
Lord of life,
hear our prayer,
and make us one in heart and mind
to serve you with joy for ever.
Amen.

cf Psalm 119

General
Church and mission
F45

[We pray for God's grace.
Lord, receive our praise
and hear our prayer.]

Lord God, through your grace we are your people:
through your Son you have redeemed us;
in your Spirit you have made us as your own.

We pray for ... (*new Christians, the Church*)
Make our hearts respond to your love.
Lord, receive our praise
and hear our prayer.

We pray for ... (*the world, society, the local community*)
Make our lives bear witness to your glory in the world.
Lord, receive our praise
and hear our prayer.

We pray for ... (*people in need, Christian service*)
Make our wills eager to obey, and our hands ready to heal.
Lord, receive our praise
and hear our prayer.

We give thanks for ...
Make our voices one with all your people
    in heaven and on earth.

Lord of life,
hear our prayer,
and make us one in heart and mind
to serve you with joy for ever.
Amen.

[We pray to the Lord.
In faith we pray.
We pray to you our God.]

That the rest of this day may be holy,
　　peaceful and full of your presence;
in faith we pray.
We pray to you our God.

That the work we have done
and the people we have met today
may bring us closer to you;
in faith we pray.
We pray to you our God.

[That we may be forgiven our sins and failures;
in faith we pray.
We pray to you our God.]

That we may hear and respond to your call
　　to peace and justice;
in faith we pray.
We pray to you our God.

That you will sustain the faith and hope of those
　　who are lonely, oppressed and anxious;
in faith we pray.
We pray to you our God.

That you will strengthen us in your service,
and fill our hearts with longing for your kingdom;
in faith we pray.
We pray to you our God.

God of mercy,
**you know us and love us
and hear our prayer:
keep us in the eternal fellowship of
　　Jesus Christ our Saviour.
Amen.**

God in creation
F47

[Let us pray to God,
that he will bring to fruition all that he desires
for his creation.
Father, Lord of creation,
in your mercy, hear us.]

You have created the universe by your eternal Word,
and have blessed humankind in making us
stewards of the earth.
We pray for your world,
that we may share and conserve its resources,
and live in reverence for the creation
and in harmony with one another.
Father, Lord of creation,
in your mercy, hear us.

You have given the human race a rich land,
a land of streams and springs,
wheat and barley,
vines and oil and honey.
We have made by sin a world of suffering and sorrow.
We pray for those who bear the weight of affliction,
that they may come to share the life of wholeness
and plenty.
Father, Lord of creation,
in your mercy, hear us.

In Christ you call us to a new way of life,
loving our neighbours before ourselves.
Help us to treat with care and respect the world as it is
as we live in hope and anticipation of the world
as it will be
when your kingdom comes and your will is done.
Thank you for those, living and departed,
who have shown a true respect for your creation …
Help us to follow in their footsteps,
until, with them, we see you face to face,
where all is made new in Christ our Lord.

Merciful Father,
accept these prayers
for the sake of your Son
our Saviour Jesus Christ.
Amen.

God in creation
Living in the world
F48

O God our creator,
whose good earth is entrusted to our care
            and delight and tenderness,
we pray:
May those who sow in tears
reap with shouts of joy.

For all who are in captivity to debt,
whose lives are cramped by fear
from which there is no turning
except through abundant harvest.
May those who sow in tears
reap with shouts of joy.

For all who depend on the earth for their
            daily food and fuel,
whose forests are destroyed
for the profits of a few.
May those who sow in tears
reap with shouts of joy.

For all who labour in poverty,
who are oppressed by unjust laws,
who are banned for speaking the truth,
who long for a harvest of justice.
May those who sow in tears
reap with shouts of joy.

For all who are in captivity
to greed and waste and boredom,
whose harvest joy is choked
with things they do not need.
May those who sow in tears
reap with shouts of joy.

Turn us again from our captivity
and restore our vision,
that our mouth may be filled with laughter
and our tongue with singing.
Amen.

Let us pray for our own needs and for the needs of others,
following the pattern which Jesus gave
when he taught us to pray to God our Father.

Through our love of the countryside,
through our care for animals,
through our respect for property and tools:
Father, hallowed be your name.

On our farms and in our homes,
in our colleges and schools,
where machinery is made,
and where policy is planned:
Father, your kingdom come.

By our seeking your guidance,
by our keeping your commandments,
by our living true to our consciences:
Father, your will be done.

For the millions who live in poverty and hunger,
for our own needs, and the requirements of our
    neighbours,
by cooperation, sympathy and generosity:
give us today our daily bread.

Because we have broken your commandments,
doing what we ought not to do and neglecting
    what we ought to do:
forgive us our sins.

If any have injured us by injustice, double dealing
    or exploitation:
we forgive those who sin against us.

When prosperity lulls us to false security,
or hard times prompt us to despair,
When success makes us boastful,
or failure makes us bitter:
**lead us not into temptation,
but deliver us from evil.**

In the assurance of faith,
in the confidence of hope,
in the will to serve,
help us to love Christ as Lord,
and our neighbour as ourselves.
**for the kingdom, the power,
and the glory are yours,
now and for ever.
Amen.**

[In joyful expectation of his coming
we pray to Jesus, saying,
Maranatha.*
Amen. Come, Lord Jesus.]

Come to your Church as Lord and Judge.
We pray for ...
Help us to live in the light of your coming
and give us a longing for your kingdom.
Maranatha.
Amen. Come, Lord Jesus.

Come to your world as King of the nations.
We pray for ...
Before you rulers will stand in silence.
Maranatha.
Amen. Come, Lord Jesus.

Come to your people with a message of victory
        and peace.
We pray for ...
Give us the victory over death, temptation and evil.
Maranatha.
Amen. Come, Lord Jesus.

Come to us as Saviour and Comforter.
We pray for ...
Break into our lives,
where we struggle with sickness and distress,
and set us free to serve you for ever.
Maranatha.
Amen. Come, Lord Jesus.

Come to us from heaven, Lord Jesus,
with power and great glory.
Lift us up to meet you,
with [N and] all your saints and angels,
to live with you for ever.
Maranatha.
Amen. Come, Lord Jesus.

This Aramaic word is traditionally translated, 'Our Lord, come.'

Christ's coming
F5*1*

Short biddings are offered in the form
To [the suffering; the sick; those in authority;
Mrs Smith in hospital; etc.] ...

The response is used each time
Come, Lord Jesus.

The response can be varied to suit the season
Come Holy Spirit; Come risen Lord; etc.

*These can easily be used with children present and, after a
series of biddings led by the president, further biddings could be
encouraged from the congregation, and a suitable collect used
at the end.*

Incarnation
F52

Christ, for whom there was no room in the inn,
give courage to all who are homeless;
in your mercy
hear our prayer.

Christ, who fled into Egypt,
give comfort to all refugees;
in your mercy
hear our prayer.

Christ, who fasted in the desert,
give relief to all who are starving;
in your mercy
hear our prayer.

Christ, who hung in agony on the cross,
give strength to all who suffer;
in your mercy
hear our prayer.

Christ, who died to save us,
give peace to all who seek pardon.
Lord of the Church
**hear our prayer,
and make us one in heart and mind
to serve you with joy for ever.
Amen.**

Christ, born in a stable,
give courage to all who are homeless:
Jesus, Saviour,
hear our prayer.

Christ, for whom the angels sang,
give the song of the kingdom to all who weep:
Jesus, Saviour,
hear our prayer.

Christ, worshipped by the shepherds,
give peace on earth to all who are oppressed:
Jesus, Saviour,
hear our prayer.

Christ, before whom the wise men knelt,
give humility and wisdom to all who govern:
Jesus, Saviour,
hear our prayer.

Christ, whose radiance filled a lowly manger,
give the glory of your resurrection to all who rest in you:
Jesus, Saviour,
hear our prayer.

Lord Jesus Christ,
Son of the Father,
full of the Spirit,
hear our prayer,
receive our praises,
fill our lives.
Amen.

Unto us a child is born, unto us a Son is given.
Let us offer our prayers for the needs of the world.

Wonderful Counsellor,
give your wisdom to the rulers of the nations …
Lord, in your mercy
hear our prayer.

Mighty God,
make the whole world know
that the government is on your shoulders …
Lord, in your mercy
hear our prayer.

Everlasting Father,
establish your reign of justice and righteousness
    for ever …
Lord, in your mercy
hear our prayer.

Prince of Peace,
bring in the endless kingdom of your peace ...
Lord, in your mercy
hear our prayer.

Lord of the Church,
hear our prayer,
and make us one in heart and mind
to serve you with joy for ever.
Amen.

cf Isaiah 9.6

Incarnation
F55

The phrase 'in this holy night' makes this prayer particularly
appropriate for use on Christmas Eve during the night.
With the omission of this phrase (or its replacement with
'at this holy time') it is suitable for use on other occasions
during the Christmas season.

Father, [in this holy night] your Son our Saviour
    was born as a child among us.
Renew your Church as the Body of Christ.
Holy God
hear our prayer.

[In this holy night] there was no room for your Son
    in the inn.
Protect with your love those who have no home
and all who live in poverty.
Holy God
hear our prayer.

[In this holy night] Mary, in the pain of labour,
    brought your Son to birth.
Hold in your hand [... *and*] all who are in pain or distress.
Holy God
hear our prayer.

[In this holy night] your Christ came
    as a light shining in the darkness.
Bring comfort to [... *and*] all who suffer
    in the sadness of our world.
Holy God
hear our prayer.

[In this holy night] the angels sang
    'Peace to God's people on earth'.
Strengthen those who work for peace and justice
in [... *and in*] all the world.
Holy God
hear our prayer.

[In this holy night] shepherds in the field heard
    good tidings of joy.
Give us grace to preach the gospel of Christ's redemption.
Holy God
hear our prayer.

[In this holy night] heaven is come down to earth,
and earth is raised to heaven.
Keep in safety [… *and*] all those who have
    passed through death in the hope of heaven.
Holy God
hear our prayer.

[In this holy night] Christians the world over
    celebrate his birth.
Open our hearts that he may be born in us today.
Holy God
hear our prayer.

Father,
[in this holy night] angels and shepherds worshipped at
    the manger throne.
Receive the worship we offer in fellowship with Mary,
    Joseph and the saints
through him who is your Word made flesh,
our Saviour Jesus Christ.
Amen.

Incarnation
F56

*These intercessions are particularly appropriate for use when
small children are present. The prayer should be very simple, if
possible drawing from the children the subjects for intercession.*

Jesus, born in a human family:
we pray for … *(families)*
Lord Jesus,
hear our prayer.

Jesus, cradled in a manger:
we pray for … *(homeless, refugees)*
Lord Jesus,
hear our prayer.

Jesus, sharing the stable with the animals:
we pray for … *(the creation)*
Lord Jesus,
hear our prayer.

Jesus, worshipped by shepherds and kings:
we pray for … *(nations, races, peoples)*
Lord Jesus,
hear our prayer.

Jesus, our Emmanuel:
we pray for … (*those in particular need*)
Lord Jesus,
hear our prayer.

Incarnation
F57

[Let us pray to the Lord.
Lord, come to your people.
In your mercy set us free.]

The following, bracketed, section may be omitted in Epiphany.

[Unlooked for,
Christ comes.

To shepherds,
watching their sheep through the long, dark night,
he comes with the glory of the angels' song
and in the humility of the manger.

Silence

Loving God, we pray for our community …
In the midst of our everyday lives,
surprise us with glimpses of your glorious, humble love,
at the heart of existence.

Lord, come to your people.
In your mercy set us free.]

Searched for,
Christ comes.

To the wise and powerful,
star-led to Bethlehem, seeking a king,
he comes, child of Mary,
crowned with meekness,
worthy of every gift.

Silence

Loving God, we pray for the leaders of the world …
Guide them with your light
to seek wisdom, justice and peace.

Lord, come to your people.
In your mercy set us free.

Longed for,
Christ comes.

To Anna and Simeon,
whose days are lived in faithful expectation,
he comes, a new life to the old,
a living prophecy of hope.

Silence

Loving God, we pray for the Church in all the world …
Unite us by your Spirit,
and make us faithful witnesses to the hope we have in you.

Lord, come to your people.
In your mercy set us free.

Prayed for,
Christ comes.

To men and women, girls and boys,
crying out in darkness, pain and loneliness,
he comes, at one with us,
our Saviour, healer and friend.

Silence

Loving God, we pray for those whose lives are
    hard and painful
or whose existence is sorrowful, bitter or empty …
In their need, may they know your healing touch,
reaching out to comfort, strengthen and restore.

Lord, come to your people.
In your mercy set us free.

[Unlooked for and not searched for,]
longed for and prayed for,
loving God, you come to us now
as you have come to your people in every age.
We thank you for all who have reflected
    the light of Christ.
Help us to follow their example
and bring us with them to eternal life;
through Jesus Christ our Lord.
Amen.

Incarnation
F58

Let us worship the Saviour with joy
and make our prayer to our heavenly Father.

The magi came from the east to worship your Son:
Father, grant to Christians everywhere
    the spirit of adoration …
Lord of glory,
hear our prayer.

The infant Christ received gifts of gold, incense and myrrh:
Father, accept the offering of our hearts and minds
[at the beginning of this year] …
Lord of glory,
hear our prayer.

The kingdoms of this world have become
  the kingdom of our God and of his Christ:
Father, grant an abundance of peace to your world …
Lord of glory,
hear our prayer.

The Holy Family lived in exile and in the shadow of death:
Father, look in mercy on all who are poor and powerless,
  and all who suffer …
Lord of glory,
hear our prayer.

Your Son shared the life of his home and family
  at Nazareth:
Father, protect in your love our neighbours,
our families and this community of which we are a part …
Lord of glory,
hear our prayer.

Rejoicing in fellowship with the shepherds,
the angels, the magi, the Virgin Mary, Saint Joseph
and all the faithful departed,
we commend ourselves and all people
  to your unfailing love.
Merciful Father, …

<table>
<tr><td>Cross</td></tr>
<tr><td>F59</td></tr>
</table>

Cross
F59

*If this prayer is used as a meditation or Holy Week
intercession, the silence comes best after the first line in each
section, as here; if it is used as a Sunday intercession, it may
come better before 'Lord, hear us', where particular requests
may be inserted. This is an example of a set of intercessions
which would be suitable for two people with contrasting voices:
one to read the first part of each bidding and the other to lead
the part after the silence.*

[Let us pray to the Father,
who loved the world so much that he sent
  his only Son to give us life.]

Simon from Cyrene was forced to carry the cross
  for your Son.

Silence

Give us grace to lift heavy loads from those we meet
and to stand with those condemned to die.
Lord, hear us.
Lord, graciously hear us.

Your Son watched the soldiers gamble
  to share his clothes.

Silence

Transform the hearts of those who make a profit
    from their victims,
and those whose hearts are hardened by their work.
Lord, hear us.
Lord, graciously hear us.

The thief, who was crucified with Jesus,
was promised a place in your kingdom.

Silence

Give pardon and hope, healing and peace
to all who look death in the face.
Lord, hear us:
Lord, graciously hear us.

From the cross, Jesus entrusted Mary his mother and
    John his disciple to each other's care.

Silence

Help us also to care for one another
and fill our homes with the spirit of your love.
Lord, hear us.
Lord, graciously hear us.

The centurion was astonished to recognize your glory
    in the crucified Messiah.

Silence

Open the minds of those who do not know you
to grasp in your Son the meaning of life and death.
Lord, hear us.
Lord, graciously hear us.

Joseph of Arimathea came to take your Son's body away.

Silence

Give hope and faith to the dying and bereaved,
gentleness to those who minister to them,
and courage to those whose faith is secret.
Lord, hear us.
Lord, graciously hear us.

Simon and Joseph, Mary and John,
became part of the life of your Church in Jerusalem.
Bring into your Church today a varied company of people,
to walk with Christ in the way of his passion,
and to find their salvation in the victory of his cross.
Lord of the Church:
hear our prayer,
and make us one in heart and mind
to serve you with joy for ever.
Amen.

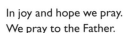

In joy and hope we pray.
We pray to the Father.
Hear our prayer.

That our risen Saviour may fill us with the joy of his
    glorious and life-giving resurrection ...
we pray to the Father.
Hear our prayer.

That isolated and persecuted churches
    may find fresh strength in the good news of Easter ...
we pray to the Father.
Hear our prayer.

That God may grant us humility
to be subject to one another in Christian love ...
we pray to the Father.
Hear our prayer.

That he may provide for those who lack food,
    work, or shelter ...
we pray to the Father.
Hear our prayer.

That by his power war and famine
    may cease through all the world ...
we pray to the Father.
Hear our prayer.

That he may reveal the light of his presence to the sick,
    the weak and the dying,
to comfort and strengthen them ...
we pray to the Father.
Hear our prayer.

That he may send the fire of the Holy Spirit upon
    his people,
so that we may bear faithful witness to his resurrection,
we pray to the Father.
Hear our prayer.

Jesus our exalted Lord has been given all authority.
Let us seek his intercession that our prayers may be
    perfected by his prayer.
Lord, hear us.
Lord, graciously hear us.

Jesus Christ, great high priest,
living for ever to intercede for us,
pray for the Church, your broken body in the world ...
Lord, hear us.
Lord, graciously hear us.

Jesus Christ, king of righteousness,
enthroned at the right hand of the majesty on high,
pray for the world, and make it subject to
your gentle rule ...
Lord, hear us.
Lord, graciously hear us.

Jesus Christ, Son of Man,
drawing humanity into the life of God,
pray for your brothers and sisters in need,
distress or sorrow ...
Lord, hear us.
Lord, graciously hear us.

Jesus Christ, pioneer of our salvation,
bringing us to glory through your death and resurrection,
surround with your saints and angels
those who have died trusting your promises ...
Lord, hear us.
Lord, graciously hear us.

Jesus Christ, Lord over all things,
ascended far above the heavens and filling the universe,
pray for us who receive the gifts you give us for
work in your service ...
Lord, hear us.
Lord, graciously hear us.

Jesus Christ,
keep the Church in the unity of the Spirit
and in the bond of peace,
and bring the whole created order
to worship at your feet;
for you are alive and reign with the Father
and the Holy Spirit,
one God, now and for ever.
Amen.

Holy Spirit
F62

[We pray to God the Holy Spirit.
Holy Spirit, come upon us.]

Come, Holy Spirit, creator,
and renew the earth.
Holy Spirit, come upon us.

Come, Holy Spirit, counsellor,
and touch our lips that we may proclaim your word.
Holy Spirit, come upon us.

Come, Holy Spirit, power from on high.
make us channels of peace and ministers of healing:
Holy Spirit, come upon us.

Come, Holy Spirit, breath of God,
give life to the dry bones around us,
and make us a living people, holy and free.
Holy Spirit, come upon us.

Come, Holy Spirit, wisdom and truth;
strengthen us to be bold in faith.
Holy Spirit, come upon us.

Holy Spirit
Relationships and healing
F63

[We pray for God to fill us with his Spirit.
Lord, come to bless us.
Fill us with your Spirit.]

Generous God, we thank you for the power
    of your Holy Spirit.
We ask that we may be strengthened to serve you better.
Lord, come to bless us.
Fill us with your Spirit.

We thank you for the wisdom of your Holy Spirit.
We ask you to make us wise to understand your will.
Lord, come to bless us.
Fill us with your Spirit.

We thank you for the peace of your Holy Spirit.
We ask you to keep us confident of your love,
wherever you call us.
Lord, come to bless us.
Fill us with your Spirit.

We thank you for the healing of your Holy Spirit.
We ask you to bring reconciliation and wholeness
where there is division, sickness and sorrow.
Lord, come to bless us.
Fill us with your Spirit.

We thank you for the gifts of your Holy Spirit.
We ask you to equip us for the work which you
    have given us.
Lord, come to bless us.
Fill us with your Spirit.

We thank you for the fruit of your Holy Spirit.
We ask you to reveal in our lives the love of Jesus.
Lord, come to bless us.
Fill us with your Spirit.

We thank you for the breath of your Holy Spirit,
given by the risen Lord.
We ask you to keep the whole Church,
living and departed,
in the joy of eternal life.
Lord, come to bless us.
Fill us with your Spirit.

Generous God,
you sent your Holy Spirit upon your Messiah
    at the River Jordan,
and upon the disciples in the upper room.
In your mercy fill us with your Spirit.
Hear our prayer,
and make us one in heart and mind
to serve you with joy for ever.
Amen.

Holy Spirit
Living in the world
F64

[We pray that God's Holy Spirit may direct our lives.
Lord, come to bless us.
Fill us with your Spirit.]

'The fruit of the Spirit is love, joy and peace.'
Father, we know that your world needs love and harmony.
Lord, come to bless us.
Fill us with your Spirit.

'The fruit of the Spirit is patience, kindness and goodness.'
Father, we know that our world is starved of love and care.
Lord, come to bless us.
Fill us with your Spirit.

'The fruit of the Spirit is faithfulness, gentleness
    and self-control.'
Father, we know that our world is short of truth
    and justice.
Lord, come to bless us.
Fill us with your Spirit.

Send us out in the power of your Spirit
to live and work to your praise and glory.
Amen.

cf Galatians 5.22,23

Church and mission
F65

[We pray that Christ may be seen in the life of the Church.
Jesus, Lord of the Church,
in your mercy, hear us.]

You have called us into the family of those who are
    the children of God.
May our love for our brothers and sisters
be strengthened by your grace.
Jesus, Lord of the Church,
in your mercy, hear us.

You have called us to be a temple
where the Holy Spirit can dwell.
Give us clean hands and pure hearts,
so that our lives will reflect your holiness.
Jesus, Lord of the Church,
in your mercy, hear us.

You have called us to be a light to the world,
so that those in darkness come to you.
May our lives shine
as a witness to the saving grace you have given for all.
Jesus, Lord of the Church,
in your mercy, hear us.

You have called us to be members of your body,
so that when one suffers, all suffer together.
We ask for your comfort and healing power
to bring hope to those in distress.
Jesus, Lord of the Church,
in your mercy, hear us.

You have called us to be the Bride,
where you, Lord, are the Bridegroom.
Prepare us for the wedding feast,
where we will be united with you for ever.
Jesus, Lord of the Church,
hear our prayer,
and make us one in heart and mind
to serve you with joy for ever.
Amen.

Christian beginnings
Father, Son and Spirit
F66

High and holy God,
robed in majesty,
Lord of heaven and earth,
we pray that you will bring justice, faith and
          salvation to all peoples.
[*Especially we pray ...*]
Lord, hear us.
Lord, graciously hear us.

You chose us in Christ to be your people
and to be the temple of your Holy Spirit;
we pray that you will fill your Church with
          vision and hope.
[*Especially we pray ...*]
Lord, hear us.
Lord, graciously hear us.

Your Spirit enables us to cry, 'Abba! Father!',
affirms that we are fellow-heirs with Christ
and pleads for us in our weakness;
we pray for all who are in need or distress.
[*Especially we pray ...*]
Lord, hear us.
Lord, graciously hear us.

In the baptism and birth of Jesus,
you have opened heaven to us
and enabled us to share in your glory:
the joy of the Father, Son and Holy Spirit
from before the world was made.
[*Especially we remember ...*]
May your whole Church, living and departed,
come to a joyful resurrection in your city of light.
Lord, hear us.
Lord, graciously hear us.

Relationships and healing
Resurrection
F67

[We pray to Jesus who is present with us to eternity.
Jesus, Lord of life,
in your mercy, hear us.]

Jesus, light of the world,
bring the light and peace of your gospel to
        the nations ...
Jesus, Lord of life,
in your mercy, hear us.

Jesus, bread of life,
give food to the hungry ...
and nourish us all with your word.
Jesus, Lord of life,
in your mercy, hear us.

Jesus, our way, our truth, our life,
be with us and all who follow you in the way ...
Deepen our appreciation of your truth
and fill us with your life.
Jesus, Lord of life,
in your mercy, hear us.

Jesus, Good Shepherd who gave your life for the sheep,
recover the straggler,
bind up the injured,
strengthen the sick
and lead the healthy and strong to new pastures.
Jesus, Lord of life,
in your mercy, hear us.

Jesus, the resurrection and the life,
we give you thanks for all who have lived and
believed in you ...
Raise us with them to eternal life.
Jesus, Lord of life,
in your mercy, hear us,
accept our prayers, and be with us always.
Amen.

Relationships and healing
Church and mission
F*68*

[We pray for the family of the Church,
for loving relationships,
and for the life of families around us.
Jesus, Lord of love,
in your mercy, hear us.]

Jesus, born in poverty and soon a refugee,
be with families today who are poor
and live in hunger and want ...
Jesus, Lord of love,
in your mercy, hear us.

Jesus, as you grew in wisdom and in favour with
God and the people
in the family of Joseph the carpenter,
bring wisdom and the presence of God
into the work and growth of families today ...
Jesus, Lord of love,
in your mercy, hear us.

Jesus, as you blessed marriage in the wedding at Cana,
be with those preparing for marriage
and with those who come to the end of
their resources ...
Jesus, Lord of love,
in your mercy, hear us.

Jesus, as you healed Peter's mother-in-law,
bring healing to those in our families who are ill today ...
Jesus, Lord of love,
in your mercy, hear us.

Jesus, when you were dying you called Mary and John to
care for one another.
Provide today for those who lose their families:
the bereaved and childless, orphans and widows ...
Jesus, Lord of love,
in your mercy, hear us.

Jesus, as you ate breakfast on the beach with
		your disciples
after you were raised from the dead,
bring the whole Church on earth and in heaven
into your risen presence to eat at the eternal banquet.
Jesus, Lord of love,
in your mercy, hear us,
accept our prayers and be with us always.
Amen.

Relationships and healing
Christian beginnings
F69

[Let us pray to God, our heavenly Father.
Father of all
hear your children's prayer.]

Sovereign Lord,
your Son has revealed you as our heavenly Father,
from whom every family in heaven and on earth is named.
Father of all
hear your children's prayer.

You have made your Church a spiritual family,
a household of faith.
Through baptism we are reborn as the brothers and
		sisters of Christ.
Deepen our unity and fellowship in him.
Father of all
hear your children's prayer.

You sent your Son to give his life
as a ransom for the whole human family.
Give justice, peace and racial harmony to the
		world he died to save.
Father of all
hear your children's prayer.

You gave your Son a share in the life of a
		family in Nazareth.
Help us to value our families, to be thankful for them,
and to live sensitively within them.
Father of all
hear your children's prayer.

Your Son drew around him a company of friends.
Bring love and joy to all who are alone.
Help us all to find in the brothers and sisters of Christ
		a loving family.
Father of all
hear your children's prayer.

You are the God of the dead as well as of the living.
In confidence we remember those of the household of
        faith who have gone before us.
Bring us with them to the joy of your home in heaven.
Father of all
hear your children's prayer.

Living in the world
Cross
F70

[We pray to the Lord for the courage to give ourselves to
        him [this Lent].
Lord, meet us in the silence.
Give us strength and hear our prayer.]

Give us the courage to look beyond ourselves
        to mission in your world.
[We pray for N our bishop and …]

May the blood and water flowing from the side of Jesus
bring forgiveness to your people
and help us to face the cost of proclaiming salvation.
Lord, meet us in the silence.
Give us strength and hear our prayer.

Give us the courage to give up war, bitterness and hatred,
and to seek peace.
[*We pray for* …]

May the shoulders of the risen Jesus,
once scourged by soldiers,
bear the burden of political and military conflict in
        our world.
Lord, meet us in the silence.
Give us strength and hear our prayer.

Give us the courage to give up quarrels, strife and jealousy
in our families, neighbourhoods and communities.
[*We pray for* …]

May the presence of the risen Jesus,
his body once broken and now made whole,
bring peace and direction as we live with one another.
Lord, meet us in the silence.
Give us strength and hear our prayer.

Give us the courage to live for others,
giving time, care and comfort to the sick
        and those in need.
[*We pray for* …]

May the wounded hands of Jesus bring his healing,
and the light of his presence fill their lives.
Lord, meet us in the silence.
Give us strength and hear our prayer.

Give us the courage to give up our fear of death
and to rejoice with those who have died in faith.
[*Especially we hold … in our minds.*]

May the risen Lord Jesus,
whose feet were once nailed to the cross,
walk alongside the dying and bereaved,
and lead them and all your Church through death
 to the gate of glory.
Lord, meet us in the silence.
Give us strength and hear our prayer,
here and in eternity.
Amen.

Living in the world
F71

[We pray for God's faithfulness to be known in our world.
Faithful God
glorify your name.]

In a world of change and hope,
of fear and adventure;
faithful God
glorify your name.

In human rebellion and obedience,
in our seeking and our finding;
faithful God
glorify your name.

In the common life of our society,
in prosperity and need;
faithful God
glorify your name.

As your Church proclaims your goodness in
 words and action;
faithful God
glorify your name.

Among our friends
and in our homes;
faithful God
glorify your name.

In our times of joy,
in our days of sorrow;
faithful God
glorify your name.

In our strengths and triumphs,
in our weakness and at our death;
faithful God
glorify your name.

In your saints in glory
and on the day of Christ's coming;
faithful God
glorify your name.

Living in the world
Christ's coming
F72

[We pray for the coming of God's kingdom.
Father, by your Spirit
bring in your kingdom.]

You sent your Son to bring good news to the poor,
sight to the blind,
freedom to captives
and salvation to your people:
anoint us with your Spirit;
rouse us to work in his name.
Father, by your Spirit
bring in your kingdom.

Send us to bring help to the poor
and freedom to the oppressed.
Father, by your Spirit
bring in your kingdom.

Send us to tell the world
the good news of your healing love.
Father, by your Spirit
bring in your kingdom.

Send us to those who mourn,
to bring joy and gladness instead of grief.
Father, by your Spirit
bring in your kingdom.

Send us to proclaim that the time is here
for you to save your people.
Father, by your Spirit
bring in your kingdom.

God of mercy,
you know us and love us
and hear our prayer:
keep us in the eternal fellowship of
     Jesus Christ our Saviour.
Amen.

cf Isaiah 61.1-3

[In the power of the Spirit let us pray to the Father
through Christ the saviour of the world.
Let us pray to the Lord.
Lord, have mercy.]

For forgiveness for the many times we have denied Jesus,
let us pray to the Lord.
Lord, have mercy.

For grace to seek out those habits of sin
    which mean spiritual death,
and by prayer and self-discipline to overcome them,
let us pray to the Lord.
Lord, have mercy.

For Christian people,
that through the suffering of disunity
there may grow a rich union in Christ,
let us pray to the Lord.
Lord, have mercy.

For those who make laws, interpret them
    and administer them,
that our common life may be ordered in justice and mercy,
let us pray to the Lord.
Lord, have mercy.

For those who still make Jerusalem a battleground,
let us pray to the Lord.
Lord, have mercy.

For those who have the courage and honesty
to work openly for justice and peace,
let us pray to the Lord.
Lord, have mercy.

For those in the darkness and agony of isolation,
that they may find support and encouragement,
let us pray to the Lord.
Lord, have mercy.

For those who, weighed down with hardship,
    failure, or sorrow,
feel that God is far from them,
let us pray to the Lord.
Lord, have mercy.

For those who are tempted to give up the way of the cross,
let us pray to the Lord.
Lord, have mercy.

That we, with those who have died in faith,
may find mercy in the day of Christ,
let us pray to the Lord.
Lord, have mercy.

This may also be used

Holy God,
holy and strong,
holy and immortal,
have mercy upon us.

Heaven
Resurrection
F74

[Let us pray to the Lord, who has conquered death.
Hear us, risen Lord,
our resurrection and our life.]

Jesus, bread from heaven,
you satisfy the hungry with good things:
grant us a share with all the faithful departed
in the banquet of your kingdom.
Hear us, risen Lord,
our resurrection and our life.

Jesus, the light of the world,
you gave the man born blind the gift of sight:
open the eye of faith
and bring us from darkness
to your eternal light and glory.
Hear us, risen Lord,
our resurrection and our life.

Jesus, Son of the living God,
you summoned your friend Lazarus from death to life:
raise us at the last to full and eternal life with you.
Hear us, risen Lord,
our resurrection and our life.

Jesus, crucified Saviour,
in your dying you entrusted each to the other,
Mary your mother and John your beloved disciple:
sustain and comfort all who mourn.
Hear us, risen Lord,
our resurrection and our life.

Jesus, our way and truth and life,
you drew your disciple Thomas from doubt to faith:
reveal the resurrection faith to the doubting and the lost.
Hear us, risen Lord,
our resurrection and our life.

May God in his infinite love and mercy
bring the whole Church,
living and departed in the Lord Jesus,
to a joyful resurrection
and the fulfilment of his eternal kingdom.
Amen.

United in the company of all the faithful
and looking for the coming of the kingdom,
let us offer our prayers to God,
the source of all life and holiness.

Merciful Lord,
strengthen all Christian people by your Holy Spirit,
that we may live as a royal priesthood and a holy nation
to the praise of Jesus Christ our Saviour.
Lord, have mercy.

Bless *N* our bishop, and all ministers of your Church,
that by faithful proclamation of your word
we may be built on the foundation of the apostles
        and prophets
into a holy temple in the Lord.
Lord, have mercy.

Empower us by the gift of your holy and life-giving Spirit,
that we may be transformed into the likeness of Christ
from glory to glory.
Lord, have mercy.

Give to the world and its peoples
the peace that comes from above,
that they may find Christ's way of freedom and life.
Lord, have mercy.

Hold in your embrace all who witness to your love in the
        service of the poor and needy;
all those who minister to the sick and dying;
and all who bring light to those in darkness.
Lord, have mercy.

Touch and heal all those whose lives are scarred by sin
        or disfigured by pain,
that, raised from death to life in Christ,
their sorrow may be turned to eternal joy.
Lord, have mercy.

Remember in your mercy all those gone before us,
who have been well-pleasing to you from eternity;
preserve in your faith your servants on earth,
guide us to your kingdom,
and grant us your peace at all times.
Lord, have mercy.

Hasten the day when many will come
from east and west, from north and south,
and sit at table in your kingdom.
Lord, have mercy.

We give you thanks
for the whole company of your saints in glory,
with whom in fellowship we join our prayers and praises;
by your grace may we, like them,
    be made perfect in your love.

**Blessing and glory and wisdom,
thanksgiving and honour and power,
be to our God for ever and ever.
Amen.**

(or)

Merciful Father,
**accept these prayers
for the sake of your Son,
our Saviour Jesus Christ.
Amen.**

Heaven
F76

*These intercessions are especially suitable for a service
for the commemoration of the faithful departed, but may
appropriately be used at other times.*

[In faith and hope we pray,
Lord of mercy,
Lord, hear us.]

Almighty God,
you bring your chosen people together
    in one communion,
in the body of your Son, Jesus Christ our Lord.
We rejoice in your light and your peace
with your whole Church in heaven and on earth.
Lord of mercy,
Lord, hear us.

[Give to all who mourn a sure confidence
    in your loving care,
that we may cast all our sorrow on you
and know the consolation of your love.
Lord of mercy,
Lord, hear us.]

Give your faithful people pardon and peace,
that we may be cleansed from all our sins
and serve you with a quiet mind.
Lord of mercy,
Lord, hear us.

Give us strength to meet the days ahead
in the joyful expectation of eternal life
        with those you love.
Lord of mercy,
Lord, hear us.

Give to us who are still in our pilgrimage,
and who walk as yet by faith,
your Holy Spirit to lead us in holiness and righteousness
all our days.
Lord of mercy,
Lord, hear us.

May all who have been made one with Christ
in his death and in his resurrection
die to sin and rise to newness of life.
Lord of mercy,
Lord, hear us.

praise and thanksgiving

G Praise and Thanksgiving

Stories from the four churches

St Ann's Evening Praise replaced Evening Prayer some years ago when
people were looking for something much freer in their worship. The service
this evening includes some teaching in preparation for an evangelistic event in
a few weeks' time, and is punctuated at intervals by one of the acclamations:

> Christ in you, the hope of glory:
> **this is the gospel we proclaim.**

A Service of the Word provides the structure which holds everything
together, including some dance to the psalm, interviews with a couple just
moving to a new job and wanting to thank the congregation for their
support, some praise songs and a time of extempore thanksgiving. The
service moves to a climax of sung and spoken praise using one of the longer
Thanksgivings, ending with the Sanctus. Other things they have used at the
climax of the service have been traditional sung texts like the Te Deum and
the Gloria, and the first section of one of the Eucharistic Prayers, ending with
the Sanctus.

The Worship Planning Group at **St Bartholomew's** are leading worship
based on Evening Prayer on Sunday from *Common Worship*. They have been
grappling with the problem – and opportunity – of how to deal with the
Advent theme of heaven, when one of the older people in the village has just
died. While preparing for the funeral they came across the thematic material
for a vigil on pages 247–252 of *Common Worship: Pastoral Services* and decided
to use the psalm (116), with its psalm prayer ('We walk through eternity in
your presence'), and the canticle 'A Song of the Justified' from Romans 4 and
5, concluding with the Prayers of Thanksgiving from the Memorial Service
(*Pastoral Services,* page 340) and one of the Resurrection Thanksgivings (G38
below) as an alternative Thanksgiving section for the end of Evening Prayer.
At the end of the service there is an almost tangible silence as people feel
they have been caught up to heaven and are reluctant to come back to earth
again.

The Eucharist at **St Christopher's** today uses two items from this section
of *New Patterns*. The theme is justification by faith, using the first of the two
lectionary modules from Romans (pages 119–120 above). They have been
using the acclamation there ('I am not ashamed of the gospel …') for the last
two weeks, and today they use one of the responsive acclamations on this
theme (G45) as a Gospel acclamation, and one of the Thanksgivings (G75)

replaces the preface in Eucharistic Prayer E. The clergy have read Note 18 to *Common Worship* Holy Communion, which says that Extended Prefaces may be used with Eucharistic prayers A, B and E for Order One and that they replace the entire text between the opening dialogue and the Sanctus.

The **St Dodo's** Praise Service has no apparent structure at all – and so, one or two people say, must be led by the Spirit. There is little content, with only one of the lectionary readings (irrelevant to the theme of praise) and the sermon is replaced by long introductions by four different people to four of the hymns. People in the congregation are encouraged to suggest items to give thanks for or to sing (sometimes without the congregation having the words because it is assumed everyone knows them), with the inevitable result that there is no development in the service and no one quite knows when it should come to an end. But a liturgical structure used without preparation can produce equally bad results. Last week the president got a bit lost in Eucharistic Prayer E, used a Short Preface rather than an extended one, with the result that no one knew when to come in with 'Holy, holy …'

Notes to the resources

Acclamations and praise responses

Where to use them

These may be used
* at the beginning of the service;
* at the end of worship;
* after a reading; or
* acclamations may be repeated at various points in a service as a reminder of the theme.

Finding some more

There are more acclamations and responses in the Gathering and Greeting section.

See the Lectionary modules in Resource Section C for some specific acclamations which relate to the readings there.

Further appropriate forms can be devised locally. The key principles in constructing your own are:
* look at the readings for the service and especially the psalm as a possible source for words and ideas;
* keep the length of sentences short (especially for the congregation's part);

* match the length of the response to the length of the leader's text;
* take care over words that people may not be sure how to pronounce in the congregation's text (even something like 'blessed' can cause uncertainty).

Songs

Some of the praise responses are suitable for saying or singing together, rather than in responsive form. These are marked with an asterisk*.

Thanksgivings

* These may be used at any suitable point in A Service of the Word, but they are particularly appropriate for use as the climax to the service or part of the response to the Liturgy of the Word.

* They may also be used as a proper preface in the Eucharistic Prayer: in this case, the introduction 'Father, we give you thanks and praise through Jesus Christ our Lord' should be used only where indicated.

* The Benedictus qui venit ('Blessed is he who comes …') may be added to the Sanctus in any of these thanksgivings where it is not printed.

* If it is desired to shorten the Thanksgivings, the lines in brackets may be omitted.

* If the Preface is specially composed, the president says,
    'And now we give you thanks …'
and then offers brief thanksgivings in the form 'We thank you that …' or similar words. They normally include thanksgiving for
* creation;
* redemption;
* the continuing work of the Spirit.

* They should not conclude with 'Amen'. The president concludes by saying
    'Therefore with angels and archangels …' (Prayers A, B and C)
    (or)
    'And so we gladly thank you, with saints and angels …' (Prayer E)
Eucharistic Prayers D, G and H are not suitable for this approach.

Short Prefaces

These short seasonal or thematic Prefaces are for use at the appropriate points in any authorized Eucharistic Prayer on suitable occasions. They may be inserted in Prayers A, B and C in Order One and, suitably amended, in both prayers in Order One in Traditional Language. They may also be used (suitably amended: see Note 28 to the *Common Worship* services of Holy Communion) with Order Two and Order Two in Contemporary Language.

Praise

Acclamations

General **G**1	Rejoice in the Lord always **and again I say, 'Rejoice'.** *cf Philippians 4.4*
General **G**2	The Lord of hosts is with us; **the God of Jacob is our stronghold.** *cf Psalm 46.7*
Christ's coming *Incarnation* **G**3	Jesus Christ is the Light of the world: **a light no darkness can quench.** *cf John 8.12*
Incarnation **G**4	The Word was made flesh and lived among us **and we have seen his glory.** *cf John 1.14*
Cross **G**5	The Son of man came not to be served, but to serve: **to give up his life as a ransom for many.** *cf Mark 10.45*
Cross **G**6	Jesus is the Lamb of God **who takes away the sins of the world.** **[Alleluia.]** *cf John 1.29*
Resurrection *Heaven* **G**7	Jesus is the resurrection and the life: **those who believe in him shall never die.** **Alleluia.** *cf John 11.25*
Ascension **G**8	We have a great high priest who has passed through the heavens. **We come boldly to the throne of grace.** *cf Hebrews 4.14,16*
Word *Living in the world* **G**9	Your word is a lantern to my feet **and a light upon our path.** *cf Psalm 119.105*
Word **G**10	O Lord, your word is everlasting: **it stands firm for ever in the heavens.** *cf Psalm 119.89*

Church and mission **G**11	The love of Christ compels us. **We are ambassadors for him.**	
		cf 2 Corinthians 5.14,20
Church and mission *Cross* **G**12	God forbid that we should glory **save in the cross of Christ our Lord.**	
		cf Galatians 6.14
Church and mission *Holy Spirit* *Father, Son and Spirit* **G**13	Jesus said, 'Receive the Spirit: as the Father sent me, so I send you.' **Alleluia. Thanks be to God.**	
		cf John 20.21,22
Christian beginnings *Church and mission* *Christ's coming* **G**14	Christ in you, the hope of glory. **This is the gospel we proclaim.**	
		cf Colossians 1.27,28
Christian beginnings *Incarnation* **G**15	Christ has brought us out of darkness **to dwell in his marvellous light.**	
		cf 1 Peter 2.9
Christian beginnings *Church and mission* **G**16	There is one body and one Spirit, **one Lord, one faith, one baptism.**	
		cf Ephesians 4.4,5
Relationships and healing *Cross* **G**17	Christ himself carried our sins in his body on the cross. **By his wounds we have been healed.**	
		cf 1 Peter 2.24
Relationships and healing *General (morning)* **G**18	God's saving power will rise like the sun **bringing healing like the sun's rays.**	
		cf Malachi 4.2
Living in the world **G**19	A city on a hill cannot be hidden. **We are the light of the world.**	
		cf Matthew 5.14
Living in the world *Church and mission* **G**20	Declare God's glory among the nations, **his wonders among all peoples.**	
		cf Psalm 96.3
Heaven *Christian beginnings* *Resurrection* **G**21	We have died together with Christ. **We rise united with him.**	
		cf Romans 6.5

Praise responses

Responses which are suitable for saying or singing together, rather than in responsive form, are marked with an asterisk*.

General

G22

Let us give thanks to the God of our Lord Jesus Christ,
who has blessed us in Christ
    with every spiritual blessing.
Before the world was made, God chose us in Christ,
that we might be holy and blameless before him.
Let us praise God for the glory of his grace,
for the free gift he gave us in his dear Son.
To Father, Son and Holy Spirit
give praise and dominion, honour and might,
for ever and ever.
Amen.

cf Ephesians 1.3-6

General

Incarnation

G23

See what love the Father has given us,
that we should be called the children of God.
You are my sons and daughters,
this day I have begotten you.
See what love the Father has given us.
As many as received him,
to them he gave power to become the children of God.
See what love the Father has given us.
Glory to the Father and to the Son
and to the Holy Spirit.
See what love the Father has given us,
that we should be called the children of God.

cf 1 John 3.1

General

Heaven*

G24

Great is the Lord and greatly to be praised,
there is no end to his greatness.
One generation shall praise your works to another
and shall declare your power.
All your works praise you, Lord,
and your faithful servants bless you.
They make known the glory of your kingdom
and speak of your power.
My mouth shall speak the praise of the Lord:
let all flesh bless his holy name for ever and ever.

cf Psalm 145.3,4,10-12

General (evening)
God in creation
G25

Blessed are you, Lord God, King of the universe.
Your word calls forth the dusk of evening.
Your wisdom creates both night and day.
You determine the cycles of time.
You arrange the succession of seasons
and establish the stars in their heavenly courses.
Lord of the starry hosts is your name.
Living and eternal God, rule over us always.
**Blessed be the Lord, whose word makes
evening fall.**

Father, Son and Spirit
God in creation
Heaven
G26

You are worthy, our Lord and God,
to receive glory and honour and power.
For you have created all things,
and by your will they have their being.
You are worthy, O Lamb, for you were slain,
**and by your blood you ransomed for God
saints from every tribe and language and nation.**
You have made them to be a kingdom and priests
serving our God,
and they will reign with you on earth.

To the One who sits on the throne and to the Lamb
**be blessing and honour, glory and might,
for ever and ever.
Amen.**

cf Revelation 4.11; 5.9,10,13

Christ's coming
G27

The Lord is my light and my salvation.
The Lord is my light and my salvation.
The Lord is the strength of my life.
The Lord is my light and my salvation.
Glory to the Father and to the Son
and to the Holy Spirit.
The Lord is my light and my salvation.

Incarnation*
G28

Blessed be the Lord, the God of Israel.
He has come to his people and set them free.
Light has sprung up for the righteous
and joyful gladness for those who are faithful.
Glory to God in the highest
and peace to his people on earth.

Incarnation
G29

I bring you good news of great joy:
a Saviour has been born to you. Alleluia.
Unto us a child is born, a Son is given. Alleluia.

Incarnation
G30

This may be used on Christmas Day with G67 below, or as a Greeting.

Today [*This night/day*] Christ is born:
Alleluia.

Today [*This night/day*] the Saviour comes:
Alleluia.

Today [*This night/day*] the angels sing on earth:
Alleluia. Glory to God in the highest.

Incarnation
G31

The glory of the Lord has been revealed
and all flesh shall see it together.

[A candle may be lit.]

Jesus Christ is the light of the world,
a light no darkness can quench.

The shepherds kept watch by night
and your glory shone around them.

The darkness is not dark to you,
the night is as bright as the day.

Let your light scatter the darkness
and fill your Church with your glory.

Incarnation
G32

'Do I not fill heaven and earth?' says the Lord.
**Now the Word is made flesh
and laid in a narrow manger.**
From eternity to eternity you are God,
and now we see you as a newborn child.

Incarnation
G33

The people who walked in darkness
have seen a great light.
For to us a child is born,
to us a Son is given.
His name will be called
Wonderful, Counsellor, Mighty God,
**the Everlasting Father,
the Prince of Peace.**
Glory to God in the highest
and peace to his people on earth.

cf Isaiah 9.2,6

Church and mission
Word
Incarnation
G34

The Word of life which was from the beginning
we proclaim to you.
The darkness is passing away
and the true light is already shining;
the Word of life which was from the beginning.
That which we heard, which we saw with our eyes,
and touched with our hands,
we proclaim to you.
For our fellowship is with the Father,
and with his Son, Jesus Christ our Lord.
The Word of life which was from the beginning
we proclaim to you.

cf 1John 1.1-3

Cross
Lament
Relationships and healing
G35

Christ became obedient unto death for us,
even death upon a cross.
He was pierced for our sins,
bruised for no fault but our own.
His punishment has brought us peace.
By his wounds we are healed.
Worthy is the Lamb that was slain
to receive power and riches and wisdom,
strength and honour, glory and praise.
Amen.

Cross
Church and mission
Relationships and healing
G36

O Lord, open my lips
and my mouth shall proclaim your praise.
When we were still helpless
Christ died for the ungodly.
The proof of God's amazing love is this:
while we were still sinners, Christ died for us.

cf Romans 5.6,8

Resurrection
Church and mission
G37

Alleluia. Christ is risen.
He is risen indeed. Alleluia.
Praise the God and Father of our Lord Jesus Christ.
He has given us new life and hope.
He has raised Jesus from the dead.
God has claimed us as his own.
He has brought us out of darkness.
He has made us light to the world.
Alleluia. Christ is risen.
He is risen indeed. Alleluia.

Resurrection
G38

Alleluia. Christ is risen.
He is risen indeed. Alleluia.
Blessed are those who have not seen him
    and yet have believed.
He is our Lord and our God.
We have seen his glory,
the glory which he had as the Father's only Son,
full of grace and truth.
The Lord says to us, 'Do you love me?'
Our hearts reply, 'You know that we love you.'
Jesus says, 'Whoever comes to me shall never hunger.
Whoever believes in me shall never thirst.'
This is the Lamb of God
who takes away the sins of the world.
Jesus is the resurrection and the life:
those who believe in him shall never die.
Yes! Christ is risen.
He is risen indeed. Alleluia.

Ascension
G39

[Christ has gone up on high.
Alleluia.]

God raised Christ from the dead
and enthroned him at his right hand in the
    heavenly realms.
God put all things in subjection beneath his feet
and gave him as head over all things to the Church.
We died, and our life lies hidden with Christ in God.
We set our minds on things above.
When Christ, who is our life, is revealed,
we too will be revealed with him in glory.

[Christ has gone up on high.
Alleluia.]
cf Ephesians 1.20,23; Colossians 3.1-4

Church and mission
Christ's coming
Incarnation
G40

Blessed are you, Lord our God, King of the universe.
To you be glory and praise for ever.
From the rising of the sun to its setting
your name is proclaimed in all the world.
To you be glory and praise for ever.
When the time had fully come
you sent the Sun of Righteousness.
In him the fullness of your glory dwells.
To you be glory and praise for ever.

There are varieties of gifts,
but the same Spirit.
There are varieties of service,
but the same Lord.
There are different kinds of working,
but the same God is at work in all.

cf 1 Corinthians 12.4-6

This may be used with G41 above.

There is one body, one Spirit, one hope in God's call,
one Lord, one faith, one baptism.
There is one God, Father of all, over all and in all,
to whom Christ ascended on high.
And through his Spirit he gives us gifts:
some are apostles, some are his prophets.
Evangelists, pastors and teachers he gives us,
so we can minister together
to build up his body,
to be mature in the fullness of Christ.

cf Ephesians 4.4-13

The love of God has been poured into our hearts
through the Holy Spirit who has been given to us.
We dwell in him and he in us.
Give thanks to the Lord and call upon his name,
make known his deeds among the peoples.
Sing to him, sing praises to him,
and speak of all his marvellous works.
Holy, holy, holy is the Lord God almighty,
who was and is and is to come.

Here are words you may trust.
Remember Jesus Christ, risen from the dead:
he is our salvation, our eternal glory.
If we die with him, we shall live with him;
if we endure, we shall reign with him.
If we deny him, he will deny us;
if we are faithless, he keeps faith.
For he has broken the power of death
**and brought life and immortality to light through
    the gospel.**

cf 2 Timothy 2.11-13

Christian beginnings
Holy Spirit
G45

Now that we have been put right with God through faith,
**we have peace with God through
our Lord Jesus Christ.**
He has brought us by faith into the grace of God.
We rejoice in the hope of sharing God's glory.
This hope does not deceive us:
**God has poured his love into our hearts
by the gift of his Spirit.**

cf Romans 5.1-2

Christian beginnings
Cross
Resurrection
G46

Since we have died with Christ,
we believe that we will also live with him.
For we know that Christ has been raised from death:
he will never die again.
We have been buried with him by baptism into death,
so that we might walk with him in newness of life.

cf Romans 6.4,8,9

Lament
Christ's coming
G47

Restore us, Lord God of hosts.
Turn the light of your face to us and save us.
Will you not give us life again,
that your people may rejoice in you?
Show us your mercy, O Lord,
and grant us your salvation.
Blessed is the King who comes in the name of the Lord.
Peace in heaven and glory in the highest.

Lament
G48

Lord, we are clay
and you are the potter.

We are all the work of your hand;
do not remember our sins for ever.

Look upon us in your mercy,
for we are your people.

cf Isaiah 64.8,9

Lament
Relationships
and healing
G49

Cast your burden upon the Lord:
he will sustain you.
Create in us clean hearts, O God;
renew a right spirit within us.
Cast us not away from your presence;
take not your Holy Spirit from us.
Give us the joy of your saving help;
sustain us with your life-giving Spirit.
[Blessed be the Lord day by day:
the God of our salvation, who bears our burdens.]

Relationships and healing*
G50

This is love, not that we loved God,
but that he loved us and sent his Son.
He is the sacrifice for our sins,
that we might live through him.
If God loves us so much
we ought to love one another.
If we love one another
God lives in us.

cf 1 John 4.10-12

Relationships and healing
G51

I saw water flowing from the threshold of the temple.
Where the river flows everything will spring to life.
On the banks of the river grow trees
    bearing every kind of fruit;
their leaves will not wither nor their fruit fail.
Their fruit will serve for food,
their leaves for the healing of the nations,
for the river of the water of life
flows from the throne of God and of the Lamb.

cf Ezekiel 47.1,9; Revelation 22.1-3

Relationships and healing
Living in the world
G52

God is light.
In him there is no darkness.
If we live in the light,
as God is in the light,
we have fellowship with one another
and the blood of Jesus, his Son,
    purifies us from all sin.

cf 1 John 1.5,7

Living in the world
General (morning)
G53

A thousand years in God's sight are like a single day:
like an evening that has already gone.
Christ is the first and the last,
the beginning and the end.
You hold the key to God's way of justice.
Open to us your kingdom of peace.

Blessed are you, Lord our God, King of the universe.
**You have given us a share in the inheritance
of the saints in light.**

In the darkness of this age
your saints proclaim the glory of your kingdom.
Chosen as lights in the world,
they surround our steps as we journey on
towards that eternal city of light
where they sing the triumphal song.
Open our eyes to behold your glory
and free our tongues to join their song:

**Great and wonderful are your deeds,
Lord God almighty;
just and true are your ways,
King of the ages.
To you be praise and glory,
now and for ever.
Amen.**

In the city of God, night shall be no more:
the people of God need no light of lamp or sun.
For the Lord God will be their light
and they will reign for ever and ever.

cf Revelation 22.5

G 11 Thanksgiving

Thanksgivings

General
G56

Father, we give you thanks and praise
through Jesus Christ your Son, our Lord.

Jesus is Lord of all creation.
We worship and adore you.

A

Jesus made his home among us.
We worship and adore you.

B

Jesus died to set us free.
We worship and adore you.

C

Jesus was raised to life again.
We worship and adore you.

D

Jesus reigns in glory now.
We worship and adore you.

We worship and adore you with angels and archangels
and all the company of heaven, *saying:*
Holy, holy, holy Lord,
God of power and might,
heaven and earth are full of your glory.
Hosanna in the highest.

One or more sentences in the following form, with the response 'We worship and adore you', may be used at the points indicated by the letters in the text above. Choosing one from A, one from B etc. will maintain the balance; choosing more than one will provide the opportunity for seasonal and thematic emphasis.

A

He was born of the Virgin Mary.

He was cradled in a manger.

He's our Saviour, Christ the Lord.

He is God in human flesh.

Jesus is Emmanuel.

B   He was lifted up for us.

Jesus stretches out his arms.

Jesus died for a dying world.

Jesus bore our sins and griefs.

C   Jesus lay within the tomb.

Jesus rose to life in triumph.

Jesus conquers death for us.

D   He is Lord of life and death.

He's the Lamb upon the throne.

He is crowned, in glory seated.

Jesus always pleads for us.

Jesus comes again in glory.

Jesus claims his kingdom here.

B, C, D   Jesus is the Son of God.

He's the Light of all the world.

Jesus is the bread of heaven.

He's our way, our truth, our life.

Jesus is the door to life.

Jesus is the first and last.

Jesus is the Lord of all.

He's our wisdom from above.

Jesus is the King of kings.

Jesus is our friend and brother.

He's the healer of the sick.

Alleluia. Praise the Lord!

Almighty God, Father of all mercies,
we your unworthy servants give you most humble and
    hearty thanks
for all your goodness and loving kindness.
We bless you for our creation, preservation, and
    all the blessings of this life;
but above all for your immeasurable love
in the redemption of the world by our Lord Jesus Christ,
for the means of grace, and for the hope of glory.
And give us, we pray, such a sense of all your mercies
that our hearts may be unfeignedly thankful,
and that we show forth your praise,
not only with our lips but in our lives,
by giving up ourselves to your service,
and by walking before you in holiness and
    righteousness all our days;
through Jesus Christ our Lord,
to whom, with you and the Holy Spirit,
be all honour and glory,
for ever and ever.
Amen.

Glory to the Father, the God of love,
who created us;
who continually preserves and sustains us;
who has loved us with an everlasting love,
and given us the light of the knowledge of his glory
in the face of Jesus Christ.

Blessed be God for ever.

Glory to Jesus Christ our Saviour,
who, though he was rich,
yet for our sake became poor,
and was tested in every way as we are,
yet without sin;
who proclaimed the good news of the kingdom,
and was obedient to the point of death,
even death on a cross;
who was raised from the dead and is alive for ever,
and has opened the kingdom of heaven
to all who trust in him;
who is seated at God's right hand in glory,
and will come to be our judge.

Blessed be God for ever.

Glory to the Holy Spirit,
the Lord, the giver of life,
by whom we are born into the family of God,
and made members of the body of Christ;
whose witness confirms us;
whose wisdom teaches us;
whose power enables us:
who will do for us more than we can ask or think.

Blessed be God for ever.

Holy, holy, holy Lord,
God of power and might,
heaven and earth are full of your glory.
Hosanna in the highest.

General
G59

Let us give thanks to God.

For the love of our Father, the maker of all,
the giver of all good things,
let us bless the Lord.

Thanks be to God.

For Jesus Christ our Saviour,
who lived and worked among us,
let us bless the Lord.

Thanks be to God.

For his suffering and death on the cross
and his resurrection to new life,
let us bless the Lord.

Thanks be to God.

For his rule over all things
and his presence in the world,
let us bless the Lord.

Thanks be to God.

For the Holy Spirit, the giver of life,
who teaches and guides us,
let us bless the Lord.

Thanks be to God.

For the grace of the Spirit
in the work of the Church
and the life of the world,
let us bless the Lord.

Thanks be to God.
Amen.

We thank you, O God,
for you are gracious.
You have loved us from the beginning of time
and you remember us in times of trouble and of joy.

Your mercy endures for ever.

We thank you, O God,
for you came to us in Jesus Christ,
who has redeemed the world
and saves us from our sins.

Your mercy endures for ever.

We thank you, O God,
for you have sent your Holy Spirit,
who comforts us and leads us into all truth.

Your mercy endures for ever.
Amen.

Blessed are you, Holy God,
creator, redeemer and life-giver;
you have spoken the world into being
and filled it with wonder and beauty.

For every blessing we have received
we give you thanks and praise.

Blessed are you, Holy God,
for people of every language and culture
and for the rich variety you give to life.

For every blessing we have received
we give you thanks and praise.

Blessed are you, Holy God,
for Jesus Christ our Saviour,
truly divine and truly human,
living and dying for us,
and going before us into heaven.

For every blessing we have received
we give you thanks and praise.

Blessed are you, Holy God,
for your Spirit,
the fire of love burning in our hearts,
bringing us to faith,
and calling us to holiness
in the Church and in the world.

For every blessing we have received
we give you thanks and praise.

Other thanksgivings, appropriate to the season or the situation,
may be added here. Prefaces for eucharistic prayers, suitably
adapted, may provide appropriate material.

Therefore, we worship you
    with all the company of heaven.
Holy, holy, holy Lord,
God of power and might,
heaven and earth are full of your glory.
Hosanna in the highest.

General
God in creation
G62

We thank God for the world he has made,
and for all his love and care.

For the warmth of the sun,
Father in heaven
we give you thanks and praise.

For the rain which makes things grow,
Father in heaven
we give you thanks and praise.

For the woods and the fields,
Father in heaven
we give you thanks and praise.

For the sea and the sky,
Father in heaven
we give you thanks and praise.

For the flowers and the animals,
Father in heaven
we give you thanks and praise.

For families and holidays,
Father in heaven
we give you thanks and praise.

For all your gifts,
Father in heaven
we give you thanks and praise.
Amen.

We give thanks to God for all his gifts to us.

Father, we give you thanks and praise
     through Jesus Christ our Lord.
For birth and life and strength of body,
for safety and shelter and food,
we give you thanks:
we praise your holy name.

For sight and hearing and the beauty of nature,
for words and music and the power of thought,
we give you thanks:
we praise your holy name.

For work and leisure and the joy of achieving,
for conscience and will and depth of feeling,
we give you thanks:
we praise your holy name.

For grace and truth in Jesus Christ,
for the gifts of the Spirit and the hope of heaven,
we give you thanks:
we praise your holy name.

**Holy, holy, holy Lord,
God of power and might,
heaven and earth are full of your glory.
Hosanna in the highest.**

Father, Son and Spirit
G64

This may be said or sung in three voices.

1   Glory to the Holy and Undivided Trinity;
2   Father, Son and Holy Spirit;
3   Three persons and one God.

1   Perfectly one from before time began;
2   One in being and one in glory;
3   Dwelling in love; three persons, one God.

1   Incarnate Son, in suffering forsaken;
2   Father, giving and forgiving;
3   Spirit, bond in joy and pain.

1   Eternal Father, the Fountain of Life;
2   Risen Son, the Prince of Life;
3   Spirit of freedom, Giver of Life.

1   Truth, Word and Power;
2   Lover, Beloved and Friend;
3   Hope without end; Joy beyond words.

All Glory to God, Father, Son and Holy Spirit.

Father, Son and Spirit
Ascension
G65

Father, we are in your Spirit and hear your voice:
'I am the first and the last,
who is, who was, and who is to come.'
Before the worlds were made,
Jesus Christ the living one was reigning with you and the
    Holy Spirit.
Through Christ you created everything
    in heaven and earth,
the whole universe created through him and for him.
Lord of glory
we worship and adore you.

You sent him,
the visible likeness of the invisible God,
to reflect the brightness of your glory,
to sustain the universe with his word of power,
to achieve forgiveness for the sins of all.
Lord of glory
we worship and adore you.

And now he rules in heaven, mighty risen Lord,
[his hair as white as snow, his eyes like fire,
his feet like polished brass, his hands full of stars,
his face bright as the noonday sun,]
his voice like a roaring waterfall:
'I am the living one!
I was dead but now I am alive for ever and ever.'

So, with angels and archangels,
and all the company of heaven,
we praise you for ever, *saying*:
Holy, holy, holy Lord,
God of power and might,
heaven and earth are full of your glory.
Hosanna in the highest.

The acclamation 'We worship and adore you'
may be repeated between each line of the paragraph
beginning 'And now he rules'.

cf Colossians 1.15-20; Hebrews 1.3; Revelation 1.14-18

God in creation
G66

You, Christ, are the image of the unseen God,
the firstborn of all creation.
You created all things in heaven and on earth:
everything visible and everything invisible,
thrones, dominions, sovereignties, powers,
all things were created through you and for you.
Lord of all creation
we worship and adore you.

You are the radiant light of God's glory:
you hold all creation together by your word of power.

Lord of all creation
we worship and adore you.

You are the first to be born from the dead.
All perfection is found in you,
and all things were reconciled through you and for you,
everything in heaven and everything on earth,
when you made peace by your death on the cross.
Lord of all creation
we worship and adore you.

The Church is your body,
you are its head.
You take your place in heaven
at the right hand of the divine majesty,
where we worship and adore you
with all your creation, *singing*:
Holy, holy, holy Lord,
God of power and might,
heaven and earth are full of your glory.
Hosanna in the highest.
Blessed is he who comes in the name of the Lord.
Hosanna in the highest.

cf Colossians 1.15-18

If this Thanksgiving is used as an extended preface to a
eucharistic prayer it should be in this form

Father, we give you thanks and praise
for your Son, Jesus Christ our Lord.
He is the image of the unseen God,
the firstborn of all creation.
He created all things in heaven and on earth:
everything visible and everything invisible,
thrones, dominions, sovereignties, powers,
all things were created through him and for him.
Lord of all creation
we worship and adore you.

He is the radiant light of your glory:
he holds all creation together by his word of power.
Lord of all creation
we worship and adore you.

He is first to be born from the dead.
All perfection is found in him,
and all things were reconciled through him and for him,
everything in heaven and everything on earth,
when he made peace by his death on the cross.
Lord of all creation
we worship and adore you.

The Church is his body,
he is its head.
He takes his place in heaven
at your right hand,
where we worship you with all of your creation, *singing:*
Holy, holy, holy Lord,
God of power and might,
heaven and earth are full of your glory.
Hosanna in the highest.
Blessed is he who comes in the name of the Lord.
Hosanna in the highest.

cf Colossians 1.15-18

Incarnation
G67

Blessed are you, God of all glory,
through your Son the Christ.
His name is Jesus,
because he saves his people from their sins.

He will be called Emmanuel:
God is with us. Alleluia.

Let us praise the Lord, the God of Israel:
he has come to his people and set them free.

He gave up all the glory of heaven
and took the form of a servant.

In humility he walked the path of obedience,
even to death on the cross.

God raised him to the highest place above
and gave him the name above every name:
Jesus Christ is Lord!

So all beings in heaven and earth will fall at his feet,
and proclaim to the glory of God:
Jesus Christ is Lord!

[So, with angels and archangels,
and all the company of heaven,
we praise you for ever, *saying:*
Holy, holy, holy Lord,
God of power and might,
heaven and earth are full of your glory.
Hosanna in the highest.]

cf Matthew 1.21,23; Philippians 2.9-11

G30 could be inserted before the final section
on Christmas Day.

Gracious God,
we give you thanks and praise for Jesus Christ our Lord,
for he was the Word before all creation.
Through him all things come to be;
not one thing has its being but through him.

Jesus, light of the world,
we worship and adore you.

His life is the light that shines in the dark,
a light that darkness cannot overpower.

Jesus, light of the world,
we worship and adore you.

[The Word was the true light coming into the world.
He was in the world
that had its being through him,
and the world did not know him.

Jesus, light of the world,
we worship and adore you.]

He came to his own, and they did not accept him.
But to all who accept him
he gives power to become children of God.

Jesus, light of the world,
we worship and adore you.

The Word was made flesh and lived among us,
and we have seen his glory,
as the only Son of the Father,
full of grace and truth.

Jesus, light of the world,
we worship and adore you.

To God our creator,
born as one of us,
be all praise and glory.
With all the company of heaven, we worship you, *saying:*
Holy, holy, holy Lord,
God of power and might,
heaven and earth are full of your glory.
Hosanna in the highest.

cf John 1

Incarnation
G69

Blessed are you, God of all glory,
through your Son Jesus Christ.
We worship and adore you.

He is the heavenly king, born of Mary.
We worship and adore you.

He is the Word of the Father, crying as a baby.
We worship and adore you.

He is robed in glory, wrapped in infant clothes.
We worship and adore you.

He is Lord of heaven and earth, laid in a manger.
We worship and adore you.

Strong in weakness,
glorious in humility,
to him be all praise and glory.
We join with all the company of heaven,
worshipping you and *saying:*
Holy, holy, holy Lord,
God of power and might,
heaven and earth are full of your glory.
Hosanna in the highest.
Blessed is he who comes in the name of the Lord.
Hosanna in the highest.

Incarnation
G70

Glory to Christ, Son of Mary;
born a child,
he shares our humanity.
Glory to God in the highest.

Glory to Christ, Son of David;
born to rule,
he receives gifts from the wise.
Glory to God in the highest.

Glory to Christ, Son of Man;
born our Saviour,
he is the light of the world.
Glory to God in the highest.

We celebrate the coming of our God
with all the voices of heaven:
Holy, holy, holy Lord,
God of power and might,
heaven and earth are full of your glory.
Hosanna in the highest.
Blessed is he who comes in the name of the Lord.
Hosanna in the highest.

Incarnation
G71

Glory to Christ, Son of Mary;
born a child,
you are one with us.
Glory to God in the highest.
Glory to Christ, Son of David;
born to rule,
you reign in our hearts.
Glory to God in the highest.

Glory to Christ, Son of man;
born to save,
you are the light of the world.
Glory to God in the highest.

Incarnation
G72

Blessed are you, God our Father,
through your Son the Christ.
His name is Jesus.
God is with us. Praise the Lord.

Jesus came and shared our life.
God is with us. Praise the Lord.

Jesus' touch made people whole.
God is with us. Praise the Lord.

Jesus raised the dead to life.
God is with us. Praise the Lord.

Jesus died to set us free.
God is with us. Praise the Lord.

Jesus rose to life again.
God is with us. Praise the Lord.

Jesus is our King on high.
God is with us. Praise the Lord.

Cross
Lament
G73

We give you thanks and praise, Father in heaven,
through Jesus Christ, your only Son, our Lord.
Through him you created the world.
Through his word the universe is sustained.

Father in heaven
we give you thanks and praise.

Through him we come near to you,
with sincere heart and sure faith.
Because of the death of Jesus
we come into the holy place.

Father in heaven
we give you thanks and praise.

[He is our high priest.
He knows and feels our weaknesses.
He was tempted in every way, like us, but did not sin.

Father in heaven
we give you thanks and praise.]

By his own blood
he entered once and for all into the holy place.
He obtained eternal salvation for us.
He is our perfect sacrifice.

Father in heaven
we give you thanks and praise.

So we come by that living way,
the new way he opened for us,
to receive mercy and grace,
and to join with angels and archangels
and all the company of heaven, *saying*:
Holy, holy, holy Lord,
God of power and might,
heaven and earth are full of your glory.
Hosanna in the highest.

cf Hebrews 1.3; 4.15,16; 9.12; 10.19-22

Cross
Lament
G*74*

Blessed are you, Lord our God:
through your Son Jesus Christ
you have known our pain
and show us your mercy.

Surely he has borne our griefs;
he has carried our sorrows.
Surely he has borne our griefs;
he has carried our sorrows.

He was despised, he was rejected;
a man of sorrows and acquainted with grief.
Surely he has borne our griefs;
he has carried our sorrows.

He was pierced for our sins,
bruised for no fault but ours.
Surely he has borne our griefs;
he has carried our sorrows.

His punishment has bought our peace,
and by his wounds we are healed.
Surely he has borne our griefs;
he has carried our sorrows.

We had all strayed like sheep,
but the Lord has laid on him the guilt of us all.
Surely he has borne our griefs;
he has carried our sorrows.

So, with angels and archangels
and all the company of heaven,
we praise you for ever, *saying*:
Holy, holy, holy Lord,
God of power and might,
heaven and earth are full of your glory.
Hosanna in the highest.

cf Isaiah 53

Cross

G*75*

Thanks and praise be to you, almighty God.
You justify us through faith
and give us peace in our Lord Jesus Christ.

Through faith
we are saved by grace.

Through him you brought us by faith
into this experience of grace in which we live,
where we rejoice in the hope of sharing your glory.

Through faith
we are saved by grace.

Not only so, but we also rejoice in our sufferings,
because we know that suffering produces perseverance;
perseverance, character; and character, hope.

Through faith
we are saved by grace.

And hope does not disappoint us,
because you have poured out your love
into our hearts by the Holy Spirit.

Through faith
we are saved by grace.

You show us how much you love us:
while we were helpless, Christ died for the ungodly;
while we were still sinners, Christ died for us.

Through faith
we are saved by grace.

And through faith we stand in heaven and worship you
with angels and archangels, *saying*:
Holy, holy, holy Lord,
God of power and might,
heaven and earth are full of your glory.
Hosanna in the highest.

cf Romans 5.1-9

Father, you loved the world so much
that you sent your only Son
to die that we might live through him.
For his words from the cross,
we bring you thanks and praise:

'Forgive them …'
He forgave in the face of bitter hatred.
We give you thanks:
we praise your holy name.

'Today you shall be with me in paradise.'
He promised heaven to the forgiven sinner.
We give you thanks:
we praise your holy name.

'Mother, behold your Son …'
He loved his Mother to the last.
We give you thanks:
we praise your holy name.

'I thirst.'
He shared in our physical suffering and longing.
We give you thanks:
we praise your holy name.

'Why have you forsaken me?'
He entered into our testing and desolation.
We give you thanks:
we praise your holy name.

'It is finished!'
He completed his saving work,
and made the new covenant of love between God
        and his world.
We give you thanks:
we praise your holy name.

'Into your hands I commit my spirit.'
He won the victory over sin and death for ever.
We give you thanks:
we praise your holy name.

The words of Jesus from the cross could be omitted if necessary. Not every section need be used.

Our Lord Jesus Christ, risen from death,
we praise you for changed lives and new hopes at Easter.

You come to Mary in the garden,
and turn her tears into joy.
For your love and mercy we give you thanks:
we praise your holy name.

You come to the disciples in the upper room,
and turn their fear into courage.
For your love and mercy we give you thanks:
we praise your holy name.

You come to the disciples by the lakeside,
and turn their failure into faith.
For your love and mercy we give you thanks:
we praise your holy name.

You come to the disciples on the Emmaus road,
and turn their despair into hope.
For your love and mercy we give you thanks:
we praise your holy name.

You come to your people now,
and turn our weakness into triumph.
For your love and mercy we give you thanks:
we praise your holy name.

We give you thanks and praise
for the gospel we have received.
Christ died for our sins. Alleluia.
He is risen indeed. Alleluia.

Death comes to all through Adam,
and sin reigns for a time.
New life without end comes through Christ,
and he reigns for ever. Alleluia.
He is risen indeed. Alleluia.

Death, where is your victory?
Death, where is your sting?
Death is swallowed up in victory,
the victory you give us in Christ. Alleluia.
He is risen indeed. Alleluia.

We have been crucified with Christ,
and live his risen life,
to praise you for ever with angels and archangels:
**Holy, holy, holy Lord,
God of power and might,
heaven and earth are full of your glory.
Hosanna in the highest.**

cf 1 Corinthians 15

Thanks and praise to you,
Jesus Christ, Lord of all,
given the name above every other name.
Jesus, Lord of all,
we worship and adore you.

King of righteousness, King of peace,
enthroned at the right hand of Majesty on high;
Jesus, Lord of all,
we worship and adore you.

Great high priest, living for ever to intercede for us;
Jesus, Lord of all,
we worship and adore you.

Pioneer of our salvation, you bring us to glory
through your death and resurrection;
Jesus, Lord of all,
we worship and adore you.
Every knee bows to you;
every tongue confesses, you are Lord,
to the glory of God the Father.
Blessed is he who comes in the name of the Lord.
Hosanna in the highest.

If this Thanksgiving is used as an extended preface to a
eucharistic prayer, it should follow this form

Thanks and praise be to you, Lord of heaven,
for Jesus Christ your Son our Lord.
You gave him the name above every name,
so that we *say:*

Jesus is Lord of all:
we worship and adore you.

King of righteousness, King of peace,
enthroned at the right hand of Majesty on high;
Jesus is Lord of all:
we worship and adore you.

Great high priest, living for ever to intercede for us;
Jesus is Lord of all:
we worship and adore you.

Pioneer of our salvation, bringing us to glory
through death and resurrection;
Jesus is Lord of all:
we worship and adore you.
Every knee bows to him;
every tongue confesses, Jesus is Lord,
to the glory of God the Father.
Blessed is he who comes in the name of the Lord.
Hosanna in the highest.

Father, while all your creation groans with pain
like the pain of childbirth,
and longs to share the freedom of the children of God,
your Spirit pleads for us
in groans words cannot express.

Father in heaven
we give you thanks and praise.

The law of the Spirit brings us life in Christ,
and sets us free from the law of sin and death.

Father in heaven
we give you thanks and praise.

Like all who are led by your Spirit,
we are your children.
By your Spirit's power we cry, 'Abba, Father.'

Father in heaven
we give you thanks and praise.

[The Spirit confirms that we are your children,
fellow-heirs with Christ,
sharing his suffering now,
that we may share his glory.

Father in heaven
we give you thanks and praise.]

So by your Spirit we praise you for ever
and proclaim your glory with all the company of heaven,
    saying:
Holy, holy, holy Lord,
God of power and might,
heaven and earth are full of your glory.
Hosanna in the highest.

cf Romans 8.2, 14-25

*If this Thanksgiving is used as an extended preface to a
eucharistic prayer it begins with the first section, and 'Almighty
God ...' is omitted. If not, it begins with 'Almighty God ...'.*

[Father, we give you thanks and praise
through Jesus Christ our Lord
because you are God almighty,
creator of the world and everything in it,]

[Almighty God, creator of the world
and everything in it,]

Lord of heaven and earth,
you made the whole human race.
You have shown to us in Christ the mystery
    of your purpose:

you chose us all in Christ
to praise his glory.

You will bring all things together under Christ,
all things in heaven, all things on earth,
under him as head:
you chose us all in Christ
to praise his glory.

We have heard the word of truth,
the good news of salvation,
you have stamped us with the seal of your
     Spirit of promise:
you chose us all in Christ
to praise his glory.

We who once were far away
have been brought near by the blood of Christ:
you chose us all in Christ
to praise his glory.

He is the peace between us,
and has broken down the barrier of hostility.
He has made us one new humanity
and reconciled us to you by the cross:
you chose us all in Christ
to praise his glory.

He killed hostility and brought peace,
peace to all near at hand, peace to all far away:
you chose us all in Christ
to praise his glory.

Through him we come, by the Spirit,
to you, our Father in heaven, *singing*:
Holy, holy, holy Lord,
God of power and might,
heaven and earth are full of your glory.
Hosanna in the highest.
         cf Acts 17.25,26; Ephesians 1.9-13; 2.13-17

Church and mission
G82

Sovereign Lord, creator of heaven and earth and sea,
and everything in them,
we are your people, we give you thanks.
We praise your holy name.

You shake us and fill us with your Spirit,
you stretch out your hand to heal,
to do signs and wonders through the name of Jesus.
We are your people, we give you thanks.
We praise your holy name.

Jesus is the author of life,
handed over to be killed for us.
You raised him from the dead,
and made us whole in him.
We are your people, we give you thanks.
We praise your holy name.

Not many of us are wise by human standards,
not many are influential,
not many of noble birth.
We are your people, we give you thanks.
We praise your holy name.

You choose the foolish to shame the wise,
you choose the weak to shame the strong,
the lowly and despised so no one may boast before you.
We are your people, we give you thanks.
We praise your holy name.

Your strength is made perfect in our weakness.
Your grace is enough for us.
We are your people, we give you thanks.
We praise your holy name.

cf Acts 4.24,30,31; 3.15,13;
1 Corinthians 1.26-29; 2 Corinthians 12.9

Christian beginnings
Holy Spirit
G83

Father, for your gift of water in creation
we give you thanks and praise.

For your Spirit, sweeping over the waters,
bringing light and life
we give you thanks and praise.

For your Son, Jesus Christ our Lord,
baptized in the river Jordan
we give you thanks and praise.

For your new creation,
brought to birth by water and the Spirit
we give you thanks and praise.

For your grace bestowed upon us your children,
washing away our sins
we give you thanks and praise.

[So, Father, accept our sacrifice of praise;
by the power of your life-giving Spirit
bless these waters of your new creation.
Lord, receive our prayer.

May your servants who are washed in them
be made one with your Son,
who took the form of a servant.
Lord, receive our prayer.

May your Holy Spirit,
who has brought us to new birth in the family of
    your Church,
raise us in Christ, our anointed Lord,
to full and eternal life.
Lord, receive our prayer.]

For all might, majesty and dominion are yours,
now and for ever.
Alleluia. Amen.

*The paragraphs in brackets should be omitted when this
section is not being used in connection with sacramental water.*

Christian beginnings
Resurrection
G84

Blessed are you,
God and Father of our Lord Jesus Christ.
By your great mercy we have been born anew
        to a living hope
through the resurrection of your Son from the dead,
and to an inheritance which is imperishable, undefiled,
        and unfading.
Once we were no people, but now we are your people,
declaring your wonderful deeds in Christ,
who called us out of darkness into his marvellous light.

By the baptism of his death and resurrection
you gave birth to your Church,
delivered us from slavery to sin and death,
and made with us a new covenant.
At his ascension
you exalted him to sit at your right hand,
where according to his promise he is with us always,
baptizing us with the Holy Spirit and with fire.

The joy of resurrection fills the whole world,
and therefore we join with angels and archangels
and the whole company of heaven,
in the song of unending praise, *saying*:
Holy, holy, holy Lord,
God of power and might,
heaven and earth are full of your glory.
Hosanna in the highest.

Father, you gave up your Son for us all.
You give us all things with him;
you call us, justify us, glorify us.
Father in heaven
we give you thanks and praise.

Jesus Christ died, was raised to life,
and pleads for us at your right hand.
Who can separate us from your love?
Father in heaven
we give you thanks and praise.

For your sake we face death all day long.
In your world we face trouble and hardship,
persecution, famine, nakedness, danger and death.
Father in heaven
we give you thanks and praise.

But nothing separates us from your love:
neither death nor life,
neither angels nor demons,
neither the present nor the future,
nor any heavenly powers,
neither the world above nor the world below:
nothing in all creation can separate us
from your love in Jesus Christ.
Father in heaven
we give you thanks and praise.

In all these things we are more than conquerors
through him who loves us,
and has freed us from our sins
and made us a kingdom and priests
to serve you for ever,
with all the company of heaven, *saying*:
Holy, holy, holy Lord,
God of power and might,
heaven and earth are full of your glory.
Hosanna in the highest.

cf Romans 8.23-39

Living in the world
G86

Living God, Father of light,
hope of nations, friend of sinners,
builder of the city that is to come:
your love is made visible in Jesus Christ,
you bring home the lost, restore the sinner
and give dignity to the despised.

In the face of Jesus Christ
your light shines out,
flooding lives with goodness and truth,
gathering into one a divided and broken humanity.

With people from every race and nation,
with the Church of all the ages,
with apostles, evangelists and martyrs
we join the angels of heaven
in their unending song:
Holy, holy, holy Lord,
God of power and might,
heaven and earth are full of your glory.
Hosanna in the highest.

Heaven
G87

Blessed are you, gracious God,
creator of heaven and earth.
In the multitude of your saints,
you have surrounded us with a great
cloud of witnesses.
The glorious company of apostles praise you.
The noble fellowship of prophets praise you.
The white-robed army of martyrs praise you.
We your holy Church acclaim you.
In communion with angels and archangels,
and with all those who have served you
in every age,
and worship you now in heaven,
we raise our voices to proclaim your glory,
for ever praising you and *saying*:
Holy, holy, holy Lord,
God of power and might,
heaven and earth are full of your glory.
Hosanna in the highest.

Short prefaces

<table>
<tr><td>General
G88</td><td>And now we give you thanks
because as a mother tenderly gathers her children
you embraced a people as your own,
that with all the powers of heaven
we might find a voice to sing your praise.</td></tr>
</table>

General
G88

And now we give you thanks
because as a mother tenderly gathers her children
you embraced a people as your own,
that with all the powers of heaven
we might find a voice to sing your praise.

God in creation
G89

And now we give you thanks
because all things are of your making,
all times and seasons obey your laws,
but you have chosen to create us in your own image,
setting us over the whole world in all its wonder.
You have made us stewards of your creation,
to praise you day by day
for the marvels of your wisdom and power:
so earth unites with heaven
to sing the new song of creation:

All   **Holy, holy, holy Lord...**

Christ's coming
G90

And now we give you thanks
as we look forward to the day
when you will make all things new
as you come to judge the world.

Christ's coming
G91

And now we give you thanks
because when he humbled himself
to come among us in human flesh,
he fulfilled the plan you formed long ago
and opened for us the way of salvation.
So now we watch for the day,
knowing that the salvation promised us will be ours
when Christ our Lord will come again in glory.

Christ's coming
G92

And now we give you thanks
because you prepared the way of your Son Jesus Christ
by the preaching of your servant John the Baptist,
who proclaimed him as the Lamb of God, our Saviour.

Christ's coming
G93

And now we give you thanks
because your Son our Lord was awaited by the prophets,
announced by an angel,
conceived by a virgin,
and proclaimed at last to men and women of every race.

Christ's coming
G94

And now we give you thanks
because in his coming the day of our
    deliverance has dawned;
and through him you will make all things new,
as he comes in power and triumph to judge the world.

Christ's coming
G95

And now we give you thanks
because you sent him to redeem us from sin and death
and to make us inheritors of everlasting life;
that when he shall come again in power and great triumph
    to judge the world,
we may with joy behold his appearing,
and in confidence may stand before him.

Christ's coming
Heaven
G96

And now we give you thanks
that he is the King of glory,
who overcomes the sting of death
and opens the kingdom of heaven to all believers.
He is seated at your right hand in glory
and we believe that he will come to be our judge.

Christ's coming
G97

And now we give you thanks
because he came among us as a servant,
to be Emmanuel, your presence with us.

Christ's coming
G98

And now we give you thanks
as we await the promise of salvation,
the desire of all the nations,
and the fulfilment of your good purposes
before the world began.

Incarnation
G99

And now we give you thanks
because he shared our life in human form
from the warmth of Mary's womb
to the stillness of the grave.

Incarnation
G100

And now we give you thanks
because he was born in the poverty of a stable,
to make known the riches of your kingdom.

Incarnation **G**/0/	And now we give you thanks because, in the incarnation of the Word, a new light has dawned upon the world; you have become one with us that we might become one with you in your glorious kingdom.
Incarnation **G**/02	And now we give you thanks because, by the power of the Holy Spirit, he took our nature upon him and was born of the Virgin Mary his mother, that being himself without sin, he might make us clean from all sin.
Incarnation (Epiphany) **G**/03	And now we give you thanks because you have brought us from darkness to light and made your light shine in our hearts. You bring us to know your glory in the face of Jesus Christ. <div align="right">*cf 2 Corinthians 4.6*</div>
Incarnation (Epiphany) **G**/04	And now we give you thanks because in the wonder of the incarnation your eternal Word has brought to the eyes of faith a new and radiant vision of your glory. In him we see our God made visible and so are caught up in love of the God we cannot see.
Cross **G**/05	And now we give you thanks because he is the true passover lamb offered for us to take away the sin of the world.
Cross **G**/06	And now we give you thanks because you give us the spirit of discipline, that we may triumph over evil and grow in grace, as we prepare to celebrate the paschal mystery with mind and heart renewed.
Cross **G**/07	And now we give you thanks because each year you give us this joyful season when we prepare to celebrate the paschal mystery with mind and heart renewed. You give us a spirit of loving reverence for you and of willing service to our neighbour. As we recall the saving acts that give new life in Christ, you bring the image of your Son to perfection within our hearts.

Cross **G**108	And now we give you thanks because, for our salvation, he was obedient even to death on the cross. The tree of shame was made the tree of glory; and where life was lost, there life has been restored.

Cross **G**109	And now we give you thanks because for our sins he was lifted high upon the cross, that he might draw the whole world to himself; [and, by his suffering and death, became the source of eternal salvation for all who put their trust in him].

Cross *Ascension* **G**110	And now we give you thanks because you anointed Jesus Christ, your only Son, as priest and king. Crowned with thorns, he offered his life upon the cross, that he might draw all people into that kingdom where he now reigns in glory.

Cross **G**111	And now we give you thanks because you anointed Jesus Christ, your only Son, as the eternal priest and king of all. As a priest he offered up his life on the cross, that by his one sacrifice he might present to you an eternal kingdom; a kingdom of truth and life; a kingdom of justice, love and peace.

Resurrection **G**112		And now we give you thanks because Christ is the victim who dies no more, the Lamb, once slain, who lives for ever, our advocate in heaven to plead our cause, exalting us there to join the angels and archangels, with all the company of heaven for ever praising you and *saying*:
	All	**Holy, holy, holy Lord …**

Resurrection **G**113	And now we give you thanks because by his death he broke the power of sin and made us holy through his blood.

Resurrection
G114

And now we give you thanks
because by his death he has destroyed death,
and by his rising again he has restored to us eternal life.

Resurrection
G115

And now we give you thanks
because by his victory over the grave
he burst the gates of death for ever.

Resurrection
G116

But chiefly are we bound to praise you
because you raised him gloriously from the dead.
For he is the true paschal lamb who was offered for us,
and has taken away the sin of the world.
By his death he has destroyed death,
and by rising to life again he has restored to us
    everlasting life.

Ascension
G117

And now we give you thanks
because you have highly exalted him,
and given him the name which is above all other names,
that at the name of Jesus every knee shall bow.

Ascension
Living in the world
G118

And now we give you thanks
because Jesus has been given all authority,
in heaven and on earth,
to present to you, his Father,
a kingdom of truth, holiness and everlasting love.

Ascension
G119

And now we give you thanks
because he humbled himself to die on a cross;
but you raised him high
and gave him the name above all other names,
Jesus Christ our Lord.

cf Philippians 2.8,9

Ascension
G120

And now we give you thanks
because, after his most glorious resurrection,
he appeared to his disciples,
and in their sight ascended into heaven
    to prepare a place for us;
that where he is, thither we might also ascend,
and reign with him in glory.

Holy Spirit **G121**	And now we give you thanks because through him we receive the Spirit of adoption, affirming us as your children, and crying 'Abba, Father'. <div align="right">*cf Romans 8.15*</div>

Holy Spirit
Ascension
G122
	And now we give you thanks
	that, after he had ascended far above all heavens,
	and was seated at the right hand of your majesty,
	he sent forth upon the universal Church your holy
	    and life-giving Spirit;
	that through his glorious power
	the joy of the everlasting gospel might go forth
	    into all the world.

Holy Spirit *Church and mission* **G123**	And now we give you thanks because he breathed upon his disciples the power of your Spirit to proclaim the good news to all peoples. <div align="right">*cf John 20.21,22*</div>
Word **G124**	And now we give you thanks because the wisdom of your word sustains all things and reveals you to us in your fullness.
Church and mission **G125**	And now we give you thanks because by the Holy Spirit you lead us into all truth, and give us power to proclaim your gospel to the nations and to serve you as a royal priesthood.
Church and mission **G126**	And now we give you thanks because he is the true vine, your chosen one, in whom we are joined to bear fruit in plenty.
Christian beginnings **G127**	And now we give you thanks because through him we are saved for ever and baptized into your service.
Lament *Cross* **G128**	And now we give you thanks because he was tempted in every way as we are, yet did not sin. By his grace we are able to triumph over every evil, and to live no longer for ourselves alone, but for him who died for us and rose again.

Relationships and healing
Incarnation
G129

And now we give you thanks
because in his earthly childhood
you entrusted him to the care of a human family.
In Mary and Joseph you give us an example of love and
    devotion to him,
and also a pattern of family life.

Relationships and healing
G130

And now we give you thanks
because [a man leaves his father and mother
and is joined to his wife:
you make them one flesh;
and because] you put us together in families,
to grasp your love and forgiveness,
reflected in those around us,
and as we grow,
you prepare to bring us into the glorious freedom
    of your children,
as brothers and sisters of Jesus Christ.

Genesis 2.24; Romans 8.17,22

Relationships and healing
G131

And now we give you thanks
because you have made the union between Christ
    and his Church
a pattern for the marriage between husband and wife.

Relationships and healing
G132

All glory, honour, thanks and praise
be given to you, creator of heaven and earth.
When you made us in your image,
creating us male and female,
you gave us the gift of marriage.
When sin marred that image
you healed our brokenness,
giving your Son to die for us.
Therefore we raise our voices,
with all who have served you in every age,
to proclaim the glory of your name:

All **Holy, holy, holy Lord ...**

Relationships and healing
G133

And now we give you thanks
because in the covenant of marriage
you show us your divine love,
a mirror of your will for all creation
made new and united to you for ever.

Relationships and healing
G134

And now we give you thanks
because you provide medicine to heal our sickness,
and the leaves of the tree of life
for the healing of the nations,
anointing us with your healing power
so that we may be the first fruits of your new creation.

Relationships and healing
G135

And now we give you thanks
that, taking upon himself our human nature,
he shared our joy and our tears,
bore all our sickness,
and carried all our sorrows.
Through death he brought us
to the life of his glorious resurrection,
giving for frailty eternal strength,
and restoring in us the image of your glory.

Relationships and healing
Lament
G136

And now we give you thanks
that you have shown the greatness of your love for us
by sending him to share our human nature
and accomplish our forgiveness.
He embraces us in our weakness,
he suffers with the sick and the rejected,
and, bringing your healing to the world,
he rescues us from every evil.

Relationships and healing
G137

And now we give you thanks
that through him the sick are healed:
the blind regain their sight,
the deaf hear,
the lame walk,
and the outcast are brought home;
the poor receive good news
and the dead are raised to life.

Relationships and healing
Lament
G138

It is right to give you thanks
in sickness and in health,
in suffering and in joy,
through Christ our Saviour and our Redeemer,
who, as the Good Samaritan,
tends the wounds of body and spirit.
He stands by us and pours out for our healing
the oil of consolation and the wine of renewed hope,
turning the darkness of our pain
into the dawning light of his kingdom.
And now we join with saints and angels
for ever praising you and *saying*:

All   **Holy, holy, holy Lord …**

Living in the world G139	And now we give you thanks because he broke bread with those whom others scorned and when the multitude were hungry he fed them abundantly.
Living in the world G140	And now we give you thanks because you are one God in three persons and you draw us into the unity of your kingdom, where all divisions of age or achievement, race or language are overcome by your love.
Living in the world G141	And now we give you thanks because you call us to live in your city while we look for the city which is to come, designed and built by you, with eternal foundations, to which we journey as citizens of heaven. *Hebrews 13.14; 11.10*
Living in the world G142	And now we give you thanks because he gave up his life outside the city gate and opened for all the way to heaven. *Hebrews 13.12*
Heaven G143	And now we give you thanks because in him you have received us as your sons and daughters, joined us in one fellowship with the saints, and made us citizens of your kingdom.
Heaven G144	And now we give you thanks through Jesus Christ our Lord. In him who rose from the dead our hope of resurrection dawned. The sting of death has been removed by the glorious promise of his risen life.
Heaven G145	Blessed are you, gracious God, creator of heaven and earth, giver of life, and conqueror of death. By his death on the cross, your Son Jesus Christ offered the one true sacrifice for sin, breaking the power of evil and putting death to flight.

[With all your saints
we give you thanks and praise.]

Through his resurrection from the dead
you have given us new birth into a living hope,
into an inheritance which is imperishable,
undefiled, and unfading.
[With all your saints
we give you thanks and praise.]

The joy of resurrection fills the universe,
and so we join with angels and archangels,
with [*N and*] all your faithful people,
evermore praising you and *saying*:

All　　**Holy, holy, holy Lord…**

Heaven
G146

And now we give you thanks
for the hope to which you call us in your Son,
that following in the faith of all your saints,
we may run with perseverance the race that is
　　　set before us,
and with them receive the unfading crown of glory.

Heaven
G147

And now we give you thanks
because through him you have given us the hope of a
　　　glorious resurrection;
so that, although death comes to us all,
yet we rejoice in the promise of eternal life;
for to your faithful people life is changed, not taken away;
and when our mortal flesh is laid aside
an everlasting dwelling place is made ready for us in heaven.

Heaven
G148

And now we give you thanks
through Jesus Christ our Lord.
In him who rose from the dead
our hope of resurrection dawned.
The sting of death has been drawn
by the glorious promise of his risen life.

the peace

H   The Peace

Stories from the four churches

At **St Ann's** the Peace is the climax to which the first half of the service moves. Today the president uses a versicle and response echoing the theme of the service. This is used for a month or more during the same teaching theme or season of the Church's year and is printed on the notice sheet. Members of the congregation are encouraged to greet one another with it outside the church – or even over the telephone! The response 'and also with you' is the signal for a lot of movement in the church as people shake hands, hug or greet one another in other ways. There is some sensitivity to people who want to remain on their own, though the PCC recently rejected a suggestion that one corner of the church be set aside as a peace-free zone. It is good to see people using the time to share with others something of what God has said to them through the preaching, and to discover what the younger members of the church have been doing in their groups. People have been taught what the Peace is for and how to use it (see pages 270–271). At present they are experimenting with the Peace lasting for fifteen to twenty minutes, with refreshments being served, after which some who are not yet communicants leave. This has helped to encourage enquirers and those seeking baptism for their children, for instance, to experience a freer style of service which is shorter and does not commit them to receiving communion. Some, however, say that communion feels like an afterthought rather than the climax of the service. The service begins again with some gentle music and chorus singing, during which people take their seats as they prepare for the Thanksgiving.

At **St Bartholomew's** today the service has been led by one of the lay people. At the end of the intercessions she glances at her watch. The vicar is taking the service at one of the other churches in the group and often arrives here towards the end of the intercessions. If he does, it is natural for him to say the words of the Peace and it acts partly as a greeting announcing his arrival. But he must have met sheep on the road or have been talking too long at the other church, so the lay leader says the words of the Peace and the small congregation spend a few moments greeting one another. If they are short of time, the Peace can be briefer and more formal – living together in a village means they have already greeted one another today. Enter the vicar, at speed, just as the hymn is being announced. 'Peace be with you all!' he shouts, with a wave of the hand, and they all reply. Much better than 'Good morning everyone'!

The clergy at **St Christopher's** use a full range of seasonal introductory words to the Peace, occasionally following the pattern of the Maundy Thursday service in the seasonal material, using a short collect about peace instead of the introductory sentence. The deacon says, 'Let us offer one another a sign of peace' and sometimes wonders why people need this reminder what to do: why can't they just get on with it? But when they were moving away from the (bad old?) days when the Peace was first exchanged in the sanctuary and then brought down to the people by a server greeting the person at the end of each row, these action words were needed to give people permission to move on their own. And occasionally they have the Peace later in the service, before the distribution. Some say that a general handshake is not appropriate at that point, so the 'Let us offer ...' words are not used.

The vicar at **St Dodo's** is used to commanding his congregation, but has been having a battle over the Peace, with some resisting his attempts to make it more demonstrative. 'We will all stand for the Peace. The peace ...' he bellows ...'We will all exchange a sign of peace.' And when one couple on the front row remain kneeling (in peace), he marches over, lays a hand on each head and says, 'The peace of the Lord be with you!' which is not quite a demonstration of peace. There has never been any teaching on why or how to exchange the Peace (see section below). There is embarrassment as one lady, taught in a more formal church, extends both hands tentatively towards a large man bearing down on her with arms flung out ready to hug her. She ducks. In one corner, some of the younger people don't seem to have been taught the difference between the Peace and snogging. And those who know one another well are engaging in noisy back-slapping and handshaking, ignoring those who are not known to them, who stand in sheepish silence waiting for the thing to be over. But that is the problem. The vicar is deep in (no doubt important) conversation with the church treasurer and has not thought how to announce the next hymn over the hubbub. So he shouts ... .

What the Peace is for and how to use it

Some of the things people at **St Ann's** have been taught:

* time to get straight with God before coming to communion (so you may need to be on your own, perhaps grappling with something from the sermon);
* time to get straight with other people before coming to communion (so you may need to go and make your peace, or ask forgiveness from someone at the other end of the church). This is what the Prayer Book calls being 'in love and charity with your neighbours';

* time to share with others something for prayer (so you may need to ask one of the leaders for the laying on of hands for healing, or some other individual ministry, later in the service);
* time to share with others something for praise (so you may have something that God has been doing with you during the week that will contribute to the praise of the whole church);
* time to greet people you do not know (so you may need to help someone else, perhaps someone new to the church, feel part of the Christian family at communion, rather than greeting only your close friends);
* time to be sensitive to the mood of others (so you may need to refrain from approaching someone who is clearly putting themselves right with God).

How to stop the Peace

Some suggestions:
* When announcing the Peace, announce the hymn after it: 'At the end of the Peace we shall sing ...'. Then all that is needed is a nod to the organist, or an agreement that the organist takes the decision when to start.
* The organist plays the opening bars of the hymn, and stops while the announcement is made.
* Some gentle music is played, perhaps a chorus which people can join in. As this ends the hymn is announced.

Note to the resources

Note 16 in *Common Worship* Holy Communion provides for the Peace to be used at other points than the one provided. It can be used as the opening greeting, or as part of the Communion rite before the breaking of bread or the Dismissal. The Peace may be introduced with a suitable sentence; some are provided in the seasonal provisions, and more here. The pattern is easy to copy, for instance to provide words for special occasions or to echo some particular teaching in the sermon. The introductory words should not normally be a prayer but an encouragement, based on Scripture, to minister peace to one another. The second sentence, 'The peace of the Lord be always with you', is best kept as a standard introduction to the response, but may be seasonally varied, as for example, 'The peace of the risen Lord be always with you.'

Introductory words to the Peace

General
H1
God will speak peace to his people,
to those who turn to him in their hearts.
The peace of the Lord be always with you.

cf Psalm 85.8; 1 Samuel 12.20

General
H2
God has called us to live in peace.
The peace of the Lord be always with you.

cf 1 Corinthians 7.17

General
H3
The Apostle Paul said:
'Aim for perfection,
be of one mind, live in peace.
Greet one another with a holy kiss.'
The peace of the Lord be always with you.

cf 2 Corinthians 13.11

General
H4
Let the peace of Christ rule in your hearts,
since as members of one body you are called to peace.
The peace of the Lord be always with you.

cf Colossians 3.15

General
H5
Blessed are the peacemakers:
they shall be called children of God.
We meet in the name of Christ and share his peace.
The peace of the Lord be always with you.

cf Matthew 5.19

General
H6
God is love
and those who live in love live in God
and God lives in them.
The peace of the Lord be always with you.

General
H7
'Where two or three are gathered together in my name,'
says the Lord, 'there am I in the midst of them.'
The peace of the Lord be always with you.

General
H8
We are all one in Christ Jesus.
We belong to him through faith,
heirs of the promise of the Spirit of peace.
The peace of the Lord be always with you.

| General
Heaven
H9 | Jesus says to his disciples,
'Peace I leave with you; my peace I give you.
Not as the world gives do I give to you.
Let not your hearts be troubled or afraid.'
The peace of the Lord be always with you. |

cf John 14.27

| Father, Son
and Spirit
H10 | Peace to you from God who is our Father.
Peace from Jesus Christ who is our peace.
Peace from the Holy Spirit who gives us life.
The peace of the triune God be always with you. |

| Christ's coming
H11 | In the tender mercy of our God,
the dayspring from on high shall break upon us,
to give light to those who dwell in darkness
and in the shadow of death,
and to guide our feet into the way of peace.
The peace of the Lord be always with you. |

cf Luke 1.78,79

| Christ's coming
H12 | May the God of peace make you completely holy,
ready for the coming of our Lord Jesus Christ.
The peace of the Lord be always with you. |

cf 1 Thessalonians 5.23

| Christ's coming
H13 | Blessed is the king who comes in the name of the Lord.
Peace in heaven and glory in the highest.
The peace of the Lord be always with you. |

| Incarnation
H14 | Glory to God in the highest,
and peace on earth to all on whom his favour rests.
The peace of the Lord be always with you. |

cf Luke 2.14

| Incarnation
H15 | Unto us a child is born, unto us a son is given,
and his name shall be called the Prince of Peace.
The peace of the Lord be always with you. |

cf Isaiah 9.6

| Incarnation
H16 | Christ came and proclaimed the gospel,
peace to those who are far off
and peace to those who are near.
The peace of the Lord be always with you. |

Incarnation	Our Saviour Christ is the Prince of Peace.
H17	Of the increase of his government and of peace
	there shall be no end.
	The peace of the Lord be always with you.

cf Isaiah 9.6,7

Cross	Since we are justified by faith,
H18	we have peace with God through our Lord Jesus Christ,
	who has given us access to his grace.
	The peace of the Lord be always with you.

cf Romans 5.1

Cross	Once we were far off
H19	but now in union with Christ Jesus we have been brought near
	through the shedding of Christ's blood,
	for he is our peace.
	The peace of the Lord be always with you.

cf Ephesians 2.13

Cross	Jesus says: 'Peace I leave with you; my peace I give to you.
H20	Do not let your hearts be troubled, neither let them be afraid.'
	The peace of the Lord be always with you.

cf John 14.27

Cross	Christ is our peace.
H21	He has reconciled us to God
	in one body by the cross.
	We meet in his name and share his peace.
	The peace of the Lord be always with you.

cf Ephesians 2.15,16

Resurrection	The risen Christ came and stood among his disciples
H22	and said, 'Peace be with you.'
	Then were they glad when they saw the Lord. Alleluia.
	The peace of the Lord be always with you.

cf John 20.19

Ascension	Jesus says: 'Peace I leave with you; my peace I give to you.
H23	If you love me, rejoice because I am going to the Father.' Alleluia.
	The peace of the Lord be always with you.

Ascension	The risen Lord now reigns at God's right hand.
H24	He is the Prince of Peace.
	The peace of the risen Lord be always with you.

Holy Spirit	We are baptized into Christ:
Christian	let us live in the Spirit of Christ.
beginnings	The peace of the Lord be always with you.
H25	

Holy Spirit	The mind of sinful nature is death;
H26	the mind controlled by the Spirit is life and peace.
	The peace of the Lord be always with you.

cf Romans 8.6

Holy Spirit	God has made us one in Christ.
H27	He has set his seal upon us and, as a pledge of what is to come,
	has given the Spirit to dwell in our hearts. Alleluia.
	The peace of the Lord be always with you.

cf Ephesians 1.13,14

Holy Spirit	The fruit of the Spirit is love, joy, peace.
H28	If we live in the Spirit, let us walk in the Spirit.
	The peace of the Lord be always with you.

cf Galatians 5.22,23

Church and	We are the body of Christ.
mission	**By one Spirit we were baptized into one body.**
H29	Keep the unity of the Spirit in the bond of peace.
	We are bound by the love of Christ.
	The peace of the Lord be always with you.

cf 1 Corinthians 12.13; Ephesians 4.3

Church and	We are the body of Christ.
mission	In the one Spirit we were all baptized into one body.
H30	Let us then pursue all that makes for peace
	and builds up our common life.
	The peace of the Lord be always with you.

cf 1 Corinthians 12.13; Romans 14.19

Church and	We are all one in Christ Jesus.
mission	We belong to him through faith,
H31	heirs of the promise of the Spirit of peace.
	The peace of the Lord be always with you.

cf Galatians 3.28

Church and	God has reconciled us to himself through Christ
mission	and given us the ministry of reconciliation.
H32	The peace of the Lord be always with you.

cf 2 Corinthians 5.18

Relationships
and healing
Church and
mission
H33
Jesus said:
'Love one another.
As I have loved you,
so you are to love one another.'
The peace of the Lord be always with you.

cf John 15.12

Relationships
and healing
Church and
mission
H34
Let love be genuine. Never pay back evil for evil.
As far as it lies with you, live at peace with everyone.
The peace of the Lord be always with you.

cf Romans 12.9,17,18

Relationships
and healing
Church and
mission
H35
To crown all things there must be love,
to bind all together and complete the whole.
Let the peace of Christ rule in our hearts.
The peace of the Lord be always with you.

cf Colossians 3.14,15

Living in
the world
H36
God calls us to peace:
in God's justice is our peace.
Christ calls us to be God's people:
in Christ is our peace.
The peace of the Lord be always with you.

cf Ephesians 2.14,15

Living in
the world
H37
Blessed be Christ, the Prince of Peace.
He breaks down the walls that divide us:
praise Christ who is our peace!
The peace of the Lord be always with you.

Living in
the world
Christ's coming
H38
Peacemakers who sow in peace raise a harvest of
        righteousness.
The peace of the Lord be always with you.

cf James 3.18

Holy
Communion
H39
The kingdom of God is not a matter of eating
        and drinking,
but of righteousness, peace and joy in the Holy Spirit.
The peace of the Lord be always with you.

cf Romans 14.17

Heaven
H40
We are fellow-citizens with the saints and of the household of God,
through Christ our Lord, who came and preached peace
        to those who were far off and those who were near.
The peace of the Lord be always with you.

cf Ephesians 2.17,19

Heaven
H41

May the God of peace sanctify you:
may he so strengthen your hearts in holiness
that you may be blameless before him
at the coming of our Lord Jesus with his saints.
The peace of the Lord be always with you.

cf I Thessalonians 5.23; 3.13

Heaven
Christ's coming
H42

May the God of peace make you perfect and holy,
that you may be kept safe and blameless
in spirit, soul and body,
for the coming of our Lord Jesus Christ.
The peace of the Lord be always with you.

cf I Thessalonians 5.23

action and movement

▌ Action and Movement

Stories from the four churches

Today is Pentecost Sunday at **St Ann's**. The church feels very different. Everyone is wearing something red, and it feels as if the whole church is ablaze with colour. The focus is an enormous crown suspended over the communion table, which was put there on Ascension Day to symbolize the kingship of Christ. Now there are flames all around and inside it as the theme moves on to the Lord, the Spirit. St Ann's has been having a discussion about the use of symbols and symbolic action, and divided them into three groups (see pages 280–281). Today, the small dance group interprets a hymn to the Holy Spirit while the congregation remains seated to sing, so that they can see and be involved in the movement.

At **St Bartholomew's**, just before the Peace, there is a noise at the back of the church, and the children enter in a procession with musical instruments (recorders, percussion etc.). This used to happen during the hymn after the Peace, but was brought forward so that the children could share in exchanging the Peace. At the end are two children with bread and wine which they take up to the sanctuary. The congregation have been learning about being on the move, and sometimes process outside the church, for example on Palm Sunday accompanied by a donkey.

At **St Christopher's** there is deliberate and systematic use of symbols. They have decided which symbols require explanation and which are self-explanatory: they have learnt that taking too much time to explain to people what they are doing simply interrupts the worship, and that not everything needs explaining. They have also learnt not to be minimalistic about their symbols and actions. So, for instance, the fire on the Saturday night before Easter Day, from which the candles were lit during the Easter Vigil, was a large bonfire outside the church. Similarly, the movement in church is not over-solemn and slow: they recognize that movement is necessary and should be done well. Today they are trying something different as, at the offertory, people come from different corners of the church carrying the altar cloth, chalice and ciborium, bread and wine, and proceed to lay the table which has been bare until that point.

The church is sufficiently large for the whole congregation to get up and move to different parts of it for different sections of the service. This is more like a moving group of people than a solemn two-by-two procession. They did this very successfully at Epiphany and found that the children could take part more easily in something that moved from place to place.

Though the usual symbolism at **St Dodo's** is that of dead flowers and failed light bulbs, things look brighter today with a fairly full church for the Christingle service. The children go to the sanctuary step to hand over money in return for lighted Christingles (no one seems to have thought through the implications of the symbolism of this exchange). Because things seem to be moving very slowly, with small children finding it difficult to hold the Christingle orange upright, the vicar sends some of them off in one direction and some in another, and the two processions meet amid great and dangerous confusion towards the back of the church, where angry parents, afraid of the danger, have to intervene to sort things out. They remember what happened on Palm Sunday a few years ago when an acolyte set fire to a palm frond with his candle. A server with great presence of mind picked up the burning palm but instead of throwing it on the floor and stamping the fire out, tried (solemnly but with difficulty!) to process out of church holding it in front of him, with the result that his hair was very badly singed. Remember the rule: when processing out of church with a burning palm, walk backwards.

Processions: some questions

Where is the procession going from and where to?

How will they know the way? Is it obvious or do they need leading by crucifer/acolytes/verger/musicians?

Processions should have a purpose, not just wander about. What is the purpose for this procession? What expectation do we want the procession to create? What is going to happen when it arrives? Is there a gift to receive, a banner to display, a prayer to say?

In what order are people to move off? There is no particular reason why the important people have to come at the end. It may often work best if they go first.

Symbols and actions

Symbols can be of very many different sorts:

1 **Symbols people bring with them**

For example, wearing clothes symbolizing respectability, purity, or some aspect of the season (e.g. bonnets at Easter or something white at Christmas), or simply being visually the people of God, a crowd or a number of smaller groups relating together.

2 Symbols and actions which are individual

Holding a book for worship (what is the message of that?). Bowing, making the sign of the cross, distributing nails to people on Good Friday, or candles at Candlemas: though these are individual, they also express relationship and unity among the congregation.

3 Symbols and actions uniting the congregation

Actions done together at the same time, such as standing and kneeling, exchanging the Peace, holding hands etc., are a way of drawing the congregation together.

Pictures, statues, icons, frontals and banners should be unitive and gather the attention of the congregation towards God – they can sometimes be fragmentary and disperse the congregation's thoughts and responses. Should some things be moved away for some sorts of service, as happens with the stripping of the Holy Table on Maundy Thursday?

Dance is also something which can unite or divide. It might involve one person or a group 'performing' something which is usually rehearsed, for example as an interpretation of a reading or song or prayer. It can involve spontaneous solo dancers: this is usually easier during a hymn or song, expressing praise to God and often assisting the congregation to gather up their praise and worship. Large numbers of a congregation might also dance spontaneously to praise God, sometimes moving out to occupy the aisles and other spaces in the church.

Distributing communion: stories from the four churches

At **St Ann's**, five of the leadership team come and stand around the table to receive communion, which they pass from one to the other. Then, together with the president, they distribute communion in three pairs moving right round the rail, returning round the far side of the communion table to the point at which they started. The bread is part of a loaf, which they break as they go. (They have been taught that the breaking – 'fraction' – was something functional rather than ceremonial in the New Testament descriptions, and that the custom of chopping the bread into little bits before the service starts really undermines the strong image of unity in the body conveyed by 'We break this bread … we, though many, are one body…'). As they pass the children, they lay one hand on them and pray for them; one or two of the parents break a piece off their own bread to share with their children. At the side of the long rail, one or two people remain kneeling, waiting for the ministry of the laying on of hands for healing. This is usually done by the same group of people, though others may join in or come forward to take over the distributing of communion if that seems in danger of being held up.

At **St Bartholomew's** the vicar is away, and the service is led by a Reader. During a hymn the consecrated bread and wine are brought from the church in the next village, and placed on the altar. There is no consecration prayer, but the Reader uses the service from *Public Worship with Communion by Extension*. The Reader distributes the sacrament, following the local custom of saying the longer BCP words to the whole rail of people, followed by brief words to each. The communicants at the rail wait until everyone has received, and all depart together. The sidespeople encourage forward only the right number to fill the rail each time, so there is no queue.

The distribution at **St Christopher's** is equally well organized, with one of the wardens gradually moving back down the church telling people when to go forward, and a server some yards from the rail to direct people where to go. The whole thing moves very smoothly. The three lay ministers of communion are not robed. One shares the distribution of the wafers with the president, and two follow with the cup. Everyone knows – because it is regularly announced – that those who come to the rail holding a book are not receiving the sacrament. When there is a large service, the congregation have got used to receiving communion standing, from two stations, one at the front of the church and one half way down the nave. Those who give the cup to people taller than themselves have realized that it is easier to put the cup into people's hands. At the end of the distribution, three people who have the bishop's permission to take communion to the sick come forward, with their pyxes, and after a prayer they go straight out to perform their ministry.

At **St Dodo's**, no one is quite sure who is meant to be helping the president to distribute communion, so after a hurried conversation at the back of the church (and rejecting one of the women who offers to do it, because they think she is unsuitably dressed), one of the wardens moves forward as the president glares anxiously down the church. He has to lift the centre part of the rail out in order to get into the sanctuary, and by the time he arrives the president has begun to distribute wafers to the four members of the choir at one side of the rail. The warden is not quite sure whether he has the authority to take the cup from the table, so there is a hiatus. The delay puts a certain amount of pressure on the operation, and the distribution proceeds at a rapid pace, so much so that some people do not have any time to pray when they kneel down before the wafer is thrust at them. Those distributing also have no time to pray for each person, as disasters follow thick and fast. The president drops a wafer and the warden, following close behind, puts his foot on it (or was he trying to conceal it?). He then discovers a fly struggling to get out of the cup and tries to get it out with a flick of his finger, without even turning around so that his action is not quite so visible! The warden next gives the cup to a young woman carrying a small child who immediately reaches out a violent arm, knocking the cup so that a quantity of wine spills down the woman's front. A considerable amount of embarrassment and mopping up with purificators ensues, all of which might have been avoided had the warden, perhaps wise from previous encounters, held the child's hand or retained a firm hold on the cup. Before long, the wine runs out and he simply goes to the credence table and fills up with more.

Authorization of ministers of the sacrament

Canon B 12.3 says:

> No person shall distribute the holy sacrament of the Lord's Supper to the people unless he shall have been ordained in accordance with the provisions of Canon C 1, or is otherwise authorized by Canon or unless he has been specially authorized to do so by the bishop acting under such regulations as the General Synod may make from time to time.

The Church Assembly Regulations made in 1969 are still in operation:

> 1. An application to the Bishop to authorize ... a baptized and confirmed person to distribute the Holy Sacrament in any parish shall be made in writing by the incumbent or priest-in-charge of the parish and supported by the churchwardens, and shall specify the name and give relevant particulars of the person to whom the application relates.

> 2. It shall be in the discretion of the Bishop to grant or refuse the application and to specify the circumstances or conditions in or on which the authority is to be available.

Blessings

Where children and adults who are not receiving communion are being blessed at the rail, it is good to vary the form of words used. Some possibilities are:
* 'The Lord bless you and keep you';
* 'The Lord bless you and give you joy in all you do for him';
* 'The Lord bless and take care of you *both*' (for example, with a married couple when one of them is receiving communion and the other not);
* 'The Lord bless and strengthen you as you seek to follow him' (especially suitable for those preparing for baptism or confirmation);
* 'Christ fill you with his joy and peace';
* 'The blessing of Jesus Christ rest upon you';
* 'May God be with you';
* 'May Jesus Christ bless you'.

(The last four may be more suitable for lay people to use in situations where there is some sensitivity about whether or not they may use a more direct form of blessing.)

As well as words there should be some gesture of inclusion. Some ministers prefer to lay a hand on the shoulder rather than the head, to avoid episcopal or priestly connotations, but laying hands on heads is a biblical gesture by no means confined to priests, and is unlikely to upset lay people. Another possibility is to make the sign of the cross, on the forehead for example. With very small children, rather than simply patting them on the head from on high, it may help to get down to their level and greet them briefly before blessing them. But it is best not to get into long conversations about teddy bears.

Training for those who distribute communion

This should be theological, spiritual and practical. It might include:

* Something on theology and history;
* Knowledge of differing approaches to the sacrament within the Church, so that those who distribute are prepared for different customs and can be sensitive to those with different views from their own;
* Knowing the words by heart;
* Prayer before and silently for each person during the distribution;
* Recognizing those in distress;
* How to distribute bread without dropping crumbs;
* The best way to cope with intinction (whether by the president or by the communicant taking the wafer and waiting until the cup comes round);
* Giving the cup to women with wide-brimmed hats;
* What to do if wine is spilt;
* How to tell the president quietly and without attracting attention if the bread or wine is running out;
* What to do when the distribution is finished.

Note to the resources

These, or other similar responses, may be used at the beginning of the service, at the intercessions, at the presentation of the gifts, or before the blessing and dismissal. Some of them are suitable only when gifts of money or tokens of the life and work of the people, or of some particular aspect of service, are to be collected and/or offered to God. These might be placed on a table in the middle of the congregation or presented to the presiding minister. The last three prayers here come from 'Prayers at the Preparation of the Table' on page 291 of *Common Worship,* where more prayers suitable for use in the Holy Communion may be found.

Words for dedication

Some of these responses might also be used for the dedication of church officers and leaders, PCC members, stewardship or mission visitors, etc. This may take place at the intercessions or at the Peace, and the minister may first say, 'As mission visitors (or whatever …) we dedicate *ourselves/you* to God's service.' For an Affirmation of Commitment, see page 169.

11 Christ has offered for all time a single sacrifice for sins.
    He is seated at the right hand of God.

    Through him let us offer up a sacrifice of praise to God:
    the fruit of lips that acknowledge his name.

    Do not forget to do good and share what you have.
    Such sacrifices are pleasing to God.

12 The free gift of God is eternal life in Christ Jesus our Lord.
    By his mercy we present our whole lives to God as a living sacrifice.

13 Lord Jesus Christ, you emptied yourself, taking the form of a servant.
    Through your love, make us servants of one another.

    Lord Jesus Christ, for our sake you became poor.
    May our lives and gifts enrich the life of your world.

14 Though many, we form one body in Christ.
    We belong to one another.

    By God's grace we have different gifts.
    We will use them in faith.

    Rejoice in hope, stand firm in trouble, be constant in prayer.
    Filled with his Spirit we will serve the Lord.

15 Blessed are you, Lord, God of all creation;
    through your goodness we have this money to offer,
    the fruit of our labour and of the skills you have given us.
    Take us and our possessions to do your work in the world.
    Blessed be God for ever.

16 God of all goodness and grace,
   receive the gifts we offer;
   and grant that our whole life
   may give you glory and praise;
   through Jesus Christ our Lord.
   Amen.

17 Let us pray.
   Gracious God, accept these gifts,
   and with them our lives,
   to be used in your service;
   through Jesus Christ our Lord.
   Amen.

18 Yours, Lord, is the greatness, the power,
   the glory, the splendour, and the majesty;
   for everything in heaven and on earth is yours.
   All things come from you,
   and of your own do we give you.

19 Generous God,
   creator, redeemer, sustainer,
   at your table we present this money,
   symbol of the work you have given us to do;
   use it, use us,
   in the service of your world
   to the glory of your name.
   Amen.

110 God of life, saviour of the poor,
    receive with this money
    gratitude for your goodness,
    penitence for our pride
    and dedication to your service
    in Jesus Christ our Lord.
    Amen.

conclusion

J Conclusion

Stories from the four churches

Today at **St Ann's** the whole service has been centred around the theme of God's love. After the distribution of Communion, there is silent prayer, and then the whole congregation joins together in the Post Communion prayer:

> Lord, we have broken your bread,
> and received your life.
> By the power of your Spirit
> keep us always in your love ... (J35 below)

The first verse of 'We are marching in the light of God' is sung followed by the Blessing and Dismissal from the chancel step, and then the whole congregation go out singing the rest of the hymn.

At **St Bartholomew's** today there has been a baptism, so the Baptism Post Communion prayer is used (page 362 in *Common Worship*), followed by the threefold Blessing, 'The Father, whose glory fills the heavens, cleanse you by his holiness and send you to proclaim his word ...' (J98 below). One of the churchwardens then presents a lighted candle to the parents of the baby who has just been baptized. He uses the words on page 363 of *Common Worship*. The minister says the Dismissal, and leads the baptism party out first with the candle held high, as a symbol of bearing the light of Christ into the world.

At **St Christopher's** after the Post Communion prayers there is a recessional hymn during which the choir move to the back of the church. The president pronounces the Blessing from the sanctuary, and moves to the door as the Deacon says the Dismissal from the back of the church.

The president at **St Dodo's** starts the shorter congregational Post Communion prayer and, while that is being said, fumbles with the ribbons in *Common Worship* to find the Post Communion for the day. Unfortunately he turns to the page where the traditional form of the prayer is found, when the rest of the service has been in modern English. He goes straight into the Blessing, having just invited the congregation to kneel and given them insufficient time to do so. After the Dismissal he announces the final hymn. At the end of this, everybody kneels for the final vestry prayer which is amplified for the congregation to hear. Nobody moves, as they have been taught – wrongly – that the service is not over until that point, and that they should wait for the final 'liturgical ending'.

The service should have a clear ending. This may be

* a blessing;
* a dismissal (with or without a preceding blessing);
* some other liturgical ending, including the Peace, the Grace or a suitable ascription or responsive conclusion.

This is set out in the final rubric and Note 9 to A Service of the Word. The Dismissal in Order One Holy Communion (*Common Worship*, page 183) provides for a blessing (which is optional) and a responsive dismissal (which must be used, though three options are given) after which 'The ministers and people depart'. One form of blessing is provided on page 183, but the rubric says that the seasonal or another suitable blessing may be used, and more are provided on page 299 and pages 300–329. Those planning the service will want to ensure that both the blessing and any prayer immediately before it gather up what has been going on in the service and focus on God who now sends his people out into the world.

So any prayer near the end of the service should not be general intercession, but a brief combination of thanksgiving and petition for grace to go out and serve God. Many of the Post Communion prayers (pages 376–521) are also suitable for use at the end of A Service of the Word as well, and more are provided below, divided into these two categories. Note 22 to *Common Worship* Holy Communion suggests that if two prayers are used after communion, the second should be a congregational one. If only one is used, it may be presidential or congregational, and may be one of those printed in the main text or one of those in the supplementary texts, some of which are included below. This may have a seasonal or thematic flavour.

A dismissal, ending or blessing should be the last item in any service, and should not normally be followed by a hymn or more prayers.

Notes to the resources

This section includes:

* Closing prayers, suitable for use in a non-eucharistic Service of the Word;
* Prayers suitable for use at the end of a service of Holy Communion, either as Post Communion prayers, or as part of the sending out;
* Blessings;
* Acclamations for the end of a service.

In general the congregational 'Amen', which concludes a prayer said by the leader, has not been printed here. It may need to be added if a full congregational text is being produced.

Texts in bold are suitable for congregational use.

Closing prayers

These prayers are particularly suitable as closing prayers for a non-eucharistic service. Though they do not refer explicitly to the sacrament, some of them could also be used as a Post Communion prayer, or as part of the Dismissal in a service of Holy Communion. The prayers printed in bold type are suitable for the whole congregation to join in.

General
Heaven
J1

Heavenly Father,
we share together the blessing of your presence.
Give us in this life knowledge of your truth,
and in the world to come life everlasting;
through Jesus Christ our Lord.

General (morning)
J2

Eternal God,
our beginning and our end,
accompany us in this day's journey.
Dawn on our darkness,
open our eyes to praise you for your creation
and to see the work you set before us today.
Take us and use us
to bring to others the new life you give in Jesus Christ
        our Lord.

General (evening)
J3

Lord, you have brought us through this day
to a time of reflection and rest.
Calm us,
and give us your peace to refresh us.
Keep us close to Christ
that we may be closer to one another
because of his perfect love.
In his name we pray.

General (evening)
J4

God, you are everything to us,
giving us life,
filling us with love,
and setting us free from sin
that we might live in you.
Accept the work of our hands this day,
take our lives,
give us your peace
and renew us in the service of Jesus Christ our Lord.

General (evening) J5	Gracious God, you have given us much today; grant us also a thankful spirit. Into your hands we commend ourselves and those we love. Stay with us, and when we take our rest renew us for the service of your Son Jesus Christ.
General (morning) *Lament* J6	**In darkness and in light,** **in trouble and in joy,** **help us, heavenly Father,** **to trust your love,** **to serve your purpose,** **and to praise your name;** **through Jesus Christ our Lord.**
General (time) *Christ's coming* J7	Almighty God, by your command time runs its course; forgive our impatience, perfect our faith, and, while we wait for the fulfilment of your promises, grant us to have a good hope because of your word; through Jesus Christ our Lord.
General (time) *Lament* J8	Jesus, lord of time, **hold us in your eternity.** Jesus, image of God, **travel with us the life of faith.** Jesus, friend of sinners, **heal the brokenness of our world.** Jesus, lord of tomorrow, **draw us into your future. Amen.**
Father, Son and Spirit J9	O God our mystery, you bring us to life, call us to freedom, and move between us with love. May we so participate in your dance of trinity that our lives may resonate with you, now and for ever.

Creator God,
you give seed for us to sow,
and bread for us to eat;
make us thankful for what we have received
and generous in supplying the needs of others
so all the world may give you thanks and glory,
through Jesus Christ our Lord.

Lord our God,
on the first day of creation
you made the light that scatters the darkness.
Let Christ, the light of lights,
hidden from all eternity,
shine at last on your people
and free us from the darkness of sin.
Fill our lives with joy
as we go out to welcome your Son at his coming.
We ask this in the name of Jesus the Lord.

God our Father,
[in this night] you have made known to us again
the coming of our Lord Jesus Christ:
confirm our faith and fix our eyes on him
until the day dawns
and Christ the Morning Star rises in our hearts.
To him be glory both now and for ever.
Amen.

God our Father,
your Word has come among us
in the Holy Child of Bethlehem:
may the light of faith illumine our hearts
    and shine in our words and deeds;
through him who is Christ the Lord.

Father of all,
you have given us your Son to be the Saviour of the world.
Welcome us your children into your kingdom
to enjoy your presence now and for ever.

Son of Mary, Son of God,
we have joined the worship of the angels;
may we never lose that heavenly vision.
Like the shepherds,
we have rejoiced at the news of your birth;
help us to proclaim that message in word and deed,
to your praise and glory.

God of glory,
you nourish us with your Word
who is the bread of life:
fill us with your Holy Spirit
that through us the light of your glory
may shine in all the world.
We ask this in the name of Jesus Christ our Lord.

Most merciful God,
by the death and resurrection of your Son Jesus Christ
you delivered and saved the world:
grant that by faith in him who suffered on the cross
we may triumph in the power of his victory;
through Jesus Christ your Son our Lord,
[who is alive and reigns with you,
in the unity of the Holy Spirit,
one God, now and for ever.]

Lord Jesus Christ,
you humbled yourself in taking the form of a servant,
and in obedience died on the cross for our salvation:
give us the courage to follow you
and to proclaim you as Lord and King,
to the glory of God the Father.

Jesus, Son of God, our true and only Saviour:
you died like a criminal on a cross;
but you are God who forgives.
Once broken, helpless and in pain,
you are God in whom there is hope.
You have shown us a love beyond words:
give us your forgiveness, hope and love.

Cross
Heaven
J20

Lord Jesus Christ,
Son of the living God,
set your passion, cross, and death between your
    judgement and us,
now and at the hour of our death.
Give mercy and grace to the living,
rest to the faithful departed,
to your holy Church peace and concord,
and to us sinners eternal life and glory;
for you are alive and reign with the Father
and the Holy Spirit, one God, now and for ever.

Resurrection
J21

God of our salvation,
you have restored us to life,
you have brought us back again into your love
by the triumphant death and resurrection of Christ.
Continue to heal us,
as we go to live and work
in the power of your Spirit,
to your praise and glory.

Ascension
Heaven
J22

Almighty God,
who raised Jesus from the dead
and exalted him to your right hand on high:
may we know your resurrection power in our daily lives
and look with hope to that day
when we shall see you face to face
and share in your glory,
Father, Son and Holy Spirit:
one God, now and for ever.

Holy Spirit
Christian beginnings
J23

God of power,
may the boldness of your Spirit transform us,
may the gentleness of your Spirit lead us,
may the gifts of your Spirit equip us to serve and
    worship you
now and always.

Holy Spirit
Christian beginnings
J24

Faithful God,
who fulfilled the promises of Easter
by sending us your Holy Spirit
and made known to every race and nation
the way of life eternal:
open our lips by your Spirit,
that every tongue may tell of your glory;
through Jesus Christ our Lord.

Word J25	Almighty God, we thank you for the gift of your holy word. May it be a lantern to our feet, a light to our paths, and a strength to our lives. Take us and use us to love and serve in the power of the Holy Spirit and in the name of your Son, Jesus Christ our Lord.
Church and mission J26	Keep us, Father, in this community of faith, the Church of your Son Jesus Christ, and help us to confess him as Messiah and Lord in all we say and do. We ask this in his name.
Church and mission J27	Draw your Church together, O God, into one great company of disciples, together following our Lord Jesus Christ into every walk of life, together serving him in his mission to the world, and together witnessing to his love on every continent and island.
Church and mission J28	Eternal God, giver of love and power, your Son Jesus Christ has sent us into all the world to preach the gospel of his kingdom: confirm us in this mission, and help us to live the good news we proclaim; through Jesus Christ our Lord.
Christian beginnings J29	**God of our pilgrimage,** **you have led us to the living water:** **refresh and sustain us** **as we go forward on our journey,** **in the name of Jesus Christ our Lord.**
Lament J30	God of compassion, through your Son Jesus Christ you have reconciled your people to yourself. As we follow his example of prayer and fasting, may we obey you with willing hearts and serve one another in holy love; through Jesus Christ our Lord.

Living in the world
J31

Lord God,
you hold both heaven and earth in a single peace.
Let the design of your great love
shine on the waste of our anger and sorrow,
and give peace to your Church,
peace among nations,
peace in our homes,
and peace in our hearts,
in Jesus Christ our Lord.

Living in the world
Relationships and healing
J32

Great God, you are one God,
and you bring together what is scattered
and mend what is broken.
Unite us with the scattered peoples of the earth
that we may be one family of your children.
Bind up all our wounds
and heal us in spirit,
that we may be renewed as disciples of Jesus Christ,
our Master and Saviour.

Living in the world
J33

To be said facing the open doors

To a troubled world
peace from Christ.
To a searching world
love from Christ.
To a waiting world
hope from Christ.

Heaven
J34

God and Father of our Lord Jesus Christ,
bring us to the dwelling
which your Son is preparing for all who love you.
Give us the will each day
to live in life eternal.
Let our citizenship be in heaven
with the whole company of the redeemed
and with countless angels,
praising, worshipping and adoring him
who sits upon the throne for ever and ever.

Post Communion prayers

General
J35

**Lord,
we have broken your bread
and received your life.
By the power of your Spirit
keep us always in your love;
through Jesus Christ our Lord.**

General
J36

**We thank you, Lord,
that you have fed us in this sacrament,
united us with Christ,
and given us a foretaste of the heavenly banquet
prepared for all peoples.**

Christ's coming
J37

**Generous God,
you have fed us at your heavenly table.
Set us on fire with your Spirit
that when Christ comes again
we may shine like lights before his face,
who with you and the Spirit lives for ever.**

Christ's coming
J38

Loving Father,
your Son Jesus Christ has come to us
in word and Spirit, in bread and cup.
Make us holy
and bring us to perfection,
when we stand before him
as he comes to judge the living and the dead,
Jesus Christ our Lord.

Christ's coming
J39

God our guide,
you have fed us with bread from heaven
as you fed your people Israel.
May we who have been spiritually nourished
be ready to follow you all our days;
we ask this in the name of Jesus Christ our Lord.

Incarnation
J40

We praise and thank you, creator God,
for you have not left us alone.
Every year we celebrate your coming as Emmanuel.
Every eucharist celebrates his death,
in the bread we break and the cup we share,
until that day when we shall see you face to face,
in Jesus Christ our Lord.

Cross J41	Faithful God, may we who share this banquet glory in the cross of our Lord Jesus Christ, our salvation, life and hope, who reigns as Lord now and for ever.
Resurrection J42	**God of truth,** **we have seen with our eyes** **and touched with our hands the bread of life:** **strengthen our faith** **that we may grow in love for you** **and for each other;** **through Jesus Christ our Lord.**
Holy Spirit *Christian beginnings* *Relationships and healing* J43	Father, in baptism we die to sin, rise again to new life and find our true place in your living body. Send us out sealed in Christ's blood of the new covenant, to bring healing and reconciliation to this wounded world, through Jesus Christ our Lord.
Word J44	Lord God, you feed us with the living bread from heaven; renew our faith, increase our hope, and strengthen our love. Teach us to hunger for Christ who is the true and living bread, and to live by every word that comes from your mouth, through Jesus Christ our Lord.
Church and mission J45	**Fill us, good Lord, with your Spirit of love;** **and as you have fed us with the one bread** **of heaven,** **so make us one in heart and mind,** **in Jesus Christ our Lord.**

Church and mission
J46
	Eternal God and Father,
	whose Son at supper prayed that his disciples
	    might be one,
	as he is one with you:
	draw us closer to him,
	that in common love and obedience to you
	we may be united to one another
	in the fellowship of the one Spirit,
	that the world may believe that he is Lord,
	    to your eternal glory;
	through Jesus Christ our Lord.

Lament J47	Eternal God, comfort of the afflicted and healer of the broken, you have fed us at the table of life and hope: teach us the ways of gentleness and peace, that all the world may acknowledge the kingdom of your Son, Jesus Christ our Lord.
Living in the world J48	Father of lights, from whom comes every good and perfect gift: keep us in the light of Christ, to shine in your world, that all may believe in you, through Jesus Christ our Lord. *cf James 1.17*
Living in the world J49	**Merciful God,** **you have called us to your table** **and fed us with the bread of life.** **Draw us and all people to serve your Son,** **our Saviour Jesus Christ.**

Living in the world
J50
	Father of all,
	we thank you that you have shared this feast of your
	    kingdom with all peoples
	and have united all races in your Son Jesus Christ:
	may the unity we have known here
	give us a joyful anticipation of the fullness of life
	    to which you call us;
	through Jesus Christ our Lord,
	who lives and reigns with you and the Holy Spirit,
	one God for ever and ever.

Heaven
Relationships
and healing
J51

Father of all, you gathered us here
around the table of your Son;
we have shared this meal with the saints
and the whole fellowship of the household of God.
In that new world
where the fullness of your peace will be revealed,
gather people of every race, language and way of life
to share in the one eternal banquet of
    Jesus Christ the Lord.

Blessings

The triple 'solemn blessings' included here (with Amens between each section) need particular care to ensure that the congregation know when to respond with 'Amen'. Printing the full text for the congregation is one way of doing this. Another approach is to make sure that someone taking the deacon's role has the full text and is clearly visible to give a lead to the congregation.

If a form of dismissal is used it should follow the blessing.

General J52	The almighty and merciful Lord, Father, Son, and Holy Spirit, bless us and keep us. **Amen.**

General J53	Now may the Lord of peace himself give you peace at all times and in every way. The Lord be with you all; and the blessing …

cf 2 Thessalonians 3.16

General J54	May God give to you and to all those you love his comfort and his peace, his light and his joy, in this world and the next; and the blessing …

General J55	Christ the good shepherd, who laid down his life for the sheep, draw you and all who hear his voice, to be one flock within one fold; and the blessing …

General J56	The God of all grace, who called you to his eternal glory in Christ Jesus, establish, strengthen and settle you in the faith; and the blessing …

General J57	The God of hope fill you with all joy and peace in believing; and the blessing …

General
J58

May God, who in Christ gives us a spring of water welling
    up to eternal life,
perfect in you the image of his glory;
and the blessing ...

General
J59

God, who from the death of sin raised you to new life in Christ,
keep you from falling and set you in the presence of his glory;
and the blessing ...

cf Jude 24

General
J60

God grant to the living, grace;
to the departed, rest;
to the Church, the Queen, the Commonwealth, and all humankind,
    peace and concord;
and to us and all his servants, life everlasting;
and the blessing ...

General
J61

God the Father,
who has given to his Son the name above every name,
strengthen you to proclaim Christ as Lord;
and the blessing ...

General
J62

The Lord bless you and watch over you,
the Lord make his face shine upon you
and be gracious to you,
the Lord look kindly on you
and give you peace;
and the blessing ...

cf Numbers 6.24,25

General
J63

The love of the Lord Jesus
draw you to himself,
the power of the Lord Jesus
strengthen you in his service,
the joy of the Lord Jesus fill your hearts;
and the blessing ...

General
J64

Christ, who has nourished us with himself the living bread,
make you one in praise and love,
and raise you up at the last day;
and the blessing ...

General
J65

You are called and loved by God the Father
and kept safe by Jesus Christ.
Mercy, peace and love be yours in abundance,
from God the Father, Son and Holy Spirit.
Amen.

cf Jude 1,2

General
J66

*The congregation accompanies the first three responses with a sweep of
the arm towards a cross, as if throwing the objects of the prayer; the final
response is a sweep of the arm towards heaven.*

All our problems
we send to the cross of Christ.
All our difficulties
we send to the cross of Christ.
All the devil's works
we send to the cross of Christ.
All our hopes
we set on the risen Christ;
and the blessing of God almighty …

*Father, Son
and Spirit*
J67

[The Lord bless you and keep you.
Amen.

The Lord make his face to shine upon you,
and be gracious to you.
Amen.

The Lord lift up his countenance upon you
and give you peace.
Amen.]

The Lord God almighty, Father, Son and Holy Spirit,
the holy and undivided Trinity,
guard you, save you,
and bring you to that heavenly city,
where he lives and reigns for ever and ever.
Amen.

cf Numbers 6.24,25

*Father, Son
and Spirit
Relationships
and healing*
J68

May God keep you in all your days.
May Christ shield you in all your ways.
May the Spirit bring you healing and peace.
May God the Holy Trinity drive all darkness from you
and pour upon you blessing and light.

God in creation May God the Father of our Lord Jesus Christ,
J69   who is the source of all goodness and growth,
             pour his blessing upon all things created,
             and upon you his children,
             that you may use his gifts to his glory and the welfare of all peoples;
             and the blessing …

God in creation May God
J70   who clothes the lilies and feeds the birds of the sky,
             who leads the lambs to pasture and the deer to water,
             who multiplied loaves and fishes and changed water into wine,
             lead us, feed us, multiply us,
             and change us to reflect the glory of our Creator
             now and through all eternity;
             and the blessing …

Christ's coming May God the Father,
J71   who loved the world so much that he sent his only Son
             to come among us in great humility,
             open your eyes to look for his coming again.
             Amen.

             May God the Son
             give you grace to live in the light of his coming as redeemer and judge.
             Amen.

             May God the Holy Spirit
             free you from sin,
             make you holy,
             and bring you to eternal life.
             Amen.

             And the blessing …

Christ's coming May God the Father,
J72   who loved the world so much that he sent his only Son,
             give you grace to prepare for life eternal.
             Amen.

             May God the Son,
             who comes to us as redeemer and judge,
             reveal to you the path from darkness to light.
             Amen.

             May God the Holy Spirit,
             by whose working the Virgin Mary conceived the Christ,
             help you bear the fruits of holiness.
             Amen.

             And the blessing …

Christ's coming
J73

May God the Father, Judge all-merciful,
make us worthy of a place in his kingdom.
Amen.

May God the Son, coming among us in power,
reveal in our midst the promise of his glory.
Amen.

May God the Holy Spirit make us steadfast in faith,
joyful in hope and constant in love.
Amen.

And the blessing ...

Christ's coming
J74

May God himself, the God of peace,
make you perfect and holy,
and keep you safe and blameless, in spirit, soul and body,
for the coming of our Lord Jesus Christ;
and the blessing ...

cf 1 Thessalonians 5.23

Incarnation
J75

God sent his angels from glory to bring to shepherds
the good news of Jesus' birth.
Yes! We thank you Lord.
You have heard his story, the story of God's own Son.
Yes! We thank you Lord.
May he fill you with joy to bring this good news to others today.
Yes! We thank you Lord.

And the blessing ...

Incarnation
J76

May the Father,
who has loved the eternal Son
from before the foundation of the world,
shed that love upon you his children.
Amen.

May Christ,
who by his incarnation gathered into one things earthly and heavenly,
fill you with joy and peace.
Amen.

May the Holy Spirit,
by whose overshadowing Mary became the God-bearer,
give you grace to carry the good news of Christ.
Amen.

And the blessing ...

Jesus Christ was born of the Virgin Mary,
revealed in his glory,
worshipped by angels,
proclaimed among the nations,
believed in throughout the world,
exalted to the highest heavens.
Blessed be God our strength and our salvation
now and for ever. Amen.

And the blessing ...

cf I Timothy 3.16

When the Word became flesh
earth was joined to heaven in the womb of Mary:
may the love and obedience of Mary be your example.
Amen.

May the peace of Christ
rule in your hearts and homes.
Amen.

May you be filled with the joy of the Spirit
and the gifts of your eternal home.
Amen.

And the blessing ...

Christ the Son of God perfect in you the image of his glory
and gladden your hearts with the good news of his kingdom;
and the blessing ...

May God the Father,
who led the wise men by the shining of a star
to find the Christ, the Light from Light,
lead you in your pilgrimage to find the Lord.
Amen.

May God who has brought us out of darkness
give us a place with the saints in light
in the kingdom of his Son.
Amen.

May the light of the glorious gospel of Christ
shine in your hearts and transform your lives,
to bring his light to others.
Amen.

And the blessing ...

cf Colossians 1.13; 2 Corinthians 4.4

Cross
J81

You believe that by his dying
Christ destroyed death for ever.
Amen.

You have been crucified with Christ
and live by faith in the Son of God,
who loved you and gave himself for you.
Amen.

May he send you out to glory in his cross,
and live no longer for yourselves but for him,
who died and was raised to life for us.
Amen.

And the blessing …

cf Galatians 2.20; 2 Corinthians 5.15

Cross
J82

May the Father,
who so loved the world that he gave his only Son,
bring you by faith to his eternal life.
Amen.

May Christ,
who accepted the cup of sacrifice
in obedience to the Father's will,
keep you steadfast as you walk with him the way of his cross.
Amen.

May the Spirit,
who strengthens us to suffer with Christ
that we may share his glory,
set your minds on life and peace.
Amen.

And the blessing …

Resurrection
J83

You believe Jesus has been raised from the dead in glory.
Amen.

You believe you have been raised with Christ.
Amen.

May your hearts and minds be set on things above,
where Christ is seated at the right hand of God.
Amen.

And the blessing …

God the Father,
by whose love Christ was raised from the dead,
open to you who believe the gates of everlasting life.
Amen.

God the Son,
who in bursting the grave has won a glorious victory,
give you joy as you share the Easter faith.
Amen.

God the Holy Spirit,
whom the risen Lord breathed into his disciples,
empower you and fill you with Christ's peace.
Amen.

And the blessing ...

May Christ,
who out of defeat brings new hope and a new future,
fill you with his new life;
and the blessing ...

God the Father,
by whose glory Christ was raised from the dead,
strengthen you to walk with him in his risen life;
and the blessing ...

God, who through the resurrection of our Lord Jesus Christ
has given us the victory,
give you joy and peace in your faith;
and the blessing ...

Christ our ascended King
pour upon you the abundance of his gifts
and bring you to reign with him in glory;
and the blessing ...

Christ our King make you faithful and strong to do his will,
that you may reign with him in glory;
and the blessing ...

God the Father,
who has given to his Son the name above every name,
strengthen you to proclaim Christ Jesus as Lord.
Amen.

God the Son,
who is our great high priest passed into the heavens,
plead for you at the right hand of the Father.
Amen.

God the Holy Spirit,
who pours out his abundant gifts upon the Church,
make you faithful servants of Christ our King.
Amen.

And the blessing ...

Holy Spirit
J91

May the Spirit,
who hovered over the waters when the world was created,
breathe into you the life he gives.
Amen.

May the Spirit,
who overshadowed the Virgin when the eternal Son came among us,
make you joyful in the service of the Lord.
Amen.

May the Spirit,
who set the Church on fire upon the day of Pentecost,
bring the world alive with the love of the risen Christ.
Amen.

And the blessing ...

Holy Spirit
J92

May Christ's holy, healing, enabling Spirit be with you
and guide you on your way at every change and turn;
and the blessing ...

Holy Spirit
Christian
beginnings
J93

God poured out his promised Holy Spirit in tongues of flame
on the day of Pentecost.
Amen.

You have been baptized with the Spirit and with fire.
Amen.

May that same Holy Spirit send you out to tell his story,
and give you a voice to glorify God before all people.
Amen.

And the blessing ...

cf Acts 2.1-4

Holy Spirit
Church and
  mission
J94
May the God of hope fill us with all joy and peace in believing,
through the power of the Holy Spirit;
and the blessing ...

cf Romans 15.13

Word
J95
Hear the teaching of Jesus:
'Blessed are those who hear the word of God and obey it.'
Go now to do God's will;
and the blessing ...

Church and
  mission
J96
May God, who gives patience and encouragement,
give you a spirit of unity
to live in harmony as you follow Jesus Christ,
so that with one voice
you may glorify the God and Father of our Lord Jesus Christ;
and the blessing ...

cf Romans 15.5,6

Church and
  mission
Living in
  the world
J97
May Christ draw you to humility and worship,
and bring you to see God at work;
and the blessing ...

Church and
  mission
Christian
  beginnings
J98
The Father, whose glory fills the heavens,
cleanse you by his holiness
and send you to proclaim his word.
Amen.

The Son, who has ascended to the heights,
pour upon you the riches of his grace.
Amen.

The Holy Spirit, the Comforter,
equip you and strengthen you in your ministry.
Amen.

And the blessing ...

Christian
  beginnings
Incarnation
J99
May God the Father,
who led the wise men by the shining of a star
to find the Christ, the Light from Light,
lead you also in your pilgrimage to find the Lord.
Amen.

May God the Son,
who turned water into wine at the wedding feast at Cana,
transform your lives and make glad your hearts.
Amen.

May God the Holy Spirit,
who came upon the beloved Son
at his baptism in the river Jordan,
pour out his gifts on you
who have come to the waters of new birth.
Amen.

And the blessing …

Lament
J100

May God the Father,
who does not despise the broken spirit,
give to you a contrite heart.
Amen.

May Christ,
who bore our sins in his body on the tree,
heal you by his wounds.
Amen.

May the Holy Spirit,
who leads us into all truth,
speak to you words of pardon and peace.
Amen.

And the blessing …

cf Psalm 51; Isaiah 53

Relationships
and healing
Heaven
J101

May God,
whose Son revealed his glory at a wedding in Cana,
bring you the blessings of his presence.
Amen.

May God,
whose power turned water into wine,
transform your lives and make glad your hearts.
Amen.

May God, who works miracles in our lives,
fill you with his Spirit,
and change you day by day to reflect his glory,
until that day when you see him face to face.
Amen.

And the blessing …

cf John 2.1-11

Relationships
and healing
J102

May the Father
from whom every family in earth and heaven receives its name
strengthen you with his Spirit in your inner being,
so that Christ may dwell in your hearts by faith,
[and that, knowing his love,
broad and long, deep and high beyond our knowledge,
you may be filled with all the fullness of God;]
and the blessing …

cf Ephesians 3.15-19

Living in
the world
J103

God, who has prepared for us a city with eternal foundations,
bring you to the triumphant joy of the city of the great King;
and the blessing …

Living in
the world
J104

Go forth into the world in peace;
be of good courage;
hold fast that which is good;
render to no one evil for evil;
strengthen the fainthearted; support the weak;
help the afflicted; honour everyone;
love and serve the Lord,
rejoicing in the power of the Holy Spirit;
and the blessing …

1 Thessalonians 5.13-22

Living in
the world
J105

Now may the blessing of God the Father,
who made from one every nation that occupies the earth;
of God the Son who bought us for God
from every tribe and language and people and nation;
and of God the Spirit who brings us together in unity,
be with us and remain with us always.
Amen.

cf Acts 17.26; Revelation 5.9

Holy
Communion
J106

May the Father,
who fed his children with bread and honey in the wilderness,
strengthen you in your pilgrimage to the Promised Land.
Amen.

May the Son,
who gave his flesh for food and his blood for drink,
keep you in eternal life and raise you up on the last day.
Amen.

May the Holy Spirit,
who leads us into all truth,
help you discern the Lord's body
and empower you to proclaim his death until he comes.
Amen.

And the blessing ...

Heaven
J*107*
May God, who has given you in the lives of the saints
patterns of holy living and victorious dying,
strengthen you to follow them in the way of holiness.
Amen.

May God,
who kindled the fire of his love in the hearts of the saints,
pour upon you the riches of his grace.
Amen.

May God, who calls you no longer strangers and aliens
but fellow-citizens with all the saints,
bring you to your home in heaven.
Amen.

And the blessing ...

cf Colossians 1.12; Ephesians 1.17,18; 2.14

Heaven
J*108*
God,
the Father of our Lord Jesus Christ,
give you the spirit of wisdom and revelation,
to know the hope to which he has called you.
Amen.

God,
who has shown you a pattern of holy living and holy dying
    in the lives of the saints,
bring you to share their glorious inheritance.
Amen.

God,
who calls you no longer strangers
but fellow-citizens with the saints,
set your hearts and minds on things above,
where Christ is seated at God's right hand.
Amen.

And the blessing ...

Heaven **J***109*	May God, who kindled the fire of his love in the hearts of the saints, pour upon you the riches of his grace. **Amen.**
	May he give you joy in their fellowship and a share in their praises. **Amen.**
	May he strengthen you to follow them in the way of holiness and to come to the full radiance of glory. **Amen.**
	And the blessing …

Heaven
Living in
  the world
J*110*

May Christ, who makes saints of sinners,
who has transformed those we remember today,
raise and strengthen you that you may transform the world;
and the blessing …

Heaven
J*111*

May God the Father bring us to the home
which his Son prepares for all who love him.
Amen.

May God the Son give us the will
to live for him each day in life eternal.
Amen.

May God the Holy Spirit give us the assurance
that our citizenship is in heaven
with the blessed and beloved,
and the whole company of the redeemed.
Amen.

And the blessing …

Heaven
J*112*

May God give you
his comfort and his peace,
his light and his joy,
in this world and the next;
and the blessing …

Final acclamations

These may be used on their own to conclude the act of worship, or they may precede or follow a blessing. If one of these is used with a dismissal, the dismissal should come at the very end.

General
J113

The Lord God almighty is our Father:
he loves us and tenderly cares for us.
The Lord Jesus Christ is our Saviour:
he has redeemed us and will defend us to the end.
The Lord, the Holy Spirit, is among us:
he will lead us in God's holy way.
To God almighty, Father, Son and Holy Spirit,
be praise and glory today and for ever.
Amen.

General
J114

Let us bless the Lord:
thanks be to God.
Blessing, honour and glory be yours,
here and everywhere,
now and for ever.
Amen.

General
J115

Now unto the King eternal, immortal, invisible,
the only wise God,
be honour and glory for ever and ever.
Amen.

cf 1 Timothy 1.17

General
J116

We go into the world
to walk in God's light,
to rejoice in God's love
and to reflect God's glory.

Father, Son
and Spirit
J117

To God the Father, who loved us,
and made us accepted in the Beloved:
to God the Son, who loved us,
and loosed us from our sins by his own blood:
to God the Holy Spirit,
who spreads the love of God abroad in our hearts:
to the one true God be all love and all glory
for time and for eternity.
Amen.

*Father, Son
and Spirit*
*Christian
beginnings*
J118

The Holy Trinity,
in whose name we were baptized,
preserve us,
members of Christ,
children of God,
inheritors of the kingdom of heaven,
saved by the waters,
and filled with the Spirit.
**Glory to God,
Father, Son and Holy Spirit.**

Ascension
J119

**Yours, Lord, is the greatness, the power,
the glory, the splendour, and the majesty:
for everything in heaven and on earth is yours.**

Yours, Lord, is the kingdom:
and you are exalted as head over all.
Alleluia, Alleluia. Amen.

cf 1 Chronicles 29.11

*Church and
mission*
J120

Glory to God,
**whose power, at work among us,
can do infinitely more
than all we can ask or conceive;
to him be glory in the Church and in Christ Jesus,
for ever and ever.
Amen.**

cf Ephesians 3.20,21

Heaven
J121

To him who is able to keep us from falling
and to present us without blemish
before the presence of his glory with rejoicing,
to the only God, our Saviour through Jesus Christ our Lord,
be glory, majesty, dominion and authority,
before all time and now and for ever.
Amen.

cf Jude 24,25

sample sample sample services services services

Sample Services

Contents

Introduction

The sample services are of two types:

1 'Outlines', giving the basic headings and some suggested texts. These could form the basis of your own local service, but each also acts as an illustration of how to structure a service and how to choose resource material for a particular situation.

2 Fully 'worked out' services, printed in full. These illustrate how a service might be presented when printed out for the congregation. None of these are intended to be prescriptive in terms of layout, but they do illustrate different ways of handling headings, rubrics etc.

Some of these worked out services (such as the Service for Fathers' Day) are 'one-offs' that illustrate a unique situation and would not necessarily be of use in this particular form in any other context or at any other time.

Others are more 'standard' and have been deliberately designed to be as widely applicable as possible, for regular use across a range of different churches. Examples include: An Evening Service of the Word, For all the Church Family, etc. Where appropriate, these could be copied in this form for local use. The usual rules about reproduction for local use apply, as explained in the Archbishops' Council's booklet *A Brief Guide to Liturgical Copyright* (see page 481 for more information).

Each of the services includes a page of notes that explains the thinking behind the service and gives further suggestions.

Some of the services have been designed to work as non-eucharistic Services of the Word, whereas others have been constructed as Services of the Word with a Celebration of Holy Communion. In each case the one could be adapted to produce the other. In a few cases we have provided a non-eucharistic Service of the Word, with guidance in the notes about possible resources and structural changes if a eucharistic service is required.

Songs and hymns

In most of the sample services we have not indicated places for songs and hymns, as local custom will usually determine this. Where it is especially appropriate to include a hymn, song, or group of songs at a particular point in the service, we have indicated this, but these are only suggestions.

Posture

These samples include few indications of posture, to allow for maximum adaptability to local contexts. Where particular posture has become the local norm for a part of the service, it may help visitors if this is indicated clearly in the rubrics. Where posture varies it is best to omit it from the printed version and rely on clear verbal instructions.

The Lord's Prayer

The Lord's Prayer is printed here on almost every occasion in its modern form. Churches producing their own orders of service can easily replace it with the traditional form if desired.

The Lord's Prayer is also sometimes printed with a 'cue line' (such as, 'As our Saviour taught us …') and sometimes without. Where no cue line is given this allows the leader to use one which is suitable for the particular occasion, or a simple, 'Let us say the Lord's Prayer together', as appropriate.

Standard Non-Eucharistic Services

1

Morning Praise

Notes

Type of service

¶ A non-eucharistic morning service, not necessarily 'all-age';

¶ Fully worked out sample, suitable for local reproduction;

¶ Designed to be suitable for regular use and for a variety of contexts.

Hymns and songs

Possible points for these include:
¶ during an opening procession before the greeting or after the greeting;
¶ after the sermon or after the Creed;
¶ after the Collect.

Venite

The version printed here is from *Common Worship*. Other versions (for instance, a hymn or song based on Psalm 95, or text taken from a different Bible translation) could be used. Note, for instance, that there is a very free paraphrase in the Psalms and Canticles section of this book.

Prayers

The Lord's Prayer is used in this service as an introduction to the prayers of intercession, 'setting the agenda for prayer'. The optional response in the intercessions,

Your kingdom come
Your will be done.

picks this up.

The Collect is used as the summary and conclusion of the prayers, and for this reason there is no ending to the intercessions (such as 'Merciful Father, accept these prayers …').

Morning Praise

Preparation

Greeting

The minister welcomes the people with a greeting, which may include

Grace, mercy and peace
from God our Father
and the Lord Jesus Christ
be with you

All **and also with you.**

Prayers of Penitence

The minister introduces the confession.

All **Lord God,**
we have sinned against you;
we have done evil in your sight.
We are sorry and repent.
Have mercy on us according to your love.
Wash away our wrongdoing and cleanse us from our sin.
Renew a right spirit within us
and restore to us the joy of your salvation,
through Jesus Christ our Lord.
Amen.

May the Father of all mercies
cleanse *you* from *your* sins,
and restore *you* in his image
to the praise and glory of his name,
through Jesus Christ our Lord.

All **Amen.**

Praise

Let everything be said and done in the name of the
Lord Jesus,

All **giving thanks to God through Jesus Christ.**

Sing psalms, hymns and sacred songs:

All **let us sing to God with thankful hearts.**

Open our lips, Lord:

All **and we shall praise your name.**

A canticle or song or responsory, which may include

Venite – a Song of Triumph

1   O come, let us sing to the Lord; ♦
    let us heartily rejoice in the rock of our salvation.

2   Let us come into his presence with thanksgiving ♦
    and be glad in him with psalms.

3   For the Lord is a great God ♦
    and a great king above all gods.

4   In his hand are the depths of the earth ♦
    and the heights of the mountains are his also.

5   The sea is his, for he made it, ♦
    and his hands have moulded the dry land.

6   Come, let us worship and bow down ♦
    and kneel before the Lord our Maker.

7   For he is our God; ♦
    we are the people of his pasture and the sheep of his hand.

    Glory to the Father and to the Son
    and to the Holy Spirit;
    as it was in the beginning is now
    and shall be for ever. Amen.

Word

A psalm or song based on a passage of Scripture may be used.

Reading(s)

After each reading this response may be used

This is the word of the Lord.
All   **Thanks be to God.**

Sermon

This, or an authorized Affirmation of Faith, is used.

All   **I believe in God, the Father almighty,
creator of heaven and earth.**

**I believe in Jesus Christ, his only Son, our Lord,
who was conceived by the Holy Spirit,
born of the Virgin Mary,
suffered under Pontius Pilate,
was crucified, died, and was buried;
he descended to the dead.
On the third day he rose again;
he ascended into heaven,
he is seated at the right hand of the Father,
and he will come to judge the living and the dead.**

**I believe in the Holy Spirit,
the holy catholic Church,
the communion of saints,
the forgiveness of sins,
the resurrection of the body,
and the life everlasting.
Amen.**

Prayers

The Lord's Prayer

As our Saviour taught us, so we pray

All   **Our Father in heaven,
hallowed be your name,
your kingdom come,
your will be done,
on earth as in heaven.
Give us today our daily bread.
Forgive us our sins
as we forgive those who sin against us.
Lead us not into temptation
but deliver us from evil.
For the kingdom, the power,
and the glory are yours
now and for ever.
Amen.**

One of these responses may be used

Your kingdom come.

All **Your will be done.**

(or)

Loving God, we look to you.

All **Receive our prayer.**

The Collect

The Collect, the prayer of the day, is said.

Conclusion

A blessing may be given.

The service ends with the Grace, or another ending.

All **The grace of our Lord Jesus Christ,**
and the love of God,
and the fellowship of the Holy Spirit,
be with us all evermore.
Amen.

2

For all the Church Family

Notes

Type of service

¶ A non-eucharistic service designed for use when all ages are present throughout;

¶ Fully worked out sample, suitable for local reproduction;

¶ Designed to be suitable for regular use and for a variety of contexts.

This service follows the same structure as the Morning Praise sample service, but makes different choices of texts and uses headings of a different style.

Opening Prayer

If it is desired to make connections between this service and services of Holy Communion, the opening prayer printed here could be replaced by the Prayer of Preparation from *Common Worship* Order One.

Praise

The rubrics have been phrased to allow a hymn or songs either to *replace* or to *follow* the 'Blessed is the Lord ...' responses.

Readings

No responses have been printed after the readings. This would not necessarily mean that they could not be used.

Prayers

The Lord's Prayer is used in this service to sum up the prayers of intercession.

The 'Lord in your mercy hear our prayer' response, and the concluding 'Merciful Father, accept these prayers ...' have been included as options to facilitate connections being made between this service and celebrations of Holy Communion. If these forms are not used in communion services, other choices could be made.

Dismissal

The use of 'Go in peace ...' is designed to connect with Holy Communion services. Other options could be used instead.

If it is desired to give a blessing, the section, 'Let us bless the Lord ...' should be omitted.

For all the Church Family

*We say together the words printed in **bold**.*

Gathering to worship God

Greeting

Let us worship God: Father, Son and Holy Spirit.

All **Amen.**

The Lord be with you

All **and also with you.**

This is the day that the Lord has made.

All **We will rejoice and be glad in it.**

Words of welcome and introduction may follow.

Opening Prayer

All **Lord, direct our thoughts, and teach us to pray.
Lift up our hearts to worship you in spirit and in truth,
through Jesus Christ our Lord.
Amen.**

Hymns or songs may be sung.
Silence is kept and the Collect, the prayer of the day, is said.

Saying sorry to God

Confession

God our Father,
we come to you in sorrow for our sins.

For turning away from you,
and ignoring your will for our lives;
Father, forgive us:

All **save us and help us.**

For behaving just as we wish,
without thinking of you;
Father, forgive us:

All **save us and help us.**

For failing you by what we do
and think and say;
Father, forgive us:

All   **save us and help us.**

For letting ourselves be drawn away from you
by temptations in the world about us;
Father, forgive us:

All   **save us and help us.**

For living as if we were ashamed to belong to your Son;
Father, forgive us:

All   **save us and help us.**

The minister declares God's forgiveness.

Praise

These words may be said

Blessed is the Lord

All   **for he has heard the voice of our prayer;**

therefore shall our hearts dance for joy

All   **and in our song we will praise our God.**

A hymn or song(s) may be sung.

Hearing and responding to the Word of God

Reading(s)

A psalm, hymn or songs may be sung between readings or before or after the Response.

Response

*This may include a sermon or talk, discussion, and activities for different age groups.
It continues with the Affirmation of Faith and the Prayers.*

Do you believe and trust in God the Father,
source of all being and life,
the one for whom we exist?

All **We believe and trust in him.**

Do you believe and trust in God the Son,
who took our human nature,
died for us and rose again?

All **We believe and trust in him.**

Do you believe and trust in God the Holy Spirit,
who gives life to the people of God
and makes Christ known in the world?

All **We believe and trust in him.**

This is the faith of the Church.

All **This is our faith.**
We believe and trust in one God,
Father, Son and Holy Spirit.
Amen.

Prayers of Intercession

The prayers may include one of these responses

Lord, in your mercy

All **hear our prayer.**

(or)

Lord, hear your people

All **and answer our prayers.**

The prayers may end with

Merciful Father,

All **accept these prayers**
for the sake of your Son,
our Saviour Jesus Christ.
Amen.

All **Our Father in heaven,
hallowed be your name,
your kingdom come,
your will be done,
on earth as in heaven.
Give us today our daily bread.
Forgive us our sins
as we forgive those who sin against us.
Lead us not into temptation
but deliver us from evil.
For the kingdom, the power,
and the glory are yours
now and for ever.
Amen.**

Going out to serve God

A hymn or song(s) may be sung.

This prayer may be said

Let us bless the Lord:

All **thanks be to God.
Blessing, honour and glory be yours,
here and everywhere,
now and for ever.
Amen.**

Go in peace to love and serve the Lord.

All **In the name of Christ. Amen.**

3

An Evening Service of the Word

Notes

Type of service

¶ A non-eucharistic evening service;

¶ A fully worked out sample, suitable for local reproduction;

¶ Designed to be suitable for regular use and for a variety of contexts.

Hymns and songs

Suggested places have been indicated. Note that the second response in the Greeting section might need to be changed if a hymn or song precedes, rather than follows, the Greeting.

Penitence

Note that the confession and absolution have been used as part of the response to the Word, rather than at the beginning of the service.

Prayers

A form of prayers of intercession has been included. Other forms can be used. Thanksgiving could use set prayers (such as the General Thanksgiving (G57) or one of the sets of acclamations (G22–G55)) or might be an opportunity for extempore prayer if the size of congregation and acoustics of the building are suitable.

Creed

If this service forms the principal service on a Sunday or Principal Holy Day then one of the authorized Creeds or Affirmations of Faith would need to be included. It might be added to the response to the Word, coming after the Confession and Praise and before the Prayers.

An Evening Service of the Word

We say together the words printed in **bold.**

Preparation

Greeting

The light and peace of Jesus Christ be with you
All **and also with you.**

The glory of the Lord has risen upon us.
All **Let us rejoice and sing God's praise for ever.**

Song(s) or a hymn may be sung.

Opening Prayer

Faithful one, whose word is life:
come with saving power
to free our praise,
inspire our prayer
and shape our lives
for the kingdom of your Son,
Jesus Christ our Lord.
All **Amen.**

(or)

O Lord, we call to you: come to us quickly.
All **Hear us when we cry to you.**
Let our prayers rise up before you like incense.
All **Let our lifted hands be like an evening sacrifice.**
Glory to the Father and to the Son
and to the Holy Spirit;
All **as it was in the beginning is now
and shall be for ever.
Amen.**

The Word

Psalm

A psalm, or a song or hymn based on a passage of Scripture, may be used.

Reading(s)

At the end of each reading this response may be used

This is the word of the Lord.

All **Thanks be to God.**

Response to God's Word

Sermon

Song(s) or a hymn may be sung.

Confession and Forgiveness

Christ the light of the world has come to dispel
the darkness of our hearts.
In his light let us examine ourselves and confess our sins.

Silence may be kept.

Let us admit to God the sin which always confronts us.

All **Lord God,**
we have sinned against you;
we have done evil in your sight.
We are sorry and repent.
Have mercy on us according to your love.
Wash away our wrongdoing and cleanse us from our sin.
Renew a right spirit within us
and restore us to the joy of your salvation,
through Jesus Christ our Lord.
Amen.

The minister declares God's forgiveness.

Blessed are you, Lord our God, King of the universe.

All **To you be glory and praise for ever.**
From the rising of the sun to its setting
your name is proclaimed in all the world.

All **To you be glory and praise for ever.**
When the time had fully come
you sent the Sun of Righteousness.

All **In him the fullness of your glory dwells.**
To you be glory and praise for ever.

Song(s) or a hymn may be sung.

Prayers

Prayers of Thanks and Intercession

This, or some other form, may be used:

(We pray to the Lord:
in faith we pray.

All **We pray to you our God.)**

That the rest of this day may be holy,
    peaceful and full of your presence;
in faith we pray.

All **We pray to you our God.**

That the work we have done and the people we have met today
may bring us closer to you;
in faith we pray.

All **We pray to you our God.**

That we may hear and respond to your call to peace and justice;
in faith we pray.

All **We pray to you our God.**

That you will sustain the faith and hope of those who are lonely,
    oppressed and anxious;
in faith we pray.

All **We pray to you our God.**

That you will strengthen us in your service,
and fill our hearts with longing for your kingdom;
in faith we pray.

All **We pray to you our God.**

God of mercy,

All **you know us and love us**
and hear our prayer:
keep us in the eternal fellowship of Jesus Christ our Saviour.
Amen.

The prayer of the day is said.

All **Our Father in heaven,**
hallowed be your name,
your kingdom come,
your will be done,
on earth as in heaven.
Give us today our daily bread.
Forgive us our sins
as we forgive those who sin against us.
Lead us not into temptation
but deliver us from evil.
For the kingdom, the power,
and the glory are yours
now and for ever.
Amen.

Conclusion

All **In darkness and in light,**
in trouble and in joy,
help us, heavenly Father,
to trust your love,
to serve your purpose,
and to praise your name;
through Jesus Christ our Lord.
Amen.

A blessing, the Grace or the sharing of the Peace may conclude the service, or these responses may be used

Jesus Christ is the light of the world:

All **a light no darkness can quench.**

Stay with us, Lord, for it is evening:

All **and the day is almost over.**

The darkness is not dark to you:

All **the night is as bright as the day.**

Let your light scatter the darkness:

All **and fill your church with your glory. Amen.**

Communion Services

4

Christ is our Peace

Notes

Type of service

¶   A Service of Holy Communion;

¶   A fully worked out sample, suitable for local reproduction;

¶   Designed to be suitable for regular use and for a variety of contexts.

This straightforward order of service follows the basic structure of *Common Worship* Order One in a simple way, with minimal rubrics.

Eucharistic Prayer

¶   This order is suitable for use with Eucharistic Prayers A, B, C, E and G. The full text of the Eucharistic Prayer is *not* included. The order is not suitable in this form for use with Eucharistic Prayers D, F or H;

¶   Only one of the four memorial acclamations is included in this order of service.

Christ is our Peace

A Service of Holy Communion

We say together the words printed in **bold.**

We gather

Greeting

The minister welcomes the people with a greeting, which may include

The Lord be with you

All **and also with you.**

Prayer of Preparation

This prayer may be used

All **Almighty God,**
to whom all hearts are open,
all desires known,
and from whom no secrets are hidden:
cleanse the thoughts of our hearts
by the inspiration of your Holy Spirit,
that we may perfectly love you,
and worthily magnify your holy name;
through Christ our Lord.
Amen.

Confession and Forgiveness

All **Almighty God, our heavenly Father,**
we have sinned against you
and against our neighbour
in thought and word and deed,
through negligence, through weakness,
through our own deliberate fault.
We are truly sorry
and repent of all our sins.
For the sake of your Son Jesus Christ,
who died for us,
forgive us all that is past
and grant that we may serve you in newness of life
to the glory of your name.
Amen.

The president declares God's forgiveness.

This, or another song, may be said or sung

All **Glory to God in the highest,
and peace to his people on earth.**

**Lord God, heavenly King,
almighty God and Father,
we worship you, we give you thanks,
we praise you for your glory.**

**Lord Jesus Christ, only Son of the Father,
Lord God, Lamb of God,
you take away the sin of the world:
have mercy on us;
you are seated at the right hand of the Father:
receive our prayer.**

**For you alone are the Holy One,
you alone are the Lord,
you alone are the Most High, Jesus Christ,
with the Holy Spirit,
in the glory of God the Father.
Amen.**

The Collect

The president says the Collect, the prayer of the day.

We listen to God's Word

There will be two or three readings from the Bible.
The final reading is the Gospel. Psalms or songs may also be used.

Reading(s)

At the end of the reading(s) this response may be used

This is the word of the Lord.
All **Thanks be to God.**

Gospel Reading

Before the Gospel reading this response may be used

Hear the Gospel of our Lord Jesus Christ according to N.
All **Glory to you, O Lord.**

This is the Gospel of the Lord.

All **Praise to you, O Christ.**

Sermon

Creed

All **I believe in God, the Father almighty,**
creator of heaven and earth.

I believe in Jesus Christ, his only Son, our Lord.
who was conceived by the Holy Spirit,
born of the Virgin Mary,
suffered under Pontius Pilate,
was crucified, died, and was buried;
he descended to the dead.
On the third day he rose again;
he ascended into heaven,
he is seated at the right hand of the Father,
and he will come to judge the living and the dead.

I believe in the Holy Spirit,
the holy catholic Church,
the communion of saints,
the forgiveness of sins,
the resurrection of the body,
and the life everlasting.
Amen.

We pray

Prayers of Intercession

The prayers of intercession may include the response

Lord, in your mercy

All **hear our prayer.**

and may end with

Merciful Father,

All **accept these prayers**
for the sake of your Son,
our Saviour Jesus Christ.
Amen.

We share in Holy Communion

The Peace

After the introductory words

The peace of the Lord be always with you
All **and also with you.**

The Eucharistic Prayer

One of the authorized Eucharistic Prayers is used.

The Lord be with you   *(or)*   The Lord is here.
All **and also with you.**   **His Spirit is with us.**

Lift up your hearts.
All **We lift them to the Lord.**

Let us give thanks to the Lord our God.
All **It is right to give thanks and praise.**

The president continues the prayer, praising God.

All join in the words

All **Holy, holy, holy Lord,**
God of power and might,
heaven and earth are full of your glory.
Hosanna in the highest.
[Blessed is he who comes in the name of the Lord.
Hosanna in the highest.]

The prayer continues and may include this acclamation

Great is the mystery of faith:
All **Christ has died:**
Christ is risen:
Christ will come again.

The Eucharistic Prayer ends with

All **Amen.**

(or)

All **Blessing and honour and glory and power**
be yours for ever and ever.
Amen.

As our Saviour taught us, so we pray

All **Our Father in heaven,**
hallowed be your name,
your kingdom come,
your will be done,
on earth as in heaven.
Give us today our daily bread.
Forgive us our sins
as we forgive those who sin against us.
Lead us not into temptation
but deliver us from evil.
For the kingdom, the power,
and the glory are yours
now and for ever.
Amen.

Breaking of the Bread

We break this bread
to share in the body of Christ.

All **Though we are many, we are one body,**
because we all share in one bread.

Giving of Communion

The president invites the people to receive communion.
Each communicant replies **Amen** *to the words of distribution.*

After Communion

The president may use a post communion prayer
and then this prayer may be said together

All **Almighty God,**
we thank you for feeding us
with the body and blood of your Son Jesus Christ.
Through him we offer you our souls and bodies
to be a living sacrifice.
Send us out
in the power of your Spirit
to live and work
to your praise and glory.
Amen.

We go out to serve God

A blessing may be given, and the service ends with

Go in peace to love and serve the Lord.

All **In the name of Christ. Amen.**

(or)

Go in the peace of Christ.

All **Thanks be to God.**

A service from New Patterns for Worship. *Compilation copyright © The Archbishops' Council 2002.*

5

The Lord is Here

Notes

Type of service

¶ A Service of Holy Communion;

¶ A fully worked out sample, suitable for local reproduction;

¶ Makes less 'standard' choices of texts and is likely to be suitable for regular, but probably not weekly, use.

Responsive style

The dominant style in this service is responsive. If the suggestions here are replaced with other options this should be borne in mind. The biddings during the intercessions should be kept brief in order to maintain this sense of movement.

Confession

A Kyrie form of confession has been included. Attention is drawn to the note in *Common Worship* (Note 10, page 331) which states that this form of confession 'should not be the norm on Sundays'.

Note that the absolution is followed by the acclamation, 'Thanks be to God'.

Gloria in Excelsis

The form printed here is designed for responsive speaking. If possible, a sung version or another song of praise should be used.

Gospel acclamation

A form of acclamation is suggested which is different from that in *Common Worship*.

The Peace

A standard introduction to the Peace has been used, but it has been turned into a responsive form.

Prayers at the Preparation of the Table

The use of the 'With this bread that we bring ...' responses requires careful consideration of the practicalities. The leader's text here could be said by those bringing the bread and wine forward as they bring them – in which case care must be taken not to drown this out with a hymn at that point. Alternatively they could be said after any hymn either by those who have brought the elements forward, or by the president or another minister.

Eucharistic Prayer

Because of the responsive nature of the whole service, Prayer H has been chosen and is printed in full. Other suitable prayers that could be used (if printed) might include Prayers A (with optional responses), D or F. Alternatively, Prayers A, B or E could be used with a responsive thanksgiving from this book as a long Proper Preface.

After Communion

The 'Father of all ...' prayer has been used, not as printed in *Common Worship*, but turned into a responsive form.

The Lord is Here

A Service of Holy Communion

We say together the words printed in **bold.**

The Gathering

The Greeting

We meet in the name of God:
All **Father, Son and Holy Spirit.**

The Lord be with you
All **and also with you.**

(or)

Be with us, Spirit of God;
All **nothing can separate us from your love.**

Breathe on us, breath of God;
All **fill us with your saving power.**

Speak in us, wisdom of God;
All **bring strength, healing and peace.**

Silence is kept.

The Lord is here.
All **His Spirit is with us.**

Words of welcome or introduction may follow.

Prayers of Penitence

A minister invites the congregation to confession using this form or other suitable words

The Spirit of truth will convict the world
   of guilt about sin, righteousness and judgement.
All **We have grieved the Holy Spirit.**

In sorrow we confess our sins.

Silence is kept for reflection.

The Kyries are used, with penitential sentences inserted between each section

Lord, have mercy.

All **Lord, have mercy.**

Christ, have mercy.

All **Christ, have mercy.**

Lord, have mercy.

All **Lord, have mercy.**

May God our Father forgive *us our* sins,
and bring *us* to the fellowship of his table
with his saints for ever.

All **Amen. Thanks be to God.**

Gloria in Excelsis

Glory to God in the highest.

All **Glory to God in the highest.**

Glory to God in the highest,
and peace to his people on earth.

All **Glory to God in the highest.**

Lord God, heavenly King,
almighty God and Father,

All **Glory to God in the highest.**

we worship you, we give you thanks,
we praise you for your glory.

All **Glory to God in the highest.**

Lord Jesus Christ, only Son of the Father,
Lord God, Lamb of God,

All **Glory to God in the highest.**

you take away the sin of the world:
have mercy on us;
you are seated at the right hand of the Father:
receive our prayer.

All **Glory to God in the highest.**

For you alone are the Holy One,
you alone are the Lord,
you alone are the Most High, Jesus Christ,
with the Holy Spirit,
in the glory of God the Father.

All **Glory to God in the highest.**
Amen.

The president introduces a period of silent prayer.
The Collect is said, and all respond

All   **Amen.**

The Liturgy of the Word

Reading(s)

This response may be used

This is the word of the Lord.
All   **Thanks be to God.**

A psalm or canticle may follow the first reading; other hymns and songs may be used between the readings.

Gospel Reading

Praise the Lord.
All   **Alleluia.**

A sentence from Scripture is added here.

Alleluia.
All   **Praise the Lord.**

When the Gospel is announced the reader says

Hear the Gospel of our Lord Jesus Christ according to *N*.
All   **Glory to you, O Lord.**

At the end

This is the Gospel of the Lord.
All   **Praise to you, O Christ.**

Sermon

Creed

Do you believe and trust in God the Father?
All   **I believe in God, the Father almighty,**
       creator of heaven and earth.

Do you believe and trust in his Son Jesus Christ?

All **I believe in Jesus Christ, his only Son, our Lord,**
who was conceived by the Holy Spirit,
born of the Virgin Mary,
suffered under Pontius Pilate,
was crucified, died, and was buried;
he descended to the dead.
On the third day he rose again;
he ascended into heaven,
he is seated at the right hand of the Father,
and he will come to judge the living and the dead.

Do you believe and trust in the Holy Spirit?

All **I believe in the Holy Spirit,**
the holy catholic Church,
the communion of saints,
the forgiveness of sins,
the resurrection of the body,
and the life everlasting.
Amen.

Prayers of Intercession

This, or some other, response may be used

In faith we pray.

All **We pray to you our God.**

The Liturgy of the Sacrament

The Peace

We are the body of Christ.

All **In the one Spirit we were all baptized into one body.**

Let us then pursue all that makes for peace

All **and builds up our common life.**

The peace of the Lord be always with you

All **and also with you.**

Let us offer one another a sign of peace.

All may exchange a sign of peace.

A hymn may be sung.

This prayer at the preparation of the table may be said.

With this bread that we bring
All **we shall remember Jesus.**

With this wine that we bring
All **we shall remember Jesus.**

Bread for his body,
wine for his blood,
gifts from God to his table we bring.
All **We shall remember Jesus.**

The Eucharistic Prayer

The Lord be with you   *(or)*   The Lord is here.
All **and also with you.**   **His Spirit is with us.**

Lift up your hearts.
All **We lift them to the Lord.**

Let us give thanks to the Lord our God.
All **It is right to give thanks and praise.**

It is right to praise you, Father, Lord of all creation;
in your love you made us for yourself.

When we turned away
you did not reject us,
but came to meet us in your Son.
All **You embraced us as your children
and welcomed us to sit and eat with you.**

In Christ you shared our life
that we might live in him and he in us.
All **He opened his arms of love upon the cross
and made for all the perfect sacrifice for sin.**

On the night he was betrayed,
at supper with his friends
he took bread, and gave you thanks;
he broke it and gave it to them, saying:
Take, eat; this is my body which is given for you;
do this in remembrance of me.
All **Father, we do this in remembrance of him:
his body is the bread of life.**

At the end of supper, taking the cup of wine,
he gave you thanks, and said:
Drink this, all of you; this is my blood of the new covenant,
which is shed for you for the forgiveness of sins;
do this in remembrance of me.

All **Father, we do this in remembrance of him:
his blood is shed for all.**

As we proclaim his death and celebrate his rising in glory,
send your Holy Spirit that this bread and this wine
may be to us the body and blood of your dear Son.

All **As we eat and drink these holy gifts
make us one in Christ, our risen Lord.**

With your whole Church throughout the world
we offer you this sacrifice of praise
and lift our voice to join the eternal song of heaven:

All **Holy, holy, holy Lord,
God of power and might,
Heaven and earth are full of your glory.
Hosanna in the highest.**

The Lord's Prayer

As our Saviour taught us, so we pray

All **Our Father in heaven,
hallowed be your name,
your kingdom come,
your will be done,
on earth as in heaven.
Give us today our daily bread.
Forgive us our sins
as we forgive those who sin against us.
Lead us not into temptation
but deliver us from evil.
For the kingdom, the power,
and the glory are yours
now and for ever.
Amen.**

Every time we eat this bread
and drink this cup,

All **we proclaim the Lord's death
until he comes.**

The Agnus Dei may be used as the bread is broken

Jesus, Lamb of God,

All **have mercy on us.**

Jesus, bearer of our sins,

All **have mercy on us.**

Jesus, redeemer of the world,

All **grant us peace.**

This invitation is given

God's holy gifts for God's holy people.

All **Jesus Christ is holy,
Jesus Christ is Lord,
to the glory of God the Father.**

Father of all,
we give you thanks and praise,
that when we were still far off
you met us in your Son and brought us home.
Dying and living, he declared your love,
gave us grace, and opened the gate of glory.

All **May we who share Christ's body live his risen life;
we who drink his cup bring life to others;
we whom the Spirit lights give light to the world.**
Keep us firm in the hope you have set before us,
so we and all your children shall be free,
and the whole earth live to praise your name;
through Christ our Lord.

All **Amen.**

A hymn may be sung.

The Dismissal

This ending or a suitable blessing may be used

The Lord God almighty is our Father:

All **he loves us and tenderly cares for us.**

The Lord Jesus Christ is our Saviour:

All **he has redeemed us and will defend us to the end.**

The Lord, the Holy Spirit, is among us:

All **he will lead us in God's holy way.**
To God almighty, Father, Son and Holy Spirit,
be praise and glory today and for ever.
Amen.

A minister may say

Go in peace to love and serve the Lord.

All **In the name of Christ. Amen.**

A service from New Patterns for Worship. *Compilation copyright* © *The Archbishops'
Council 2002.*

6

This is our Story

Notes

Type of service

¶ A Service of the Word with Holy Communion;

¶ A fully worked out sample, suitable for local reproduction;

¶ Makes less 'standard' choices of texts and structure and is not intended for regular Sunday use.

Style and mood

The style of the service is generally informal.

The Gathering

This is seen as the time in the service to share news, including learning themes for adults and young people.

The Bible (or Gospel book) which is placed on the lectern could have been carried in by a member of the congregation (perhaps a child) and the responses could be led by that person before the Bible is placed on the lectern.

Candles on stands near the lectern could be lit. These could be moved to stand beside the holy table during the peace, when the focus of the service moves from lectern to table. If this is done, it is not appropriate to have candles alight on the holy table from the beginning of the service.

Opening Prayer

The responsive form printed could be replaced by the Prayer of Preparation from *Common Worship* Order One, or another suitable prayer.

Praise

The song of praise could be a version of the Gloria in Excelsis.

The Prayers

The prayers begin with the penitential material (which is used there, as part of the response to the Word, rather than at the beginning of the service) and then move on to intercession. The Lord's Prayer is used as the conclusion to the intercessions, and is used there rather than after the Eucharistic Prayer.

Eucharistic Prayer

This service is designed to use Prayer D, but another prayer could be used.

This is our Story

A Service of the Word
with a Celebration of Holy Communion

We say together the words printed in **bold.**

Gathering as the People of God

Greeting

Welcome in the name of Christ!
God's grace, mercy and peace be with you
All **and also with you.**

The president introduces the service.
A hymn or song may be sung.

Preparing for the Word

We worship with Christians near and far,
living and departed, old and young.
God's word is for all of us.
All **May it be a lamp to our feet**
and a light to our path.

A Bible is placed on the lectern and candles near it are lit.

Sit. News and learning themes for different age groups are shared.

Opening Prayer

Lord, speak to us
All **that we may hear your word.**
Move among us
All **that we may behold your glory.**
Receive our prayers
All **that we may learn to trust you.**
Amen.

Praise

A song or hymn of praise is sung.

The Collect

The president introduces a time of silent prayer and then says the Collect,
the prayer of the day.

Proclaiming the Word of the Lord

Reading(s)

At the end of the reading(s) this response is used

This is the word of the Lord.

All **Thanks be to God.**

Silence is kept for reflection.

Gospel Reading

Before the Gospel reading this response is used

Hear the Gospel of our Lord Jesus Christ according to N.

All **Glory to you, O Lord.**

After the Gospel

This is the Gospel of the Lord.

All **Praise to you, O Christ.**

Sermon

A hymn or song(s) may be sung.

Creed

The Apostles' Creed is used

All **I believe in God, the Father almighty,**
creator of heaven and earth.

I believe in Jesus Christ, his only Son, our Lord,
who was conceived by the Holy Spirit,
born of the Virgin Mary,
suffered under Pontius Pilate,
was crucified, died, and was buried;
he descended to the dead.
On the third day he rose again;
he ascended into heaven,
he is seated at the right hand of the Father,
and he will come to judge the living and the dead.

I believe in the Holy Spirit,
the holy catholic Church,
the communion of saints,
the forgiveness of sins,
the resurrection of the body,
and the life everlasting.
Amen.

Come, let us return to the Lord and say:

All **Lord our God,**
in our sin we have avoided your call.
Our love for you is like a morning cloud,
like the dew that goes away early.
Have mercy on us;
deliver us from judgement;
bind up our wounds and revive us;
in Jesus Christ our Lord.
Amen.

The president declares God's forgiveness.

Praying for Others

The prayers of intercession may include the response

In faith we pray.
All **We pray to you our God.**

and may end with

Lord of the Church:
All **hear our prayer,**
and make us one in heart and mind
to serve you with joy for ever.
Amen.

The Lord's Prayer

As our Saviour taught us, so we pray

All **Our Father in heaven,**
hallowed be your name,
your kingdom come,
your will be done,
on earth as in heaven.
Give us today our daily bread.
Forgive us our sins
as we forgive those who sin against us.
Lead us not into temptation
but deliver us from evil.
For the kingdom, the power,
and the glory are yours
now and for ever.
Amen.

Sharing at the Table of the Lord

After the introductory words

The peace of the Lord be always with you

All　**and also with you.**

The Eucharistic Prayer

One of the authorized Eucharistic Prayers is used.

The Lord be with you　　*(or)*　　The Lord is here.

All　**and also with you.**　　　　　**His Spirit is with us.**

Lift up your hearts.

All　**We lift them to the Lord.**

Let us give thanks to the Lord our God.

All　**It is right to give thanks and praise.**

The president continues the prayer, praising God.

All join in the words

All　**Holy, holy, holy Lord,**
God of power and might,
heaven and earth are full of your glory.
Hosanna in the highest.
[Blessed is he who comes in the name of the Lord.
Hosanna in the highest.]

Father of all, we give you thanks
　　for every gift that comes from heaven.

To the darkness Jesus came as your light.
With signs of faith and words of hope
he touched untouchables with love and washed the guilty clean.

This is his story.

All　**This is our song:**
Hosanna in the highest.

The crowds came out to see your Son,
　　yet at the end they turned on him.
On the night he was betrayed
he came to table with his friends
　　to celebrate the freedom of your people.

This is his story.

All　**This is our song:**
Hosanna in the highest.

Jesus blessed you, Father, for the food;
he took bread, gave thanks, broke it and said:
This is my body, given for you all.
Jesus then gave thanks for the wine;
he took the cup, gave it and said:
This is my blood, shed for you all
    for the forgiveness of sins.
Do this in remembrance of me.

This is our story.

All **This is our song:**
Hosanna in the highest.

Therefore, Father, with this bread and this cup
we celebrate the cross
on which he died to set us free.
Defying death he rose again
and is alive with you to plead for us and all the world.

This is our story.

All **This is our song:**
Hosanna in the highest.

The prayer continues, concluding with

All **Blessing and honour and glory and power**
be yours for ever and ever.
Amen.

Breaking of the Bread

We break this bread
to share in the body of Christ.

All **Though we are many, we are one body,**
because we all share in one bread.

Giving of Communion

The president invites the people to receive communion.
Each communicant replies **Amen** *to the words of distribution.*

The president may use a post communion prayer and then this prayer may be said together

All **Lord,**
we have broken your bread
and received your life.
By the power of your Spirit
keep us always in your love
through Jesus Christ our Lord.
Amen.

Going out to serve the Lord

A blessing may be given, and the service ends with

Go in peace to love and serve the Lord.

All **In the name of Christ. Amen.**

A service from New Patterns for Worship. *Compilation copyright © The Archbishops' Council 2002.*

7

Believe and Trust:
Holy Communion with Baptism

Notes

Type of service

¶ A fully worked out sample, suitable for local reproduction
(note that it does *not* include all the words required by the president);

¶ Designed to be suitable for regular use and for a variety of contexts.

This service is designed for use at the baptism of infants. It could be adapted for use with adult candidates.

The candidates with their parents, and also those who are the ministers in this service, will need careful preparation.

This form of the service is a fairly simple version of the Baptism service, within a celebration of Holy Communion, for use by the congregation. It may help to give the parents, godparents and others a copy of the service, in this simplified form, to study at home.

For the Baptism of Children at A Service of the Word (without a celebration of Holy Communion), see *Common Worship: Initiation Services.*

Some points to note

¶ The presentation of the candidates has been placed in its alternative position, near the beginning of the service, rather than immediately before the Decision.

¶ Other people – parents, sponsors, godparents – may be invited to sign the candidate with the cross.

¶ Careful thought should be given to the location for each part of the service, and to the movement of ministers, parents, godparents and candidates to and from the font.

¶ Some points are suggested for hymns, but they may come elsewhere. A hymn might be sung, for instance, while those taking part – or the whole congregation – move to the font.

¶ Eucharistic Prayer E gives the opportunity for a short Eucharistic Prayer with a Proper Preface relating to baptism (see *Common Worship*, page 362), but Eucharistic Prayers A, B, C and G are also suitable for use with the service printed out in this form.

¶ If there is a Blessing, it should come before the Giving of a Lighted Candle.

If a local leaflet is being produced for this service, it may be helpful to include the Pastoral Introduction to Holy Baptism from page 345 of *Common Worship*, which is printed below.

Pastoral Introduction

This may be read by those present before the service begins.

Baptism marks the beginning of a journey with God which continues for the rest of our lives, the first step in response to God's love. For all involved, particularly the candidates but also parents, godparents and sponsors, it is a joyful moment when we rejoice in what God has done for us in Christ, making serious promises and declaring the faith. The wider community of the local church and friends welcome the new Christian, promising support and prayer for the future. Hearing and doing these things provides an opportunity to remember our own baptism and reflect on the progress made on that journey, which is now to be shared with this new member of the Church.

The service paints many vivid pictures of what happens on the Christian way. There is the sign of the cross, the badge of faith in the Christian journey, which reminds us of Christ's death for us. Our 'drowning' in the water of baptism, where we believe we die to sin and are raised to new life, unites us to Christ's dying and rising, a picture that can be brought home vividly by the way the baptism is administered. Water is also a sign of new life, as we are born again by water and the Spirit. This reminds us of Jesus' baptism. And as a sign of that new life, there may be a lighted candle, a picture of the light of Christ conquering the darkness of evil. Everyone who is baptized walks in that light for the rest of their life.

As you pray for the candidates, picture them with yourself and the whole Church throughout the ages, journeying into the fullness of God's love.

Jesus said, 'I came that they may have life, and have it abundantly.'

John 10.10

Believe and Trust: Holy Communion with Baptism

*Texts printed in **bold** without 'All' in the margin are spoken by candidates, parents and godparents alone.*

Greeting

Singing, Scripture sentence, Greeting, Introduction or Prayer, which includes

The grace of our Lord Jesus Christ,
the love of God
and the fellowship of the Holy Spirit
be with you

All **and also with you.**

Presentation of the Candidate(s)

The candidate(s) may be presented to the congregation.

The president addresses the whole congregation

Faith is the gift of God to his people.
In baptism the Lord is adding to our number
    those whom he is calling.
People of God, will you welcome *these children*
    and uphold *them* in *their* new life in Christ?

All **With the help of God, we will.**

The president says to the parents and godparents

Parents and godparents, the Church receives *these children* with joy.
Today we are trusting God for *their* growth in faith.
Will you pray for *them,*
draw *them* by your example into the community of faith
and walk with *them* in the way of Christ?
With the help of God, we will.

In baptism *these children* begin *their* journey in faith.
You speak for *them* today.
Will you care for *them,*
and help *them* to take *their* place within the life and worship of Christ's Church?
With the help of God, we will.

The president says the Collect.

At the end of each reading this response may be used

This is the word of the Lord.

All **Thanks be to God.**

A psalm or scriptural song may follow.

When the Gospel reading is announced the reader says

Hear the Gospel of our Lord Jesus Christ according to N.

All **Glory to you, O Lord.**

At the end of the Gospel reading this response is used

This is the Gospel of the Lord.

All **Praise to you, O Christ.**

The president addresses the candidate(s) through the parents
and godparents

In baptism, God calls us out of darkness into his marvellous light.
To follow Christ means dying to sin and rising to new life with him.
Therefore I ask:

Do you reject the devil and all rebellion against God?
I reject them.

Do you renounce the deceit and corruption of evil?
I renounce them.

Do you repent of the sins that separate us from God and neighbour?
I repent of them.

Do you turn to Christ as Saviour?
I turn to Christ.

Do you submit to Christ as Lord?
I submit to Christ.

Do you come to Christ, the way, the truth and the life?
I come to Christ.

A minister makes the sign of the cross on the forehead of the candidate(s) using these words

Christ claims you for his own.
Receive the sign of his cross.

The president may invite parents, godparents and sponsors to sign the candidates with the cross. When all the candidates have been signed, the president says

Do not be ashamed to confess the faith of Christ crucified.
All **Fight valiantly as a disciple of Christ**
against sin, the world and the devil,
and remain faithful to Christ to the end of your life.

May almighty God deliver you from the powers of darkness,
restore in you the image of his glory,
and lead you in the light and obedience of Christ.
All **Amen.**

Prayer over the Water

The ministers and candidate(s) gather at the font.

Praise God who made heaven and earth,
All **who keeps his promise for ever.**

Let us give thanks to the Lord our God.
All **It is right to give thanks and praise.**

The prayer over the water follows.

This response may be used

Saving God
All **give us life.**

The prayer ends

All **Amen.**

The president addresses the congregation

Brothers and sisters, I ask you to profess
together with *these candidates*
the faith of the Church.

Do you believe and trust in God the Father?

All **I believe in God, the Father almighty,
creator of heaven and earth.**

Do you believe and trust in his Son Jesus Christ?

All **I believe in Jesus Christ, his only Son, our Lord,
who was conceived by the Holy Spirit,
born of the Virgin Mary,
suffered under Pontius Pilate,
was crucified, died, and was buried;
he descended to the dead.
On the third day he rose again;
he ascended into heaven,
he is seated at the right hand of the Father,
and he will come to judge the living and the dead.**

Do you believe and trust in the Holy Spirit?

All **I believe in the Holy Spirit,
the holy catholic Church,
the communion of saints,
the forgiveness of sins,
the resurrection of the body,
and the life everlasting.
Amen.**

Baptism

*The president or another minister dips each candidate in water,
or pours water on them, saying*

N, I baptize you
in the name of the Father,
and of the Son,
and of the Holy Spirit.

All **Amen.**

The president says

May God, who has received you by baptism into his Church,
pour upon you the riches of his grace,
that within the company of Christ's pilgrim people
you may daily be renewed by his anointing Spirit,
and come to the inheritance of the saints in glory.

All **Amen.**

Commission

A minister addresses the congregation, parents and godparents, and prays for them.

Prayers of Intercession

The Welcome and Peace

There is one Lord, one faith, one baptism:
N and N, by one Spirit we are all baptized into one body.

All   **We welcome you into the fellowship of faith;
we are children of the same heavenly Father;
we welcome you.**

The congregation may greet the newly baptized.

The president introduces the Peace

The peace of the Lord be always with you

All   **and also with you.**

Preparation of the Table

The table is prepared and bread and wine are placed upon it.
These responses may be used

With this bread that we bring

All   **we shall remember Jesus.**

With this wine that we bring

All   **we shall remember Jesus.**

Bread for his body,
wine for his blood,
gifts from God to his table we bring.

All   **We shall remember Jesus.**

The Eucharistic Prayer

The Lord be with you   *(or)*   The Lord is here.

All   **and also with you.**   **His Spirit is with us.**

Lift up your hearts.

All   **We lift them to the Lord.**

Let us give thanks to the Lord our God.

All   **It is right to give thanks and praise.**

All **Holy, holy, holy Lord,**
God of power and might,
heaven and earth are full of your glory.
Hosanna in the highest.
[Blessed is he who comes in the name of the Lord.
Hosanna in the highest.]

The president recalls the Last Supper.
This acclamation may be used

[Praise to you, Lord Jesus:]
All **Dying you destroyed our death,**
rising you restored our life:
Lord Jesus, come in glory.

The Prayer continues and concludes
either

All **Amen.**

(or)

All **Blessing and honour and glory and power**
be yours for ever and ever.
Amen.

The Lord's Prayer

As our Saviour taught us, so we pray

All **Our Father in heaven,**
hallowed be your name,
your kingdom come,
your will be done,
on earth as in heaven.
Give us today our daily bread.
Forgive us our sins
as we forgive those who sin against us.
Lead us not into temptation
but deliver us from evil.
For the kingdom, the power,
and the glory are yours
now and for ever.
Amen.

We break this bread
to share in the body of Christ.

All **Though we are many, we are one body,
because we all share in one bread.**

The president invites the people to receive communion.
Authorized words of distribution are used and the communicant replies **Amen**.
A prayer follows the distribution of communion.

Each candidate may be given a lighted candle.
When they have each received a candle, the minister says

God has delivered us from the dominion of darkness
and has given us a place with the saints in light.

You have received the light of Christ;
walk in this light all the days of your life.

All **Shine as a light in the world
to the glory of God the Father.**

Go in the light and peace of Christ.

All **Thanks be to God.**

A service from New Patterns for Worship. *Compilation copyright © The Archbishops'
Council 2002.*

Seasonal Services

Seasonal Services

8

Come, Lord Jesus:
Holy Communion in Advent

Notes

Type of service

¶ A Service of the Word with a Celebration of Holy Communion for use in Advent;

¶ A fully worked out sample, suitable for local reproduction (note that it does *not* include all the words required by the president).

Advent ring

A position is suggested for the lighting of appropriate candles on the Advent ring (if there is one). Other possible positions for this would be:
¶ after the sermon;
¶ before the peace;
¶ before the dismissal.

There are several different patterns of 'meanings' suggested for the four or five candles of the ring. Care needs to be taken that the congregation understands what the candles are signifying.

If words are said and a song sung, care is needed to maintain a sense of event. A suggested pattern is:
¶ Congregation stands;
¶ Words are said (either words of explanation, or a sentence of Scripture, or a versicle and response);
¶ Candle is lit;
¶ Song is sung.

Where the Collect follows, the congregation remain standing in silence before the president prays the Collect.

Intercessions

The response printed is F72 from the intercessions ('We pray for the coming of God's kingdom ...'), but any form of intercessions could be used with the same response.

Eucharistic Prayer

This order is suitable as printed, for use with Prayers A, B, C, E and G, though Prayer G does not allow for a seasonal Proper Preface.

Come, Lord Jesus

A Service of the Word with a Celebration of Holy Communion in Advent

We say together the words printed in **bold.**

The Gathering

The Greeting

The Lord be with you

All **and also with you.**

One of these sentences may be used

Break forth together into singing, you waste places of Jerusalem,
for the Lord has comforted his people.   *Isaiah 52.9*

Lift up your heads, O gates; lift them high, O everlasting doors, and
the king of glory shall come in.   *Psalm 24.7*

Watch at all times, praying for the strength to stand with confidence
before the Son of Man.   *Luke 21.36*

Look up and raise your heads, because your redemption is drawing
near.   *Luke 21.28*

Our Lord says 'Surely I come quickly.' Even so; Come, Lord Jesus.
                                                      Revelation 22.20

Prayer of Preparation

All **Almighty God,**
to whom all hearts are open,
all desires known,
and from whom no secrets are hidden:
cleanse the thoughts of our hearts
by the inspiration of your Holy Spirit,
that we may perfectly love you,
and worthily magnify your holy name;
through Christ our Lord.
Amen.

Christ the Light of the world has come to dispel the darkness of our hearts.
In his light let us examine ourselves and confess our sins.

All **Most merciful God,**
Father of our Lord Jesus Christ,
we confess that we have sinned
in thought, word and deed.
We have not loved you with our whole heart.
We have not loved our neighbours as ourselves.
In your mercy
forgive what we have been,
help us to amend what we are,
and direct what we shall be;
that we may do justly,
love mercy,
and walk humbly with you, our God.
Amen.

The president declares God's forgiveness.

Advent Ring

If there is an Advent ring, candles on it may be lit at this point.

The Collect

The Liturgy of the Word

Reading(s)

After each reading

This is the word of the Lord.
All **Thanks be to God.**

This, or another psalm or scriptural song, may be used

Out of the depths I have called to you, Lord.
Let your ears be open to hear my voice.
All　**My hope is in God's word.**

If you recorded all our sins
who could come before you?
All　**My hope is in God's word.**

There is forgiveness with you:
therefore you shall be feared.
All　**My hope is in God's word.**

My soul is longing for the Lord,
more than those who watch for daybreak.
All　**My hope is in God's word.**

O Israel, wait for the Lord,
for with the Lord there is mercy.
All　**My hope is in God's word.**

Glory to the Father, and to the Son, and to the Holy Spirit.
All　**My hope is in God's word.**

Gospel Reading

When the Gospel is announced the reader says

Hear the Gospel of our Lord Jesus Christ according to *N*.
All　**Glory to you, O Lord.**

and at the end

This is the Gospel of the Lord.
All　**Praise to you, O Christ.**

Affirmation of Faith

This, or a creed or other authorized Affirmation of Faith is used

We say together in faith
All　**Holy, holy, holy**
is the Lord God almighty,
who was, and is, and is to come.

We believe in God the Father, who created all things:
All　**for by his will they were created**
and have their being.

We believe in God the Son,
who was slain:

All **for with his blood,
he purchased us for God,
from every tribe and language,
from every people and nation.**

We believe in God the Holy Spirit:

All **the Spirit and the Bride say, 'Come!'
Even so come, Lord Jesus!
Amen.**

Prayers of Intercession

This response is used

We pray for the coming of God's kingdom, saying:
Father, by your Spirit

All **bring in your kingdom.**

The prayers conclude

Lord of the Church

All **hear our prayer,
and make us one in heart and mind
to serve you with joy for ever.
Amen.**

The Lord's Prayer

The Lord's Prayer may be said here or after the Eucharistic Prayer

Let us pray for the coming of God's kingdom
in the words our Saviour taught us.

All **Our Father in heaven,
hallowed be your name,
your kingdom come,
your will be done,
on earth as in heaven.
Give us today our daily bread.
Forgive us our sins
as we forgive those who sin against us.
Lead us not into temptation
but deliver us from evil.
For the kingdom, the power,
and the glory are yours
now and for ever.
Amen.**

The Liturgy of the Sacrament

In the tender mercy of our God,
the dayspring from on high shall break upon us,
to give light to those who dwell in darkness
and in the shadow of death,
and to guide our feet into the way of peace.
The peace of the Lord be always with you

All **and also with you.**

Let us offer one another a sign of peace.

All may exchange a sign of peace.

If the Service of the Word is to end here, the Dismissal takes place here.

Preparation of the Table

Taking of the Bread and Wine

This prayer may be used

Blessed be God,
who feeds the hungry,
who raises the poor,
who fills our praise.

All **Blessed be God for ever.**

The Eucharistic Prayer

The Lord be with you.   *(or)*   The Lord is here.

All **and also with you.**   **His Spirit is with us.**

Lift up your hearts.

All **We lift them to the Lord.**

Let us give thanks to the Lord our God.

All **It is right to give thanks and praise.**

The president praises God for his mighty acts, ending

All **Holy, holy, holy Lord,**
God of power and might,
heaven and earth are full of your glory.
Hosanna in the highest.
[Blessed is he who comes in the name of the Lord.
Hosanna in the highest.]

The president recalls the Last Supper.

Praise to you, Lord Jesus:

All **Dying you destroyed our death,
rising you restored our life:
Lord Jesus, come in glory.**

The Prayer ends

All **Amen.**

(or)

All **Blessing and honour and glory and power
be yours for ever and ever.
Amen.**

The Lord's Prayer is said here if not already used.

Breaking of the Bread

Every time we eat this bread
and drink this cup,

All **we proclaim the Lord's death
until he comes.**

The Agnus Dei ('Lamb of God') may be said or sung.

Giving of Communion

The president invites the people to receive communion.

Prayer after Communion

Silence is kept.

One or both of these prayers may be said

Loving Father,
your Son Jesus Christ has come to us
in word and Spirit, in bread and cup.
Make us holy
and bring us to perfection,
when we stand before him
as he comes to judge the living and the dead,
Jesus Christ our Lord.

All **Amen.**

All **Generous God,**
you have fed us at your heavenly table.
Set us on fire with your Spirit
that when Christ comes again
we may shine like lights before his face;
who with you and the Spirit lives for ever.
Amen.

The Dismissal

These words may be said

Our Lord says, I am coming soon.
All **Amen. Come Lord Jesus.**

May the Lord, when he comes, find us watching and waiting.
All **Amen.**

The president may use this seasonal blessing

May God himself, the God of peace,
make you perfect and holy;
and keep you all safe and blameless, in spirit, soul and body,
for the coming of our Lord Jesus Christ.
And the blessing …

Go in peace to love and serve the Lord.
All **In the name of Christ. Amen.**

A service from New Patterns for Worship. *Compilation copyright © The Archbishops'*
Council 2002.

9

Peace to God's People: Holy Communion during the Christmas Season

Notes

Type of service

¶ A service of Holy Communion for use at and after Christmas;

¶ A fully worked out sample, suitable for local reproduction (note that it does *not* include all the words required by the president).

Response

The response

> The Word was made flesh and lived among us:
> **and we have seen his glory.**

is used in several places in the service as a common thread.

Prayers of Intercession

A suitable seasonal form should be chosen (for example F53) and any response clearly explained to the congregation.

Eucharistic Prayer

This order is suitable as printed, for use with Prayers A, B, C, E and G, though Prayer G does not allow for a seasonal Proper Preface.

Prayer after Communion

This prayer has been printed as a presidential prayer, but the congregation could be invited to join in with it if desired.

Blessing

If a blessing is required, a suitable seasonal form could be used.

Peace to God's People

Holy Communion during the Christmas Season

We say together the words printed in **bold.**

The Greeting

I bring you good news of great joy:

All   **a Saviour has been born to you. Alleluia.**

Unto us a child is born,

All   **unto us a Son is given. Alleluia.**

He is Christ the Lord. Alleluia.

All   **We worship and adore him. Alleluia.**

Prayers of Penitence

Hear the words of the angel to Joseph:
'You shall call his name Jesus,
for he will save his people from their sins.'
Therefore let us seek the forgiveness of God
through Jesus the Saviour of the world.

Lord of grace and truth,
we confess our unworthiness
to stand in your presence as your children.
We have sinned:

All   **forgive and heal us.**

The Virgin Mary accepted your call
to be the mother of Jesus.
Forgive our disobedience to your will.
We have sinned:

All   **forgive and heal us.**

Your Son our Saviour
was born in poverty in a manger.
Forgive our greed and rejection of your ways.
We have sinned:

All   **forgive and heal us.**

The shepherds left their flocks
to go to Bethlehem.
Forgive our self-interest and lack of vision.
We have sinned:

All   **forgive and heal us.**

The wise men followed the star
to find Jesus the King.
Forgive our reluctance to seek you.
We have sinned:

All **forgive and heal us.**

May the God of all healing and forgiveness
draw *us* to himself,
and cleanse *us* from all our sins
that *we* may behold the glory of his Son,
the Word made flesh,
Jesus Christ our Lord.

All **Amen.**

The Word was made flesh and lived among us:

All **and we have seen his glory.**

Gloria in Excelsis

All **Glory to God in the highest,
and peace to his people on earth.**

**Lord God, heavenly King, almighty God and Father,
we worship you, we give you thanks,
we praise you for your glory.**

**Lord Jesus Christ, only Son of the Father,
Lord God, Lamb of God,
you take away the sin of the world:
have mercy on us;
you are seated at the right hand of the Father:
receive our prayer.**

**For you alone are the Holy One,
you alone are the Lord,
you alone are the Most High, Jesus Christ,
with the Holy Spirit,
in the glory of God the Father.
Amen.**

The Collect

Reading(s)

After each reading

This is the word of the Lord.

All **Thanks be to God.**

The Word was made flesh and lived among us:

All **and we have seen his glory.**

When the Gospel is announced

Hear the Gospel of our Lord Jesus Christ according to *N*.

All **Glory to you, O Lord.**

and at the end

This is the Gospel of the Lord.

All **Praise to you, O Christ.**

Sermon

This response may follow the sermon

The Word was made flesh and lived among us:

All **and we have seen his glory.**

Affirmation of Faith

This, or another authorized Affirmation of Faith or Creed, is used

Let us affirm our faith in Jesus Christ the Son of God.

All **Though he was divine,**
he did not cling to equality with God,
but made himself nothing.
Taking the form of a slave,
he was born in human likeness.
He humbled himself
and was obedient to death,
even the death of the cross.
Therefore God has raised him on high,
and given him the name above every name:
that at the name of Jesus
every knee should bow,
and every voice proclaim that Jesus Christ is Lord,
to the glory of God the Father.
Amen.

The Word was made flesh and lived among us:

All **and we have seen his glory.**

A hymn may be sung.

Prayers of Intercession

Unto us a child is born, unto us a son is given,
and his name shall be called the Prince of Peace.
The peace of the Lord be always with you

All **and also with you.**

All may exchange a sign of peace.

Preparation of the Table

A hymn may be sung.

The table is prepared and bread and wine are placed upon it.
This prayer may be said

Blessed be God,
by whose grace creation is renewed,
by whose love heaven is opened,
by whose mercy we offer our sacrifice of praise.

All **Blessed be God for ever.**

The Eucharistic Prayer

The Lord be with you.   *(or)*   The Lord is here.

All **and also with you.**   **His Spirit is with us.**

Lift up your hearts.

All **We lift them to the Lord.**

Let us give thanks to the Lord our God.

All **It is right to give thanks and praise.**

The president praises God for his mighty acts, ending with

All **Holy, holy, holy Lord,**
God of power and might,
heaven and earth are full of your glory.
Hosanna in the highest.
[Blessed is he who comes in the name of the Lord.
Hosanna in the highest.]

The president recalls the Last Supper.

This acclamation may be used

Jesus Christ is Lord:

All **Lord, by your cross and resurrection
you have set us free.
You are the Saviour of the world.**

The Prayer ends

All **Amen.**

(or)

All **Blessing and honour and glory and power
be yours for ever and ever.
Amen.**

The Lord's Prayer

As our Saviour taught us, so we pray

All **Our Father in heaven,
hallowed be your name,
your kingdom come,
your will be done,
on earth as in heaven.
Give us today our daily bread.
Forgive us our sins
as we forgive those who sin against us.
Lead us not into temptation
but deliver us from evil.
For the kingdom, the power,
and the glory are yours
now and for ever.
Amen.**

Breaking of the Bread

We break this bread
to share in the body of Christ.

All **Though we are many, we are one body,
because we all share in one bread.**

Giving of Communion

*The president invites the people to communion.
When the bread and wine are received each communicant replies*

All **Amen.**

Silence is kept.

This prayer may be said

Son of Mary, Son of God,
we have joined the worship of the angels;
may we never lose that heavenly vision.
Like the shepherds,
we have rejoiced at the news of your birth;
help us to proclaim that message in word and deed,
to your praise and glory.

All **Amen.**

The Dismissal

A hymn may be sung.

A blessing may be given.

This response is used

The Word was made flesh and lived among us:

All **and we have seen his glory.**

Go in peace to love and serve the Lord.

All **In the name of Christ. Amen.**

A service from New Patterns for Worship. *Compilation copyright © The Archbishops' Council 2002.*

10

Light to the World: Holy Communion in Epiphany

Notes

Type of service

¶ A Service of the Word with a celebration of Holy Communion for use in the period between the Epiphany and the Presentation of Christ (Candlemas);

¶ A fully worked out sample, suitable for local reproduction (note that it does *not* include all the words required by the president).

General

Because this is a service for the season of Epiphany, rather than the Feast of the Epiphany, the particular texts chosen reflect the general themes of 'revelation' and light, rather than focusing on the more specific Epiphany themes of the wise men, the baptism of Christ or the miracle at the wedding at Cana.

Points to note:

¶ The Gloria takes the place of the opening hymn;

¶ The prayers of penitence are in the alternative place before the prayers of intercession, to allow people to respond to God's word.

Eucharistic Prayer

This order is suitable as printed for use with Prayers A, B, C, E and G, though Prayer G does not allow for a seasonal Proper Preface.

Light to the World

Holy Communion in Epiphany

We say together the words printed in **bold.**

The Greeting

The Lord be with you

All   **and also with you.**

God in Christ has revealed his glory.

All   **Come let us worship.**

From the rising of the sun to its setting

All   **the Lord's name is greatly to be praised.**

Give him praise, you servants of the Lord.

All   **O praise the name of the Lord!**

Gloria in Excelsis

All   **Glory to God in the highest,**
and peace to his people on earth.

Lord God, heavenly King, almighty God and Father,
we worship you, we give you thanks,
we praise you for your glory.

Lord Jesus Christ, only Son of the Father,
Lord God, Lamb of God,
you take away the sin of the world:
have mercy on us;
you are seated at the right hand of the Father:
receive our prayer.

For you alone are the Holy One,
you alone are the Lord,
you alone are the Most High, Jesus Christ,
with the Holy Spirit,
in the glory of God the Father.
Amen.

The Collect

Reading(s)

After each reading

This is the word of the Lord.
All **Thanks be to God.**

Gospel Reading

When the Gospel is announced the reader says

Hear the Gospel of our Lord Jesus Christ according to N.
All **Glory to you, O Lord.**

and at the end

This is the Gospel of the Lord.
All **Praise to you, O Christ.**

Sermon

Affirmation of Faith

This, or some other, authorized Affirmation of Faith, or a Creed, may be used

Let us affirm our faith in Jesus Christ the Son of God.

All **Though he was divine,**
he did not cling to equality with God,
but made himself nothing.
Taking the form of a slave,
he was born in human likeness.
He humbled himself
and was obedient to death,
even the death of the cross.
Therefore God has raised him on high,
and given him the name above every name:
that at the name of Jesus
every knee should bow,
and every voice proclaim that Jesus Christ is Lord,
to the glory of God the Father.
Amen.

When the Lord comes,
he will bring to light the things now hidden in darkness,
and will disclose the purposes of the heart.
Therefore in the light of Christ let us confess our sins.

God be gracious to us and bless us,
and make your face shine upon us:
Lord, have mercy.

All   **Lord, have mercy.**

May your ways be known on the earth,
your saving power among the nations:
Christ, have mercy.

All   **Christ, have mercy.**

You, Lord, have made known your salvation,
and reveal your justice in the sight of the nations:
Lord, have mercy.

All   **Lord, have mercy.**

The president declares God's forgiveness.

Prayers of Intercession

This response may be used

Lord, in your mercy

All   **hear our prayer.**

The prayers may conclude

Merciful Father,

All   **accept these prayers**
for the sake of your Son,
our Saviour Jesus Christ.
Amen.

The Lord's Prayer may be said here or after the Eucharistic Prayer.

As our Saviour taught us, so we pray

All   **Our Father in heaven,**
hallowed be your name,
your kingdom come,
your will be done,
on earth as in heaven.
Give us today our daily bread.
Forgive us our sins
as we forgive those who sin against us.
Lead us not into temptation
but deliver us from evil.
For the kingdom, the power,
and the glory are yours
now and for ever.
Amen.

The service may end here with Blessing and Dismissal.

The Peace

Christ came and proclaimed the gospel,
peace to those who are far off
and peace to those who are near.

The peace of the Lord be always with you

All   **and also with you.**

Let us offer one another a sign of peace.

All may exchange a sign of peace.

Preparation of the Table

Taking of the Bread and Wine

This prayer may be said

Look upon us in mercy, not in judgement;
draw us from hatred to love;
make the frailty of our praise
a dwelling place for your glory.

All   **Amen.**

The Lord be with you   *(or)*   The Lord is here.
All   **and also with you.**   **His Spirit is with us.**

Lift up your hearts.
All   **We lift them to the Lord.**

Let us give thanks to the Lord our God.
All   **It is right to give thanks and praise.**

The president praises God for his mighty acts, ending with

All   **Holy, holy, holy Lord,**
God of power and might,
heaven and earth are full of your glory.
Hosanna in the highest.
[Blessed is he who comes in the name of the Lord.
Hosanna in the highest.]

The president recalls the Last Supper.

This acclamation may be used

Great is the mystery of faith:
All   **Christ has died:**
Christ is risen:
Christ will come again.

The Prayer ends

All   **Amen.**

(or)

All   **Blessing and honour and glory and power**
be yours for ever and ever.
Amen.

The Lord's Prayer should be said here if it has not been used earlier.

Breaking of the Bread

We break this bread
to share in the body of Christ.
All   **Though we are many, we are one body,**
because we all share in one bread.

The Agnus Dei ('Lamb of God') may be said or sung.

The president invites the people to receive communion.

Silence is kept.

God of glory,
you nourish us with your Word
who is the bread of life.
Fill us with your Holy Spirit,
that through us the light of your glory
may shine in all the world.
We ask this in the name of Jesus Christ our Lord.

All **Amen.**

All **Almighty God,**
we thank you for feeding us
with the body and blood of your Son Jesus Christ.
Through him we offer you our souls and bodies
to be a living sacrifice.
Send us out
in the power of your Spirit
to live and work
to your praise and glory.
Amen.

May Christ draw you to humility and worship,
and bring you to see God at work;
and the blessing of God almighty,
the Father, the Son, and the Holy Spirit,
be among you and remain with you always.

All **Amen.**

Let us go in peace.

All **We go into the world**
to walk in God's light,
to rejoice in God's love
and to reflect God's glory.
Amen.

A service from New Patterns for Worship. *Compilation copyright © The Archbishops'
Council 2002.*

11

In Penitence and Faith: a Service in Lent

Notes

Type of service

¶ A non-eucharistic service for use in Lent;

¶ A fully worked out sample, suitable for local reproduction;

¶ Designed to be suitable for regular use, though not for every Sunday in Lent.

The Beatitudes

The Beatitudes here are used as part of the preparation for the service rather than part of the fuller penitential material which occurs later in the service. They can be enhanced by the use of two voices, one taking the first half of each Beatitude and the other responding with the second half.

The version printed here is the *Common Worship* form, but another form or a different Bible translation could be used.

As an alternative, the 'comfortable words' could be used.

Psalm

A version of Psalm 130 is printed in the order of service (another version, or a different psalm could be used instead). This is intended to give the congregation a chance to become familiar with one particular psalm, which has a seasonal 'flavour'.

Agnus Dei

Agnus Dei is suggested as part of the preparation for confession. Where a congregation is familiar with a sung setting from the Eucharist, this should be used. If not, a setting could be learnt, or a suitable simple penitential song could be sung instead.

Affirmation of Faith

Placing this in the concluding part of the service helps make the shift from the penitential mood of the rest of the service to preparing to go out into the world full of faith and hope.

Final Prayer

This could be used as a congregational prayer.

In Penitence and Faith

A Service of the Word in Lent

We say together the words printed in **bold.**

Preparation

The Greeting

The Lord our redeemer be with you
All **and also with you.**

Further words of welcome and introduction may be given.

Opening Prayer

God of our days and years,
we set this time apart for you.
Form us in the likeness of Christ
so that our lives may glorify you.
All **Amen.**

The Beatitudes

Let us hear our Lord's blessing on those who follow him.

Blessed are the poor in spirit,
for theirs is the kingdom of heaven.

Blessed are those who mourn,
for they shall be comforted.

Blessed are the meek,
for they shall inherit the earth.

Blessed are those who hunger and thirst after righteousness,
for they shall be satisfied.

Blessed are the merciful,
for they shall obtain mercy.

Blessed are the pure in heart,
for they shall see God.

Blessed are the peacemakers,
for they shall be called children of God.

Blessed are those who suffer persecution for righteousness' sake,
for theirs is the kingdom of heaven.

Silence is kept.

All **Almighty God,**
to whom all hearts are open,
all desires known,
and from whom no secrets are hidden:
cleanse the thoughts of our hearts
by the inspiration of your Holy Spirit,
that we may perfectly love you,
and worthily magnify your holy name;
through Christ our Lord.
Amen.

The Word

Reading(s)

After each reading

This is the word of the Lord.
All **Thanks be to God.**

Psalm 130

This psalm is used between the readings

Out of the depths I have called to you, Lord.
Let your ears be open to hear my voice.
All **My hope is in God's word.**

If you recorded all our sins
who could come before you?
All **My hope is in God's word.**

There is forgiveness with you:
therefore you shall be feared.
All **My hope is in God's word.**

My soul is longing for the Lord,
more than those who watch for daybreak.
All **My hope is in God's word.**

O Israel, wait for the Lord,
for with the Lord there is mercy.
All **My hope is in God's word.**

Glory to the Father, and to the Son, and to the Holy Spirit.
All **My hope is in God's word.**

Sermon

Confession and Forgiveness

Our Lord Jesus Christ said:
The first commandment is this:
'Hear, O Israel, the Lord our God is the only Lord.
You shall love the Lord your God with all your heart,
with all your soul, with all your mind,
and with all your strength.'

The second is this: 'Love your neighbour as yourself.'
There is no other commandment greater than these.
On these two commandments hang all the law and the prophets.

All **Amen. Lord, have mercy.**

The Agnus Dei may be said or sung

All **Lamb of God,
you take away the sin of the world,
have mercy on us.**

**Lamb of God,
you take away the sin of the world,
have mercy on us.**

**Lamb of God,
you take away the sin of the world,
grant us peace.**

Compassion and forgiveness belong to the Lord our God,
though we have rebelled against him.
Let us then renounce our wilfulness and ask his mercy
by confessing our sins in penitence and faith.

Wash away all my iniquity

All **and cleanse me from my sin.**

Lord, have mercy.

All **Lord, have mercy.**

Against you, you only have I sinned

All **and done what is evil in your sight.**

Christ, have mercy.

All **Christ, have mercy.**

Create in me a pure heart, O God,

All **and renew a steadfast spirit within me.**

Lord, have mercy.

All **Lord, have mercy.**

The president declares God's forgiveness in these or other authorized words

May almighty God,
who sent his Son into the world to save sinners,
bring *you* his pardon and peace, now and for ever.

All **Amen.**

A hymn or song(s) may be sung.

Prayers

The Lord's Prayer

As our Saviour taught us, so we pray

All **Our Father in heaven,**
hallowed be your name,
your kingdom come,
your will be done,
on earth as in heaven.
Give us today our daily bread.
Forgive us our sins
as we forgive those who sin against us.
Lead us not into temptation
but deliver us from evil.
For the kingdom, the power,
and the glory are yours
now and for ever.
Amen.

Prayers of Intercession

This response may be used

Lord, meet us in the silence:
All **and hear our prayer.**

The Collect

The Collect is said.

Conclusion

Let us affirm our faith in Jesus Christ the Son of God.

All **Though he was divine,**
he did not cling to equality with God,
but made himself nothing.
Taking the form of a slave,
he was born in human likeness.
He humbled himself
and was obedient to death,
even the death of the cross.
Therefore God has raised him on high,
and given him the name above every name:
that at the name of Jesus
every knee should bow,
and every voice proclaim that Jesus Christ is Lord,
to the glory of God the Father.
Amen.

A hymn or song(s) may be sung.

Final Prayer

God of compassion,
through your Son Jesus Christ
you have reconciled your people to yourself.
As we follow his example of prayer and fasting,
may we obey you with willing hearts
and serve one another in holy love;
through Jesus Christ our Lord.

All **Amen.**

Let us bless the Lord.

All **Thanks be to God.**

12

Christ is Risen: a Service in Easter

Notes

Type of service

¶ A non-eucharistic service for use in the weeks between Easter Sunday and Pentecost;

¶ A fully worked out sample, suitable for local reproduction;

¶ Designed to be suitable for regular use.

This service is not designed for Easter Sunday itself (though it could form the basis of any non-eucharistic service on that day), but to meet the need for something that keeps the Easter flavour in the Sundays of the Easter season.

Opening Acclamation

The acclamation which is used as the greeting is also used (with an additional clause) as an acclamation of praise immediately prior to the dismissal (which, in this case, is the Peace). The service is therefore sandwiched between two great acclamations of the resurrection of Christ.

Penitence

The prayers of penitence could be led from the Easter candle. Children could be invited to gather there with the minister leading that part of the service.

Gloria in Excelsis

This is used as part of the concluding praise. If it is not used (or is said, rather than sung) a hymn or song of praise may be added.

The Peace

The Peace is used here as the dismissal. Other options could be used if this were not appropriate.

Combining the service with Holy Communion

If on occasion this service is combined with Holy Communion, the Gloria in Excelsis and the Praise acclamation that follows it should be moved to form part of the Post Communion and Dismissal respectively. The Peace would then lead into the preparation of the table and the Eucharistic Prayer.

If desired, the Lord's Prayer could be moved to come after the Eucharistic Prayer.

Christ is Risen

A Service of the Word in Easter

We say together the words printed in **bold**.

The minister greets the people and says

Alleluia. Christ is risen.

All **He is risen indeed. Alleluia.**

Praise the God and Father of our Lord Jesus Christ.

All **He has given us new life and hope.**
He has raised Jesus from the dead.

Alleluia. Christ is risen.

All **He is risen indeed. Alleluia.**

Opening Prayer

All **Faithful one, whose word is life:**
come with saving power
to free our praise,
inspire our prayer
and shape our lives
for the kingdom of your Son,
Jesus Christ our Lord.
Amen.

Prayers of Penitence

Jesus Christ, risen Master and triumphant Lord,
we come to you in sorrow for our sins,
and confess to you our weakness and unbelief.

We have lived by our own strength,
and not by the power of your resurrection.
In your mercy, forgive us.

All **Lord, hear us and help us.**

We have lived by the light of our own eyes,
as faithless and not believing.
In your mercy, forgive us.

All **Lord, hear us and help us.**

We have lived for this world alone,
and doubted our home in heaven.
In your mercy, forgive us.

All **Lord, hear us and help us.**

May the God of love and power
forgive *you* and free *you* from *your* sins,
heal and strengthen *you* by his Spirit,
and raise *you* to new life in Christ our Lord.

All **Amen.**

The Collect

The Collect is said.

Reading(s)

After each reading

This is the word of the Lord.

All **Thanks be to God.**

Sermon

Affirmation of Faith

This Affirmation of Faith or an authorized Creed is used

Let us declare our faith
in the resurrection of our Lord Jesus Christ.

All **Christ died for our sins
in accordance with the Scriptures;
he was buried;
he was raised to life on the third day
in accordance with the Scriptures;
afterwards he appeared to his followers,
and to all the apostles:
this we have received,
and this we believe.
Amen.**

A hymn may be sung.

Prayers of Intercession

This response may be used

Jesus, Lord of life:

All **in your mercy, hear us.**

Gathering our prayers and praise into one, let us pray as our Saviour taught us

All **Our Father in heaven,**
hallowed be your name,
your kingdom come,
your will be done,
on earth as in heaven.
Give us today our daily bread.
Forgive us our sins
as we forgive those who sin against us.
Lead us not into temptation
but deliver us from evil.
For the kingdom, the power,
and the glory are yours
now and for ever.
Amen.

Gloria in Excelsis

This song may be said or sung

All **Glory to God in the highest,**
and peace to his people on earth.

Lord God, heavenly King,
almighty God and Father,
we worship you, we give you thanks,
we praise you for your glory.

Lord Jesus Christ, only Son of the Father,
Lord God, Lamb of God,
you take away the sin of the world:
have mercy on us;
you are seated at the right hand of the Father:
receive our prayer.

For you alone are the Holy One,
you alone are the Lord,
you alone are the Most High, Jesus Christ,
with the Holy Spirit,
in the glory of God the Father.
Amen.

Alleluia. Christ is risen.

All **He is risen indeed. Alleluia.**

Praise the God and Father of our Lord Jesus Christ.

All **He has given us new life and hope.**
He has raised Jesus from the dead.

God has claimed us as his own.

All **He has brought us out of darkness.**
He has made us light to the world.

Alleluia. Christ is risen.

All **He is risen indeed. Alleluia.**

The Peace

The risen Christ came and stood among his disciples
and said, 'Peace be with you.'
Then were they glad when they saw the Lord. Alleluia.

The peace of the Lord be always with you

All **and also with you.**

All may exchange a sign of peace.

A service from New Patterns for Worship. *Compilation copyright © The Archbishops'*
Council 2002.

Special Days and Occasions

Special Days and Occasions

13

A Service for St Valentine's Day

Notes

Type of service

¶   Non-eucharistic;

¶   A fully worked out example, *not* intended to be reproduced locally in this particular form.

Aim

To reflect on the sacrificial love of God in Christ as an example for the human love between men and women.

Introduction

It is important to capture something of God's love, as well as the celebration of human love, at the start of the service. The 'further words of introduction' might, for instance, include something like:

> This is the day when we celebrate the martyrdom of St Valentine, in Rome around AD 269 under the Emperor Claudius. There is nothing to connect his death with the choosing of a 'Valentine' of the opposite sex, other than that it coincided with a rather jolly Roman pagan festival in mid-February.

Sharing experiences

As part of the response to the readings, and possibly as part of the sermon, there might be an opportunity to interview one or two people with a particular story to tell about how God has brought them together, or deepened their love, or overwhelmed them with his love in Christ.

The Peace

The service moves towards a climax at the Peace. This needs careful introduction, perhaps focusing on that unity in Christian fellowship, because of what Christ has done for us, of which St Paul speaks in the introductory words. People should also be encouraged to greet one another in whatever way is most natural and comfortable for them — and for those they are greeting! The more adventurous worship planners might want to provide some symbol – coloured paper hearts, or flowers, for example, which members of the congregation might give to one another as reminders of the love and generosity of God.

Marriage Vows

It may be a good occasion on which to combine this service with some of the material for the Renewal of Marriage Vows in the Thanksgiving for Marriage section of *Common Worship: Pastoral Services,* page 184ff. The concluding congregational prayer is – slightly amended – from that service. One of the prayers from the *Common Worship* Marriage Service, placed where it will sum up the Intercessions and prepare for the Peace, is used in place of a collect.

A Service for St Valentine's Day

This sample service is *not* intended to be reproduced locally in this particular form.

We say together the words printed in **bold.**

Preparation

Greeting

Praise God! For the Lord our God the almighty reigns!

All **Let us rejoice and be glad and give him the glory.**
Happy are those who have been invited
to the wedding-feast of the Lamb.

All **Amen. Praise the Lord!**

Further words of welcome and introduction follow.

Praise

A hymn or song of praise may be sung.

Confession

The minister may introduce the confession

God shows his love for us
in that, while we were still sinners, Christ died for us.
Let us then show our love for him
by confessing our sins in penitence and faith.

Silence may be kept.

(Come, let us return to the Lord and say)

All **Lord our God,**
in our sin we have avoided your call.
Our love for you is like a morning cloud,
like the dew that goes away early.
Have mercy on us;
deliver us from judgement;
bind up our wounds and revive us;
in Jesus Christ our Lord.
Amen.

May the God of love
bring *us* back to himself,
forgive *us our* sins,
and assure *us* of his eternal love
in Jesus Christ our Lord.

All **Amen.**

The Word

Psalm

A psalm, or a song or hymn based on a passage of Scripture, may be used.

Reading(s)

This acclamation may herald a reading from the Gospel

Alleluia, alleluia.
God is love;
let us love one another
as God has loved us.

All **Alleluia.**

At the end of each reading this response may be used

This is the word of the Lord.

All **Thanks be to God.**

Response to God's Word

Sermon

Song(s) or Hymn

This Affirmation of Faith, or the Apostles' Creed, or another authorized Affirmation of Faith is used

Let us declare our faith in God:

All   **We believe in God the Father,
from whom every family
in heaven and on earth is named.**

**We believe in God the Son,
who lives in our hearts through faith,
and fills us with his love.**

**We believe in God the Holy Spirit,
who strengthens us
with power from on high.**

**We believe in one God;
Father, Son and Holy Spirit.
Amen.**

Prayers

The Lord's Prayer

Lord, remember us in your kingdom,
as we pray in the words you gave us

All   **Our Father in heaven,
hallowed be your name,
your kingdom come,
your will be done,
on earth as in heaven.
Give us today our daily bread.
Forgive us our sins
as we forgive those who sin against us.
Lead us not into temptation
but deliver us from evil.
For the kingdom,
the power, and the glory are yours
now and for ever.
Amen.**

This form, or some other form, may be used

(We pray for the family of the Church,
for loving relationships, and for the life of families around us, saying
Jesus, Lord of love,

All   **in your mercy, hear us.)**

Jesus, born in poverty and soon a refugee,
be with families today who are poor
and live in hunger and want …
Jesus, Lord of love,

All   **in your mercy, hear us.**

Jesus, as you grew in wisdom and in favour with God and the people
in the family of Joseph the carpenter,
bring wisdom and the presence of God
into the work and growth of families today …
Jesus, Lord of love,

All   **in your mercy, hear us.**

Jesus, as you blessed marriage in the wedding at Cana,
be with those preparing for marriage
and with those who come to the end of their resources …
Jesus, Lord of love,

All   **in your mercy, hear us.**

Jesus, as you healed Peter's mother-in-law,
bring healing to those in our families who are ill today …
Jesus, Lord of love,

All   **in your mercy, hear us.**

Jesus, when you were dying you called Mary and John
    to care for one another,
provide today for those who lose their families:
the bereaved and childless, orphans and widows …
Jesus, Lord of love,

All   **in your mercy, hear us.**

Jesus, as you ate breakfast on the beach with your disciples
after you were raised from the dead,
bring the whole Church on earth and in heaven
into your risen presence to eat at the eternal banquet.
Jesus, Lord of love,

All   **in your mercy, hear us,**
    accept our prayers and be with us always.
    Amen.

God of wonder and of joy:
grace comes from you,
and you alone are the source of life and love.
Without you, we cannot please you;
without your love, our deeds are worth nothing.
Send your Holy Spirit,
and pour into our hearts
that most excellent gift of love,
that we may worship you now
with thankful hearts
and serve you always with willing minds;
through Jesus Christ our Lord.

All **Amen.**

Ending

The Peace

The minister may introduce the Peace with these words

To crown all things there must be love,
to bind all together and complete the whole.
Let the peace of Christ rule in our hearts.
The peace of the Lord be always with you

All **and also with you.**

Song(s) or Hymn

Concluding Prayers

Eternal God, we offer our thanks that through our earthly lives
you speak of your eternal life.
We rejoice in the wonder of creation,
the gift of human life
and the many blessings that our relationships bring.
Renew in us the fruits of your Holy Spirit;
that love, joy and peace may abound in our homes,
through Jesus Christ our Lord.

All **Amen.**

All   **Heavenly Father,**
We offer you our souls and bodies,
our thoughts and words and deeds,
our love for one another.
Unite our wills in your will,
that we may grow
in love and peace
all the days of our life;
through Jesus Christ our Lord.
Amen.

Sending Out

God the Holy Trinity make you strong in faith and love,
defend you on every side, and guide you in truth and peace;
and the blessing of God almighty,
the Father, the Son, and the Holy Spirit,
be among you and remain with you always.

All   **Amen.**

14

A Service for Mothering Sunday

Notes

Type of service

¶ Non-eucharistic, with suggestions for combining with Holy Communion;

¶ A fully worked out example, *not* intended to be reproduced locally in this particular form.

A good deal will depend on whether this service is intended to be the main Sunday service for the Fourth Sunday of Lent or a 'special' service at some other time on that day.

Acclamation

The acclamation

> Praise God who loves us.
> **Praise God who cares.**

is used throughout the service as a unifying thread.

Using different voices

In the section 'Praising and thanking God' the acclamations may be led by different voices from different parts of the church building. If a large candle is lit at this point the first section is used. A child might be invited to light the candle. Alternatively, a candle might be lit at the absolution.

Sharing experiences

The chance to let members of the congregation speak of their experiences and their faith can be an excellent way of connecting the worship to the rest of life, and can especially help visitors to see how our faith is worked out in practice. Before the sermon (or as part of it) it might be possible and appropriate to include such an element of 'testimony'. This might include, for instance:

¶ asking a pregnant woman to talk about the frustration and excitement of waiting for a baby to be born, or a new mother to describe the difference being a mother has made to her life and her faith;

¶ inviting someone to share (sensitively) their experience of having a mother who let them down badly, and the difference that knowing God's love has made to them;

¶ inviting a grandmother to speak about what it is like to be a grandparent, including any advice she has for new parents, or any things she wishes she had done differently when her children were young.

It might be particularly appropriate to conclude such sharing with the Affirmation of Faith.

The giving of flowers or other gifts

It is important that this element of the service is conducted with sensitivity towards those present who do not have children.

In addition to the giving of gifts of flowers (or other gifts) to mothers in the congregation, it may be appropriate to place flowers near a statue of Mary, the mother of our Lord.

Posture needs to be thought through beforehand. If the response at the beginning of the section is led by children it would be easier to see them if everyone sits. It is probably better if everyone remains seated for the giving of the flowers or other gifts, and the mothers (or all the women) stand for the **Thank you** ... prayer at the end. Of course local custom and architecture may suggest another arrangement.

Combining the service with Holy Communion

If the service is to be eucharistic it could follow this order:

The Gathering

¶ Including the 'Praising and Thanking God' and Confession material.

The Liturgy of the Word

¶ This might include the Song of Saint Anselm, the Affirmation of Faith and the Prayers of Intercession;

¶ This Gospel Acclamation could be used before the Gospel reading:

> Praise to you, O Christ, King of eternal glory.
> This child is the light to enlighten the nations
>   and the glory of your people Israel.
> **Praise to you, O Christ, King of eternal glory.**

The Liturgy of the Sacrament

¶ The Peace is introduced using the suggested words, or another suitable introduction;

¶ Eucharistic Prayer G is particularly appropriate;

¶ The Prayer for Mothers could be included after the Post Communion prayers.

Dismissal

¶ Use suggested material.

A Service for Mothering Sunday

This sample service is *not* intended to be reproduced locally in this particular form.

We say together the words printed in **bold.**

A hymn or song may be sung.

Greeting

This acclamation may be used as part of the greeting

Praise God who loves us.

All   **Praise God who cares.**

Praising and Thanking God

[A large candle may be lit.

We light this candle to remind us that the love of God is like a light in our darkness.

All   **Blessed be God for ever.]**

We praise you, our God, for all mothers who have loved and laughed and laboured as they cared for their children;

All   **Blessed be God for ever.**

We praise you, our God, for all mothers who have wept in sorrow and joy for their children:

All   **Blessed be God for ever.**

We praise you, our God, for Jesus, born of a woman and nurtured in her love, and for Mary, a reminder of your patient, waiting love.

All   **Blessed be God for ever.**

Confession

Let us call to mind our sin, our failure to value the love of others
and our failure to love as Christ has loved us.

Silence for reflection

Your love gives us life from the moment of conception.
    We fail to live as your children.
Lord, have mercy.

All   **Lord, have mercy.**

You call us to do good. We seek our own good.
Christ, have mercy.

All   **Christ have mercy.**

You hear us when we cry for help. We ignore the cries of others.
Lord, have mercy.

All **Lord, have mercy.**

If a candle was not lit earlier, it might be lit at this point.

May the Father of all mercies
cleanse *us* from *our* sins,
and restore *us* in his image
to the praise and glory of his name,
through Jesus Christ our Lord.

All **Amen.**

A hymn of praise may be sung.

The Collect

Praise God who loves us.

All **Praise God who cares.**

The Collect for Mothering Sunday is said.

Reading(s)

At the end this response may be used

This is the word of the Lord.

All **Thanks be to God.**

This canticle, or some other appropriate hymn, song or canticle, may be used

A Song of St Anselm

This refrain may be used at the beginning and end of the canticle and, in addition, between verses or groups of verses.

All **Gather your little ones to you, O God,**
 as a hen gathers her brood to protect them.

1 Jesus, like a mother you gather your people to you; ♦
 you are gentle with us as a mother with her children.

2 Often you weep over our sins and our pride, ♦
 tenderly you draw us from hatred and judgement.

3 You comfort us in sorrow and bind up our wounds, ♦
 in sickness you nurse us and with pure milk you feed us.

4 Jesus, by your dying, we are born to new life; ♦
 by your anguish and labour we come forth in joy.

5   Despair turns to hope through your sweet goodness; ◆
    through your gentleness we find comfort in fear.

6   Your warmth gives life to the dead, ◆
    your touch makes sinners righteous.

7   Lord Jesus, in your mercy heal us; ◆
    in your love and tenderness remake us.

8   In your compassion bring grace and forgiveness, ◆
    for the beauty of heaven may your love prepare us.

All **Glory to the Father and to the Son**
    and to the Holy Spirit;
    as it was in the beginning is now
    and shall be for ever.
    Amen.

Sermon

A hymn or song may be sung.

Affirmation of Faith

Praise God who loves us.
All **Praise God who cares.**

This, or another Creed or authorized Affirmation of Faith is used

Let us declare our faith in God.

All **We believe in God the Father,**
    from whom every family
    in heaven and on earth is named.

    We believe in God the Son,
    who lives in our hearts through faith,
    and fills us with his love.

    We believe in God the Holy Spirit,
    who strengthens us
    with power from on high.

    We believe in one God;
    Father, Son and Holy Spirit.
    Amen.

As children of a loving God who always listens to our cries, let us pray to our Father in heaven.

After each section this response may be used

God of love,

All **hear our prayer.**

Loving God, you have given us the right to be called children of God. Help us to show your love in our homes that they may be places of love, security and truth.

Loving God, Jesus, your Son, was born into the family of Mary and Joseph; bless all parents and all who care for children; strengthen those families living under stress and may your love be known where no human love is found.

Loving God, we thank you for the family of the Church. We pray that all may find in her their true home; that the lonely, the marginalized, the rejected may be welcomed and loved in the name of Jesus.

Loving God, as we see the brokenness of our world we pray for healing among the nations; for food where there is hunger; for freedom where there is oppression; for joy where there is pain; that your love may bring peace to all your children.

The Lord's Prayer

As God's children, and heirs with Christ
we cry in the Spirit, 'Abba', Father.

All **Our Father in heaven,**
hallowed be your name,
your kingdom come,
your will be done,
on earth as in heaven.
Give us today our daily bread.
Forgive us our sins
as we forgive those who sin against us.
Lead us not into temptation
but deliver us from evil.
For the kingdom, the power,
and the glory are yours
now and for ever.
Amen.

Loving God, accept the cries of our heart as we offer you prayers;
through them transform us and all creation until you are in all and through all.
We ask these and all our prayers in the name of Jesus.

All **Amen.**

Praise God who loves us.
All **Praise God who cares.**

Through the prophet Isaiah, God says,
'As a mother comforts her child, so I will comfort you.'
The peace of the Lord be always with you
All **and also with you.**

The congregation share the Peace.

A hymn or song may be sung.

Prayer for Mothers and Distribution of Flowers

Praise God who loves us.
All **Praise God who cares.**

Children may lead the following responsory

For the care of mothers;
All **Thanks be to God.**

For their patience when tested;
All **Thanks be to God.**

For their love when tired;
All **Thanks be to God.**

For their hope when despairing;
All **Thanks be to God.**

For their service without limit;
All **Thanks be to God.**

Other words of thanksgiving may be added as appropriate.

Hymns or songs of praise may be sung during the distribution of flowers to the congregation.

At the end of the distribution of flowers we all say this prayer. Everyone sits except mothers, who are asked to remain standing.

All **Thank you God for the love of our mothers:**
thank you God for their care and concern;
thank you God for the joys they have shared with us;
thank you God for the pains they have borne for us;
thank you God for all that they give us;
through Jesus Christ our Lord.
Amen.

Praise God who loves us.

All **Praise God who cares.**

May God, who gave birth to all creation, bless *us*:
may God, who became incarnate by an earthly mother, bless *us*:
may God, who broods as a mother over her children, bless *us*.
May almighty God bless *us*, Father, Son and Holy Spirit,
now and for ever.

All **Amen.**

The Dismissal

Go in peace to love and serve the Lord.

All **In the name of Christ. Amen.**

A hymn or song may be sung.

15

A Service for Fathers' Day

Notes

Type of service

¶ Non-eucharistic;

¶ A fully worked out example, *not* intended to be reproduced locally in this particular form.

The Ten Commandments

The Commandments have been included for their reference to 'obeying your father and mother'. Care needs to be taken that their inclusion does not make the service feel too 'heavy', especially if many visitors have been invited and the overall feel of the service is one of celebration. The Commandments have been included here in a brief form, with only two responses. They could further be 'lightened' by the use of different voices, or by the careful choice of a different Bible translation from which they could be taken.

Sharing experiences

The chance to let members of the congregation speak of their experiences and their faith can be an excellent way of connecting the worship to the rest of life, and can especially help visitors to see how our faith is worked out in practice. Before the sermon (or as part of it) it might be possible and appropriate to include such an element of 'testimony'. This might include, for instance:

¶ asking a new dad to describe the difference being a father has made to his life and his faith;

¶ inviting someone to share (sensitively) their experience of having a father who let them down badly, and the difference that knowing God's love has made to them;

¶ inviting a grandfather to speak about what it is like to be a grandparent, including any advice he has for new parents, or any things he wishes he had done differently when his children were young.

It might be particularly appropriate to conclude such sharing with the Affirmation of Faith.

Giving gifts to fathers

If you intend to give symbolic gifts (or cards) to fathers, this might appropriately happen at the end of the prayers of intercession. This element of the service needs to be conducted with sensitivity. Music might be played or a hymn or song be sung while this takes place. Fathers present might be asked to stand during the prayer, 'Heavenly Father, you entrusted your Son Jesus …'.

A Service for Fathers' Day

This sample service is *not* intended to be reproduced locally in this particular form.

We say together the words printed in **bold.**

Preparation

Greeting

Grace, mercy and peace
from God our Father
and the Lord Jesus Christ
be with you

All **and also with you.**

Further words of welcome and introduction follow.

Praise

This responsory may be used, and/or a hymn or song of praise may be sung (if a hymn has not preceded the Greeting)

See what love the Father has given us

All **that we should be called the children of God.**

You are my sons and daughters:
this day have I begotten you.

All **See what love the Father has given us.**

As many as received him,
to them he gave power to become the children of God.

All **See what love the Father has given us.**

Glory to the Father, and to the Son,
and to the Holy Spirit.

All **See what love the Father has given us
that we should be called the children of God.**

The Collect

The minister introduces a time of silent prayer, which concludes with the Collect.

God spoke these words and said: I am the Lord your God;
you shall have no other gods but me.
You shall not make for yourself any idol,
whether in the form of anything that is in heaven above,
or that is on the earth beneath, or that is in the water under the earth.
You shall not bow down to them or worship them.
You shall not take the name of the Lord your God in vain.
Remember the Sabbath day, and keep it holy.
For six days you shall labour and do all your work.
But the seventh day is a Sabbath to the Lord your God.

All **Lord, have mercy upon us,**
and incline our hearts to keep this law.

Honour your father and your mother.
You shall not murder.
You shall not commit adultery.
You shall not steal.
You shall not bear false witness.
You shall not covet.

All **Lord, have mercy upon us,**
and write all these your laws in our hearts.

Silence may be kept.

Confession

Let us return to the Lord our God and say to him

All **Father,**
we have sinned against heaven and against you.
We are not worthy to be called your children.
We turn to you again.
Have mercy on us,
bring us back to yourself
as those who once were dead
but now have life through Christ our Lord.
Amen.

May the God of love
bring *us* back to himself,
forgive *us our* sins,
and assure *us* of his eternal love
in Jesus Christ our Lord.

All **Amen.**

The Word

Psalm

A psalm, or a song or hymn based on a passage of Scripture, may be used.

Reading(s)

At the end of each reading this response may be used

This is the word of the Lord.

All **Thanks be to God.**

Response to God's Word

Sermon

Song(s) or Hymn

Affirmation of Faith

This Affirmation of Faith, or the Apostles' Creed, or another authorized Affirmation of Faith is used

Let us declare our faith in God.

All **We believe in God the Father,**
from whom every family
in heaven and on earth is named.

We believe in God the Son,
who lives in our hearts through faith,
and fills us with his love.

We believe in God the Holy Spirit,
who strengthens us
with power from on high.

We believe in one God;
Father, Son and Holy Spirit.
Amen.

Prayers

Jesus taught us to call God our Father,
so in faith and trust we pray

All **Our Father in heaven,**
hallowed be your name,
your kingdom come,
your will be done,
on earth as in heaven.
Give us today our daily bread.
Forgive us our sins
as we forgive those who sin against us.
Lead us not into temptation
but deliver us from evil.
For the kingdom, the power,
and the glory are yours
now and for ever.
Amen.

Prayers of Thanksgiving and Intercession

This form, or some other form, may be used

Sovereign Lord,
your Son has revealed you as our heavenly Father,
from whom every family in heaven and on earth is named.
Father of all
All **hear your children's prayer.**

You have made your Church a spiritual family,
a household of faith.
Through baptism we are reborn as the brothers and sisters of Christ.
Deepen our unity and fellowship in him.
Father of all
All **hear your children's prayer.**

You sent your Son to give his life
as a ransom for the whole human family.
Give justice, peace and racial harmony to the world he died to save.
Father of all
All **hear your children's prayer.**

You gave your Son a share in the life of a family in Nazareth.
Help us to value our families, to be thankful for them,
and to live sensitively within them.
Father of all
All **hear your children's prayer.**

Your Son drew around him a company of friends.
Bring love and joy to all who are alone.
Help us all to find in the brothers and sisters of Christ a loving family.
Father of all

All **hear your children's prayer.**

You are the God of the dead as well as of the living.
In confidence we remember those of the household of
    faith who have gone before us.
Bring us with them to the joy of your home in heaven.
Father of all

All **hear your children's prayer.**

This or some other prayer of thanksgiving may be used

Blessed are you Lord our God,
creator and redeemer of all;
to you be glory and praise for ever.

All **[Blessed be God for ever.]**

You father us from all eternity giving life to creation
and pouring your love into all you have made.

All **[Blessed be God for ever.]**

From the beginning we have known you as 'Father',
and all our families have their origin in you.

All **[Blessed be God for ever.]**

Through the love of earthly fathers you give us a glimpse
    of your everlasting love.
Their guidance and wisdom reveal to us the eternal life of heaven.

All **[Blessed be God for ever.]**

In following their example we become more like you,
 growing into the people your heart longs for us to be.

All **[Blessed be God for ever.]**

May the love of our fathers draw us ever nearer to you
and perfect in us the image of your Son Jesus Christ our Lord.
Blessed be God, Father, Son and Holy Spirit.

All **Blessed be God for ever.**

If symbolic gifts are to be distributed to fathers, this should take place before the following prayer

Heavenly Father,
you entrusted your Son Jesus,
the child of Mary,
to the care of Joseph, an earthly father.
Bless *all fathers*
as they care for their families.
Give them strength and wisdom,
tenderness and patience;
support them in the work they have to do,
protecting those who look to them,
as we look to you for love and salvation,
through Jesus Christ our rock and defender.

All   **Amen.**

Ending

Song(s) or Hymn

Final Prayer

All   **In darkness and in light,**
in trouble and in joy,
help us, heavenly Father,
to trust your love,
to serve your purpose,
and to praise your name;
through Jesus Christ our Lord.
Amen.

Sending Out

A blessing, the Grace or the sharing of the Peace may conclude the service, or these responses may be used

The Lord God almighty is our Father:
All   **he loves us and tenderly cares for us.**
The Lord Jesus Christ is our Saviour:
All   **he has redeemed us and will defend us to the end.**
The Lord, the Holy Spirit, is among us:
All   **he will lead us in God's holy way.**
To God almighty, Father, Son and Holy Spirit,
be praise and glory today and for ever.
Amen.

16

Harvest (outline)

Notes

Type of service

¶   An outline, with suggestions for resources to use within it.

This shows a possible structure for a service in which the 'talk' (in whatever form it takes) is divided into three short sections, one in each of the three main sections of the service.

Harvest

Greeting

A suitable greeting would be **A**26

God is good …

Hymn

Bible Reading 1

Talk part 1

Canticle or other Song of Praise

For instance, the version of the Benedicite **D**30

Glory to God above …

or the **response** *from* **G**25 *could be used*

Blessed are you, Lord God, King of the universe …

Collect

Talk part 2

[Sentence of Scripture]

G1 *or another suitable sentence*

[Rejoice in the Lord always …]

Confession

B56 *might be used with an appropriate absolution*

We confess to you our lack of care …

Song, Hymn or Psalm

*For instance, this version of Psalm 66 (***D**9)

Let the praises of God ring out …

[Bible Reading 2]

Talk part 3

[Affirmation of Faith]

This Affirmation of Faith may be used (Affirmation 1, E6)

**Do you believe and trust in God the Father,
source of all being and life ...**

Song or Hymn

Intercessions

For instance, the form F47

Let us pray to God, that he will bring to fruition ...

The Lord's Prayer

Song or Hymn

Blessing or Dismissal

If a blessing is given, this form may be suitable (J69)

May God the Father of our Lord Jesus Christ ...

17

A Saint's Day: a Celebration of St Luke

Notes

Type of service

¶ Non-eucharistic;

¶ A fully worked out example, *not* intended to be reproduced locally in this particular form.

Different kinds of saints

Each saint is different. While we always need to remember we are worshipping God our Father, through his Son Jesus Christ in the power of the Spirit, the life of the saint concerned, and the gift he or she brought to the Church, should guide the theme and direction of the worship.

This particular service has been built around a celebration of the Feast of St Luke, evangelist and doctor. Over the centuries his feast day has been an opportunity for the Church to focus on its healing ministry, so following this tradition an opportunity for the thanksgiving for the healing ministry of the Church has been incorporated into the service. Note 8 on page 58 of *Common Worship* applies. (See also pages 439–442 below.)

However, some saints are missionaries, others teachers, others bishops, others martyrs and so on. The content, style and ethos of each service should reflect the saint who is being celebrated. For example, if the saint is a martyr, the service might focus on commitment and use elements from the Thanksgiving for Baptism.

Exciting Holiness (Canterbury Press, 1997) may be used as a suitable resource for details of the saints and suggested texts for use with their celebrations.

The presentation of the life of the saint

This may vary from a simple comment by the leader, or some other suitable person, to a dramatic presentation of the saint's life by a number of people.

The first reading

This may be about the saint concerned or from his own writings but it should not repeat the points made in the introduction. Alternatively, it may be an Old Testament or New Testament reading.

The response to God's word

This should include an authorized Affirmation of Faith, a confession if one has not been used earlier in the service, and intercession, and may include some symbolic action relating to the life, ministry and gifting of the saint being celebrated. For example, this service celebrating St Luke incorporates an opportunity for the ministry of healing.

A Celebration of St Luke

This sample service is *not* intended to be reproduced locally in this particular form.

Preparation

We stand before the throne of God
with countless crowds
from every nation and race, tribe and language.

All **Blessing and glory and wisdom,
thanksgiving and honour, power and might
be to our God for ever and ever.
Amen.**

Song or Hymn

Greeting

*The leader greets the people with a suitable greeting.
Informal greetings may also be included.*

A brief explanation of the life of the saint may be offered.

Opening Prayer

Let us pray.

All **Come, Holy Spirit,
fill the hearts of your faithful people,
and kindle in us the fire of your love;
through Jesus Christ our Lord.
Amen.**

Prayers of Penitence

The minister introduces the confession with these words

God the Father forgives us in Christ and heals us by the Holy Spirit.
Let us therefore put away all anger and bitterness,
all slander and malice,
and confess our sins to God our redeemer.

Silence for reflection

We have wandered from your paths, yet your truth leads us home.
Lord, have mercy.

All **Lord, have mercy.**

We have failed to live as your children, yet your love restores us.
Christ, have mercy.

All **Christ, have mercy.**

We are disfigured by our sin, yet your power heals us.
Lord, have mercy.

All **Lord, have mercy.**

The minister says the absolution

May the God of all healing and forgiveness
draw *us* to himself,
and cleanse *us* from all *our* sins
that *we* may behold the glory of his Son,
the Word made flesh,
Jesus Christ our Lord.

All **Amen.**

Song of Praise

related to the saint

The Collect

for St Luke's Day

The Word

Reading(s) from the Bible

At the end of each reading this response may be used

This is the word of the Lord.

All **Thanks be to God.**

Hymn, Song, Psalm or Canticle

Verses from Psalm 34

O magnify the Lord with me;
let us exalt his name together.

All **O magnify the Lord with me;
let us exalt his name together.**

I sought the Lord and he answered me;
he delivered me from all my fears.

All **O magnify the Lord with me.**

In my weakness I cried to the Lord;
he heard me and saved me from my troubles.

All   **Let us exalt his name together.**

Glory to the Father, and to the Son
and to the Holy Spirit.

All   **O magnify the Lord with me;
let us exalt his name together.**

Sermon

Response to God's Word

Song(s) or Hymn

Thanksgiving for the Healing Ministry of the Church

Bless the Lord, O my soul;

All   **and forget not all his benefits;**

Who forgives all your sins

All   **and heals all your infirmities;**

Who redeems your life from the Pit;

All   **and crowns you with faithful love and compassion.**

This prayer of thanksgiving may be said

Blessed are you, sovereign God, gentle and merciful,
creator of heaven and earth.
Your Word brought light out of darkness.
In Jesus Christ you proclaim good news to the poor,
liberty to captives, sight to the blind
and freedom for the oppressed.
Daily your Spirit renews the face of the earth,
bringing life and health, wholeness and peace.
In the renewal of our lives
you make known your heavenly glory.
Blessed be God, Father, Son and Holy Spirit:

All   **Blessed be God for ever.**

This or another authorized Creed or Affirmation of Faith may be used.

Let us declare our faith in God.

All **We believe in God the Father,**
from whom every family
in heaven and on earth is named.

We believe in God the Son,
who lives in our hearts through faith,
and fills us with his love.

We believe in God the Holy Spirit,
who strengthens us
with power from on high.

We believe in one God;
Father, Son and Holy Spirit.
Amen.

Prayers of Intercession

Intercessions for those in need and those who care for them may be offered in this or another form

Holy God, in whom we live and move and have our being,
we make our prayer to you, saying,
Lord, hear us.

All **Lord, graciously hear us.**

Grant to all who seek you
the assurance of your presence, your power and your peace.
Lord, hear us.

All **Lord, graciously hear us.**

Grant your healing grace to all who are sick
that they may be made whole in body, mind and spirit.
Lord, hear us.

All **Lord, graciously hear us.**

Grant to all who minister to the suffering
wisdom and skill, sympathy and patience.
Lord, hear us.

All **Lord, graciously hear us.**

Sustain and support the anxious and fearful
and lift up all who are brought low.
Lord, hear us.

All **Lord, graciously hear us.**

Hear us, Lord of life.

All **Heal us, and make us whole.**

Almighty God,
whose Son revealed in signs and miracles
the wonder of your saving presence:
renew all your people
with your heavenly grace,
and in all our weakness
sustain us by your mighty power,
through Jesus Christ our Lord.

All **Amen.**

The Lord's Prayer

All **Our Father in heaven,**
hallowed be your name,
your kingdom come,
your will be done,
on earth as in heaven.
Give us today our daily bread.
Forgive us our sins
as we forgive those who sin against us.
Lead us not into temptation
but deliver us from evil.
For the kingdom, the power,
and the glory are yours
now and for ever.
Amen.

Prayer for Healing

The Ministry of Healing may take place here using these or other suitable prayers. Hymns and songs may be sung during the prayers.

Be with us, Spirit of God;

All **nothing can separate us from your love.**

Breathe on us, breath of God;

All **fill us with your saving power.**

Speak in us, wisdom of God;

All **bring strength, healing and peace.**

The Lord is here.

All **His Spirit is with us.**

The laying on of hands may be administered using the authorized words on page 52 of Common Worship *or other suitable words.*

If anointing is administered by an authorized minister, the authorized words on pages 52–53 of Common Worship *or other suitable words may be used.*

The almighty Lord,
who is a strong tower for all who put their trust in him,
whom all things in heaven, on earth, and under the earth obey,
be now and evermore your defence.
May you believe and trust that the only name under heaven
given for health and salvation
is the name of our Lord Jesus Christ.

All **Amen.**

The Peace

Peace to you from God our Father who hears our cry.
Peace from his Son Jesus Christ whose death brings healing.
Peace from the Holy Spirit who gives us life and strength.
The peace of the Lord be always with you

All **and also with you.**

Song(s) or Hymn

Conclusion

God give you grace to follow his saints
in faith and hope and love;
and the blessing ...

All **Amen.**

18

Facing Pain: a Service of Lament

Notes

Type of service

¶   Non-eucharistic;

¶   An example of a 'one-off' service, *not* designed to be used without adaptation.

This service will need to be adapted to the particular circumstance that has caused the community to lament. It might be the passing of someone significant in the community; a major incident resulting in death, which affects many people; the effects of an industrial policy; or something of that kind.

Use of symbols and actions

If appropriate, and possible, something that symbolizes the event might be brought in and placed on or near the Holy Table, or in some other appropriate place, during the opening hymn.

A cross should be prominent.

The ministers could enter in silence.

Naming the departed

If there are deaths related to the event, the names of the deceased should be read out individually. A place for this to happen is indicated in the text. For each of the deceased a candle might be lit. A light could be taken from the Easter candle or some other large candle and a small candle lit as each of the names is read out.

The Candle of Hope

If a candle is lit at the section headed 'Proclamation of Hope', it could be carried at the front of any formal procession at the end of the service.

Affirmation of Faith

Because a service like this might not be the principal service of the day, and might well not take place on a Sunday, an Affirmation of Faith is not required and has not been included, though a point in the service at which it might appropriately come has been indicated.

Facing Pain: a Service of Lament

An example of a 'one-off' service, *not* designed to be used without adaptation.

We say together the words printed in **bold.**

Welcome and Introduction

We meet in the presence of God
All **who knows our needs,
hears our cries,
feels our pain,
and heals our wounds.**

A minister introduces the service.

A hymn or song may be sung.

Let us pray.
The weight of grief bears heavily upon us
    but it is a load we need not bear alone.
Let us offer our burden to Jesus,
Lord of life and of death, of the present and of the future.

We bring before you, Lord,
our confusion in the face of shock,
our despair in the face of tragedy,
our helplessness in the face of death.

Lift from us our burden,
All **and in your power, renew us.**

We bring before you, Lord,
the tears of sorrow,
the cries for help,
the vulnerability of pain.

Lift from us our burden,
All **and in your power, renew us.**

We bring before you, Lord,
our sense of frustration,
our feeling of powerlessness,
our fears for the future.

Lift from us our burden,
All **and in your power, renew us.**

[We bring before you, Lord,
our frustrated hopes,
our unfulfilled desires,
our unfettered sadness.

Lift from us our burden,

All **and in your power, renew us.]**

The minister concludes with this prayer

God of the desolate and despairing,
your Son Jesus Christ was forced to carry the instrument
    of his own death —
the cross that became for us the source of life and healing.
Transform us in our suffering
that [*in the pain we bear*] you might be for us a fount of life
    and a spring of hope;
though him who died for us,
yet is alive and reigns with you and the Holy Spirit,
now and for ever.

All **Amen.**

Sharing the Story

Experiences of those who have been affected may be shared.

Psalm 102 — a Psalm of Lament

Turn your ear to me;
be swift to answer when I call.

All **Turn your ear to me;**
be swift to answer when I call.

Lord, hear my prayer,
and let my cry come before you:

All **be swift to answer when I call.**

Do not hide your face from me
in the day of my trouble:

All **be swift to answer when I call.**

You, Lord, endure for ever,
and your name from age to age:

All **be swift to answer when I call.**

You will be moved to have compassion on Zion,
for it is time to have pity on her:

All **be swift to answer when I call.**

Glory to the Father and to the Son and to the Holy Spirit.

All **Turn your ear to me;**
be swift to answer when I call.

Hear these words of comfort which the Lord our God offers to all in trouble and distress:

A short silence is kept between each of the readings.

The Israelites groaned under their slavery, and cried out. Out of the slavery their cry for help rose up to God. God heard their groaning, and God remembered his covenant with Abraham, Isaac, and Jacob. God looked upon the Israelites, and God took notice of them.

Exodus 2.23b-25

Jesus said 'Come to me, all you that are weary and are carrying heavy burdens, and I will give you rest. Take my yoke upon you, and learn from me; for I am gentle and humble in heart, and you will find rest for your souls. For my yoke is easy, and my burden is light.'

Matthew 11.29,30

When you pass through the waters, I will be with you; and through the rivers, they shall not overwhelm you; when you walk through fire you shall not be burned, and the flame shall not consume you. For I am the Lord your God, the Holy One of Israel, your Saviour.

Isaiah 43.2-3a

For I am convinced that neither death, nor life, nor angels, nor rulers, nor things present, nor things to come, nor powers, nor height, nor depth, nor anything else in all creation, will be able to separate us from the love of God in Christ Jesus our Lord.

Romans 8.38-39

Hymn or Song

Finding Hope

Reading(s)

After each reading the reader says

This is the word of the Lord.
All **Thanks be to God.**

Address

Silence for reflection

Proclamation of Hope

A minister goes to the large candle, carrying a light.

We light this candle to remind us that when God the Father raised Jesus from the dead he defeated the power of death, and his light shines in the midst of the darkness of this world.

The candle is lit as a sign of the hope of resurrection.

May the light of Christ, rising in glory,
banish all darkness from our hearts and lives.

All **Lord, by your cross and resurrection
you have defeated death,
and set your people free.
You are the Saviour of the world.**

(or)

The Lord is my light and my salvation;
The Lord is the strength of my life.

All **The Lord is my light and my salvation;
The Lord is the strength of my life.**

The light shines in the darkness
And the darkness has not overcome it.

All **The Lord is the strength of my life.**

Glory to the Father and to the Son
and to the Holy Spirit.

All **The Lord is my light and my salvation;
The Lord is the strength of my life.**

If appropriate, an authorized Affirmation of Faith could be used here.

Hymn or Song

Laying Down the Past

Prayers of Intercession

Biddings might be offered, interspersed with silence. Initially these should relate to the local incident but they should also include suffering experienced throughout the world.

The prayers end with this Collect

Lighten our darkness,
Lord, we pray,
and in your great mercy
defend us from all perils and dangers [of this night],
for the love of your only Son,
our Saviour Jesus Christ.

All **Amen.**

[Names of the deceased could be mentioned here.]

Stand.

Now, Lord, you let your servant go in peace:

All **your word has been fulfilled.**

My own eyes have seen the salvation

All **which you have prepared in the sight of every people;**

A light to reveal you to the nations

All **and the glory of your people Israel.**

All **Glory to the Father and to the Son**
and to the Holy Spirit;
as it was in the beginning is now
and shall be for ever.
Amen.

Silence is kept.

Let us pray that we may know life and hope in Jesus Christ as we say

All **Our Father, who art in heaven,**
hallowed be thy name;
thy kingdom come;
thy will be done;
on earth as it is in heaven.
Give us this day our daily bread.
And forgive us our trespasses,
as we forgive those who trespass against us.
And lead us not into temptation;
but deliver us from evil.
For thine is the kingdom,
the power and the glory,
for ever and ever.
Amen.

Moving into the Future

Blessing and Dismissal

Neither death nor life can separate us from the love of God.

All **Amen. Thanks be to God.**

God the Father,
by whose glory Christ was raised from the dead,
strengthen *you* to walk with him in his risen life;
and the blessing of God almighty,
the Father, the Son and the Holy Spirit
be among *you* and remain with *you* always.

All **Amen.**

Hymn

19

A Penitential Service (outline)

Notes

Type of service

¶ An outline structure for a service with a particularly penitential flavour, such as might be appropriate in Lent or in Advent, or at a particular stage in the life of a local church.

¶ Hymns or songs may be added at suitable points.

A Penitential Service

Gathering

Greeting

For example

A11   The Lord be with you …
A12   We come from scattered lives …

Introduction, Welcome and Explanations

The Collect

Word

Reading 1

Psalm

Psalm 51 might be suitable.

Reading 2

Sermon

Response

Act of Penitence

This might include the following: the Commandments, Jesus' summary of the Law or the Beatitudes; silence; Confession; imposition of ashes or some symbolic placing of sin at the cross; the use of water for washing or sprinkling; Kyries; Absolution.

Thanksgiving

These thanksgivings may be appropriate

G23   See what love ...
G35   Christ became obedient unto death ...

Intercessions

The Lord's Prayer

Going out

Affirmation of Faith

Blessing and Dismissal

The following may be suitable

J53   Now may the Lord of peace ...
J54   May God give to you ...

20

A Service of Healing (outline)

Notes

Type of service

¶   Non-eucharistic;

¶   This service could be used regularly or on an occasional basis as an
alternative to the provision in *Common Worship: Pastoral Services* for the
Laying on of Hands with Prayer and Anointing at a Celebration of Holy
Communion (page 26).

It falls within the suggestions in the *Common Worship* provision for Prayer for
Individuals in Public Worship (*Common Worship: Pastoral Services*, page 48), and
some of the notes there may be helpful.

This public ministry of prayer may be accompanied by laying on of hands, and
may also be accompanied by anointing with oil. It may be helpful to make
clear in advance the form of ministry that is intended. There are a number of
possibilities, such as prayer for individuals who do not explain their particular
need; prayer following a brief explanation to those who will pray with them
of a person's need or concern; or prayer following an explanation to the
whole congregation of a person's need or concern. (The Laying on of Hands
may be received on behalf of a third person who is not present.)

Care needs to be taken to integrate ministry to individuals with the
corporate prayer of the whole people.

Those who will be ministering to individuals should be offered appropriate
help in preparing for this. Before the service it is normally appropriate for
them to pray together for grace and discernment.

Anointing

Canon B 37 provides that the priest should use 'pure olive oil consecrated by
the bishop of the diocese or otherwise by the priest', for which forms are
provided in the rite for a celebration of Wholeness and Healing in *Common
Worship: Pastoral Services*, pages 20–21, and also on pages 46–47. Note 1 on
page 40 also says that whoever presides may delegate the ministry of
anointing to other ministers authorized for this ministry.

Introduction

In *Common Worship: Pastoral Services* (page 42) there are some sample introductions, one of which may be used here. These, together with some of the passages in the lectionary provision on pages 44–45 of *Common Worship: Pastoral Services*, will give some indication of themes that can be tackled in the course of teaching people over a number of months about healing, but it may well be that the words used at this point in the service are briefer and more informal.

Prayers of Intercession

It is intended that prayer for healing takes place within the wider context of the prayer of the people for other things. The litany on page 31 of *Common Worship: Pastoral Services*, or some other suitable prayers or biddings, may be used.

Conclusion

A Time to Heal: A Report by the House of Bishops on the Healing Ministry (CHP, 2000), page 243, suggests that at this point there should be a prayer of thanksgiving, an act of praise and the final blessing and dismissal: 'This helps both the congregation and those who have received ministry to depart in a spirit of faith and hope in God.'

A Service of Healing

The Gathering

The minister welcomes the people with a greeting, for example **A**34

We meet in the presence of God ...

The minister may introduce the service.

Prayers of Penitence

The minister introduces the Confession. **B**25 *may be suitable.*

A form of Confession is used. **B**65 *may be suitable*

Friend of sinners, you bring hope in our despair ...

The minister declares God's forgiveness.

The Liturgy of the Word

Readings

One or more readings from the Bible.

A Psalm or scriptural Song

Sermon

An authorized Affirmation of Faith, or Creed

Prayers of Intercession

Brief biddings may introduce prayer for the world and the Church.

The time of prayer for individuals may include one or both of these prayers

Be with us, Spirit of God;

All **nothing can separate us from your love.**

Breathe on us, breath of God;

All **fill us with your saving power.**

Speak in us, wisdom of God;

All **bring strength, healing and peace.**

The Lord is here.

All **His Spirit is with us.** **A**43

(or)

In the name of God and trusting in his might alone,
receive Christ's healing touch to make you whole.
May Christ bring you wholeness
of body, mind and spirit,
deliver you from every evil,
and give you peace.

All **Amen.**

The Collect and the Lord's Prayer are said.

Conclusion

A suitable hymn of praise and a praise item such as this versicle and response

Bless the Lord, O my soul;

All **and forget not all his benefits;**

Who forgives all your sins

All **and heals all your infirmities;**

Who redeems your life from the Pit;

All **and crowns you with faithful love and compassion.**

The service ends with the Peace

Peace to you from God our Father, who hears our cry.
Peace from his Son Jesus Christ, whose death brings healing.
Peace from the Holy Spirit, who gives us life and strength.
The peace of the Lord be always with you

All **and also with you.**

21

Worship in a Small Group
or an Intercessory Prayer Meeting (outline)

Notes

Type of service

¶ An outline structure for a home group, a Bible study group, a Lent group, an enquirers' group, a prayer meeting with a focus on intercession or another small group setting.

Worship in a Small Group

Introduction

The meeting may begin with a brief time of silence.

A prayer may be used, for example **A**39

Lord, speak to us ...

Praise

A psalm or canticle of praise may be said. Songs or hymns may be sung.

Thanksgiving

Informal sharing of answers to prayer and other reasons to thank God may take place.

This form may be used to introduce the time of giving thanks

The Lord is here.
All **His Spirit is with us.**

Lift up your hearts.
All **We lift them to the Lord.**

Let us give thanks to the Lord our God.
All **It is right to give thanks and praise.**

The Thanksgiving may conclude with a short song, or with a canticle such as Great and Wonderful *(Common Worship, page 800).*

Scripture Reading

Suitable passages from the Bible may be read. This may be followed by silence.
Sharing of reflections on the readings may take place, a brief talk may be given or a short meditation may be led.

Prayer

Needs for prayer may be shared and open prayer may follow.
The prayers may conclude with the Lord's Prayer.

The Dismissal

The canticle Nunc dimittis *(The Song of Simeon, Common Worship, page 799) may be used.*
The meeting may conclude with the saying of the Grace or the sharing of the Peace.

A Special Example

A Special Example

22

All Creation Worships (Holy Communion)

Notes

Type of service

¶ A celebration of Holy Communion;

¶ An example of a one-off service.

This service differs from the other sample services in that it is provided here in three versions. The order of service and contents are the same in each: what the three versions illustrate is three 'levels' of presentation of a service.

1 The first is a worked out order of service suitable for putting in the hands of the congregation.

2 The second is a basic outline that shows the structure and (unlike the other sample service outlines) includes in full the texts which are 'special' for this service (with the exception of those which are printed in the congregation's text). This would be for the service leaders and others with a particular role, such as musicians, sidespeople, wardens, and so on. It could be used by them during the service itself, in conjunction with the congregational version.

3 The third illustrates a fully worked out leaders' order of service, which includes all the congregational text, plus the texts and instructions needed by those leading the service or taking particular roles in it, plus indications of opportunities for creativity. This sort of sheet might be used during the planning of the service. It could act as a leaders' version for use during the service itself.

In this example it is not so much the texts, as the possibilities for creativity, which are being illustrated.

A service such as this might be used on the Second Sunday before Lent (when there is a 'creation' theme running through the readings) or elements from it might be used in Rogationtide or for Harvest Thanksgiving.

Eucharistic Prayer

Eucharistic Prayer E has been used, with an extended responsorial preface drawn from one of the acts of praise and thanksgiving in this book. Other eucharistic prayers could have been used, with this short proper preface:

> And now we give you thanks
> because all things are of your making,
> all times and seasons obey your laws,
> but you have chosen to create us in your own image,
> setting us over the whole world in all its wonder.
> You have made us stewards of your creation,
> to praise you day by day for the marvels of your wisdom and power:
> so earth unites with heaven
> to sing the new song of creation:

All   **Holy, holy, holy Lord …**

All Creation Worships – text for the congregation

The congregation say the words in **bold**.

Gathering

Greeting

In the name of the Father, and of the Son, and of the Holy Spirit.

All **Amen.**

The Lord be with you

All **and also with you.**

The Spirit of God hovered over the water

All **and brought life to all creation.**

Come, Holy Spirit

All **and renew the face of the earth.**

Silence is kept.

Prayer of Preparation

All **Almighty God,**
to whom all hearts are open,
all desires known,
and from whom no secrets are hidden:
cleanse the thoughts of our hearts
by the inspiration of your holy Spirit,
that we may perfectly love you,
and worthily magnify your holy name;
through Christ our Lord.
Amen.

Prayers of Penitence

Human sin disfigures the whole creation,
which groans with eager longing for God's redemption.
We confess our sin in penitence and faith.   **B**6

We confess to you
our lack of care for the world you have given us.
Lord have mercy.

All **Lord have mercy.**

We confess to you
our selfishness in not sharing the earth's bounty fairly.
Christ have mercy.

All **Christ have mercy.**

We confess to you
our failure to protect resources for others.
Lord have mercy.

All **Lord have mercy.** B56

The president declares God's forgiveness.

Gloria in Excelsis

All **Glory to God in the highest,
and peace to his people on earth.**

**Lord God, heavenly King,
almighty God and Father,
we worship you, we give you thanks,
we praise you for your glory.**

**Lord Jesus Christ, only Son of the Father,
Lord God, Lamb of God,
you take away the sin of the world:
have mercy on us;
you are seated at the right hand of the Father:
receive our prayer.**

**For you alone are the Holy One,
you alone are the Lord,
you alone are the Most High, Jesus Christ,
with the Holy Spirit,
in the glory of God the Father.
Amen.**

The Collect

The Collect is said.

The Liturgy of the Word

Reading(s)

At the end of each reading this response is used

This is the word of the Lord.

All **Thanks be to God.**

Gospel Reading

Alleluia, alleluia.
You are worthy, our Lord and God,
to receive glory and honour and power,
for you created all things.

All **Alleluia.**

Hear the Gospel of our Lord Jesus Christ according to *N.*

All **Glory to you, O Lord.**

At the end

This is the Gospel of the Lord.

All **Praise to you, O Christ.**

Sermon

Affirmation of Faith

We say together in faith

All **Holy, holy, holy**
is the Lord God almighty,
who was, and is, and is to come.

We believe in God the Father,
who created all things:

All **for by his will they were created**
and have their being.

We believe in God the Son,
who was slain:

All **for with his blood,**
he purchased us for God,
from every tribe and language,
from every people and nation.

We believe in God the Holy Spirit:

All **the Spirit and the Bride say, 'Come!'**
Even so come, Lord Jesus!
Amen.

E11

This response is used

Lord of creation

All **hear the cry of our hearts.**

The prayers end

Merciful Father,

All **accept these prayers
for the sake of your Son,
our Saviour Jesus Christ.
Amen.**

The Liturgy of the Sacrament

The Peace

The president introduces the Peace and then this response is used

The peace of the triune God be always with you

All **and also with you.**

Let us offer one another a sign of peace.

All may exchange a sign of peace.

Hymn

The Eucharistic Prayer

The Lord be with you

All **and also with you.**

Lift up your hearts.

All **We lift them to the Lord.**

Let us give thanks to the Lord our God.

All **It is right to give thanks and praise.**

The president praises God for his mighty acts.

This response recurs during this part of the prayer

Lord of all creation

All **we worship and adore you.**

… where we worship you with all of your creation, singing:

All **Holy, holy, holy Lord,**
God of power and might,
heaven and earth are full of your glory.
Hosanna in the highest.
Blessed is he who comes in the name of the Lord.
Hosanna in the highest.

The president recalls the Last Supper, and this acclamation is used

Jesus Christ is Lord:
All **Lord, by your cross and resurrection**
you have set us free.
You are the Saviour of the world.

At the conclusion of the Prayer, all say

All **Amen.**

The Lord's Prayer

As our Saviour taught us, so we pray

All **Our Father in heaven,**
hallowed be your name,
your kingdom come,
your will be done,
on earth as in heaven.
Give us today our daily bread.
Forgive us our sins
as we forgive those who sin against us.
Lead us not into temptation
but deliver us from evil.
For the kingdom, the power,
and the glory are yours
now and for ever.
Amen.

Breaking of the Bread

We break this bread
to share in the body of Christ.
All **Though we are many, we are one body,**
because we all share in one bread.

The Agnus Dei is used as the bread is broken

All **Jesus, Lamb of God,**
have mercy on us.

Jesus, bearer of our sins,
have mercy on us.

Jesus, redeemer of the world,
grant us peace.

Giving of Communion

God's holy gifts
for God's holy people.

All **Jesus Christ is holy,**
Jesus Christ is Lord,
to the glory of God the Father.

The president and people receive communion.

Prayer after Communion

Silence is kept.

Blessed are you, Lord our God, King of the universe,
creator of light and giver of life,
to you be glory and praise for ever.
In Jesus your light has shone out;
and you have given your Holy Spirit
as a mighty stream of life-giving water
to refresh and renew the face of the earth.
Let your light shine in us
that we may be beacons of justice
and bearers of hope.
Blessed be God, Father, Son and Holy Spirit.

All **Blessed be God for ever.**

Dismissal

Blessing

The Dismissal

Go in the light and peace of Christ.

All **Thanks be to God.**

A service from New Patterns for Worship. *Compilation copyright © The Archbishops' Council 2002.*

All Creation Worships –
outline and leaders' text

Gathering

Greeting

Prayer of Preparation

Penitence

Kyrie confession.

This absolution

May the Father of all mercies
cleanse *you* from *your* sins,
and restore *you* in his image
to the praise and glory of his name,
through Jesus Christ our Lord.

All **Amen.**   **B***78*

Gloria in Excelsis

or another song or hymn of praise.

The Collect

This bidding introduces the silence

In a time of silence,
let us pray that our worship will bring us closer to the one who has
    created all things.

The Liturgy of the Word

Reading(s)

Gospel Reading

This acclamation heralds the Gospel

Alleluia, alleluia.
You are worthy, our Lord and God,
to receive glory and honour and power,
for you created all things.

All **Alleluia.**

Sermon

Affirmation of Faith

We say together in faith

All **Holy, holy, holy
is the Lord God almighty ...** E11

Prayers of Intercession

The leader introduces the prayers saying

Creation groans with pain ...

This response may be used

Lord of creation

All **hear the cry of our hearts.**

The Liturgy of the Sacrament

The Peace

Peace to you from God who is our Father.
Peace from Jesus Christ who is our peace.
Peace from the Holy Spirit who gives us life.
The peace of the triune God be always with you

All **and also with you.** H10

Preparation of the Table

Taking of the Bread and Wine

Hymn

All Creation Worships **467**

This Extended Proper Preface is used

Father, we give you thanks and praise
for your Son, Jesus Christ our Lord.
He is the image of the unseen God,
the firstborn of all creation.
He created all things in heaven and on earth:
everything visible and everything invisible,
thrones, dominions, sovereignties, powers,
all things were created through him and for him.
Lord of all creation

All   **we worship and adore you.**

He is the radiant light of your glory:
he holds all creation together by his word of power.
Lord of all creation

All   **we worship and adore you**.

He is first to be born from the dead.
All perfection is found in him,
and all things were reconciled through him and for him,
everything in heaven and everything on earth,
when he made peace by his death on the cross.
Lord of all creation

All   **we worship and adore you.**

The Church is his body,
he is its head.
He takes his place in heaven
at your right hand,
where we worship you with all of your creation, singing:

All   **Holy, holy, holy ...**   **G**66

Acclamation:

Jesus Christ is Lord:

All   **Lord, by your cross and resurrection ...**

The Lord's Prayer

Modern version

This version of Agnus Dei is used

All **Jesus, Lamb of God,
have mercy on us.**

Jesus, bearer of our sins ...

Giving of Communion

God's holy gifts ...

Prayer after Communion

The deacon (or president) then lights a large candle and says the following prayer

Blessed are you, Lord our God ...

Final Hymn

The candle is taken to the door for the blessing and dismissal.

Dismissal

Blessing

May God
who clothes the lilies and feeds the birds of the sky,
who leads the lambs to pasture and the deer to water,
who multiplied loaves and fishes and changed water into wine,
lead us, feed us, multiply us,
and change us to reflect the glory of our Creator
now and through all eternity;
and the blessing ...   J70

The Dismissal

Go in the light and peace of Christ.
All **Thanks be to God.**

All Creation Worships –
full text for leaders

Gathering

Greeting

In the name of the Father, and of the Son, and of the Holy Spirit.

All **Amen.**

The Lord be with you

All **and also with you.**

The Spirit of God hovered over the water

All **and brought life to all creation.**

Come, Holy Spirit

All **and renew the face of the earth.**

Silence is kept.

Prayer of Preparation

All **Almighty God,**
to whom all hearts are open,
all desires known,
and from whom no secrets are hidden:
cleanse the thoughts of our hearts
by the inspiration of your holy Spirit,
that we may perfectly love you,
and worthily magnify your holy name;
through Christ our Lord.
Amen.

Prayers of Penitence

Human sin disfigures the whole creation,
which groans with eager longing for God's redemption.
We confess our sin in penitence and faith.   **B**6

*Our misuse of creation could be represented in some way, such as by holding up or
projecting images.*

We confess to you
our lack of care for the world you have given us.
Lord have mercy.

All **Lord have mercy.**

We confess to you
our selfishness in not sharing the earth's bounty fairly.
Christ have mercy.

All **Christ have mercy.**

We confess to you
our failure to protect resources for others.
Lord have mercy.

All **Lord have mercy.**   **B**56

May the Father of all mercies
cleanse *you* from *your* sins,
and restore *you* in his image
to the praise and glory of his name,
through Jesus Christ our Lord.

All **Amen.**   **B**78

Gloria in Excelsis

The Gloria, or some other song or hymn of praise, may be sung.

The congregation may be sprinkled with water as a sign of forgiveness during the singing.

All **Glory to God in the highest,**
and peace to his people on earth.

Lord God, heavenly King,
almighty God and Father,
we worship you, we give you thanks,
we praise you for your glory.

Lord Jesus Christ, only Son of the Father,
Lord God, Lamb of God,
you take away the sin of the world:
have mercy on us;
you are seated at the right hand of the Father:
receive our prayer.

For you alone are the Holy One,
you alone are the Lord,
you alone are the Most High, Jesus Christ,
with the Holy Spirit,
in the glory of God the Father.
Amen.

The president introduces a period of silent prayer with this bidding

In a time of silence,
let us pray that our worship will bring us closer to the one who has
     created all things.

The Collect is said, and all respond

All   **Amen.**

The Liturgy of the Word

Reading(s)

At the end of each reading

This is the word of the Lord.
All   **Thanks be to God.**

*The psalm or canticle follows the first reading; other hymns and songs may be used between
the readings.*

Gospel Reading

This acclamation heralds the Gospel

Alleluia, alleluia.
You are worthy, our Lord and God,
to receive glory and honour and power,
for you created all things.
All   **Alleluia.**

When the Gospel is announced, this response is used

Hear the Gospel of our Lord Jesus Christ according to N.
All   **Glory to you, O Lord.**

At the end

This is the Gospel of the Lord.
All   **Praise to you, O Christ.**

Sermon

We say together in faith

All **Holy, holy, holy**
is the Lord God almighty,
who was, and is, and is to come.

We believe in God the Father,
who created all things:

All **for by his will they were created**
and have their being.

We believe in God the Son,
who was slain:

All **for with his blood,**
he purchased us for God,
from every tribe and language,
from every people and nation.

We believe in God the Holy Spirit:

All **the Spirit and the Bride say, 'Come!'**
Even so come, Lord Jesus!
Amen.

E*II*

Prayers of Intercession

Creation groans with pain like the pain of childbirth,
and longs to share the freedom of the children of God,
so we offer you our prayers for the healing of all creation.
Let us pray.

This response is used

Lord of creation

All **hear the cry of our hearts.**

And at the end

Merciful Father,

All **accept these prayers**
for the sake of your Son,
our Saviour Jesus Christ.
Amen.

The Liturgy of the Sacrament

Peace to you from God who is our Father.
Peace from Jesus Christ who is our peace.
Peace from the Holy Spirit who gives us life.
The peace of the triune God be always with you

All **and also with you.**   H*10*

Let us offer one another a sign of peace.

All may exchange a sign of peace.

Preparation of the Table

A hymn may be sung.

The gifts of the people may be gathered and presented.

The table is prepared and bread and wine are placed upon it.

*If the bread, wine and water are brought forward it is appropriate that on this occasion they
are clearly visible, perhaps using see-through vessels rather than opaque ones. A glass bowl
full of soil may also be presented and placed on the altar.*

Eucharistic Prayer E

The Lord be with you
All **and also with you.**

Lift up your hearts.
All **We lift them to the Lord.**

Let us give thanks to the Lord our God.
All **It is right to give thanks and praise.**

Father, we give you thanks and praise
for your Son, Jesus Christ our Lord.
He is the image of the unseen God,
the firstborn of all creation.
He created all things in heaven and on earth:
everything visible and everything invisible,
thrones, dominions, sovereignties, powers,
all things were created through him and for him.
Lord of all creation
All **we worship and adore you.**

He is the radiant light of your glory:
he holds all creation together by his word of power.
Lord of all creation

All **we worship and adore you**.

He is first to be born from the dead.
All perfection is found in him,
and all things were reconciled through him and for him,
everything in heaven and everything on earth,
when he made peace by his death on the cross.
Lord of all creation

All **we worship and adore you.**

The Church is his body,
he is its head.
He takes his place in heaven
at your right hand,
where we worship you with all of your creation, *singing*:

All **Holy, holy, holy Lord,**
God of power and might,
heaven and earth are full of your glory.
Hosanna in the highest.
Blessed is he who comes in the name of the Lord.
Hosanna in the highest.

G66

We praise and bless you, loving Father,
through Jesus Christ, our Lord;
and as we obey his command,
send your Holy Spirit,
that broken bread and wine outpoured
may be for us the body and blood of your dear Son.

On the night before he died he had supper with his friends
and, taking bread, he praised you.
He broke the bread, gave it to them and said:
Take, eat; this is my body which is given for you;
do this in remembrance of me.

When supper was ended he took the cup of wine.
Again he praised you, gave it to them and said:
Drink this, all of you;
this is my blood of the new covenant,
which is shed for you and for many for the forgiveness of sins.
Do this, as often as you drink it, in remembrance of me.

So, Father, we remember all that Jesus did,
in him we plead with confidence his sacrifice
made once for all upon the cross.

Bringing before you the bread of life and cup of salvation,
we proclaim his death and resurrection
until he comes in glory.

Jesus Christ is Lord:

All **Lord, by your cross and resurrection**
you have set us free.
You are the Saviour of the world.

Lord of all life,
help us to work together for that day
when your kingdom comes
and justice and mercy will be seen in all the earth.

Look with favour on your people,
gather us in your loving arms
and bring us with [*N and*] all the saints
to feast at your table in heaven.

Through Christ, and with Christ, and in Christ,
in the unity of the Holy Spirit,
all honour and glory are yours, O loving Father,
for ever and ever.

All **Amen.**

The Lord's Prayer

As our Saviour taught us, so we pray

All **Our Father in heaven,**
hallowed be your name,
your kingdom come,
your will be done,
on earth as in heaven.
Give us today our daily bread.
Forgive us our sins
as we forgive those who sin against us.
Lead us not into temptation
but deliver us from evil.
For the kingdom, the power,
and the glory are yours
now and for ever.
Amen.

We break this bread
to share in the body of Christ.
All **Though we are many, we are one body,
because we all share in one bread.**

The Agnus Dei is used as the bread is broken

All **Jesus, Lamb of God,
have mercy on us.**

**Jesus, bearer of our sins,
have mercy on us.**

**Jesus, redeemer of the world,
grant us peace.**

Giving of Communion

God's holy gifts
for God's holy people.
All **Jesus Christ is holy,
Jesus Christ is Lord,
to the glory of God the Father.**

The president and people receive communion.

Prayer after Communion

Silence is kept.

The deacon (or president) then lights a large (green) candle and says the following prayer

Blessed are you, Lord our God, King of the universe,
creator of light and giver of life,
to you be glory and praise for ever.
In Jesus your light has shone out;
and you have given your Holy Spirit
as a mighty stream of life-giving water
to refresh and renew the face of the earth.
Let your light shine in us
that we may be beacons of justice
and bearers of hope.
Blessed be God, Father, Son and Holy Spirit.
All **Blessed be God for ever.**

During the final hymn the candle is taken to the door for the Blessing and Dismissal.

Dismissal

May God
who clothes the lilies and feeds the birds of the sky,
who leads the lambs to pasture and the deer to water,
who multiplied loaves and fishes and changed water into wine,
lead us, feed us, multiply us,
and change us to reflect the glory of our Creator
now and through all eternity;
and the blessing … J70

The Dismissal

A minister says

Go in the light and peace of Christ.

All **Thanks be to God.**

Authorization Details

¶ The following services and other material are authorized pursuant to Canon B 2 of the Canons of the Church of England for use until further resolution of the General Synod:

  ¶ A Service of the Word

  ¶ A Prayer of Dedication (from Prayers for Various Occasions)

  ¶ Invitations to Confession B3 (from Wholeness and Healing) and B26 (from The Marriage Service within a Celebration of Holy Communion)

  ¶ Authorized Forms of Confession and Absolution

  ¶ Creeds and Authorized Affirmations of Faith

  ¶ The Lord's Prayer

  ¶ material from The Order for the Celebration of Holy Communion also called The Eucharist and The Lord's Supper

  ¶ material from Holy Baptism

  ¶ Post Communions J12, J13, J16, J24, J28, J29, J42, J48

  ¶ Rule 7 from Rules to order how the Psalter and the rest of Holy Scripture are appointed to be read

  ¶ Benedicite – a Song of Creation (shorter version), Venite – a Song of Triumph, Jubilate – a Song of Joy, The Easter Anthems, Benedictus (The Song of Zechariah), Magnificat (The Song of Mary), Nunc dimittis (The Song of Simeon), Te Deum Laudamus

  ¶ Greeting A1 (from The Marriage Service)

  ¶ Short Prefaces G131 and G132 (from The Marriage Service within a Celebration of Holy Communion), G135–G138 (from Wholeness and Healing) and G144, G145 and G147 (from The Funeral Service within a Celebration of Holy Communion)

¶ The Sample Services comply with the provisions of

  ¶ A Service of the Word

  ¶ The Order for the Celebration of Holy Communion also called The Eucharist and The Lord's Supper

  ¶ Holy Baptism

  ¶ Prayer for Individuals in Public Worship (Wholeness and Healing)

¶ Material which appeared in *Patterns for Worship* (Church House Publishing, 1995) has been commended by the House of Bishops of the General Synod for use by the minister in exercise of his or her discretion under Canon B 5 of the Canons of the Church of England.

Under Canon B 4 it is open to each bishop to authorize, if he sees fit, the form of service to be used within his diocese. He may specify that the services shall be those commended by the House, or that a diocesan form of them shall be used. If the bishop gives no directions in this matter the priest remains free, subject to the terms of Canon B 5, to make use of the material as commended by the House.

¶ Use of the remaining material in this book falls within the discretion allowed to the minister under Canon B 5 and by the rubrics and notes in authorized forms of service.

Copyright Information

Unless otherwise indicated, the Archbishops' Council of the Church of England and the other copyright owners and administrators of texts included in *New Patterns for Worship* have given permission for the use of their material in local reproductions on a non-commercial basis which comply with the conditions for reproductions for local use set out in the Archbishops' Council's booklet, *A Brief Guide to Liturgical Copyright.* This is available from:

www.cofe.anglican.org/worship/liturgy/commonworship/copyright

Unless otherwise indicated, a reproduction which meets the conditions stated in that booklet may be made without an application for copyright permission or payment of a fee, but the following copyright acknowledgement must be included:

> *New Patterns for Worship*, material from which is included in this service, is copyright © The Archbishops' Council 2002.

Permission must be obtained in advance for any reproduction which does not comply with the conditions set out in *A Brief Guide to Liturgical Copyright.* Applications for permission should be addressed to:

The Copyright Administrator
The Archbishops' Council
Church House
Great Smith Street
London SW1P 3AZ
Telephone: 020 7898 1451
Fax: 020 7898 1449
Email: copyright@c-of-e.org.uk

Acknowledgements

The publisher gratefully acknowledges permission to reproduce copyright material in this book. Every effort has been made to trace and contact copyright holders. If there are any inadvertent omissions we apologize to those concerned and undertake to include suitable acknowledgements in all future editions.

*   *indicates adapted*

**   *indicates substantially adapted.*

Published sources include the following:

The Archbishops' Council of the Church of England: *The Prayer Book as Proposed in 1928*; *The Alternative Service Book 1980*; *The Promise of His Glory* (1991); *Common Worship: Services and Prayers for the Church of England*; *Common Worship: Pastoral Services* (2000); *Common Worship: Daily Prayer* (2001), all of which are copyright The Archbishops' Council of the Church of England.

Cambridge University Press: Extracts from *The Book of Common Prayer* (1662), the rights in which are vested in the Crown, are reproduced by permission of the Crown's Patentee, Cambridge University Press. A7*

The Revised Standard Version of the Bible (RSV) © 1946, 1952, 1971, 1973 by the Division of Christian Education of the National Council of the Churches of Christ in the USA. A15*

The Bible: Authorized Version (AV), the rights in which are vested in the Crown in the United Kingdom, by permission of the Crown's Patentee, Cambridge University Press. J115

Scripture quotations marked (CEV) are from the Contemporary English Version, copyright © 1995 by the American Bible Society. A27*, D4, D11**, D13*, D14*, D15*

Thanks are also due to the following for permission to reproduce copyright material:

Anglican Church in Aotearoa, New Zealand and Polynesia: Copyright material adapted from *A New Zealand Prayer Book – He Karakia Mihinare o Aotearoa* (1989) and used with permission A9*, A10*, F40*, H29*, H36**, H37**, J5*, J10*, J15**, J19**, J21**, J23**, J27, J28*, J40**, J43**, J85, J110

The General Synod of the Anglican Church of Canada: From (or adapted from) *The Book of Alternative Services* of the Anglican Church of Canada copyright © 1985 by the General Synod of the Anglican Church of Canada. Used with permission A16*, A44, D7*, D8*, D9*, D12, D16*, D17*, D18*, F60*, F62, F76**, G24, G28, G35, G36*, G43*, G47*, G49*, G74*, G128*, J16, J24*, J29, J30, J39, J42, J47, J49

Anglican Church of Kenya: © Anglican Church of Kenya. First published 1989 J66

Church of the Province of Southern Africa: *Liturgy 1975* © Provincial Trustees Church of the Province of Southern Africa I5

Augsburg Fortress Publishers: From *Contemporary Worship 5: Services of the Word* © 1975 Augsburg Fortress A31*; from *Manual on the Liturgy: Lutheran Book of Worship* © 1978 Augsburg Fortress G70. Reprinted by permission.

Ateliers et Presses de Taizé, France: D27, D31; music: Jacques Berthier (1923–1994) F14, F16. © Ateliers et Presses de Taizé, 71250 Taizé-Community, France

Christian Aid: © Christian Aid / Janet Morley F48

Continuum: From *In Penitence and Faith: Texts for Use with the Alternative Services*, compiled by David Silk © 1988 Continuum (Mowbray) B1*, B7*, B12*, B13*, B18, B23**, B24**, B31*, B72; from *Celebration Hymnal for Everyone*, 1994 © James J. Quinn D28; from *Services for Special Occasions* by Lawrence Jackson © Continuum (Mowbray) F49*; from *Prayers for Use at the Alternative Services*, compiled by David Silk © 1980, revised 1986 Continuum (Mowbray) J7; from *After the Third Collect*, Eric Milner-White © 1959 Continuum (Mowbray) J31*; from *Sarum Missal* © Continuum (Mowbray) J69*

The Rt Revd Timothy Dudley-Smith: *A Voice of Singing* (Hodder & Stoughton 1993) E8

GIA Publications Inc., Chicago, USA: Benedictus (Now bless the God of Israel) by Ruth Duck © 1997 by GIA Publications, Inc. All rights reserved D33; © by GIA Publications Inc. All rights reserved G25 These items are covered by a Calamus licence; otherwise permission from Decani Music (Tel: 01842 819830; sue@decanimusic.co.uk) or from GIA Publications Inc. (Fax: 001-708-496-3828; reprints@giamusic.com) is required to reproduce them.

The Grail (England): Used by permission D5

International Commission on English in the Liturgy: Excerpted from the English translation of the *Roman Missal* © 1973 International Commission on English in the Liturgy (ICEL) G89*, G104, G107, G112, G118, G133, H9, J93**; from *The Liturgical Psalter* © 1995 ICEL. All rights reserved D1, D10

Joint Liturgical Group (of Churches in Great Britain): From *The Daily Office* © Joint Liturgical Group 1968 G46, J6; source not identified J48

Jubilate Hymns: Words: © Paul Wigmore / Jubilate Hymns D6; words: © Christopher Idle / Jubilate Hymns D20, D47; words: Michael Perry © Mrs B Perry / Jubilate Hymns D23, D34, D45; from *Church Family Worship*: based on prayers by Michael Perry © Mrs B Perry / Jubilate Hymns B41**, B42**, B45**, B46*, B49*, F45**, G62*, G76**; words: © Michael Baughen / Jubilate Hymns D26; words: © David Mowbray / Jubilate Hymns D37; words: James Seddon © Mrs M Seddon / Jubilate Hymns D44; Copyright control. Author sought. Based on prayers from *Church Family Worship* F43**, F64*; from *Church Family Worship* © Based on a prayer from Emmanuel Church, Northwood G63*. All reproduced by permission of the copyright holder. Prayer material from *Church Family Worship* is reproduced by kind permission of Jubilate Hymns and Hodder & Stoughton. Application for rights outside the UK to be made to Hope Publishing Co., USA (Fax: 001-630-665-2552; hope@hopepublishing.com).

Kingsway's Thankyou Music: By Fred Dunn © 1977 Thankyou Music / Adm. by worshiptogether.com songs excl. UK & Europe, adm. by Kingsway Music. tym@kingsway.co.uk. Used by permission. D25 A CCL licence (Tel: 01323 436103; www.ccli.co.uk) or permission from Kingsway Music (Tel: 01323 437700; info@kingsway.co.uk) is required to reproduce this item: D25

Methodist Publishing House, Peterborough, UK: © Trustees for Methodist Church Purposes, used by permission of Methodist Publishing House A37*, A38, A41, A42, F11, F12, F13, F41*, F57*, G58, G61*, I6*, I7, J36, J116. From *Prayers for the Sunday Preaching Service*, Methodist Sacramental Fellowship, © 1987 C. Norman R. Wallwork G59

Janet Morley: From *All Desires Known* (MOW 1988, SPCK 1992) **J**9

National Christian Education Council: Adapted from *When You Pray with 7-10s*, edited by Hazel Snashall, with the permission of Christian Education **G**77*

OCP Publications: CELTIC ALLELUIA © 1985, Fintan O'Carroll and Christopher Walker **D**21; BENEDICTUS text © 1991, Owen Alstott. Music © 1993, Bernadette Farrell **D**35; MAGNIFICAT © 1984, Paul Inwood **D**39; MAGNIFICAT text and music © 1989, 1991, Peter Jones **D**40; MAGNIFICAT text © 1993, Owen Alstott. Music © 1993, Bernadette Farrell **D**41. Published by OCP Publications, 5536 NE Hassalo, Portland, OR 97213. All rights reserved. Used with permission. These items are covered by a Calamus licence; otherwise permission from Decani Music (Tel: 01842 819830; sue@decanimusic.co.uk) or from Oregon Catholic Press (Tel: 001-503-281-1191; liturgy@ocp.org) is required to reproduce them.

Saint Andrew Press: © Panel on Worship, Church of Scotland **A**12*, **G**69*

Society of St Francis: *The Daily Office SSF*, 1981 edition **A**13**

The Revd Stuart Thomas: © Stuart Thomas **B**73, **B**83

United Methodist Publishing House, Nashville, USA: From *At the Lord's Table* Supplementary Worship Resource No. 9, Section on Worship © 1981 by United Methodist Publishing House. Used by permission **G**84

Westminster John Knox Press, Louisville, USA: From *Daily Prayer: The Worship of God* (Supplemental Liturgical Resource 5) prepared by the Office of Worship for the Presbyterian Church (USA) and the Cumberland Presbyterian Church © 1987 The Westminster Press. **G**48*, **G**55*, **J**2, **J**3*, **J**4*, **J**32; from *The Service for the Lord's Day* (Supplemental Liturgical Resource 1) © 1984 The Westminster Press **G**60 Used by permission.

Wild Goose Resource Group/The Iona Community, Glasgow G2 3DH: From *Psalms of Patience, Protest and Praise*, words and music by John Bell **D**30; from *Enemy of Apathy* © 1988 **F**15, **F**17; from *Heaven Shall Not Wait*, words and music by John Bell © 1987 **F**18

The following have made local material available for inclusion:

Holy Trinity Church, Wealdstone: © PCC Holy Trinity Wealdstone **G**30, **G**67*

Holy Trinity, Guildford: © PCC Holy Trinity and St Mary's, Guildford **F**63*

St George's Church, Oakdale: © Michael Perham for St George's Church, Oakdale **F**47**, **J**84*, **J**91*, **J**100

Westcott House, Cambridge: © Westcott House, Cambridge **J**37, **J**38, **J**44*

The following members of the Liturgical Commission contributed material produced independently:

The Ven Trevor Lloyd: © Trevor Lloyd **F**59, **F**70*, **J**70*, **J**113

The Very Revd Michael Perham: © Michael Perham **F**55*, **F**61*, **G**39, **J**106, **J**118

The Revd Dr Bryan D Spinks: © Bryan D Spinks **B**81

The Revd Michael Vasey: © Michael Vasey 1990 **G**64

Sources and Copyright Holders

† denotes texts that have been authorized pursuant to Canon B 2 of the Canons of the Church of England for use until further resolution of the General Synod. For authorization details see page 480.

Code	Source	Copyright holder
A1†	*Common Worship: Pastoral*	Archbishops' Council
A2	Patterns Group	Archbishops' Council
A3	*Patterns for Worship 0A2*	Archbishops' Council
A4	*Patterns for Worship 0A3*	Archbishops' Council
A5	Source not identified (*Patterns for Worship 0A8*)	Freely available
A6	*Patterns for Worship 13A11**	Archbishops' Council
A7	*Book of Common Prayer**	Crown (Cambridge University Press)
A8	*Patterns for Worship 0A15*	Archbishops' Council
A9*	*Patterns for Worship**	Anglican Church in Aotearoa, New Zealand and Polynesia
A10	*Patterns for Worship**	Anglican Church in Aotearoa, New Zealand and Polynesia
A11	*Church of Scotland Common Order**	Public domain
A12	*Church of Scotland Common Order**	Panel on Worship, Church of Scotland
A13	*Celebrating Common Prayer**	Society of St Francis
A14	*Common Worship*	Archbishops' Council
A15	*Patterns for Worship 0A6** (from Revised Standard Version)	National Council of the Churches of Christ in the USA
A16	*Book of Alternative Services **	Anglican Church of Canada
A17	*Patterns for Worship 0A4*	Archbishops' Council
A18	*Patterns for Worship 0L24*	Archbishops' Council
A19	Patterns Group	Archbishops' Council
A20	Patterns Group	Archbishops' Council
A21	*Common Worship*	Archbishops' Council
A22	Patterns Group	Archbishops' Council
A23	Patterns Group	Archbishops' Council
A24	*Patterns for Worship 15A12**	Archbishops' Council
A25	*Patterns for Worship 0L27**	Archbishops' Council
A26	Unknown	Not applicable
A27	*Patterns for Worship 0A16** (from Contemporary English Version)	Bible Society
A28	*Times and Seasons*	Archbishops' Council
A29	*Times and Seasons*	Archbishops' Council
A30	*Times and Seasons*	Archbishops' Council
A31	*Contemporary Worship 5**	Augsburg Fortress
A32	Patterns Group	Archbishops' Council
A33	*Times and Seasons*	Archbishops' Council
A34	Patterns Group	Archbishops' Council
A35	*Patterns for Worship 0A20**	Diocese of Chelmsford
A36	Patterns Group	Archbishops' Council
A37	*Methodist Worship Book**	Methodist Church
A38	*Methodist Worship Book*	Methodist Church
A39	Patterns Group	Archbishops' Council
A40	Patterns Group	Archbishops' Council
A41	*Methodist Worship Book*	Methodist Church

A42	*Methodist Worship Book*	Methodist Church
A43	*Common Worship**	Archbishops' Council
A44	*Book of Alternative Services*	Anglican Church of Canada
B1	*In Penitence and Faith* (David Silk)*	Continuum (Mowbray)
B2	*Patterns Group*	Archbishops' Council
B3†	*Common Worship: Pastoral*	Archbishops' Council
B4	*Patterns for Worship 9B11**	Archbishops' Council
B5	*Patterns Group*	Archbishops' Council
B6	*Patterns for Worship 10B12**	Archbishops' Council
B7	*In Penitence and Faith* (David Silk)*	Continuum (Mowbray)
B8	*Times and Seasons Chr.A4*	Archbishops' Council
B9	*Common Worship*	Archbishops' Council
B10	*Times and Seasons Chr.A5*	Archbishops' Council
B11	*Common Worship*	Archbishops' Council
B12	*In Penitence and Faith* (David Silk)*	Continuum (Mowbray)
B13	*In Penitence and Faith* (David Silk)*	Continuum (Mowbray)
B14	*Patterns for Worship 7B8*	Archbishops' Council
B15	*Common Worship*	Archbishops' Council
B16	*Patterns for Worship 8B9*	Archbishops' Council
B17	*Common Worship*	Archbishops' Council
B18	*Enriching the Christian Year* (David Silk)	Continuum (Mowbray)
B19	*Patterns for Worship 11B13*	Freely available
B20	*Patterns for Worship 4B4*	Archbishops' Council
B21	*Patterns for Worship 4B4*	Archbishops' Council
B22	Patterns Group	Archbishops' Council
B23	*In Penitence and Faith* (David Silk)*	Continuum (Mowbray)
B24	*In Penitence and Faith* (David Silk)*	Continuum (Mowbray)
B25	*Patterns for Worship 14B15*	Freely available
B26†	*Common Worship: Pastoral*	Archbishops' Council
B27	*Patterns for Worship 8B10*	Archbishops' Council
B28	*Patterns for Worship 13B14**	Freely available
B29	*Common Worship*	Archbishops' Council
B30	*Times and Seasons Asa.A2*	Archbishops' Council
B31	*In Penitence and Faith* (David Silk)*	Continuum (Mowbray)
B32	*Common Worship*	Archbishops' Council
B33	*Common Worship*	Archbishops' Council
B34	*Common Worship*	Archbishops' Council
B35	*Common Worship*	Archbishops' Council
B36	*Common Worship*	Archbishops' Council
B37	*Common Worship*	Archbishops' Council
B38	*Common Worship*	Archbishops' Council
B39	*Common Worship*	Archbishops' Council
B40	*Common Worship: Pastoral*	Archbishops' Council
B41	*Church Family Worship**	Jubilate Hymns
B42	*Church Family Worship**	Jubilate Hymns
B43	*Common Worship*	Archbishops' Council
B44	*Common Worship*	Archbishops' Council
B45	*Church Family Worship**	Jubilate Hymns
B46	*Church Family Worship**	Jubilate Hymns
B47	*Common Worship*	Archbishops' Council
B48	cf Psalm 51	
B49	*Church Family Worship**	Jubilate Hymns
B50	*Common Worship*	Archbishops' Council
B51	*Common Worship*	Archbishops' Council

B52	*Common Worship*	Archbishops' Council
B53	*Common Worship*	Archbishops' Council
B54	*Common Worship*	Archbishops' Council
B55	*Patterns Group*	Archbishops' Council
B56	*Patterns Group*	Archbishops' Council
B57	*Patterns Group*	Archbishops' Council
B58	*Patterns Group*	Archbishops' Council
B59	*Patterns Group*	Archbishops' Council
B60	*Patterns Group*	Archbishops' Council
B61	*Common Worship*	Archbishops' Council
B62	*Common Worship*	Archbishops' Council
B63	*Patterns Group*	Archbishops' Council
B64	*Promise of His Glory**	Archbishops' Council
B65	*Patterns for Worship*	unknown
B66	*Common Worship*	Archbishops' Council
B67	*Common Worship*	Archbishops' Council
B68	*Patterns Group*	Archbishops' Council
B69	*Common Worship*	Archbishops' Council
B70	*Common Worship*	Archbishops' Council
B71	*Common Worship*	Archbishops' Council
B72	*In Penitence and Faith* (David Silk)	Continuum (Mowbray)
B73	*Common Worship*	Stuart Thomas
B74	*Common Worship*	Freely available
B75	*Common Worship*	Archbishops' Council
B76	*Common Worship*	Archbishops' Council
B77	*Common Worship*	Archbishops' Council
B78	*Common Worship*	Archbishops' Council
B79	*Common Worship*	Archbishops' Council
B80	*Common Worship*	Archbishops' Council
B81	*Common Worship*	Bryan D. Spinks
B82	*Common Worship*	Archbishops' Council
B83	*Common Worship*	Stuart Thomas
B84	*Common Worship: Pastoral*	Archbishops' Council
D1	International Commission on English in the Liturgy (response added)	ICEL
D2	*Common Worship: Daily Prayer*	Archbishops' Council
D3	*Common Worship*	Archbishops' Council
D4	Contemporary English Version	Bible Society
D5	*The Grail*	Text © The Grail
D6	Paul Wigmore	Paul Wigmore / Jubilate Hymns
D7	*Book of Alternative Services**	Anglican Church of Canada
D8	*Book of Alternative Services**	Anglican Church of Canada
D9	*Book of Alternative Services**	Anglican Church of Canada
D10	International Commission on English in the Liturgy	ICEL
D11	Contemporary English Version / *The Message**	Bible Society
D12	*Book of Alternative Services*	Anglican Church of Canada
D13	Contemporary English Version*	Bible Society
D14	Contemporary English Version*	Bible Society
D15	Contemporary English Version*	Bible Society
D16	*Book of Alternative Services**	Anglican Church of Canada
D17	*Book of Alternative Services**	Anglican Church of Canada
D18	*Book of Alternative Services**	Anglican Church of Canada
D19	*Common Worship*	Archbishops' Council

D20	Christopher Idle	Christopher Idle /Jubilate Hymns
D21	*Sing Glory* Fintan O'Carroll and Christopher Walker	OCP Publications
D22	*Common Worship*	Archbishops' Council
D23	Michael Perry	Mrs B. Perry / Jubilate Hymns
D24	*Common Worship*	Archbishops' Council
D25	Fred Dunn	Kingsway's Thankyou Music
D26	*RSCM Music for Common Worship*	Michael Baughen / Jubilate Hymns
D27	*Songs for Prayer**	Ateliers et Presses de Taizé
D28	Celebration Hymnal for Everyone	James J. Quinn/Continuum
D29	*Common Worship: Daily Prayer*	Archbishops' Council
D30	*Iona Community / Wild Goose Publications*	Iona Community / Wild Goose Publications
D31	*Songs for Prayer**	Ateliers et Presses de Taizé
D32	*Common Worship: Daily Prayer*	Archbishops' Council
D33	*RSCM Music for Common Worship*	GIA Publications Inc.
D34	*Songs from the Psalms*	Mrs B. Perry / Jubilate Hymns
D35	*Common Ground*	OCP Publications
D36	*Common Worship: Daily Prayer*	Archbishops' Council
D37	*RSCM Music for Common Worship*	David Mowbray / Jubilate Hymns
D38	Anon	N/A
D39	Paul Inwood	OCP Publications
D40	Peter Jones	OCP Publications
D41	*Common Ground*	OCP Publications
D42	*Common Worship*	Archbishops' Council
D43	*Common Worship*	Archbishops' Council
D44	*RSCM Music for Common Worship*	Mrs M. Seddon / Jubilate Hymns
D45	*Songs from the Psalms*	Mrs B. Perry / Jubilate Hymns
D46	*Common Worship*	Archbishops' Council
D47	*RSCM Music for Common Worship*	Christopher Idle / Jubilate Hymns
E1	*Common Worship*	Archbishops' Council
E2	*Common Worship*	Archbishops' Council
E3	*Common Worship*	Archbishops' Council
E4	*Common Worship*	Archbishops' Council
E5	*Common Worship*	Archbishops' Council
E6	*Common Worship*	Archbishops' Council
E7	*Common Worship*	Archbishops' Council
E8	*A Voice of Singing*	Timothy Dudley-Smith
E9	*Common Worship*	Archbishops' Council
E10	*Common Worship*	Archbishops' Council
E11	*Common Worship*	Archbishops' Council
E12	*Common Worship*	Archbishops' Council
E13	*Common Worship*	Archbishops' Council
E14	*Common Worship*	Archbishops' Council
F1	*Common Worship: Daily Prayer*	Archbishops' Council
F2	*Common Worship: Daily Prayer*	Archbishops' Council
F3	*Patterns Group*	Archbishops' Council
F4	*Common Worship: Daily Prayer*	Archbishops' Council
F5	*Common Worship: Daily Prayer*	Archbishops' Council
F6	*Patterns Group*	Archbishops' Council
F7	*Common Worship: Daily Prayer*	Archbishops' Council
F8	*Patterns Group*	Archbishops' Council
F9	*Common Worship: Daily Prayer*	Archbishops' Council
F10	*Patterns Group*	Archbishops' Council
F11	*Methodist Worship Book*	Methodist Church

F12	*Methodist Worship Book*	Methodist Church
F13	*Methodist Worship Book*	Methodist Church
F14	*Songs for Prayer*	Ateliers et Presses de Taizé
F15	*Iona Community / Wild Goose Publications*	Iona Community / Wild Goose Publications
F16	*Songs for Prayer*	Ateliers et Presses de Taizé
F17	*Enemy of Apathy*	Iona Community
F18	*Heaven shall not wait*	Iona Community
F19	*Patterns Group*	Archbishops' Council
F20	*Patterns Group*	Archbishops' Council
F21	*Patterns Group*	Archbishops' Council
F22	*Patterns Group*	Archbishops' Council
F23	*Patterns Group*	Archbishops' Council
F24	*Patterns Group*	Archbishops' Council
F25	*Patterns Group*	Archbishops' Council
F26	*Patterns Group*	Archbishops' Council
F27	*Patterns Group*	Archbishops' Council
F28	*Patterns Group*	Archbishops' Council
F29	*Patterns Group*	Archbishops' Council
F30	*Patterns Group*	Archbishops' Council
F31	*Patterns Group*	Archbishops' Council
F32	*Patterns Group*	Archbishops' Council
F33	*Patterns Group*	Archbishops' Council
F34	*Patterns Group*	Archbishops' Council
F35	*Patterns Group*	Archbishops' Council
F36	*Patterns Group*	Archbishops' Council
F37	*Patterns Group*	Archbishops' Council
F38	*Patterns Group*	Archbishops' Council
F39	*ECUSA Book of Common Prayer**	Freely available
F40	*New Zealand Prayer Book*	Anglican Church in Aotearoa, New Zealand and Polynesia
F41	*Methodist Worship Book**	Methodist Church
F42	*Patterns for Worship 0H29*	Archbishops' Council
F43	*Church Family Worship**	Jubilate Hymns
F44	*Patterns for Worship 11H16**	Archbishops' Council
F45	*Church Family Worship**	Mrs B. Perry / Jubilate Hymns
F46	*Book of Alternative Services*	Anglican Church of Canada
F47	*Enriching the Christian Year 14C1**	Michael Pe rham for St George's Church, Oakdale
F48	*Till All Creation Sings*	Christian Aid
F49	*Services for Special Occasions (Lawrence Jackson)**	Continuum (Mowbray)
F50	*Patterns for Worship 1H1*	Archbishops' Council
F51	*Patterns Group*	Archbishops' Council
F52	*Church Family Worship**	Freely available
F53	*Times and Seasons Chr.H1*	Archbishops' Council
F54	*Times and Seasons Chr.H3*	Archbishops' Council
F55	*Patterns for Worship 2H4**	Michael Perham
F56	*Times and Seasons Chr.H5*	Archbishops' Council
F57	*Methodist Worship Book**	Methodist Church
F58	*Patterns Group*	Archbishops' Council
F59	*Enriching the Christian Year*	Trevor Lloyd
F60	*Book of Alternative Services**	Anglican Church of Canada
F61	*Enriching the Christian Year**	Michael Perham
F62	*Book of Alternative Services*	Anglican Church of Canada
F63	*Patterns for Worship 8H13*	PCC Holy Trinity, Guildford

F64	*Church Family Worship**	Jubilate Hymns
F65	*Patterns for Worship 12H17*	Archbishops' Council
F66	*Patterns for Worship 9H14*	Archbishops' Council
F67	*Patterns for Worship 6H8*	Archbishops' Council
F68	*Patterns for Worship 14H19*	Archbishops' Council
F69	*Patterns for Worship 14H20*	unknown
F70	*Enriching the Christian Year**	Trevor Lloyd
F71	*Promise of His Glory*	Archbishops' Council
F72	*Patterns for Worship 16H22*	Archbishops' Council
F73	*Times and Seasons*	Archbishops' Council
F74	*Common Worship: Pastoral*	Archbishops' Council
F75	*Promise of His Glory*	Archbishops' Council
F76	*Book of Alternative Services**	Anglican Church of Canada
G1	*Patterns Group*	Archbishops' Council
G2	*Patterns Group*	Archbishops' Council
G3	*Patterns Group*	Archbishops' Council
G4	*Patterns Group*	Archbishops' Council
G5	*Patterns Group*	Archbishops' Council
G6	*Patterns Group*	Archbishops' Council
G7	*Patterns Group*	Archbishops' Council
G8	*Patterns Group*	Archbishops' Council
G9	*Patterns Group*	Archbishops' Council
G10	*Patterns Group*	Archbishops' Council
G11	*Patterns Group*	Archbishops' Council
G12	*Patterns Group*	Archbishops' Council
G13	*Patterns Group*	Archbishops' Council
G14	*Patterns Group*	Archbishops' Council
G15	*Patterns Group*	Archbishops' Council
G16	*Patterns Group*	Archbishops' Council
G17	*Patterns Group*	Archbishops' Council
G18	*Patterns Group*	Archbishops' Council
G19	*Patterns Group*	Archbishops' Council
G20	*Patterns Group*	Archbishops' Council
G21	*Patterns Group*	Archbishops' Council
G22	*Patterns for Worship 0L26*	Archbishops' Council
G23	*Times and Seasons Chr.R4*	Archbishops' Council
G24	*Book of Alternative Services*	Anglican Church of Canada
G25	*Praise God in Song*	GIA Publications Inc.
G26	*Common Worship*	Archbishops' Council
G27	*Promise of His Glory*	Archbishops' Council
G28	*Book of Alternative Services*	Anglican Church of Canada
G29	*Times and Seasons*	Archbishops' Council
G30	*Patterns for Worship 2P1*	PCC Holy Trinity, Wealdstone
G31	*Times and Seasons*	Archbishops' Council
G32	*Times and Seasons*	Archbishops' Council
G33	*Times and Seasons Chr.R1*	Archbishops' Council
G34	*Common Worship: Daily Prayer*	Archbishops' Council
G35	*Book of Alternative Services*	Anglican Church of Canada
G36	*Book of Alternative Services**	Anglican Church of Canada
G37	*Contemporary Worship 5*	Augsburg Fortress
G38	*Patterns for Worship 6L9*	Freely available
G39	*Enriching the Christian Year*	Michael Perham
G40	*Liturgical Commission*	Archbishops' Council
G41	*Patterns for Worship 8L12*	Archbishops' Council

G42	*Patterns for Worship* 8L13	Archbishops' Council
G43	*Book of Alternative Services**	Anglican Church of Canada
G44	*Patterns for Worship* 6L10	Archbishops' Council
G45	*Patterns for Worship* 8L16	Archbishops' Council
G46	*Patterns for Worship* 5L7	Joint Liturgical Group
G47	*Book of Alternative Services**	Anglican Church of Canada
G48	*Daily Prayer: The Worship of God**	Westminster John Knox Press
G49	*Book of Alternative Services**	Anglican Church of Canada
G50	*Patterns for Worship* 17L23	Archbishops' Council
G51	*Patterns for Worship* 8L15	Archbishops' Council
G52	*Patterns for Worship* 0L25	Archbishops' Council
G53	*Times and Seasons* NYr.R1*	Archbishops' Council
G54	*Patterns for Worship* 15L21	Archbishops' Council
G55	*Daily Prayer: The Worship of God**	Westminster John Knox Press
G56	*Patterns for Worship* 0P21	Archbishops' Council
G57	*Common Worship: Daily Prayer*	Archbishops' Council
G58	*Methodist Worship Book*	Methodist Church
G59	*Methodist Worship Book* (*Prayers for the Sunday Preaching Service, Methodist Sacramental Fellowship*)	C. Norman R. Wallwork
G60	*Methodist Worship Book* (*Supplemental Liturgical Resources No. 1*)	The Presbyterian Church USA
G61	*Methodist Worship Book**	Methodist Church
G62	*Church Family Worship**	Mrs B. Perry / Jubilate Hymns
G63	*Church Family Worship**	Jubilate Hymns
G64	*Patterns for Worship* 9P14	Michael Vasey
G65	*Patterns for Worship* 7P11	Archbishops' Council
G66	*Patterns for Worship* 10P15	Archbishops' Council
G67	*Patterns for Worship* 2P1*	PCC Holy Trinity, Wealdstone
G68	*Patterns for Worship* 2P2*	Archbishops' Council
G69	*Worship Now Book 1**	Panel on Worship, Church of Scotland
G70	*Lutheran Book of Worship*	Augsburg Fortress
G71	*Times and Seasons*	Archbishops' Council
G72	*Times and Seasons*	Archbishops' Council
G73	*Patterns for Worship* 4P5	Archbishops' Council
G74	*Book of Alternative Services**	Anglican Church of Canada
G75	*Patterns for Worship* 5P7	Archbishops' Council
G76	*Church Family Worship**	Mrs B. Perry / Jubilate Hymns
G77	*When you pray with 7–10s**	National Christian Education Council
G78	*Patterns for Worship* 6P9	Archbishops' Council
G79	*Patterns for Worship* 7P10	Archbishops' Council
G80	*Patterns for Worship* 8P12	Archbishops' Council
G81	*Patterns for Worship* 16P20	Archbishops' Council
G82	*Patterns for Worship* 12M10	Archbishops' Council
G83	*Patterns for Worship* 8P13	Archbishops' Council
G84	*At the Lord's Table* Supplementary Worship Resource 9	United Methodist Publishing House
G85	*Patterns for Worship* 13P17	Archbishops' Council
G86	*Patterns for Worship* 13P18	Archbishops' Council
G87	*Patterns for Worship* 15P19	Archbishops' Council
G88	*Patterns for Worship* 0N30*	Archbishops' Council
G89	*Roman Missal 1970**	ICEL
G90	*Patterns for Worship* 1N1	Archbishops' Council
G91	*Times and Seasons* Adv.L2	Archbishops' Council
G92	*Times and Seasons* Adv.L3	Archbishops' Council

G93	Patterns for Worship 1N3	Archbishops' Council
G94	Alternative Service Book 1980*	Archbishops' Council
G95	Common Worship	Archbishops' Council
G96	Common Worship	Archbishops' Council
G97	Patterns for Worship 16N27	Archbishops' Council
G98	Patterns for Worship 1N2	Archbishops' Council
G99	Patterns for Worship 2N4	Archbishops' Council
G100	Patterns for Worship 2N5	Archbishops' Council
G101	Common Worship*	Archbishops' Council
G102	Common Worship	Archbishops' Council
G103	Patterns for Worship 3N6	Archbishops' Council
G104	Roman Missal 1970	ICEL
G105	Patterns for Worship 5N9	Archbishops' Council
G106	Common Worship	Archbishops' Council
G107	Roman Missal 1970	ICEL
G108	Common Worship	Archbishops' Council
G109	Common Worship (President's)	Archbishops' Council
G110	Times and Seasons CK.L1	Archbishops' Council
G111	Times and Seasons CK.L2	Archbishops' Council
G112	Roman Missal 1970	ICEL
G113	Patterns for Worship 4N8	Archbishops' Council
G114	Patterns for Worship 6N12	Archbishops' Council
G115	Patterns for Worship 6N13	Archbishops' Council
G116	Common Worship	Archbishops' Council
G117	Alternative Service Book 1980	Archbishops' Council
G118	Roman Missal 1970	ICEL
G119	Patterns for Worship 7N14	Archbishops' Council
G120	Common Worship*	Archbishops' Council
G121	Patterns for Worship 8N15	Archbishops' Council
G122	Common Worship	Archbishops' Council
G123	Patterns for Worship 8N16	Archbishops' Council
G124	Patterns for Worship 11N22	Archbishops' Council
G125	Times and Seasons Asc.L2	Archbishops' Council
G126	Patterns for Worship 10N21	Archbishops' Council
G127	Patterns for Worship 8N18	Archbishops' Council
G128	Book of Alternative Services*	Anglican Church of Canada
G129	Times and Seasons Chr.L5	Archbishops' Council
G130	Patterns for Worship 14N25	Archbishops' Council
G131†	Common Worship: Pastoral	Archbishops' Council
G132†	Common Worship: Pastoral	Archbishops' Council
G133	Roman Missal 1970	ICEL
G134	Enriching the Christian Year	Archbishops' Council
G135†	Common Worship: Pastoral	Archbishops' Council
G136†	Common Worship: Pastoral	Archbishops' Council
G137†	Common Worship: Pastoral	Archbishops' Council
G138†	Common Worship: Pastoral	Archbishops' Council
G139	Patterns for Worship 10N20	Archbishops' Council
G140	Patterns Group	Archbishops' Council
G141	Patterns for Worship 13N23	Archbishops' Council
G142	Patterns for Worship 13N24	Archbishops' Council
G143	Patterns for Worship 15N26	Archbishops' Council
G144†	Common Worship: Pastoral	Archbishops' Council
G145†	Common Worship: Pastoral	Archbishops' Council
G146	Times and Seasons*	Archbishops' Council

G147†	Common Worship: Pastoral	Archbishops' Council
G148	Times and Seasons*	Archbishops' Council
H1	Patterns for Worship 0R24	Freely available
H2	Patterns for Worship 0R26	Freely available
H3	Patterns for Worship 0R27*	Freely available
H4	Patterns for Worship 0R28	Freely available
H5	Common Worship	Archbishops' Council
H6	Common Worship	Archbishops' Council
H7	Common Worship	Archbishops' Council
H8	Common Worship	Archbishops' Council
H9	Roman Missal 1970	ICEL
H10	Patterns for Worship 9R10	Archbishops' Council
H11	Common Worship	Archbishops' Council
H12	Patterns for Worship 1R2	Freely available
H13	Times and Seasons Adv.J4	Archbishops' Council
H14	Patterns for Worship 2R3	Freely available
H15	Common Worship	Archbishops' Council
H16	Promise of His Glory	Archbishops' Council
H17	Common Worship	Archbishops' Council
H18	Common Worship	Archbishops' Council
H19	Common Worship	Archbishops' Council
H20	Common Worship	Archbishops' Council
H21	Common Worship	Archbishops' Council
H22	Common Worship	Archbishops' Council
H23	Common Worship	Archbishops' Council
H24	Source unknown	Archbishops' Council
H25	Patterns for Worship 8R8	Freely available
H26	Patterns for Worship 8R9	Freely available
H27	Common Worship	Archbishops' Council
H28	Times and Seasons Asc.J2	Archbishops' Council
H29	New Zealand Prayer Book*	Anglican Church in Aotearoa, New Zealand and Polynesia
H30	Common Worship	Archbishops' Council
H31	Patterns for Worship 12R13	Freely available
H32	Patterns for Worship 16R17	Freely available
H33	Patterns for Worship 17R18*	Freely available
H34	Patterns for Worship 17R20	Freely available
H35	Common Worship	Archbishops' Council
H36	New Zealand Prayer Book*	Anglican Church in Aotearoa, New Zealand and Polynesia
H37	New Zealand Prayer Book*	Anglican Church in Aotearoa, New Zealand and Polynesia
H38	Patterns for Worship 10R11	Freely available
H39	Patterns for Worship 0R25	Freely available
H40	Common Worship	Archbishops' Council
H41	Common Worship	Archbishops' Council
H42	Common Worship	Archbishops' Council
I1	Patterns Group	Archbishops' Council
I2	Patterns Group	Archbishops' Council
I3	Patterns Group	Archbishops' Council
I4	Patterns Group	Archbishops' Council
I5	Liturgy 1975	Church of the Province of Southern Africa
I6	Methodist Worship Book*	Methodist Church
I7	Methodist Worship Book	Methodist Church
I8	Common Worship	Archbishops' Council

I 9	Common Worship	Archbishops' Council
I 10	Common Worship	Archbishops' Council
J1	Patterns for Worship 0J41	Archbishops' Council
J2	Daily Prayer: The Worship of God	Westminster John Knox Press
J3	Daily Prayer: The Worship of God*	Westminster John Knox Press
J4	Daily Prayer: The Worship of God*	Westminster John Knox Press
J5	New Zealand Prayer Book*	Anglican Church in Aotearoa, New Zealand and Polynesia
J6	Daily Office	Joint Liturgical Group
J7	Prayers for Use at the Alternative Services (David Silk)	Continuum (Mowbray)
J8	Times and Seasons NYr.P3	Archbishops' Council
J9	All Desires Known	Janet Morley
J10	New Zealand Prayer Book*	Anglican Church in Aotearoa, New Zealand and Polynesia
J11	Promise of His Glory	Archbishops' Council
J12†	Common Worship*	Archbishops' Council
J13†	Common Worship*	Archbishops' Council
J14	Times and Seasons Chr.P7	Archbishops' Council
J15	New Zealand Prayer Book*	Anglican Church in Aotearoa, New Zealand and Polynesia
J16†	Book of Alternative Services	Anglican Church of Canada
J17	Times and Seasons*	Archbishops' Council
J18	Times and Seasons*	Archbishops' Council
J19	New Zealand Prayer Book*	Anglican Church in Aotearoa, New Zealand and Polynesia
J20	Times and Seasons*	Archbishops' Council
J21	New Zealand Prayer Book*	Anglican Church in Aotearoa, New Zealand and Polynesia
J22	Patterns Group	Archbishops' Council
J23	New Zealand Prayer Book*	Anglican Church in Aotearoa, New Zealand and Polynesia
J24†	Book of Alternative Services*	Anglican Church of Canada
J25	Common Worship	Archbishops' Council
J26	Book of Alternative Services, adapted from ECUSA Prayer Book	Freely available
J27	New Zealand Prayer Book	Anglican Church in Aotearoa, New Zealand and Polynesia
J28†	New Zealand Prayer Book	Anglican Church in Aotearoa, New Zealand and Polynesia
J29†	Book of Alternative Services	Anglican Church of Canada
J30	Book of Alternative Services	Anglican Church of Canada
J31	After the Third Collect*	Continuum (Mowbray)
J32	Daily Prayer: The Worship of God	Westminster John Knox Press
J33	Times and Seasons NYr.P4	Archbishops' Council
J34	Patterns for Worship 6J19	Archbishops' Council
J35	Patterns for Worship 0J42	Archbishops' Council
J36	Methodist Worship Book	Methodist Church
J37	Patterns for Worship	Westcott House
J38	Patterns for Worship 1J3	Westcott House
J39	Book of Alternative Services	Anglican Church of Canada
J40	New Zealand Prayer Book*	Anglican Church in Aotearoa, New Zealand and Polynesia
J41	Times and Seasons	Archbishops' Council
J42†	Book of Alternative Services	Anglican Church of Canada
J43	New Zealand Prayer Book*	Anglican Church in Aotearoa, New Zealand and Polynesia

J44	*Patterns for Worship* 11J29*	Westcott House
J45	*Patterns for Worship* 12J35	Archbishops' Council
J46	*Common Worship (President's)*	Archbishops' Council
J47	*Book of Alternative Services*	Anglican Church of Canada
J48†	*Patterns for Worship* 14J37	Archbishops' Council
J49	*Book of Alternative Services*	Anglican Church of Canada
J50	*Patterns Group*	Archbishops' Council
J51	*Patterns for Worship* 14J38	Archbishops' Council
J52	*Patterns for Worship* 0T45	Archbishops' Council
J53	*Patterns for Worship* 0T46	Freely available
J54	*Patterns for Worship* 0T48	Archbishops' Council
J55	*Common Worship*	Archbishops' Council
J56	*Common Worship*	Archbishops' Council
J57	*Common Worship*	Archbishops' Council
J58	*Common Worship*	Archbishops' Council
J59	*Common Worship (President's)*	Archbishops' Council
J60	*Common Worship (President's)*	Archbishops' Council
J61	*Common Worship (President's)*	Archbishops' Council
J62	*Common Worship (President's)*	Archbishops' Council
J63	*Common Worship (President's)*	Archbishops' Council
J64	*Common Worship*	Archbishops' Council
J65	*Patterns for Worship* 0T47	Freely available
J66	*Holy Communion Prayer Book*	Anglican Church of Kenya
J67	*Common Worship (President's)*	Archbishops' Council
J68	*Common Worship (President's)*	Archbishops' Council
J69	*Prayers for Use at the Alternative Services*	Continuum (Mowbray) (David Silk)*
J70	*Enriching the Christian Year**	Trevor Lloyd
J71	*Patterns for Worship* 1T1	Archbishops' Council
J72	*Common Worship (President's)*	Archbishops' Council
J73	*Common Worship (President's)*	Archbishops' Council
J74	*Patterns for Worship* 1T3*	Freely available
J75	*Times and Seasons* Chr.P8*	Archbishops' Council
J76	*Promise of His Glory*	Archbishops' Council
J77	*Patterns for Worship* 2T7*	Archbishops' Council
J78	*Patterns for Worship* 2T8	Archbishops' Council
J79	*Common Worship*	Archbishops' Council
J80	*Common Worship (President's)**	Archbishops' Council
J81	*Patterns for Worship* 5T13	Archbishops' Council
J82	*Times and Seasons* Pas.P2	Archbishops' Council
J83	*Patterns for Worship* 6T14	Archbishops' Council
J84	*Enriching the Christian Year**	Michael Perham for St George's Church, Oakdale
J85	*New Zealand Prayer Book**	Anglican Church in Aotearoa, New Zealand and Polynesia
J86	*Alternative Service Book 1980*	Archbishops' Council
J87	*Common Worship (President's)*	Archbishops' Council
J88	*Common Worship (President's)*	Archbishops' Council
J89	*Common Worship*	Archbishops' Council
J90	*Common Worship (President's)*	Archbishops' Council
J91	*Patterns for Worship* 8T21*	Michael Perham for St George's Church, Oakdale
J92	*Patterns for Worship* 8T22	Archbishops' Council
J93	*Roman Missal 1970**	ICEL
J94	*Patterns for Worship* 8T23	Freely available

J95	*Patterns for Worship* 11T30	Archbishops' Council
J96	*Patterns for Worship* 12T33	Archbishops' Council
J97	*Patterns for Worship* 3T10	Archbishops' Council
J98	*Times and Seasons*	Archbishops' Council
J99	*Common Worship (President's)*	Archbishops' Council
J100	*Patterns for Worship* 4T12	Michael Perham for St George's Church, Oakdale
J101	*Patterns for Worship* 3T11*	Archbishops' Council
J102	*Patterns for Worship* 14T36	Archbishops' Council
J103	*Patterns for Worship* 13T34*	Archbishops' Council
J104	*Prayer Book 1928* (Confirmation)*	Archbishops' Council
J105	*Patterns for Worship* 16T41	Archbishops' Council
J106	*Patterns for Worship* 10T29	Michael Perham
J107	*Patterns for Worship* 15T37*	Archbishops' Council
J108	*Common Worship (President's)*	Archbishops' Council
J109	*Common Worship (President's)*	Archbishops' Council
J110	*New Zealand Prayer Book*	Anglican Church in Aotearoa, New Zealand and Polynesia
J111	*Common Worship (President's)*	Archbishops' Council
J112	*Common Worship (President's)*	Archbishops' Council
J113	*Liturgy and Death* (Grove Booklet 28)	Trevor Lloyd
J114	*Patterns for Worship* 0T49	Not identified
J115	*Patterns for Worship* 0T50 (from Authorized Version)	Crown (Cambridge University Press)
J116	*Methodist Worship Book*	Methodist Church
J117	*Patterns for Worship* 9T26	Freely available
J118	*Enriching the Christian Year*	Michael Perham
J119	*Patterns for Worship* 7T19	Freely available
J120	*Patterns for Worship* 12T32	Archbishops' Council
J121	*Patterns for Worship* 6J20	Freely available
Gloria Patri	*Common Worship*	English Language Liturgical Consultation
Reading response	*Common Worship*	Archbishops' Council
Apostles' Creed	*Common Worship*	English Language Liturgical Consultation
Lord's Prayer (modern)	*Common Worship*	English Language Liturgical Consultation
The Grace	*Common Worship*	Archbishops' Council

Index of Biblical References

Index of Biblical References

Index of Subjects and Themes

Index of Subjects and Themes

Note: Headings in **bold** type indicate liturgical seasons, while those in *italics* indicate themes. Items from the Resources sections are indexed by page number, resource section and item number; thus, item 56 in Resource section B, which appears on page 91, is indexed as **91**/B56.

as ministers of communion **29, 282, 283–4**

Lament: Blessing **311/J100**
  Closing prayers **291/J6,8, 293/J19, 295/J30**
  Confessions **87/B48-9, 88/B50-51, 93/B63, 444–5**
  Greeting **69/A34**
  Intercessions **214–15/F73, 447**
  Invitations to Confession **77/B4, 6-7, 79/B20-22, 23**
  Lord's Prayer preface **183/F29**
  Post Communion prayer **299/J47**
  Praise responses **228/G35, 231/G47-9**
  sample service **443–8**
  Short Prefaces **263/G128, 265/G136,138**
  Thanksgivings **238/G60, 246–8/G73-4**
language, inclusive **176**
Laudate Dominum (Jubilate) **143–5/D24-8**
law *see* canon law
laying on of hands **29, 271, 281, 441–2, 451**
Leah and Rachel, modular lectionary material **109**
learning, and worship **44, 61, 74, 99, 158, 356**
lectionary: authorized **9, 13, 16, 21, 99, 101, 103–4**
  and modular material **101, 103–4, 105–6, 107–123, 220, 221**
  see also Readings
Lent: Affirmation of Faith **159, 165/E9**
  and Prayers of Penitence **74**
  Service of the Word (sample service) **397–401, 449–50**
  see also Cross; Lament
Light to the World (Epiphany Holy Communion) **389–95**
lighting **17, 47, 62, 74, 100**
litanies **17, 185–218/F39-76**
Liturgy of the Sacrament **12**
Liturgy of the Word **9, 11, 12, 99–106**
  and children **39**
  and lay leadership **14, 50**
  and Thanksgiving **222**
  and theme **16**
  see also Readings; sermon
Living in the world: Absolutions **97/B81-2**
  Acclamations **223/G9, 224/G19-20**
  Blessings **310/J97, 312/J103-5, 314/J110**
  Canticle **153/D41**

Closing prayers **296/J31-3**
Confessions **89/B53, 93/B64, 94/B66-8**
Greeting **67/A25**
Intercessions **192/F48, 206/F64, 211–15/F70-73**
Introductions to the Peace **276/H36-8**
Invitation to Confession **80/B28**
Opening prayer **70/A40**
Post Communion prayers **299/J48-50**
Praise responses **232/G52-3**
Short Prefaces **262/G118, 266/G139-42**
Thanksgivings **256–7/G85-6**
Lord's Prayer **11**
  in Holy Communion **23, 402**
  and intercessions **23, 171, 320, 327, 357**
  introductions **183–4/F26-38**
  prefaces **183/F26-32**
  in Sunday service **17**
  versions **183, 320**
Luke, parables from, modular lectionary material **118**

Magnificat **150–53/D36-41**
Malachi, modular lectionary material **116**
Marriage Vows, Renewal **409**
Matthew, parables from, modular lectionary material **118**
Maundy Thursday: footwashing **19**
  and the Peace **270**
meditation **100, 101;** *see also* silence
Memorial Service, Prayers of Thanksgiving **220**
memorial services, Affirmation of Faith **159, 165/E10**
mime **100;** *see also* drama
ministers of the sacrament **282, 283**
  training **284**
Miracles of Jesus, modular lectionary material **118–19**
mission *see* Church and Mission
morning: Acclamation **224/G18**
  Closing prayers **290/J2, 291/J6**
  Greetings **65/A13 66/A14-15**
  Praise responses **226/G25, 232/G53**
Morning Praise (sample service) **322–6**
Moses, modular lectionary material **110**
Mothering Sunday (sample service) **416–23**
movement **17, 39, 41, 47, 48, 269, 279–84, 363**
music: and action **37**

and space and colour **45–7**
and structures and 'specials' **33–4**
and worship and canon law **49–51**
structure **11**, **15**, **27–8**, **53**, **221**
block **18**, **33**
conversation **19**, **33**
Summary of the Law **73**
symbols **279–81**, **409**, **443**
explaining meaning **373**
types **280–81**

Taizé canticles **144/D27**, **146/D31**
Taizé chants, as prayer responses **35**, **172**, **179/F14**
Te Deum Laudamus **140–42/D19-21**
in Praise service **220**
teaching services, in early Church **27–8**
Ten Commandments **424**, **427**
testimony **33**, **416–17**, **424**
thanksgivings **10**, **11**, **220–22**
and intercessions **173**, **174**
resources **234–57/G56-87**, **430**, **439**
responsive **33**
and Sanctus **220**, **222**
The Lord is Here (sample Communion service) **346–55**
theme: announcing **61**, **62**
examples **19**
local **16**
and music **38**
planning **19**, **24**
and readings **9**, **16**, **103**
seasonal **16**
worship theme table **39**, **41**
1 Thessalonians, modular lectionary material **121**
2 Thessalonians, modular lectionary material **121**
This is our Story (sample Communion service) **356–62**
Time: Canticles **156/D46-7**
Closing prayers **291/J7-8**
Greeting **68/A26**
Opening prayer **70/A40**
Time for a feast, modular lectionary material **117**
Trinity: Affirmation of Faith **159**, **164/E7**, **166/E11**
see also *Father, Son and Spirit*

Venite **142–3/D22-3**, **322**
Visions of Daniel, modular lectionary material **115**
visual aids **14**, **16**, **39**, **41**, **45**, **99–101**, **171**

water, sprinkling with **167**
Women in the messianic line, modular lectionary material **109**
Word, as essential ingredient **15**, **16**, **19**, **20**
Word: Acclamations **223/G9-10**
Blessing **310/J95**
Closing prayer **295/J25**
Confessions **84/B41**, **93/B62**
Intercessions **187–8/F42-3**
Invitation to Confession **79/B19**
Opening prayer **70/A39**
Post Communion prayer **298/J44**
Praise response **228/G34**
Short Preface **263/G124**
Words of Comfort **446**
worship: history **27–8**
and the law **49–53**
and learning **44**, **61**, **74**, **99**, **158**, **356**
small groups **45**, **48**, **106**, **175**, **455–6**
Worship and Doctrine Measure (1974) **24**, **49**, **52**
worship planning group **34**
and four church stories **1–2**
and provision for children **39**
and psalms **125**
and Readings **100**, **106**
terms of reference **24**, **25**
and theme and direction of service **16**, **18**, **20**
and use of space and colour **47**
see also *discussion starters; A Service of the Word, planning and preparation*
worship theme table **39**, **41**

Resource Section Themes

In each Resource Section, the resources are grouped according to theme, in the following order.

Theme	Subjects covered
General	General (morning and evening)
Father, Son and Spirit	Trinity, approach to worship
God in creation	Harvest, creation
Christ's coming	Advent
Incarnation	Christmas, Epiphany, light
Cross	Holy Week, Lent
Resurrection	Easter
Ascension	Ascension, kingship
Holy Spirit	Pentecost
Word	Word
Church and mission	Mission, ministry, unity
Christian beginnings	Baptism and Confirmation
Lament	Lent, frustration/pain/anger
Relationships and healing	Reconciliation, family, love
Living in the world	Society, city
Holy Communion	Holy Communion
Heaven	Saints, death, glory
Time	Time